W9-DJK-653

AMERICAN GOVERNMENT AND HISTORY INFORMATION GUIDE SERIES

Series Editor: Harold Shill, Chief Circulation Librarian, Adjunct Assistant Professor of Political Science, West Virginia University, Morgantown

Also in this series:

AMERICAN EDUCATIONAL HISTORY—*Edited by Timothy Walsh and Michael W. Sedlak**

AMERICA'S MILITARY PAST—*Edited by Jack C. Lane*

IMMIGRATION AND ETHNICITY—*Edited by John D. Buenker and Nicholas C. Burckel*

PROGRESSIVE REFORM—*Edited by John D. Buenker and Nicholas C. Burckel**

PUBLIC ADMINISTRATION—*Edited by John E. Rouse, Jr.**

PUBLIC POLICY—*Edited by William J. Murin, Gerald Michael Greenfield, and John D. Buenker**

SOCIAL HISTORY OF THE UNITED STATES—*Edited by Donald F. Tingley*

U.S. CULTURAL HISTORY—*Edited by Philip I. Mitterling*

U.S. FOREIGN RELATIONS—*Edited by Elmer Plischke**

U.S. POLITICS AND ELECTIONS—*Edited by David J. Maurer*

U.S. RELIGIOUS AND CHURCH HISTORY—*Edited by Garth Rosell**

URBAN HISTORY AND URBANIZATION—*Edited by John D. Buenker, Gerald Michael Greenfield, and William J. Murin**

WOMEN AND FEMINISM IN AMERICAN HISTORY—*Edited by Donald F. Tingley and Elizabeth Tingley**

*in preparation

The above series is part of the

GALE INFORMATION GUIDE LIBRARY

The Library consists of a number of separate series of guides covering major areas in the social sciences, humanities, and current affairs.

General Editor: Paul Wasserman, Professor and former Dean, School of Library and Information Services, University of Maryland

Managing Editor: Denise Allard Adzigian, Gale Research Company

U.S. Constitution

A GUIDE TO INFORMATION SOURCES

Volume 4 in the American Government and History Information Guide Series

Earlean M. McCarrick

Assistant Professor
Government and Politics
University of Maryland
College Park

Gale Research Company
Book Tower, Detroit, Michigan 48226

Copyright © 1980 by
Earlean M. McCarrick

ISBN 0-8103-1203-4
Library of Congress Catalog Card Number 74-15403

VITA

Earlean M. McCarrick is an assistant professor of government and politics at the University of Maryland in College Park. She received her B.A. in journalism and M.A. in political science from Louisiana State University, Baton Rouge. She earned her Ph.D. in political science from Vanderbilt University.

CONTENTS

INTRODUCTION

Intended for both the scholar and the more casual student of the Constitution, this annotated bibliography contains citations to primary and secondary
sources, to historical and contemporary writings, to general and specific
studies, and to sophisticated and popular works.

The first five chapters deal with broad, general categories and with the
pre-Constitutional period. Thus, chapter 1 is devoted to general materials
such as bibliographies of a broad scope and chapter 4 deals with general
interpretative works. Chapter 2 deals with the Continental Congresses, the
Declaration of Independence, and the Articles of Confederation. Chapter 3
deals with the Philadelphia convention and chapter 5 deals with works examining those enduring controversies over where to draw the line between
the various centers of governmental power. The remaining seven chapters
are organized on the basis of the Constitution itself. Chapter 6 deals with
Article 1 and Congress, chapter 7 deals with Article II and the executive
branch and chapter 8 with the judiciary. Chapter 9 deals with the other
articles in the original Constitution, chapter 10 with the first ten amendments
and with the eleventh and twelfth amendments, chapter 11 with the three
Civil War amendments, and chapter 12 with the amendments added in the
twentieth century.

Chapter 1

GENERAL SOURCES

(Bibliographies, Indexes, Catalogs, and Guides to Government Publications)

ABC POL SCI: ADVANCE BIBLIOGRAPHY OF CONTENTS: POLITICAL
SCIENCE AND GOVERNMENT. Santa Barbara, Calif.: American Bibliographic Center, Clio Press, 1969-- . 8 per yr. Annual index in December.

> This book contains abstracts of articles appearing in about one
> hundred political science and legal journals with reproductions
> of the tables of contents of about three hundred journals. Single
> copies of many of the articles abstracted are available for pur-
> chase from the American Bibliographical Center.

American Association of Law Schools. LAW BOOKS RECOMMENDED FOR
LAW LIBRARIES. 6 vols. South Hackensack, N.J.: Fred R. Rothman
and Co., 1967-70.

> Constitutional law, mostly American, some English, is covered
> in volume 2, number 13. Some popular as well as scholarly
> legal and political science works are included, especially in
> the areas of civil rights and civil liberties. Legal history is
> one of the categories covered in volume 3, number 25. Some of
> the entries are annotated.

Ames, John G.B., ed. COMPREHENSIVE INDEX TO THE PUBLICATIONS
OF THE UNITED STATES GOVERNMENT, 1881-1893. Washington, D.C.:
Government Printing Office, 1905.

> The book contains a subject index to some of the documents of
> Congress and the executive branch during the period included.
> It is a partial listing. This index is successor to the Poore
> DESCRIPTIVE CATALOGUES OF THE GOVERNMENT PUBLICA-
> TIONS OF THE UNITED STATES, 1774-1881 (see p. 9). The
> Ames index is succeeded by the MONTHLY CATALOG (see p. 8)
> which began publication in 1895.

Anderman, Nancy. UNITED STATES SUPREME COURT DECISIONS: AN
INDEX TO THEIR LOCATION. Metuchen, N.J.: Scarecrow Press, 1976.

> This is an index of reprints of and excerpts from Supreme Court
> decisions. Section 1 contains a list of the books in which the
> excerpts appear. Section 2 lists Supreme Court decisions by
> date. In section 3, the cases are alphabetized by name. There
> is a subject index in section 4.

Andriot, John L. GUIDE TO UNITED STATES GOVERNMENT SERIALS
AND PERIODICALS. 4 vols. Washington, D.C.: Government Printing
Office, 1971.

> First published in 1962, this is a guide to the publications of
> the Government Printing Office and various government agencies.
> Volume 1 contains an alphabetical listing of over two thousand
> government units with a short history of each. Volume 2 lists
> the serial publication of current government agencies. Volume 3
> lists the publications of those agencies which have been abolished.
> Volume 4 is an index. It is kept up to date by use of a loose-
> leaf format.

Beers, Henry P. BIBLIOGRAPHIES IN AMERICAN HISTORY: GUIDE TO
MATERIALS FOR RESEARCH. New York: H.W. Wilson, 1942. Reprint.
New York: Octagon, 1973.

> This bibliography is organized topically and chronologically. Es-
> pecially useful to students of government and the Constitution are
> chapters 1 (which lists general aids such as bibliographies of
> bibliographies), 2 (which deals with the colonial, revolutionary
> and confederate periods), 3 (which serves as a guide to public
> documents), and 7 (which deals with political science, the Con-
> stitution and legal history).

BIBLIOGRAPHIC GUIDE TO LAW. Boston: G.K. Hall, 1975-- . Annual.

> In this publication, each entry includes the Library of Congress
> cataloging information. Twelve subjects are covered including
> government publications and U.S. law.

A BIBLIOGRAPHY AND INDEXES OF U.S. CONGRESSIONAL COMMITTEE
PRINTS. 2 vols. Edited by Rochelle Field. Complied by Gary Halvorson,
Laura Kaminsky, Vera Waddell, and Judy Cohen. Westport, Conn.: Green-
wood Press, 1976.

> Committee prints are unofficial studies done by congressional
> committee staffs for use by congressional committee. Because
> they are unofficial, they are not automatically placed in deposi-
> tory libraries or in the MONTHLY CATALOG (see p. 8). The
> number of copies printed is also limited. This guide consists of
> a bibliography (volume 1) and indexes (volume 2). They are
> organized on the basis of the type of committee--House Standing
> Committee, House Select Committee, Joint Committee, Senate
> Standing Committee and Senate Select Committee. Within each
> category, the entries are organized alphabetically first on the
> basis of the key word in the committee's name, then by the key
> word of the subcommittee name and then by the key word of the
> title of the report. Greenwood Press also has the committee
> prints on microfiche. They cover the period from 1917 and the
> Sixty-fifth Congress to 1969 and the Ninety-first Congress.

Body, Alexander C., ed. ANNOTATED BIBLIOGRAPHY OF BIBLIOGRAPHIES
ON SELECTED GOVERNMENT PUBLICATIONS AND SUPPLEMENTARY
GUIDES TO THE SUPERINTENDENT OF DOCUMENTS CLASSIFICATIONS
SYSTEM. Kalamazoo: Western Michigan University, 1967. Supplements,
1968 and 1970.

The major portion of this work consists of an annotated bibliography of bibliographies published by government agencies. There is also an extensive list of abbreviations and symbols used by government agencies and an alphabetized list of government agencies which published the listed bibliographies.

Boyd, Anne M., ed. UNITED STATES GOVERNMENT PUBLICATIONS: SOURCES OF INFORMATION FOR LIBRARIANS. 3d ed. Revised by Rae E. Rips. New York: H.W. Wilson, 1952.

This is a guide to the publications of Congress, the courts, the executive branch, and the independent regulatory commissions organized on the basis of the sources of the documents. The index is organized on the basis of subject rather than issuing agent.

Brock, Clifton. THE LITERATURE OF POLITICAL SCIENCE: A GUIDE FOR STUDENTS, LIBRARIANS AND TEACHERS. New York: R.R. Bowker, 1969.

This guide to general information sources in political science is designed primarily for undergraduate majors in political science and for beginning graduate students as an introduction to library materials and research methods in the discipline. Although not intended for advanced specialists, it is nonetheless a useful compilation and description of the myriad of periodical literature, indexes, abstracts, national and state governmental publications, and bibliographies useful to political scientists in general and students of the Constitution in particular. The bibliography in chapter 12 on American government and politics is especially helpful.

Brooks, Alexander D. CIVIL RIGHTS AND LIBERTIES IN THE UNITED STATES: AN ANNOTATED BIBLIOGRAPHY. New York: Civil Liberties Educational Fund, 1962.

Compiled for use by high school students, this bibliography by a Rutgers professor of law nonetheless is a useful source to scholarly works dealing with individual rights published between 1940 and 1960. The second half, devoted to works of fiction and to audiovisual materials, is less useful.

CATALOG OF THE PUBLIC DOCUMENTS OF THE CONGRESS AND OF ALL DEPARTMENTS OF THE GOVERNMENT OF THE UNITED STATES FOR THE PERIOD MARCH 4, 1893 TO DECEMBER 31, 1940. 25 vols. Washington, D.C.: Government Printing Office, 1896-1945.

Commonly known as the DOCUMENTS CATALOG, this catalog is considered to be the basic and most complete guide to official documents for the period covered. Alphabetized, it is without either a table of contents or an index.

CHECKLIST OF UNITED STATES DOCUMENTS, 1789-1909. 3d ed. Washington, D.C.: Government Printing Office, 1911.

Commonly known as the CHECKLIST, this bibliography contains
a list of congressional and executive publications in the library
of the Superintendent of Documents up to 1909. No index.

Congressional Quarterly. HISTORIC DOCUMENTS. Washington, D.C.:
1973-- .

This selection of materials from government reports, court decisions, presidential statements and special studies is organized
chronologically, on the basis of months, with a subject matter
index. The first volume covering 1972 includes such materials
as the Surgeon General's report on smoking and the State of
the Union address.

CONGRESSIONAL QUARTERLY GUIDE TO CURRENT AMERICAN GOVERN-
MENT. Washington, D.C.: Congressional Quarterly Service, 1963-- .
Biannual.

This is a general review of major development in the judicial,
executive and legislative branches of the national government
during the preceding six months. It is based upon materials
used in the CONGRESSIONAL QUARTERLY WEEKLY REPORT
(see p. 93).

Corwin, Edward S. THE CONSTITUTION AND WHAT IT MEANS TODAY.
Edited by Harold W. Chase and Craig R. Ducat. Rev. ed. Princeton, N.J.:
Princeton University Press, 1975.

This is a shorter version of THE CONSTITUTION ANNOTATED,
revised and updated as warranted by changes in constitutional
interpretation.

CUMULATIVE SUBJECT GUIDE TO UNITED STATES GOVERNMENT
BIBLIOGRAPHIES, 1924-1973. 6 vols. Arlington, Va.: Carrollton Press,
1976.

Alphabetized on the basis of subject, this 6-volume guide to
government bibliographies has 18,000 entries citing bibliographies
plus 22,000 entries citing publications which have extensive
bibliographies. In compiling this guide, the editors went through
every issue of the MONTHLY CATALOG (see p. 8) since 1924.
The descriptions of the material are based on those in the
MONTHLY CATALOG and thus include such information as the
title, author and issuing agency. The format that is used is
similar to that used in the DOCUMENTS CATALOG (see p. 3).

CUMULATIVE SUBJECT INDEX TO THE MONTHLY CATALOG OF UNITED
STATES GOVERNMENT PUBLICATIONS, 1900-1971. 15 vols. Arlington,
Va.: Carrollton Press, 1974.

This massive index is organized on the basis of subject matter
and is one of the most useful means of finding a government
publication listed in the MONTHLY CATALOG (see p. 8).

Fingerhut, Eugene. THE FINGERHUT GUIDE: SOURCES IN AMERICAN
HISTORY. Santa Barbara, Calif.: American Bibliographic Center, Clio
Press, 1973.

Part 2 of this guide contains basic references to social services and history; to American history; to indexes and abstracts; to guides to government documents and publications. Each section is arranged chronologically.

Ford, Paul L., ed. SOME MATERIALS FOR A BIBLIOGRAPHY OF THE OFFICIAL PUBLICATIONS OF THE CONTINENTAL CONGRESS, 1774-1789. Brooklyn, N.Y.: By the author, 1890. Reprint. Ann Arbor, Mich,: University Microfilms, 1964.

> The chronologically organized selections include such materials as letters of members of the Continental Congress, congressional resolutions and other extracts from the JOURNAL OF THE CON-TINENTAL CONGRESS, observations on the revolution made by congressmen, the Declaration of Independence, and the Articles of Confederation.

Freidel, Frank B., ed. HARVARD GUIDE TO AMERICAN HISTORY. 2 vols. Cambridge, Mass.: Belknap Press of the Harvard University Press, 1974.

> Over 1,300 pages in length, this comprehensive work is a use-ful guide to historical literature covering the period from the colonial era through the late 1960s and to public documents of national, state, and local governments as well as to unpublished materials in state, local, and national archives.

Friend, William L. ANGLO-AMERICAN LEGAL BIBLIOGRAPHIES: AN ANNOTATED GUIDE. Introduction by Archibald MacLeish. Washington, D.C.: Government Printing Office, 1944.

> With an introduction by MacLeish who succeeded Friend as law librarian of the Library of Congress, this outdated, but still somewhat useful, work cites legal works dealing with English and American law, excluding material dealing exclusively with statutory law. Chapter 1 is a historical survey.

Garrison, Curtis W. LIST OF MANUSCRIPT COLLECTIONS IN THE LI-BRARY OF CONGRESS TO JULY 1931. Washington, D.C.: Library of Congress, 1932.

> As the largest single repository of the manuscripts and papers of public figures in the United States, the Library of Congress is a useful resource for those whose constitutional research necessitates access to unpublished manuscripts. This is a list of its holdings through the early 1930s.

Harmon, Robert B. POLITICAL SCIENCE BIBLIOGRAPHY. Metuchen, N.J.: Scarecrow Press, 1973.

> This bibliography of political science literature includes citations to works in the general area of constitutional law.

Holler, Frederick L. INFORMATION SOURCES OF POLITICAL SCIENCE. 5 vols. Santa Barbara, Calif.: American Bibliographic Center, Clio Press, 1975.

Volume 1, which is devoted to general reference sources, and volume 3, which is devoted to American government and law (including some international law), are more useful to students of the Constitution than the other volumes. Volume 2 includes citations to works in the social sciences, including anthropology, psychology, economics and geography--its political science citations are thus somewhat skimpy.

Howell, Margaret. A BIBLIOGRAPHY OF LEGAL MATERIALS. 2 vols. Woodbridge: New Jersey Appellate Printing Co., 1969.

Compiled for the use of Rutgers--the State University Law Library and arranged by subject matter, this bibliography includes sections on constitutional law and basic civil rights and liberties.

INDEX TO LEGAL PERIODICALS. New York: H.W. Wilson, 1909-- . Monthly except September.

Indexed by subject and author, this is an indispensable and comprehensive guide to law review articles dealing with constitutional law as well as other legal areas.

INDEX TO PERIODICAL ARTICLES BY AND ABOUT NEGROES. Boston: G.K. Hall, 1950-- . Annual.

Formerly entitled INDEX TO SELECTED PERIODICALS (below), this is a guide to periodical literature of various disciplines which deals not just with the law and race relations but with blacks generally. Because the meaning of the Civil War amendments has been determined in large measure by race relations cases, this is a useful source of information for students of the Constitution.

INDEX TO SELECTED PERIODICALS, DECENNIAL CUMULATION, 1950-1959. Boston: G.K. Hall, 1959.

This index of the first forty issues of the INDEX TO SELECTED PERIODICALS is now entitled INDEX TO PERIODICAL ARTICLES BY AND ABOUT NEGROES (above).

INTERNATIONAL BIBLIOGRAPHY OF POLITICAL SCIENCE. Chicago: Aldine Publishing Co., 1952-- . Annual.

Volume 3 of the INTERNATIONAL BIBLIOGRAPHY OF THE SOCIAL SCIENCES indexes articles in over 1,000 political science journals as well as articles from a few other journals and some books of particular interest to political scientists. It is organized by subject and author. Although much of political science is devoted to matters other than the Constitution, constitutional law continues to be a major concern of the discipline and its literature.

INTERNATIONAL POLITICAL SCIENCE ABSTRACTS. Oxford, Engl.: A.R. Mowbray, 1951-- . Quarterly.

This publication abstracts articles in over one hundred political science journals, including works in constitutional law. It contains a subject and author index.

Jackson, Ellen P., ed. SUBJECT GUIDE TO MAJOR UNITED STATES GOVERNMENT PUBLICATIONS. Chicago: American Library Association, 1968.

The first 158 pages list government publications by subject and include only leading publications rather than exhaustive listings. For example, under the subject heading "Civil Rights," the guide includes only two entries--the Civil Rights Commission reports entitled FREEDOM TO THE FREE and TO SECURE THESE RIGHTS. The second half of the book is a useful guide to catalogs, indexes, bibliographies, and guides to government publications. It lists and annotates all the standard guides in print such as Boyd and Schmeckebier as well as the CHECK-LIST (see p. 3) and MONTHLY CATALOG (see p. 8).

Jones, L.A., and Chipman, F.E. AN INDEX TO LEGAL PERIODICAL LITERATURE. 6 vols. Dobbs Ferry, N.Y.: Oceana, 1883-1933.

The first volume covers 1791 to 1886. The years 1887 to 1932 are covered in the other volumes. Volumes 4 to 6 are consolidations of volumes 1 through 26 of the annual INDEX TO LEGAL PERIODICALS, 1909-- .

LAW REVIEW DIGEST. Boonton, N.J.: Clark Publishing Co., 1951-- . Bimonthly.

This work abstracts articles in law reviews, including articles in constitutional law.

Leidy, William P. A POPULAR GUIDE TO GOVERNMENT PUBLICATIONS. 4th ed. New York: Columbia University Press, 1976.

Organized by topic, this is an annotated guide to government publications.

Lu, Joseph K. UNITED STATES GOVERNMENT PUBLICATIONS RELATING TO THE SOCIAL SCIENCES: A SELECTED ANNOTATED GUIDE. Beverly Hills, Calif.: Sage Publications, 1975.

In addition to guides to general catalogs, indexes, and bibliographies, this work includes guides to government publications organized on the basis of historic eras (American Revolution through the Vietnam War) as well as on the basis of broad subject areas such as Congress, federal courts, and American history.

Mersky, Roy M., and Jacobstein, J.M., eds. INDEX TO PERIODICAL ARTICLES RELATED TO LAW. 20 vols. Dobbs Ferry, N.Y.: Glanville Publishers, 1974, 1979.

General Sources

This publication indexes only those articles considered by the editors to be of research value. It includes articles not indexed in the INDEX TO LEGAL PERIODICALS. Started in response to the Public School Segregation Case in 1954 which the editors view as a catalyst in the trend toward applying the techniques of the social and behavioral sciences to the law, the first two volumes are limited to those periodicals received at Yale and Columbia but it has since been expanded. The INDEX TO PERIODICAL ARTICLES RELATED TO THE LAW--FIVE YEAR CUMULATION, published in 1974, covers the years 1969-73. The TEN YEAR INDEX TO PERIODICALS RELATED TO LAW was published in 1970. The index is organized in four parts--subject, author, articles, and list of periodicals indexed. Volumes 1-10 were published in 1970. Volumes 11-15 were published in 1974. Volumes 16-20 were published in 1979.

Millett, Stephen M. A SELECTED BIBLIOGRAPHY OF AMERICAN CONSTITUTIONAL HISTORY. Introduction by C. Herman Pritchett. Santa Barbara, Calif.: American Bibliographic Center, Clio Press, 1975.

The first three chapters of this bibliography are devoted to such primary sources as judicial decisions and presidential papers, to survey studies and commentaries, and to the origins of the Constitution. The rest of the work is organized on the basis of the organization of the Constitution. Thus, chapter 4 includes works dealing with Articles I and the Congress and the states, chapter 5 is devoted to the president and Article II, and chapter 6 deals with the judiciary and Article III.

MONTHLY CATALOG OF GOVERNMENT PUBLICATIONS. Washington, D.C.: Superintendent of Documents, 1895-- .

Publications are arranged by issuing agency. An index in each issue is arranged by subject and by title. A subject matter index entitled UNITED STATES GOVERNMENT PUBLICATIONS MONTHLY CATALOG, DECENNIAL CUMULATIVE INDEX has been published every ten years since 1941. Each of these subject matter indexes is in two volumes. There is also an author index published every ten years entitled UNITED STATES GOVERNMENT PUBLICATIONS, MONTHLY CATALOG, DECENNIAL CUMULATIVE PERSONAL AUTHOR INDEX. Both of these guides to the MONTHLY CATALOG are published by the Superintendent of Documents. The most useful tool in locating the desired document in the MONTHLY CATALOG is the CUMULATIVE SUBJECT INDEX TO THE MONTHLY CATALOG OF UNITED STATES GOVERNMENT PUBLICATIONS, 1900-1971 (see p. 4). This 15-volume, 13,500 page index is organized on the basis of subject matter.

MONTHLY DIGEST OF LEGAL ARTICLES. Greenvale, N.Y.: Research and Documentation Corp., 1969-- .

This publication digests articles on various legal problems published primarily in law journals.

Mugridge, Donald H., and McCrum, Blanche P., comps. AMERICAN HISTORY AND CIVILIZATION: A LIST OF GUIDES AND ANNOTATED OR

SELECTED BIBLIOGRAPHIES. 2d rev. ed. Washington, D.C.: Library of Congress, General Reference and Bibliography Division, 1951.

> This is a list of bibliographies of works in the broad area of American history. Although the focus is not upon constitutional development, it lists guides to materials dealing with constitutional questions and is therefore a useful tool for research in constitutional law and constitutional history.

Mugridge, Donald H., and McCrum, Blanche P., eds., prepared under the direction of Roy P. Basler. A GUIDE TO THE STUDY OF THE UNITED STATES OF AMERICA: REPRESENTATIVE BOOKS REFLECTING THE DEVELOPMENT OF AMERICAN LIFE AND THOUGHT. Washington, D.C.: Library of Congress, General Reference and Bibliography Division, 1960.

> Three chapters of this extensive--1,193 pages--work are devoted to the Constitution and American national government. Chapter 29 deals with "Constitution and Government," chapter 30 with "Law and Justice," and chapter 31 with "Politics, Parties, Elections." The Supplement is similarly organized--thus chapter 9 covers the "Constitution and Government." The 1956 Supplement, published in 1976, was prepared by Oliver H. Orr, Jr. under the direction of Roy P. Basler.

New York University School of Law. ANNUAL SURVEY OF AMERICAN LAW. Dobbs Ferry, N.Y.: Oceana, 1942-- .

> This publication is a survey of major developments in the law in the preceding year.

Palic, Vladimir M. GOVERNMENT PUBLICATIONS: A GUIDE TO BIBLIOGRAPHIC TOOLS. Washington, D.C.: Library of Congress, 1975.

> This is a guide to bibliographies of government publications and documents.

Peltason, Jack W. CORWIN AND PELTASON'S UNDERSTANDING THE CONSTITUTION. 5th ed. New York: Holt, Rinehart and Winston, 1950.

> Organized on the basis of the Constitution, this work briefly discusses for the general audience what each provision of the Constitution means as interpreted by the Supreme Court.

Pimsleur, Meira G., ed. LAW BOOKS PUBLISHED. Dobbs Ferry, N.Y.: Glanville Publishers, 1976.

> Part 1 lists law books by author and title, part.2 lists books by subject and series, and part 3 lists publishers and distributors along with their addresses. Pimsleur, along with J. Myron Jacobstein, also compiled and edited LAW BOOKS IN PRINT (Dobbs Ferry, N.Y.: Glanville Publishers, 1965) which is kept up to date by supplements.

Poore, Benjamin P., ed. DESCRIPTIVE CATALOGUES OF THE GOVERNMENT PUBLICATIONS OF THE UNITED STATES, 1774-1881. Washington, D.C.: Government Printing Office, 1885.

This is the predecessor of the Ames COMPREHENSIVE INDEX (see p. 1) and the MONTHLY CATALOG (see p. 8) which serves as a guide to the period up to 1881.

_____. THE FEDERAL AND STATE CONSTITUTIONS, COLONIAL CHARTERS, AND OTHER ORGANIZED LAWS OF THE U.S. COMPILED UNDER AN ORDER OF THE UNITED STATES SENATE. 2d ed. 2 vols. 1878. Reprint. New York: Burt Franklin, 1972.

This is an official collection of the national Constitution and the fundamental laws--grants, charters, constitutions--of each of the states arranged chronologically and alphabetically by state. There is an introductory note to most of the documents.

PREVIEW OF UNITED STATES SUPREME COURT CASES. Philadelphia: Association of American Law Schools and the American Law Institute--American Bar Association Committee on Continuing Professional Education, 1974-- . 6 per month, September-May.

PREVIEW contains brief memoranda of each case the Supreme Court is to consider during each term with the name of the case to be considered, the docket number, the issue, the background and significance of the case and the arguments of both the petitioner and the respondent. An index is published at the end of each court session.

Schmeckebier, Laurence F., and Eastin, Roy B. GOVERNMENT PUBLICATIONS AND THEIR USE. 2d rev. ed. Washington, D.C.: Brookings Institution, 1969.

This is a comprehensive guide to government publications. It includes sections on catalogs and indexes; bibliographies; availability of publications; congressional publications; federal and state constitutions; federal laws, state laws; court decisions; administrative regulations and departmental rulings; presidential papers such as messages, speeches, and proclamations; foreign affairs; periodicals; and microfilm editions of government publications.

SHEPARD'S LAW REVIEW CITATIONS: A COMPILATION OF CITATIONS TO LAW REVIEWS AND LEGAL PERIODICALS. Colorado Springs, Colo.: Shepard's Citations, 1974.

This is a compilation of law review citations which appear in opinions in the U.S. REPORTS, the FEDERAL REPORTER, the FEDERAL SUPPLEMENT, FEDERAL RULES and state court opinions. It is organized on the basis of the law review in which the cited article appears.

SHEPARD'S UNITED STATES CITATIONS: A COMPILATION OF CITATIONS TO UNITED STATES SUPREME COURT CASES. New York: Frank Shepard Co., 1943-71. Colorado Springs: Shepards Citations, Inc., 1971-- . Quarterly. Supplements.

This work covers citations of Supreme Court decisions by lower federal courts, state courts, and by other government agencies.

SOCIAL SCIENCE CITATION INDEX. Philadelphia: Institute for Scientific Information, 1970-- . Annual.

This index primarily concerns the literature of the social and behavioral sciences. The PERMUTERM SUBJECT INDEX, published annually, is an index to the SSCI.

Tompkins, Hamilton B. BURR BIBLIOGRAPHY: A LIST OF BOOKS RELATING TO AARON BURR. New York: Historical Printing Club, 1892. Reprint. New York: Burt Franklin, 1970.

This bibliography of books about Burr includes reference to his trial for conspiracy, a trial which raised questions of continuing constitutional significance such as judicial authority to subpoena a president.

Tseng, Henry P. COMPLETE GUIDE TO LEGAL MATERIALS IN MICROFILM. Washington, D.C.: University Publications of America, 1976. SUPPLEMENT, 1977, 1979.

This is a guide to both American and foreign legal materials such as periodicals, archives, government documents, and manuscripts that are on microfilm. The 1975 guide contains about 17,000 entries and the 1976 paperback supplement contains about 8,000 entries.

U. S. Library of Congress. NATIONAL UNION CATALOG OF MANUSCRIPT COLLECTIONS. Washington, D.C.: 1959-- . Irregular.

This lists, describes, and notes the location of manuscripts held not only by the Library of Congress but throughout the United States. It also includes information about oral history holdings--the oral reminiscences of those who participated in some event of historical importance. The issues in the series are identified by the year in which the descriptions were cataloged. The first volume includes materials cataloged from 1959 through 1961 and was issued in 1962. The latest listing is 1975.

U. S. Library of Congress. National Referral Center. A DIRECTORY OF INFORMATION RESOURCES IN THE UNITED STATES: SOCIAL SCIENCES. Rev. ed. Washington, D.C.: 1973.

The National Referral Center serves as a guide to sources of information available to the researcher. Although it does not itself provide substantive research aid or bibliographic assistance, it can direct the researcher to whoever possesses the information. Researchers can call or write the National Referral Center for such aid. This directory of resources lists the name of organizations (government agencies, universities, associations, libraries, and other sources), their addresses, areas of interest, publications, and the kind of information services offered by each organization. The directory also includes a subject index.

Wynkoop, Sally. SUBJECT GUIDE TO GOVERNMENT REFERENCE BOOKS. Littleton, Colo.: Libraries Unlimited, 1972.

This is an annotated guide to reference materials published by the Government Printing Office and government agencies. Intended primarily for librarians as an aid in the selection of reference works, it includes such materials as bibliographies, catalogs, and guides. The selections on law, political science, race relations and history are useful to the student of the Constitution.

Chapter 2

BACKGROUND OF THE CONSTITUTION

(The Continental Congresses, The Declaration of Independence and The Articles of Confederation)

Adams, John. A DEFENCE OF THE CONSTITUTIONS OF GOVERNMENTS OF THE UNITED STATES OF AMERICA. 1787. Reprint. New York: Da Capo Press, 1971.

> In 1778, Turgot, the philosopher and French Minister of Finance, criticized the separation of powers system used by the states in the United States and argued for an integrated system. In response to this criticism in Turgot's LETTERS as well as criticism by other writers such as Macaulay in his HISTORY and Burgh's POLITICAL DISQUISITION, Adams wrote this defense of the constitutions of the American states and particularly of the separation of powers doctrine incorporated in those documents. Written before the adoption of the national Constitution, the DEFENCE was an analysis of various forms of government. The DEFENCE is also included in volume 6 of THE WORKS OF JOHN ADAMS, edited by Charles Francis Adams and published by Little, Brown in 1856.

Bailyn, Bernard. THE IDEOLOGICAL ORIGINS OF THE AMERICAN REVOLUTION. Cambridge, Mass.: Harvard University Press, 1967.

> This is an examination of the political and constitutional ideals of the colonists which propelled them to rebellion and an analysis of the relationship between American political thought and European tradition.

Bancroft, George. HISTORY OF THE FORMATION OF THE CONSTITUTION OF THE UNITED STATES OF AMERICA. 2 vols. New York: D. Appleton and Co., 1882.

> Written in a florid nineteenth-century style, this leisurely history traces developments from the seventeenth century in the colonies through the period of preparations for the Philadelphia convention. Volume 1, entitled THE CONFEDERATION, discusses such matters as the effect of the Revolution of 1688, William Penn's proposals for a federal union and Pitt's relationship to the colonies. Volume 2, entitled ON THE WAY TO A FEDERAL CONVENTION, deals with the period from 1783 to 1787. The appendix includes the letters and papers of public figures which were used in preparing the history.

Background of the Constitution

Becker, Carl. THE DECLARATION OF INDEPENDENCE: A STUDY IN THE HISTORY OF POLITICAL IDEAS. New York: Knopf, 1960.

> Originally published in 1922, this analysis of the events and ideas in America between 1764 and 1776 examines the manner in which the political theories of the colonists were shaped and modified by fluid political conditions.

Beloff, Max, ed. THE DEBATE ON THE AMERICAN REVOLUTION: A SOURCEBOOK. 1761-1783. New York: Harper and Row, 1965.

> A collection of readings focusing on the controversy over separation from Great Britain.

Boyd, Julian. THE DECLARATION OF INDEPENDENCE. Princeton, N.J.: Princeton University Press, 1945.

> An analysis of the provisions of the Declaration of Independence as submitted to, revised and adopted by the Continental Congress.

Burnett, Edmund Cody. THE CONTINENTAL CONGRESS. New York: Macmillan, 1941.

> A history of the Continental Congress from its inception in 1774 to its extinction when the Congress under the new Constitution first gathered in March 1789. Viewing the Continental Congress as "the central stage" for the enactment of "the more significant phases of the drama called the American Revolution," the editor of the LETTERS OF MEMBERS OF THE CONTINENTAL CONGRESS (below) assesses the ideas, debates, conflicts, and forces which propelled Americans toward a break with England, the political philosophy which led to the adoption of the Declaration of Independence and the Articles of Confederation, and the operation of constitutional government under that first organic law as these took shape within the Congress.

_____. "The 'More Perfect Union': The Continental Congress Seeks a Formula." CATHOLIC HISTORICAL REVIEW 24 (April 1938): 1-29.

> In this brief overview of the preconstitutional period written for the 150th anniversary of the Constitution, Burnett looks first at the period from September 1774 to the adoption of the Articles in 1781 and discusses in somewhat more detail the period from the Articles to the adoption of the Constitution within the framework of the idea of unity.

_____, ed. LETTERS OF MEMBERS OF THE CONTINENTAL CONGRESS. 9 vols. Washington, D.C.: Government Printing Office, 1921-38.

> This is the most extensive collection of letters written by the delegates to the Continental Congress and contains many useful materials on the activities of the Congress and the attitudes of Congressmen toward the crisis with England and the move to draft a constitution to govern the new nation.

Dargo, George. ROOTS OF THE REPUBLIC: A NEW PERSPECTIVE ON EARLY AMERICAN CONSTITUTIONALISM. New York: Praeger Publishers, 1974.

> Although the Constitution of 1789 sought to assure constitutionalism by a written constitution which placed limitations on the powers of government, guaranteed the rights of individuals and divided power among governmental units to prevent its abuse, Dargo argues that constitutionalism was deeply embedded in the American system in that half of our history before the adoption of the Constitution and suggests that the written Constitution embodied the ideas of the colonial period.

Dumbauld, Edward. THE DECLARATION OF INDEPENDENCE AND WHAT IT MEANS TODAY. Norman: University of Oklahoma Press, 1950.

> This is an analysis of the provisions of the Declaration of Independence in terms of the historical background of each and its significance to American political theory and constitutional law.

Ferguson E. James, and Catanzariti, John, eds. THE PAPERS OF ROBERT MORRIS, 1781-1784. 3 vols. Pittsburgh: University of Pittsburgh Press, 1977.

> The papers are organized chronologically. Volume 1 covers the period from 7 February to 31 July 1781. Volume 2 covers from August through September of 1781 and volume 3 covers 1 October 1781 to 10 January 1782.

Ford, Paul L. "The Association of the First Congress." POLITICAL SCIENCE QUARTERLY 6 (1891): 613-25.

> In this examination of the problems facing the Continental Congress, Ford points to the ad hoc, extralegal nature of its establishment and the domestic destructiveness of the economic weapons designed to cripple British trade which Congress relied upon to protest the policies of the English parliament.

Ford, W.D., ed. JOURNALS OF THE CONTINENTAL CONGRESS, 1774-1789. 34 vols. Washington, D.C.: Government Printing Office, 1904-37.

> This is a record of the official proceedings of the Continental Congress and the debates on such questions as independence and framing of the Articles of Confederation. The National Archives has a complete set of the papers and proceedings of the Congress on microfilm. There is also a 25-volume edition of the JOURNALS published in 1937 by the Government Printing Office.

Friedenwald, Herbert. THE DECLARATION OF INDEPENDENCE: AN INTERPRETATION AND AN ANALYSIS. 1904. Reprint. Introduction by Carl Ubbelohde. New York: Da Capo Press, 1974.

> This work is an analysis of the political events from 1774 to July of 1776 and of the document which emerged in that month. The first half of the book is an analysis of the Continental Congress, its increasing power and growing popular acceptance, its committees and their work and the movement for independence within that

body culminating in the writing, adoption and signing of the
Declaration of Independence. The second half is an analysis
of the document itself--the philosophy of the Declaration of
Independence, its purpose, its literary merits, and the basis
for its claims of oppression by the British.

Friedrich, Carl J., and McCloskey, Robert G., eds. FROM THE DECLARA-
TION OF INDEPENDENCE TO THE CONSTITUTION: THE ROOTS OF
AMERICAN CONSTITUTIONALISM. New York: Liberal Arts Press, 1954.

The first half of the book is a discussion of the political theories such as federalism, the natural rights of men, separation
of powers and constitutionalism which influenced the framers
and of the process of adoption of the Declaration of Independence,
the Articles of Confederation and the Constitution. The second
half is a collection of basic documents including the Declaration
of Independence, the various proposals presented to the constitutional convention, the Constitution as adopted, the Bill of
Rights and the amendments added through the Twenty-Second.

Gephart, Ronald M., comp. PERIODICAL LITERATURE ON THE AMERI-
CAN REVOLUTION: HISTORICAL RESEARCH AND CHANGING INTERPRE-
TATIONS, 1895-1970. Washington, D.C.: Library of Congress, General
Reference and Bibliographic Division, 1971.

Published in conjunction with the bicentennial of the American
Revolution, this is a selected bibliography of 1,100 essays and
periodical literature dealing with the period from the Revolution
through the Constitution published during the past seventy-five
years. Organized topically and chronologically, the chapters
on the confederate period, the Constitution and political and
legal developments are most useful.

Hawke, David. A TRANSACTION OF FREE MEN: THE BIRTH AND COURSE
OF THE DECLARATION OF INDEPENDENCE. New York: Charles Scribner's
Sons, 1964.

This is an analysis of the Declaration of Independence as a
product of the leading members of the Continental Congress responsible for its framing, with emphasis upon the thinking and
roles of John Adams and Thomas Jefferson.

Hazelton, John H. THE DECLARATION OF INDEPENDENCE: ITS HIS-
TORY. 1906. Reprint. New York: Da Capo Press, 1970.

This is an account of the deliberations of the Continental Congress on the issue of independence and on the drafting and
adoption of the Declaration of Independence. The second half
of this extensively documented work consists of footnotes. The
appendix includes Jefferson's notes on the deliberations of the
Congress on independence, letters of some of the delegates
concerning the debates on independence, various drafts of the
Declaration and Dickinson's VINDICATION, his answer to the
charge that as a member of the Continental Congress he had
opposed the Declaration of Independence.

Jameson, John Franklin, ed. ESSAYS IN THE CONSTITUTIONAL HIS-
TORY OF THE UNITED STATES IN THE FORMATIVE PERIOD, 1775-1789.
1889. Reprint. New York: Da Capo Press, 1970.

> These essays examine a number of constitutional issues of the
> preconstitutional period such as the predecessor of the Supreme
> Court, the movement toward a constitutional convention, the
> development of the executive departments and the status of the
> slave from 1775 to 1789.

Jefferson, Thomas. A SUMMARY VIEW OF THE RIGHTS OF BRITISH
AMERICA. Edited by Paul Leicester Ford. Brooklyn: Historical Printing
Club, 1892. Reprint. New York: Burt Franklin, 1971.

> Circulated anonymously in 1774, this pamphlet in which Jefferson
> expounds his views on the conflict between the colonies and
> Great Britain was published in limited number (one hundred) in
> 1892.

Jensen, Merrill. THE AMERICAN REVOLUTION WITHIN AMERICA. New
York: New York University Press, 1974.

> Originally delivered as the Anson G. Phelps Lectures at New
> York University in 1973, this work examines the internal politi-
> cal and constitutional process of constructing a new nation in
> terms of the clashes between colonists in the period before 1776,
> the internal resistance to independence and the "revolution of
> 1787" at Philadelphia.

_____. THE ARTICLES OF CONFEDERATION: AN INTERPRETATION
OF THE SOCIAL-CONSTITUTIONAL HISTORY OF THE AMERICAN
REVOLUTION 1774-1781. 1940. Reprint. Madison: University of Wiscon-
sin Press, 1966.

> This is an analysis of the social and political struggles within
> the colonies which culminated in the Declaration of Independence
> from Great Britain and the adoption of the Articles of Confedera-
> tion. It is Jensen's position that the same forces and philosophies
> which led to independence were given expression in the Articles.

_____. "The Articles of Confederation: A Re-Interpretation." PACIFIC
HISTORICAL REVIEW 6 (June 1937): 120-42.

> In this examination of the prolonged conflict over the framing
> of the Articles of Confederation, Jensen argues that the conser-
> vative revolutionaries who supported a strong central government
> selected on the basis of population rather than on the basis of
> the equality of the states were victorious in the first draft of
> the Articles. They lost to the radical revolutionaries who sup-
> ported the concept of sovereign, independent states. In turn,
> the nationalists were ultimately victorious in their fight to dis-
> card the Articles for the Constitution and to establish a federal
> system.

_____. THE FOUNDING OF A NATION: A HISTORY OF THE AMERICAN
REVOLUTION, 1763-1776. New York: Oxford University Press, 1968.

Background of the Constitution

This history of the challenges to British authority, culminating
in the decision to withdraw from the British Empire, emphasizes
the political actions of the prewar period but deals also with the
political and constitutional theories which justified those actions
in the view of the colonists.

_____, ed.   TRACTS OF THE AMERICAN REVOLUTION, 1763-1776.
Indianapolis: Bobbs-Merrill, 1967.

With an introduction by the author in which he outlines the
events occurring between 1763 and 1776 and discusses the role
of the pamphlet writers of the period, this is a collection of
seventeen pamphlets and newspaper articles, most reprinted in
their entirety, representative of the kinds of basic political and
constitutional arguments made by the colonists against English
policies after 1763 and in support of or in opposition to the
notion of independence between 1774 and 1776. The collection
includes not only the better known and available works such as
Paine's COMMON SENSE and Jefferson's SUMMARY VIEW OF
THE RIGHTS OF BRITISH AMERICANS but also less available
tracts.

Kammen, Michael. DEPUTIES AND LIBERTY: THE ORIGINS OF REPRE-
SENTATIVE GOVERNMENT IN COLONIAL AMERICA. New York: Philadelphia Book Co., 1969.

This is an analysis of the beginnings of representative government
in the seventeenth century which served as the basis for the evolution of governmental institutions in the latter colonial and constitutional periods.

Kasson, John A. THE EVOLUTION OF THE CONSTITUTION OF THE
UNITED STATES OF AMERICA AND HISTORY OF THE MONROE DOC-
TRINE. Boston: Houghton Mifflin Co., 1904.

Written originally at the request of the Constitutional Centennial
Commission for the 1887 celebration, this is an examination of
the debates and plans considered by the Continental Congress
which led to the adoption of the Declaration of Independence and
the Articles of Confederation, the infirmities of the Articles of
Confederation, the demands for a new Constitution, the debates
at the Philadelphia convention, an analysis of the major provisions of the Constitution, and an account of the process of
proposing and adopting the Bill of Rights and subsequent amendments.

Latham, Earl, ed.   THE DECLARATION OF INDEPENDENCE AND THE
CONSTITUTION. Problems of American Civilization Series. Rev. ed.
Lexington, Mass.: D.C. Heath, 1964.

With an introduction by the editor, this brief volume contains
twelve excerpts from the writings of such scholars as Merrill
Jensen, Charles A. Beard, Charles Warren, and Edward S.
Corwin, comparing and contrasting the ideals and principles
embodied in these two expressions of American ideals of government.

Leder, Lawrence H. THE MEANING OF THE AMERICAN REVOLUTION. New York: New Viewpoints, 1968.

> This collection of 23 articles from the NEW YORK TIMES deals with various facets of the American Revolution, including the nature of the Declaration of Independence, the Constitution, and the Bill of Rights.

Mably, Gabriel Donnot de. REMARKS CONCERNING THE GOVERNMENT AND LAWS OF THE UNITED STATES OF AMERICA IN FOUR LETTERS ADDRESSED TO MR. ADAMS FROM THE FRENCH OF THE ABBE DE MABLY. 1785. Reprint. New York: Burt Franklin, 1964.

> This is a collection of letters to John Adams in which the Abbe de Mably analyzes and comments upon the Articles of Confederation and the constitutions of the states.

McDonald, Forrest, and McDonald, Ellen Shapir, eds. CONFEDERATION AND CONSTITUTION, 1781-1789. Columbia: University of South Carolina Press, 1968.

> This is a collection of documents relevant to what the editors consider the dominant question in the period between 1781 and 1789--whether the former colonists and new states would form one nation. Included are such materials as the Articles of Confederation, the Treaty of Peace between the United States and Great Britain, town meeting resolutions, congressional committee reports, the Northwest Ordinance, excerpts from debates at the constitutional convention, Madison's "Federalist No. 10," Lee's "Letter of a Federal Farmer," and the accepted and rejected proposals for the Bill of Rights.

McIlwain, Charles H. THE AMERICAN REVOLUTION. A CONSTITUTIONAL INTERPRETATION. Ithaca, N.Y.: Cornell University Press, 1966.

> Originally published in 1923 and reissued in 1958, this study of the American revolution examines the mutually exclusive and incompatible interpretations of the British constitution put forth by the colonists and by the English Parliament. The author argues that a revolution erupted from this constitutional argument when the Parliament rejected the colonists' attempts to recover rights and redress grievances. In May 1776 when the colonists directed their attack toward the crown, they transformed the struggle from a constitutional dispute with the Parliament into a revolution against England.

Marks, Frederick W. III. INDEPENDENCE ON TRIAL: FOREIGN AFFAIRS AND THE MAKING OF THE CONSTITUTION. Baton Rouge: Louisiana State University Press, 1973.

> In this analysis of the confederate period within the context of foreign affairs, the author argues that a prime factor in the decision to replace the Articles with the Constitution was the inability of the Confederate Congress to cope, militarily or commercially, with foreign governments.

MISCELLANEOUS PAPERS OF THE CONTINENTAL CONGRESS, 1774-1789. Washington, D.C.: National Archives. Microfilms M332. 9 rolls.

> This contains papers relating to foreign affairs (diplomatic dispatches from foreign ministers such as Adams and Franklin), papers relating to naval affairs, papers relating to specific states, the credentials of delegates from each of the states, papers kept by officials of the Congress, and the JOURNAL OF THE CONGRESS.

Montross, Lynn. THE RELUCTANT REBELS: THE STORY OF THE CONTINENTAL CONGRESS, 1774-1789. New York: Harper and Brothers, 1950.

> This is an analysis of the process of the drafting of the Declaration of Independence and the Articles of Confederation as well as of the forces important in the development of the principles of the Northwest Ordinance and in the call for a constitutional convention.

Morison, Samuel, ed. SOURCES AND DOCUMENTS ILLUSTRATING THE AMERICAN REVOLUTION, 1764-1788 AND THE FORMATION OF THE FEDERAL CONSTITUTION. 2d ed. New York: Oxford University Press, 1965.

> This is an extensive collection of materials relating to the Revolution, the Articles of Confederation, and the adoption of the Constitution.

Nichols, Marie A. "The Evolution of the Articles of Confederation, 1775-1781." SOUTHERN QUARTERLY 2 (July 1964): 307-40.

> In this analysis of the conflicts within the Continental Congress which prolonged adoption of the Articles of Confederation, Nichols cites the disputes over the basis of representation and taxation, the disagreements between nationalists and state sovereignists, and the struggle over control of western lands. In addition, she notes such special interests as land speculators in the Congress who contributed to the prolongation of deliberations.

Niles, Hezekiah, ed. PRINCIPLES AND ACTS OF THE REVOLUTION IN AMERICA: OR AN ATTEMPT TO COLLECT AND PRESERVE SOME OF THE SPEECHES, ORATIONS, AND PROCEEDINGS. 1822. Reprint. New York: Burt Franklin, 1971.

> This is an extensive collection of various primary sources (such as the JOURNAL OF THE STAMP ACT CONGRESS) which details the arguments used to challenge the legality of the English concept of the relationship between the colonies and the mother country in the revolutionary period.

PAPERS OF THE CONTINENTAL CONGRESS, 1774-89. Washington, D.C.: National Archives. Microfilm. M247. 204 rolls.

> This includes such materials as the rough journals of the Congress from 1774-89, the secret journals from 1775-79, reports of congressional committees, letters and petitions from citizens,

and communications and reports from American representatives
abroad and from military authorities.

Rodick, Burleigh C. AMERICAN CONSTITUTIONAL CUSTOM: A FOR-
GOTTEN FACTOR IN THE FOUNDING. New York: Philosophical Library,
1953.

> This is an analysis of the constitutional customs, traditions,
> habits and thoughts which influenced the generation which chal-
> lenged the king's interference with the legal rights of the colo-
> nists, fought a revolution, adopted a Constitution and established
> a government in the name of those traditions and customs.

Rossiter, Clinton. SEEDTIME OF THE REPUBLIC: THE ORIGIN OF THE
AMERICAN TRADITION OF POLITICAL LIBERTY. New York: Harcourt,
Brace and World, 1953.

> A study of the political ideas that supported independence in the
> colonial and revolutionary period, this work analyzes the rise
> of liberalism in the colonies and the ideas of those--such as
> William Hooker, Roger Williams, and Benjamin Franklin--who
> were influential in shaping American political thought. A
> shortened version with no footnotes or bibliography was pub-
> lished as THE FIRST AMERICAN REVOLUTION: THE AMERI-
> CAN COLONIES ON THE EVE OF INDEPENDENCE (New York:
> Harcourt, Brace and World, 1953, 1956).

Shy, John, ed. THE AMERICAN REVOLUTION. Goldentree Bibliographies
in American History Series, edited by Arthur S. Link. Northbrook, Ill.:
AHM Publishing Corp., 1973.

> This is a bibliography of books, articles and Ph.D. dissertations
> dealing with the colonial period through the postwar era in which
> stability and the reorganization of government were attempted.
> It is organized chronologically and topically and has an author
> index.

Smith, Dwight, ed. ERA OF THE AMERICAN REVOLUTION: A BICEN-
TENNIAL BIBLIOGRAPHY. Santa Barbara, Calif.: American Bibliographic
Center, Clio Press, 1975.

> Each of the signed abstracts of the 1,400 entries is written by
> a different scholar. Chapter 9, which deals with the period
> of the Articles of Confederation, and chapter 10, which focuses
> on the framing and ratification of the Constitution, are especially
> useful. There is a combined index of author, bibliographical,
> geographical, and subject entries.

U.S. Continental Congress. JOURNALS OF THE CONTINENTAL CONGRESS,
1774-1789. 34 vols. Edited by W.C. Ford, Gaillard Hunt, John C. Fitzpatrick, and Roscoe R. Hill. Washington, D.C.: Government Printing Office,
1904-37.

> This is edited from the original records in the Library of Con-
> gress.

_____. SECRET JOURNALS OF THE ACTS AND PROCEEDINGS OF CONGRESS FROM THE FIRST MEETING THEREOF TO THE DISSOLUTION OF THE CONFEDERATION, BY THE ADOPTION OF THE CONSTITUTION OF THE UNITED STATES. 4 vols. Boston: Thomas B. Wait, 1821.

> Published at the direction of the Congress by an 1818 resolution, volume 1 of the JOURNALS contains the HISTORY OF THE CONFEDERATION and covers domestic affairs. Volumes 2, 3, and 4 cover foreign affairs. The original five manuscript volumes are deposited at the State Department.

U. S. Library of Congress. THE AMERICAN REVOLUTION: A SELECTED READING LIST. Washington, D.C.: 1968.

> This is a brief bibliography of books dealing with the period from the origins of the controversy with England to the postwar years of the 1780s. Intended for the general reader, this is the first of three projected Library of Congress bibliographic contributions to the bicentennial celebration. The second is the Gephart selected bibliography of scholarly periodical literature. The Library of Congress is also preparing a comprehensive bibliography of the period from 1763 to 1789.

U.S. National Archives. THE FORMATION OF THE UNION: AN EXHIBIT OF THE DECLARATION OF INDEPENDENCE, THE CONSTITUTION, THE BILL OF RIGHTS TOGETHER WITH OTHER DOCUMENTS REFLECTING EVENTS THAT LED TO AMERICAN INDEPENDENCE AND THE ESTABLISHMENT OF THE FEDERAL UNION. Washington, D.C.: 1970.

> This is a documentary history of the early years of the republic based upon an exhibit in the National Archives building.

Wood, Gordon S. THE CREATION OF THE AMERICAN REPUBLIC, 1776–1787. Chapel Hill: University of North Carolina Press, 1964.

> This is a study of the political culture of late eighteenth–century America which gave rise to a distinctively American system of government.

Wright, Benjamin F. CONSENSUS AND CONFORMITY, 1775–1787. Boston: Boston University Press, 1958.

> This analysis of the period from the Declaration of Independence to the framing of the Constitution leads the author to conclude that the same forces that were responsible for the adoption of the Articles of Confederation were responsible for rejecting the Articles in favor of the Constitution.

Chapter 3

FRAMING, RATIFICATION, AND FORMATIVE YEARS

Bloom, Sol. HISTORY OF THE FORMATION OF THE UNION UNDER THE CONSTITUTION: WITH LIBERTY DOCUMENTS AND REPORT OF THE COMMISSION. Washington, D.C.: Sesquicentennial Commission, 1935.

This publication of the Constitutional Sesquicentennial Commission contains the addresses of various public figures at the national sesquicentennial celebration, various "liberty" documents such as the Magna Carta, the Habeas Corpus Act, the English and American Bills of Rights¹, the Declaration of Independence and Washington's Farewell Address as well as an alphabetical analysis of the provisions of the Constitution, and materials pertaining to the adoption of the Constitution and the organization of government under the Constitution.

Borden, Morton, ed. THE ANTI-FEDERALIST PAPERS. East Lansing: Michigan State University Press, 1965.

This is a collection of 85 short essays representing the anti-Federalist arguments against ratification of the Constitution which originally appeared as letters to the press or speeches by such men as George Mason, Richard Henry Lee, Patrick Henry, George Clinton and Robert Yeats. The organization is similar to that used in the essays by Alexander Hamilton, James Madison and John Jay which are collected as the FEDERALIST PAPERS. The anti-Federalist papers here did not, however, represent the kind of systematic exposition of the Constitution as did the essays in the FEDERALIST PAPERS.

Bower, Catherine Drinker. MIRACLE AT PHILADELPHIA: THE STORY OF THE CONSTITUTIONAL CONVENTION, MAY TO SEPTEMBER, 1787. Boston: Little, Brown, 1956.

Based upon contemporary reports of the convention from newspapers, diaries, letters, and the words of the delegates, this is an account of the drafting of the Constitution--the conflicts and compromises between the nationalists and the state sovereignists, north and south, east and west. The last three chapters on ratification focus upon the battles in Massachusetts, Virginia, and New York.

Butzner, Jane. CONSTITUTIONAL CHAFF: REJECTED SUGGESTION OF THE CONSTITUTIONAL CONVENTION OF 1787 WITH EXPLANATORY ARGUMENT. New York: Columbia University Press, 1941.

This work contains each of the provisions of the Constitution along with the proposals that would have replaced or modified it and the arguments that were made on behalf of the rejected proposals.

Chidsey, Donald Barr. THE BIRTH OF THE CONSTITUTION: AN INFOR-MAL HISTORY. New York: Crown Publishers, 1964.

Designed for the general reader and thus without footnotes or bibliography, this work traces the events leading to the Philadelphia convention and the framing and ratification of the Constitution.

Corwin, Edward S. "The Progress of Constitutional Theory Between the Declaration of Independence and the Philadelphia Convention." AMERICAN HISTORICAL REVIEW 30 (April 1925): 511-36.

In this analysis of constitutional theories from the Declaration of Independence to the period of the constitutional convention, Corwin argues that the solutions which the framers of the Constitution furnished for the problems which plagued the country under the Articles of Confederation stemmed more from the political philosophies of the delegates and the influence of the Age of Rationalism than from the experience derived from actual institutions. It is within the framework of this view of the role of the delegates' political theories that the author examines such problems and conflicts as the controversy over the status of state power, the need for protecting liberty against the tyranny of the majority, and the view that an expansion of national power, including national judicial power, would protect rather than threaten individual rights.

Davis, Joseph L. SECTIONALISM IN AMERICA, 1774-1787. Madison: University of Wisconsin Press, 1976.

This is an analysis of the sectional conflicts which shaped the revolutionary and confederate eras and the move to the constitutional convention.

DePauw, Linda Grant. THE ELEVENTH PILLAR: NEW YORK STATE AND THE FEDERAL CONSTITUTION. Ithaca, N.Y.: Cornell University Press for the American Historical Association, 1966.

This is an analysis of the process by which the Federalists secured ratification of the Constitution in a state in which anti-Federalists constituted a substantial popular majority and in which anti-Federalists held a two to one majority in the ratifying convention that arrived in Poughkeepsie. The deliberations in New York lasted longer than in any other state and resulted in a close vote in favor of accepting the Constitution in a state that was as crucial to the success of the new government as was Virginia.

Diamond, Martin. "Democracy and the Federalist: A Reconsideration of the Framers' Intent." AMERICAN POLITICAL SCIENCE REVIEW 53 (March 1959): 52-68.

Relying upon the FEDERALIST PAPERS as a major source for
determining the political philosophy of the framers of the Constitution, Diamond rejects the view that the Constitution as it
emerged from Philadelphia was an anti-democratic document. He
argues that the framers were deeply committed to the democratic
ideals of the Declaration of Independence and that the principles
of the Declaration were embedded in the Constitution.

DOCUMENTARY HISTORY OF THE CONSTITUTION OF THE UNITED
STATES OF AMERICA. Washington, D.C.: U.S. Department of State, Bu-
reau of Rolls and Library, 1786-1870. 5 vols. Reprint. Washington, D.C.:
U.S. Department of State, 1894. Reprint. New York: Johnson Reprint
Corp., 1965.

These volumes contain the literal print of the documents deposited
in the Bureau of Rolls and the Library of the State Department
relating to the formation of the Constitution. The materials included range from the proceedings of the Annapolis Convention
to letters and debates concerning the adoption of the Fourteenth
and Fifteenth Amendments. It also includes a bibliography of all
publications in the Department of State relating to the formation
of the Constitution.

Eidelberg, Paul. THE PHILOSOPHY OF THE CONSTITUTION: A REIN-
TERPRETATION OF THE INTENTIONS OF THE FOUNDING FATHERS:
New York: Free Press, 1968.

This is an examination of the politics and the political philosophy
underlying the proposals, debates and conflicts at the Constitutional Convention with particular emphasis upon the structure
of the national government--the mode of electing members of the
House and Senate, the tenure of members of each house, and
the intended role of the President and the Supreme Court.
Eidelberg argues that the framers intended to establish a national
government of mixed ingredients rather than a simple democracy,
an intention which provides for continued tension between the
Constitution's democratic and oligarchic ingredients.

Elliot, Jonathan, ed. THE DEBATES, RESOLUTIONS, AND OTHER PRO-
CEEDINGS, IN CONVENTION, IN THE SEVERAL STATE CONVENTIONS
ON THE ADOPTION OF THE FEDERAL CONSTITUTION, AS RECOMMENDED
BY THE GENERAL CONVENTION AT PHILADELPHIA ON THE 17TH OF
SEPTEMBER 1787: WITH THE YEAS AND NAYS ON THE DECISION OF
THE MAIN QUESTION, COLLECTED AND REVISED FROM CONTEMPORARY
PUBLICATIONS BY JONATHAN EDWARDS. 5 vols. Philadelphia: Lippincott,
1861. Reprint. New York: Oxford University Press, 1920.

Volume 1 of this work, known generally as ELLIOT'S DEBATES,
consists of the JOURNAL OF THE FEDERAL CONVENTION,
Martin's letters and Yates's minutes. Volumes 2, 3, and 4
deal with the debates in state convention and volume 5 is a
supplement to the other 4.

Farrand, Max. THE FRAMING OF THE CONSTITUTION OF THE UNITED
STATES. New Haven, Conn.: Yale University Press, 1913.

This is an analysis of the activities of the constitutional convention by the editor of THE RECORDS OF THE FEDERAL CONVENTION (below).

_____, ed. THE RECORDS OF THE FEDERAL CONVENTION OF 1787. 4 vols. Rev. ed. New Haven, Conn.: Yale University Press, 1937.

Collected and published for the first time in 1911, THE RECORDS contains the journal of the convention, Madison's notes, and other materials emanating from or concerning the convention. Volumes 1 and 2 contain the proceedings of the convention, volume 3 contains the texts of such materials as the Virginia Plan and other such proposals, and the letters and other writings of the 55 delegates. In the 1937 revision, volume 4 was added in which corrections were made and additional materials provided.

Ford, Paul L. BIBLIOGRAPHY AND REFERENCE LIST OF THE HISTORY AND LITERATURE RELATING TO THE ADOPTION OF THE CONSTITUTION OF THE UNITED STATES, 1787-1788. Brooklyn, N.Y.: the Author, 1896.

This is a bibliography of letters, essays, and pamphlets written during the controversy over the adoption of the Constitution.

_____, ed. ESSAYS ON THE CONSTITUTION OF THE UNITED STATES, PUBLISHED DURING ITS DISCUSSION BY THE PEOPLE, 1787-1788. Brooklyn, N.Y.: Historical Printing Club, 1892. Reprint. New York: Burt Franklin, 1970.

This is a selection of seventeen essays written for and published anonymously (under pseudonyms such as "Cato," "Cassius," and "Caesar") by newspapers between 1787 and 1788 on the question of the desirability of the adoption of the Constitution, many by participants either in the federal constitutional convention or state ratifying conventions and some by signers of the Declaration of Independence. It includes essays by such men as Elbridge Gerry, Oliver Ellsworth, Roger Sherman, George Clinton, and Robert Yates. There is also a bibliography and reference list of the history and literature of the Constitution.

_____. PAMPHLETS ON THE CONSTITUTION OF THE UNITED STATES PUBLISHED DURING ITS DISCUSSION BY THE PEOPLE, 1787-1788. Brooklyn: n.p., 1888.

This is a selection of fourteen pamphlets written during the debate over the adoption of the constitution by such men as Elbridge Gerry, Noah Webster, John Jay, James Wilson, John Dickinson, and Richard Henry Lee.

Hofstadter, Richard. "Beard and the Constitution: The History of an Idea." AMERICAN QUARTERLY 2 (Fall 1950): 195-213.

This is an examination of Charles A. Beard's AN ECONOMIC INTERPRETATION OF THE CONSTITUTION OF THE UNITED STATES (see p. 36) not in terms of the controversial thesis of that book but in terms of the intellectual, historical, and political context within which that thesis took shape, the innovativeness of Beard's methodology, the underlying ambiguity of

the exact nature of the role of economic interests in framing the
Constitution, and Beard's changing attitude in the 1930s and
1940s toward his earlier emphasis on the Constitution as a
product of a class struggle.

Jensen, Merrill. THE MAKING OF THE AMERICAN CONSTITUTION.
New York: Van Nostrand Reinhold Co., 1964.

This is an analysis of the drafting and ratification of the Constitution against a backdrop of the experiences of the colonial
and confederate periods. The author draws upon the debates
of the Philadelphia convention and the state ratifying convention
and upon newspapers and letters of the period.

Jensen, Merrill, and Becker, Robert A., eds. THE DOCUMENTARY HIS-
TORY OF THE FIRST FEDERAL ELECTIONS. Madison: University of
Wisconsin Press, 1976.

This is the first volume of an extensive collection of materials
relating to the first national elections in which those who would
shape the Constitution in its formative years were selected.

_____, eds. THE DOCUMENTARY HISTORY OF THE RATIFICATION OF
THE CONSTITUTION. Madison: State Historical Society of Wisconsin,
1976-- .

In 1976, the first two volumes of this projected fifteen-volume
work were published. Volume 1, entitled CONSTITUTIONAL
DOCUMENTS AND RECORDS, 1776-1787, contains such material
as the Declaration of Independence, the Articles of Confederation,
Ratification of the Articles, Amendments to the Articles, the
call to the Philadelphia convention, appointment of delegates to
the Constitutional Convention, the resolutions and proposals considered at the convention and the Report of the Convention.
Volume 2 focuses on the ratification process in Pennsylvania.
Of the yet to be published volumes, volumes 3 through 10 will
focus on the ratification process in the various states, whereas
volumes 12 through 15 will be concerned with public and private
reactions to the proposed Constitution.

Jillson, Calvin, and Anderson, Thornton. "Realignments in the Convention
of 1787: The Slave Trade Compromise." JOURNAL OF POLITICS 39
(August 1977): 712-29.

Using factor analysis, this article examines George Mason's
charge that in the closing days of the Philadelphia convention
some New England and southern states formed a coalition to
push through the Commerce and Slave Trade Compromise. It
also explores the effects of that compromise.

Kenyon, Cecelia M., ed. THE ANTI-FEDERALISTS. Indianapolis: Bobbs-
Merrill, 1966.

This is a presentation of some of the basic anti-Federalist arguments against the Constitution, such as "The Impossibility of a
National Republican Government over a Large Area and a Heter-

ogeneous Population," and the "Inadequacy of Representation
and the Probable Effect Thereof," coupled with a collection of
anti-Federalist documents such as Richard Henry Lee's "Letters
from a Federal Farmer" and the letters of "Cato" and "Brutus."

Lansing, John. THE DELEGATE FROM NEW YORK; OR, PROCEEDINGS
OF THE FEDERAL CONVENTION OF 1787: FROM THE NOTES OF JOHN
LANSING JR. Edited by Joseph R. Strayer. Reprint. Port Washington,
N.Y.: Kennikat Press, Scholarly Reprints, 1939.

This is a record of the notes kept by John Lansing of the proceedings at the constitutional convention.

Lefler, Hugh T., ed. A PLEA FOR FEDERAL UNION. 1788. Reprint.
Charlottesville: University of Virginia, 1947.

With an introduction by the editor, this is a reprint of two pamphlets addressed to the people of North Carolina urging adoption
of the Constitution. One is by James Iredell. Authorship of
the other is unknown.

Lewis, John D., ed. ANTI-FEDERALISTS V. FEDERALISTS: SELECTED
DOCUMENTS. San Francisco: Chandler Publishing Co., 1967.

This selection of documents urging adoption of or rejection of a
new Constitution includes such "minority reports from the Philadelphia convention" as the letters of Robert Yates and John
Lansing explaining their reasons for leaving the convention,
Edmund Randolph's letter to the Virginia legislature and Lee's
"Letters of the Federal Farmer" and such defenses of the Constitution as those in the FEDERALIST PAPERS.

Libby, Orin Grant. THE GEOGRAPHICAL DISTRIBUTION OF THE VOTE
OF THE THIRTEEN STATES ON THE FEDERAL CONSTITUTION, 1787-
1789. Reprint. New York: Burt Franklin, 1969.

Originally published in 1894, this is an analysis of the geographic
voting patterns of the states on the question of ratification of the
Constitution.

McDonald, Forrest. "The Anti-Federalists, 1781-1789." WISCONSIN
MAGAZINE OF HISTORY 156 (Spring 1963): 206-14.

This is a brief analysis of the backgrounds, interests, ambitions,
and attitudes of the varied individuals and groups who opposed
adoption of the Constitution by the author of WE THE PEOPLE:
THE ECONOMIC ORIGINS OF THE CONSTITUTION (see p. 47).

McGee, Dorothy H. FRAMERS OF THE CONSTITUTION. New York:
Dodd, Mead and Co., 1968.

The first three chapters discuss briefly the Articles of Confederation and the adoption of the Constitution and the Bill of
Rights. The rest of the work focuses upon the delegates from
each state with a brief biographical sketch of each, outlining

their political activities prior to and during the convention and
the role of each at the convention. The latter section is organized on the basis of the states represented at Philadelphia.

Madison, James. JOURNAL OF THE FEDERAL CONVENTION. Edited by
E.H. Scott. Washington, D.C.: Langtree and O'Sullivan, 1940.

This is a copy of the notes kept by Madison at the Philadelphia
convention.

_____. THE PAPERS OF JAMES MADISON, PURCHASED BY ORDER OF
CONGRESS: BEING HIS CORRESPONDENCE AND REPORTS OF DEBATES
DURING THE CONGRESS OF THE CONFEDERATION AND HIS REPORTS
OF DEBATES IN THE FEDERAL CONVENTION: NOW PUBLISHED FROM
THE ORIGINAL MANUSCRIPTS DEPOSITED IN THE DEPARTMENT OF
STATE, BY DIRECTION OF THE JOINT LIBRARY COMMITTEE OF CON-
GRESS UNDER THE SUPERINTENDENCE OF HENRY D. GELPIN. 3 vols.
Washington, D.C.: Government Printing Office, 1942.

This collection of papers includes Madison's notes on the 1776
debates in the Continental Congress, on the Declaration of
Independence and some of the debates in the Continental Congress,
on the framing of the Articles of Confederation as well as debates
in Congress over the Articles and Madison's letters and notes
concerning the debates in the constitutional convention.

Main, Jackson Turner. THE ANTI-FEDERALISTS: CRITICS OF THE
CONSTITUTION, 1781-1788. Chapel Hill: University of North Carolina
Press, 1961.

An examination of the political controversies in the states which
culminated in the struggle between the nationalists and the anti-
Federalists over the question of the ratification of the Constitution. Main's analysis reveals significant differences in the social
and political backgrounds of the two factions which account for
the different attitudes toward preservation of the confederation.
In addition, he argues that the anti-Federalists did not share
one philosophy of government but that opposition to the Constitution came from those generally opposed to a strong central
government and from those who supported democratic, majority
control. A paperback edition was published by Norton in 1974.
Originally a Ph.D. dissertation, the work contains a good bibliographic essay.

Matteson, David M. THE ORGANIZATION OF THE GOVERNMENT UNDER
THE CONSTITUTION. New York: Da Capo Press, 1970.

This was a reprint of a work written in the 1940s and originally
published as part of Sol Bloom's HISTORY OF THE FORMATION
OF THE UNION UNDER THE CONSTITUTION. Relying upon
and quoting extensively from original letters and documents of
the period, this is an account of the establishment of the government after the ratification of the Constitution when the Congress
under the Articles went out of existence and the new legislative,
executive, and judicial branches came to power. It deals with
such events as the first congressional elections, the election of

Washington, the organization of the House and Senate, the creation of the executive departments, presidential appointments and the establishment of the Cabinet.

Meyers, Marvin, ed. THE MIND OF THE FOUNDER: SOURCES OF THE POLITICAL THOUGHT OF JAMES MADISON. Indianapolis: Bobbs-Merrill, 1973.

With an introduction and commentaries by the editor, this is a one-volume collection of letters, addresses and essays of Madison which reflect his political ideas.

Miller, John C. THE FEDERALIST ERA, 1789–1801. New American Nation Series, edited by Henry Steele Commager and Richard B. Morris. New York: Harper and Row, 1960.

This volume is an examination of the formative years of the new Constitution under the Washington and Adams administrations and of such key elements in the development of constitutional theories and practices as the quarrels between Jefferson and Hamilton, the establishment of the U.S. Bank, the Whiskey Rebellion and the Alien and Sedition Acts.

Padover, Saul K., ed. TO SECURE THESE BLESSINGS: THE GREAT DEBATES OF THE CONTINENTAL CONGRESS, ARRANGED ACCORDING TO TOPICS. New York: Washington Square Press and Ridge Press, 1962.

Relying principally upon Elliot's DEBATES ON THE ADOPTION OF THE FEDERAL CONSTITUTION IN THE CONVENTION HELD AT PHILADELPHIA, IN 1787, WITH A DIARY OF THE DEBATES OF THE CONGRESS OF THE CONFEDERATION AS REPORTED BY JAMES MADISON (see p. 25), this simplified and shortened rendition of the debates which omits recordings of votes and other materials Padover considers technicalities and repetitions, is organized topically, rather than chronologically as in Farrand (see p. 25) and Elliot, and on the basis of the organization of the Constitution. Chapter 1 presents the various plans and proposals such as the Randolph plan and the Connecticut Compromise, chapter 2 presents the debates on the powers of congress; chapter 3 focuses on the House and Senate; chapter 4 upon the executive branch, chapter 5 the judiciary, and chapters 6 and 7 upon the amendment and ratification debates.

Prescott, Arthur T., comp. DRAFTING THE FEDERAL CONSTITUTION. Baton Rouge: Louisiana State University Press, 1941.

This is a rearrangement of Madison's notes supplemented by additional documents pertinent to the developments at Philadelphia and to the process of ratification by the state.

Roche, John P. "The Founding Fathers: A Reform Caucus in Action." AMERICAN POLITICAL SCIENCE REVIEW 55 (December 1961): 799–816.

Viewing the framers of the Constitution as democratic-minded revolutionaries whose constitutional principles were derived from experience rather than as property-minded conservatives whose constitutional ideals stemmed from abstract political theories, Roche argues that there was fundamental agreement at the convention on the need for reform and for appealing to public opinion to convince the states to accept reduction of their powers and enlargement of national authority.

Rogow, Arnold A. "The Federal Convention: Madison and Yates." AMERI-CAN HISTORICAL REVIEW 60 (January 1955): 323-35.

In this comparison between Madison's notes, generally considered the most complete of the records kept by any of the delegates, and those of Robert Yates, who left the convention early in July, Rogow analyzes the discrepancies between the two. Among the more obvious differences are the greater emphasis in the Yates notes on the antirepublicanism of Hamilton and the Hamiltonian views expressed by Madison in his speeches to the convention.

Rossiter, Clinton. 1787: THE GRAND CONVENTION. New York: Macmillan, 1966.

This is an analysis of the constitutional convention within the framework of three basic themes: first, the author views the convention as an exercise in the art of democratic politics by delegates he labels "superb politicians"; second, he analyzes the convention as a self-conscious and successful attempt at nation-building by a group of elites who feared that the country was on the brink of dissolution; and third, he examines the convention within the framework of the recurring question of whether men make history or are controlled by circumstances. There is also a paperback edition published by Mentor.

Rutland, Robert A. THE ORDEAL OF THE CONSTITUTION: THE ANTI-FEDERALISTS AND THE RATIFICATION STRUGGLE OF 1787-1788. Norman: University of Oklahoma Press, 1966.

This scholarly work by the author of THE BIRTH OF THE BILL OF RIGHTS and GEORGE MASON, RELUCTANT STATESMAN is an analysis of the personalities of the anti-Federalists, the problems they encountered in opposing the politically sophisticated Federalists and their vision of political democracy. Based upon manuscript collections and the printed collections of letters and papers of both Federalists and anti-Federalists, this work appeared shortly after the publication of Main's THE ANTI-FEDERALISTS (see p. 29).

Smith, David G. THE CONVENTION AND THE CONSTITUTION: THE POLITICAL IDEAS OF THE FOUNDING FATHERS. New York: St. Martin's Press, 1965.

This is an analysis of the theories of government entertained by the framers of the Constitution and embodied in that document in 1787. The author argues that despite the lack of national unity and the disharmonious political, social and economic environment of the times, the delegates succeeded in their attempt to provide for a balanced system--one in which the government is strong but is restrained by adequate safeguards against the abuse of power.

Solbert, Winton U., ed. THE FEDERAL CONVENTION AND THE FORMATION OF THE UNION OF AMERICAN STATES. New York: Liberal Arts Press, 1958.

> With an introduction and commentaries by the editor, this source book contains extensive selections from Madison's notes of the constitutional convention as well as other basic documents. It was also reprinted as one of the American Heritage Series by Bobbs-Merrill under the general editorship of Leonard W. Levy and Alfred Young.

Thorpe, Francis Newton, comp. THE FEDERAL AND STATE CONSTITU-TION, COLONIAL CHARTERS, AND OTHER ORGANIC LAWS OF THE STATES, TERRITORIES AND COLONIES, NOW OR HERETOFORE FORMING THE UNITED STATES OF AMERICA. 7 vols. Washington, D.C.: Government Printing Office, 1909.

> These volumes contain all of the documents enumerated in the title up to 1909.

U.S. Constitutional Convention. NOTES OF DEBATES IN THE FEDERAL CONVENTION OF 1787 REPORTED BY JAMES MADISON. Introduction by Adrienne Koch. Athens: Ohio University Press, 1966.

> This is a reprint of Madison's notes.

Van Doren, Carl C. THE GREAT REHEARSAL: THE STORY OF THE MAKING AND RATIFYING OF THE CONSTITUTION OF THE UNITED STATES. New York: Viking Press, 1948.

> This is a history of the framing and ratification of the Constitu-tion based upon an analysis of the various records of the federal and state conventions as well as upon the letters, diaries and papers of the participants.

Warren, Charles. THE MAKING OF THE CONSTITUTION. Boston: Little, Brown, 1929. Reprint. New York: Barnes and Noble, 1967.

> This is an analysis of the debates at the constitutional convention organized chronologically and topically, together with a discussion of the factors leading to the convention and the process of ratifi-cation after the convention. It includes an outline of major con-stitutional developments after 1789.

White, Leonard D. THE JEFFERSONIANS: A STUDY IN ADMINISTRATIVE HISTORY, 1801-1829. New York: Macmillan, 1951.

> By the author of THE JACKSONIANS: A STUDY IN ADMINIS-TRATIVE HISTORY, 1829-1861 and THE REPUBLICAN ERA, 1860-1901, this work views the Jefferson era from the perspec-tive of public administration rather than political history.

Yates, Robert. SECRET PROCEEDINGS AND DEBATES OF THE CONVEN-TION ASSEMBLED AT PHILADELPHIA IN THE YEAR 1787, FOR THE PUR-POSE OF FORMING THE CONSTITUTION OF THE UNITED STATES OF AMERICA. FROM THE NOTES TAKEN BY THE LATE ROBERT YATES

⟋AND COPIED BY JOHN LANSING INCLUDING "THE GENUINE INFORMA-
TION" LAID BEFORE THE LEGISLATURE OF MARYLAND BY LUTHER
MARTIN, AND OTHER HISTORICAL DOCUMENTS RELATIVE TO THE
FEDERAL COMPACT OF THE NORTH AMERICAN UNION. Albany, N.Y.:
Webster and Skinners, 1821. Reprint. Richmond, Va.: Wilbur Curtis,
1839.

> Although the Yates notes are less complete than are Madison's
> notes, these two editions are among several verbatim publications
> of his notes of the debates at Philadelphia.

Young, Alfred F., ed. THE DEBATE OVER THE CONSTITUTION, 1787-
1789. Berkeley Series in American History. Chicago: Rand McNally, 1965.

> This short pamphlet contains brief excerpts from the letters and
> speeches of some of the supporters and opponents of the Con-
> stitution and from such sources as Elliot's DEBATES (see
> p. 25).

Chapter 4

GENERAL INTERPRETATIVE WORKS

Adair, Douglass. FAME AND THE FOUNDING FATHERS. Edited by Trevor
Colburn. Personal memoir by Caroline Robbins. Bibliographic essay by
Robert E. Shalhope. New York: W.W. Norton for the Institute of Early
American History and Culture, 1974.

> These essays include some of his writings on such matters
> as the disputed authorship of the FEDERALIST PAPERS and
> various facets of the role and contributions to constitutional
> development of Madison, Hamilton and Jefferson.

_____. "The Tenth Federalist Revisited." WILLIAM AND MARY QUARTERLY
8 (January 1951): 48-67.

> This is a criticism of Beard's use or misuse of "Federalist No.
> 10" to launch a progressive attack upon the Constitution and
> to support his thesis that economic interests, not political
> theories, accounted for the conservatism of the Constitution.

Association of American Law Schools. SELECTED ESSAYS ON CONSTITU-
TIONAL LAW. 4 vols. Chicago: Foundation Press, 1938.

> Each of the four volumes in this series is over 1,550 pages
> long, contains between 75 and 90 essays and deals with a dif-
> ferent aspect of constitutional law, such as federalism and judi-
> cial review. An updated selection entitled SELECTED ES-
> SAYS ON CONSTITUTIONAL LAW, 1938-1962 (St. Paul: West
> Publishing, 1963) contains 41 essays which originally appeared
> in law reviews and other journals.

Auerbach, Jerold S. UNEQUAL JUSTICE: LAWYERS AND SOCIAL CHANGE
IN MODERN AMERICA. New York: Oxford University Press, 1977.

> In contrast to the more conventional focus of modern works
> upon the role of lawyers and litigation in bringing about con-
> stitutional change, this is a criticism of lawyers whose interest
> in protecting and advancing their own power and status tends to
> perpetuate rather than alleviate injustice in the existing con-
> stitutional system.

Bauer, Elizabeth. COMMENTARIES ON THE CONSTITUTION, 1790-1860.
New York: Columbia University Press, 1952.

This is a historical study of constitutional commentaries published
in book form by American commentators prior to the Civil War.
It thus excludes foreign commentators such as de Tocqueville as
well as American commentators who reached their audiences
through speeches, pamphlets, and newspapers. In addition to
an analysis of the nature, use, role, and historical setting of
the commentaries and a brief historical sketch of the commentators whose works are examined, three chapters of this work
deal with the work of individual commentators of three major
regions: those of the middle states (such as James Wilson), the
New England nationalists (such as Joseph Story), and the states'
rights school of the South (such as John Taylor of Carolina).
Two chapters deal with a major subject of nineteenth-century
commentaries—the location of sovereignty and the conflict between the compact theory and the nationalist theory.

Baxter, Maurice G. DANIEL WEBSTER AND THE SUPREME COURT. Amherst: University of Massachusetts Press, 1966.

This study of Webster's influence on the course of constitutional
development is organized on the basis of the cases and causes
he participated in as a lawyer arguing cases before the Supreme
Court, usually as a nationalist and as a protector of property
rights. The cases and topics examined are the Dartmouth College
Case; the contract clause cases; property cases; the second
Bank of the United States cases, especially McCulloch v. Maryland; and the commerce clause cases, especially Gibbons v.
Ogden and Cooley. There is an introductory biographical chapter, one chapter deals with the general question of the relationship between court and counsel and a concluding chapter examines
the role of the constitutional lawyer in the American political
system.

Beard, Charles A. AN ECONOMIC INTERPRETATION OF THE CONSTITU-
TION OF THE UNITED STATES. New York: Macmillan, 1913.

The major thesis of this classic analysis of the Constitution is
that it was the product of the conservative class whose wealth
was in personal rather than real property, and that the framers
sought to protect the economic and essentially antidemocratic
interests of the class they represented. Since its publication,
this work has been subject to constant analysis and criticism.

_____. THE REPUBLIC: CONVERSATIONS ON FUNDAMENTALS. New
York: Viking Press, 1962.

Originally published in 1943, this is a series of fictional conversations ranging over a wide field of constitutional issues
from the establishment of constitutionalism at the time of the
American Revolution through the constitutional guarantees of
free speech, press, and religion to the constitutional powers of
the Congress, the president, and the judiciary.

Beck, James M. THE CONSTITUTION OF THE UNITED STATES: YES-
TERDAY, TODAY—AND TOMORROW? New York: George H. Doran Co.,
1924.

With a brief look at the preconstitutional period, this is largely
an account of the proceedings at the constitutional convention
and the process of ratification from the perspective of an economic conservative concerned about national impairment of property rights and invasion of the powers reserved to the states.
The author is especially critical of adoption of the Sixteenth
Amendment which he views as a danger to the Constitution of
the framers and to the freedom of the individual.

Beck, James M., and Thorpe, Merle. NEITHER PURSE NOR SWORD.
New York: Macmillan, 1936.

Written during the first administration of Franklin D. Roosevelt,
this is a constitutional criticism by a former solicitor general
and an editor of a business magazine of the centralization of
power in Washington at the expense of the power reserved to
the states and at the expense of the economic freedom of the
individual. The authors support the Supreme Court and its invalidation of such New Deal legislation as the National Industrial Recovery Act and the Agricultural Adjustment Act and argue
that the Court, working alone, cannot hold the president and the
Congress at bay.

Benson, Lee. TURNER AND BEARD: AMERICAN WRITING RECONSIDERED.
Glencoe, Ill.: Free Press, 1960.

Of the three major parts of this book, part 3, entitled "A Critique
of Beard and His Critics," is the most relevant to constitutional
interpretations. In opposition to the Beard economic thesis which
Benson relates to the Progressive era and to the Court's economic
conservatism, Benson argues that it was opposing ideologies
stemming from differing social circumstances which divided the
Federalists and anti-Federalists. The other two essays deal
with the influence of the Italian economist Achille Loria on
American economic thought and with the historical background
of Frederick Jackson Turner's frontier thesis.

Bizzell, William Bennett. JUDICIAL INTERPRETATION OF POLITICAL
THEORY: A STUDY IN THE RELATION OF THE COURTS TO THE
AMERICAN PARTY SYSTEM. New York: Burt Franklin, 1974.

Originally published in 1914, this is a revised version of law
school lectures which examine the influence of the Court in
developing basic American political theories regarding the power
of the Court, the nature of constitutional construction and of the
Constitution, as well as theories regarding the United States
Bank, legal tender, protective tariffs, the income tax, direct
elections and the recall of judicial decisions.

Black, Charles L., Jr. THE OCCASIONS OF JUSTICE: ESSAYS MOSTLY
ON LAW. New York: Macmillan, 1963.

This is a collection of about twenty five of the author's articles,
speeches and book reviews dealing with various aspects of law,
the Constitution, courts and judges, racial equality and freedom.

_____. PERSPECTIVES IN CONSTITUTIONAL LAW. 2d ed. New York: Prentice-Hall, 1970.

This is a brief introductory overview of some basic issues of constitutional law such as the court's jurisdiction and self-imposed restraints, federalism, relations between the president and Congress, foreign affairs and war and individual rights.

_____. STRUCTURE AND RELATIONSHIP IN CONSTITUTIONAL LAW. Baton Rouge: Louisiana State University Press, 1969.

Originally delivered as the Edward Douglass White Lectures at Louisiana State University, this work examines the structural relations of state, nation and people, the substantive implications of these relations and the impact of these relations on the practice of judicial review. Professor Black suggests that it is the total structure of these relations that determines constitutional law. Judicial inference from structure is illustrated in McCulloch v. Maryland, for example, in which Marshall rests the power to establish a bank not on the "necessary and proper" clause or any one express power but upon the structure of the relations of state, nation and people.

Bragdon, Henry W.; McCutchen, Samuel P.; and Brown, Stuart G., eds. FRAME OF GOVERNMENT. New York: Macmillan, 1962.

A collection of documents ranging from the Declaration of Independence to the Public School Segregation Case of 1955, this work contains an introductory essay pertaining to each document and general interpretation of the ideas and development pertinent to each document as well as explanatory notes giving information about internal details.

Brown, Robert E. CHARLES BEARD AND THE CONSTITUTION: A CRITICAL ANALYSIS OF "AN ECONOMIC INTERPRETATION OF THE CONSTITUTION." Princeton, N.J.: Princeton University Press, 1956.

In this criticism of the Beard thesis (see p. 36), Brown argues that at the time of the framing of the Constitution the United States was essentially classless and that the Constitution reflected the middle-class, democratic nature of the society for which it was written.

_____. REINTERPRETATION OF THE FORMATION OF THE AMERICAN CONSTITUTION. Boston: Boston University Press, 1963.

In this published version of the Gaspar G. Bacon Lectures on the Constitution of the United States, Brown discusses the structure of colonial society, the nature of the American Revolution and the drafting and ratification of the Constitution.

Burgess, John W. THE CIVIL WAR AND THE CONSTITUTION, 1859-1865. 2 vols. 1901. Reprint. Port Washington, N.Y.: Kennikat Press, 1971.

This is a study of constitutional developments before and during the Civil War and in the period immediately following the collapse of Southern armies.

_____. RECENT CHANGES IN AMERICAN CONSTITUTIONAL THEORY. New York: Columbia University Press, 1923. Reprint. New York: Arno Press, 1972.

This is a criticism of the expansion of governmental power in the period before and during World War I, expansions which the author viewed as unconstitutional infringements of individual freedom. The governmental actions under attack include the levying of an income tax, the suppression of free speech, and the military draft.

Chipman, Nathaniel. PRINCIPLES AND GOVERNMENT: A TREATISE ON FREE INSTITUTIONS, INCLUDING THE CONSTITUTION OF THE UNITED STATES. 1833. Reprint. New York: Da Capo Press, 1970.

This is an interpretation of the Constitution by a Vermont Federalist.

Commager, Henry Steele. MAJORITY RULE AND MINORITY RIGHTS. Gloucester, Mass.: Peter Smith, 1958.

Originally delivered as the James W. Richards Lectures in History at the University of Virginia, this slim volume is an analysis of the dilemma posed by a constitutional system rooted in the democratic notion of majority rule and in the equally strong principle of limited government. Commager examines the two proposed solutions, one accepted and the other consistently asserted but rejected, judicial review and the Jeffersonian solution of nullification by state legislatures of national government action which exceed its delegated power or infringed protected rights.

_____, ed. DOCUMENTS OF AMERICAN HISTORY. 8th ed. New York: Appleton-Century-Crofts, 1968.

This massive work contains 670 documents ranging from the "Privileges and Prerogatives Granted to Columbus" on 30 April 1492 to Ginzburg v. U.S. in 1966.

Commons, John R. LEGAL FOUNDATIONS OF CAPITALISM. New York: Macmillan, 1924. Reprint. Madison: University of Wisconsin Press, 1967.

This is an examination of the evolution and variations of basic legal concepts important in the development of capitalism from the Magna Carta to common and constitutional law. Thus, for example, the police power of the state, derived from the ancient prerogative of the king, was a kind of power early recognized in American law: the physical power of a sovereign over subjects. Distinct from this kind of power was that which was recognized in Munn v. Illinois: the economic power of citizen over citizen. Similarly, the liberty of the Magna Carta, a grant of power to participate in a privilege, is viewed as distinct from the common law right to equal treatment among individuals who belong to the same class whether privileged or not.

Cooley, Thomas M. CONSTITUTIONAL LIMITATIONS: A TREATISE ON THE CONSTITUTIONAL LIMITATIONS WHICH REST UPON THE LEGISLATIVE POWER OF THE STATE OF THE AMERICAN UNION. 1868. Reprint. New York: Da Capo Press, 1972.

This work either influenced or anticipated the judicial development of the due process clause of the Fourteenth Amendment as
a limitation upon the authority of the state to regulate in the
socioeconomic area.

Cooper, Thomas. TWO ESSAYS: ON THE FOUNDATION OF CIVIL GOVERN-
MENT. ON THE CONSTITUTION OF THE UNITED STATES. 1826. Reprint. New York: Da Capo Press, 1970.

The first of these two brief essays was delivered in England in
1787 and deals with the question of whether political power de-
rives from the consent of the people. The second and longer
essay addresses such basic questions of constitutional interpretation as the implied power doctrine, the treaty—making power,
the doctrine of contempt, the admission of new states, the federal
judiciary and states' rights, and the legitimacy of sedition laws.
The appendix includes a list of English precedents for parliamentary intervention in judicial sedition and libel decisions and
the 1825 petition by the author to the Senate to overturn his
1800 conviction for libel for a printed attack on President John
Adams.

Corwin, Edward S. "The Constitution as Instrument and as Symbol."
AMERICAN POLITICAL SCIENCE REVIEW 30 (December 1936): 1071-85.

In this brief Tercentenary Address at Harvard, Corwin suggests
that the Constitution has two aspects. As an instrument it is
future oriented and as such is a source of power to be used in
the interest of the public. As symbol, it looks to the past and
functions to protect private interest against public power. It
is the question of the relationship between these two aspects of
the Constitution that Corwin here considers. Written in the
period in which the Court narrowly construed both national and
state power to regulate in the socioeconomic area, Corwin urges
judicial expansion of governmental power to deal with economic
problems.

_____. "The 'Higher Law' Background of American Constitutional Law."
HARVARD UNIVERSITY LAW REVIEW 42 (1928): 149-85, 365-409.

This is an analysis of the evolution of the idea of the Constitution as a supreme or higher law. Corwin traces the notion of
a law superior to the will of human governors from the Ciceronian
idea of natural law to John of Salisburg and other English legal
commentators, through the development of English common law as
an embodiment of judicial right reason and the influence of Magna
Carta and Locke upon American constitutionalism. This article
was reprinted under the same title by the Cornell University
Press in 1957.

Crosskey, William W. POLITICS AND THE CONSTITUTION. Chicago:
University of Chicago Press, 1953.

The scholarly controversy aroused by this searing analysis of
the Constitutional Convention and Madison's notes was prompted
in part by his conclusion that judicial review was forbidden by
the Philadelphia convention and that the framers intended to

establish a unitary rather than a federal form of government.

CURRENT CONSTITUTIONAL ISSUES: A SYMPOSIUM. New York: Da Capo Press, 1971.

> This is a collection of six essays, originally published in the WILLIAM AND MARY LAW REVIEW 9, no. 1 (1967), dealing with a variety of constitutional problems. The topics include the Privileges and Immunities Clause of the Fourth Amendment, racial discrimination in "private" schools, church-state relations, and the conflict between free speech and individual rights protected by libel laws.

Curtis, George Ticknor. CONSTITUTIONAL HISTORY OF THE UNITED STATES: FROM THEIR DECLARATION OF INDEPENDENCE TO THE CLOSE OF THEIR CIVIL WAR. 2 vols. New York: Harper and Brothers, 1903.

> This work, which first appeared in 1854, became a standard and influential nineteenth-century history. The late nineteenth-century revision, volume 2 of which was edited after the author's death at the age of 82 in 1894, incorporated the 1854 version and updated the work to the Civil War. The appendix includes documents ranging from debates in the Continental Congress, the Declaration of Independence, debates on ratification of the Constitution, antislavery tracts, and an oration by the author to the proclamations announcing the adoption of the Thirteenth, Fourteenth and Fifteenth Amendments.

Dewey, Donald O., ed. UNION AND LIBERTY: A DOCUMENTARY HISTORY OF AMERICAN CONSTITUTIONALISM. New York: McGraw-Hill, 1969.

> An extensive collection of documents beginning with the First Charter of Virginia and the Mayflower Compact and concluding with the civil rights and civil liberties activities of the 1960s, with the focal point of the collection aimed at the theme of balancing union and liberty.

Dietz, Gottfried. THE FEDERALIST: A CLASSIC ON FEDERALISM AND FREE GOVERNMENT. Baltimore: Johns Hopkins Press, 1960.

> This analysis of the FEDERALIST PAPERS suggests that Madison, Jay, and Hamilton "elevated federalism to a form of constitutionalism." The author argues that they viewed federalism as a means of achieving popular government, the rule of law, and personal freedom.

Duer, William A. A COURSE OF LECTURES ON THE CONSTITUTIONAL JURISPRUDENCE OF THE UNITED STATES. 2d rev. ed. 1856. Reprint. New York: Burt Franklin, 1971.

> This is a collection of the lectures delivered each year to the senior class at Columbia by the president of that college. This nineteenth-century commentary on the Constitution was widely used as a text in Constitutional Law.

Dumbauld, Edward. THE CONSTITUTION OF THE UNITED STATES. Norman: University of Oklahoma Press, 1964.

> Organized on the basis of the text of the Constitution, the author discusses the origin of each clause, the arguments over each clause at the convention, the changes made as the result of debate, and the meaning of the clause as interpreted by the Supreme Court.

Eckhardt, Bob, and Black, Charles L., Jr. THE TIDES OF POWER: CONVERSATIONS ON THE AMERICAN CONSTITUTION. New Haven, Conn.: Yale University Press, 1976.

> This is a freewheeling dialogue between a Texas congressman and a Yale law professor on such matters as congressional and judicial powers, roles, and relationships.

Ferguson, E. James. NATIONAL UNION ON TRIAL, 1781-1816. Readings in American History Series. New York: Random House, 1970.

> This volume contains nine essays focusing upon the formative years of the Union and includes sections dealing with the Constitution in political and economic terms, the ethical basis of partisanship, the Jeffersonian coalition of slaveholders and mechanics, and an interpretation of the War of 1812.

Fisher, Sidney G. THE TRIAL OF THE CONSTITUTION. New York: Negro Universities Press, 1969.

> Written by a nationalist during the Civil War, this analysis of the Constitution during that crisis is primarily concerned with the more burning constitutional questions associated with that conflict—the nature of the Union and of American democracy, the status of slavery, and the powers of the president.

Friedman, Lawrence M. A HISTORY OF AMERICAN LAW. New York: Simon and Schuster, 1973.

> This is a general survey or "social history" of American state and local common, statutory, civil, and criminal law from the seventeenth through the nineteenth centuries with an epilogue on twentieth-century law.

Garvey, Gerald. CONSTITUTIONAL BRICOLAGE. Princeton, N.J.: Princeton University Press, 1971.

> In contrast to the more conventional view that the judiciary wrought vast social and political changes in the 1950s and 1960s, Garvey argues that constitutional interpretation in this, as in earlier periods, had retardative and frequently reactionary results. The reason is judicial reliance upon a limited set of doctrines. He urges a new syntax which more accurately reflects change but sees little prospect for such a development.

Gilmore, Grant. THE AGES OF AMERICAN LAW. New Haven, Conn.: Yale University Press, 1977.

This is an analysis of American law within the framework of what the author views as the three major developmental periods-- the Age of Discovery (the pre-Civil War period) during which law and society were pluralistic and fluid; the Age of Faith (from the Civil War to the First World War) characterized by a more rigid formalism; and the Age of Anxiety (the period from the First World War to the present), a long period of un- certainty and breakdown.

Goldfarb, Ronald L. THE CONTEMPT POWER. New York: Columbia University Press, 1963.

This is an analysis of the power of government to punish for contempt, an act defined as one of disobedience or disrespect toward judicial or legislative bodies or interference with their orderly processes. The author looks at the history of this power in Anglo-American law, the various forms and uses of the power (principally in American law), and the expansions of the power, traditionally exercised by judicial and legislative bodies, to administrative agencies which exercise quasilegislative and quasijudical powers. In addition, the constitutional problems presented by use of the power--especially First, Fifth, and Eighth Amendment problems--and the judicially and legislatively imposed limitations on the power are examined.

Hamilton, Alexander; Jay, John; and Madison, James. THE FEDERALIST: A COMMENTARY ON THE CONSTITUTION OF THE UNITED STATES, BEING A COLLECTION OF ESSAYS WRITTEN IN SUPPORT OF THE CON- STITUTION AGREED UPON SEPTEMBER 17, 1787 BY THE FEDERAL CON- VENTION. Introduction by Edward Mead Earle. New York: Random House Modern Library, 1937. Appendix.

There are many editions of this collection of the classic eighty- five essays written by Hamilton, Jay, and Madison in an effort to obtain support for the ratification of the Constitution by the New York legislature. The essays originally appeared individually in New York newspapers, were collected and published for the first time in two volumes in 1788 and are still considered one of the ablest and most authoritative defenses and interpretations of the original Constitution. This modern library edition has an appendix which includes the Articles of Confederation, the call for the constitutional convention, the resolution transmitting the Constitution to Congress, the Constitution, and the Declaration of Independence.

Harding, Arthur L., ed. ORIGINS OF THE NATURAL LAW TRADITION. Dallas: Southern Methodist University Press, 1954. Reprint. Port Wash- ington, N.Y.: Kennikat Press, 1971.

This is a report of the proceedings of a Conference on Law in Society at which the role of natural law concepts in American law was discussed.

Hill, Frederick Trevor. DECISIVE BATTLES OF THE LAW: NARRATIVE STUDIES OF EIGHT LEGAL CONTESTS AFFECTING THE HISTORY OF THE UNITED STATES BETWEEN THE YEARS 1800 AND 1886. New York: Harper and Row, 1906.

This is a leisurely early twentieth-century account of such domestic contests as the Callender free press case, the Burr treason
case, the Johnson impeachment trial, the Hayes-Tilden election
dispute and the international "Alabama" conflict between envoy
John Adams and the English government.

Holt, Wythe, ed. ESSAYS IN NINETEENTH-CENTURY AMERICAN LEGAL
HISTORY. Westport, Conn.: Greenwood Press, 1976.

This is a collection of twenty-three essays dealing with various
facets of legal theory and practice in the nineteenth century.
In addition to Justice Holmes's classic "The Path of the Law,"
this work includes "Reality and Social Reform: The Transition
from Laissez-Faire to the Welfare State," by Calvin Woodward;
"The Impact of the Anti-Slavery Movement Upon Styles of Judicial Reasoning in Nineteenth Century America," by William A.
Nelson; "Law and the Failure of Reconstruction: The Case of
Thomas Cooley," by Phillip S. Paladan; and "The Constitution
in the Gilded Age: The Beginnings of Constitution Realism in
American Scholarship," by Herman Belz.

Hurst, James W. THE LAW OF TREASON IN THE UNITED STATES:
COLLECTED ESSAYS. Westport, Conn.: Greenwood Press, 1971.

Treason is the only crime which the Constitution itself defines
and for which it specifies standards of evidence. This is a
collection of essays dealing with various facets of this crime.

Hyman, Harold M. A MORE PERFECT UNION: THE IMPACT OF THE
CIVIL WAR AND RECONSTRUCTION ON THE CONSTITUTION. The
Impact of the Civil War Series. New York: Knopf, 1973.

This work examines pre-Civil War quarrels and conflicts that
shaped, limited, and expanded the Constitution that was to be
shaped by the Civil War and Reconstruction. The author suggests
that the conflicts within the national government during the war
and Reconstruction took place largely within the framework of
the tradition of constitutionalism and that the Constitution emerged
largely intact, partly because its protection of individual rights
and its distribution of governmental authority had served the
nation so well during the crisis. Those changes in the Constitution that occurred served principally to strengthen the basic
principles of the prewar Constitution, the nation and the rights
of individuals.

Jacobs, Clyde E. LAW WRITERS AND THE COURTS; THE INFLUENCE
OF THOMAS M. COOLEY, CHRISTOPHER G. TIEDEMAN AND JOHN F.
DILLON UPON AMERICAN CONSTITUTIONAL LAW. Berkeley and Los
Angeles: University of California Press, 1954. Reprint. New York: Da
Capo Press, 1973.

Jacobs argues that these three writers were instrumental in the
development of the two major constitutional theories adopted by
the judiciary to limit governmental power in the economic realm.
He sees Cooley and Tiedeman as prime agents in the development
of substantive due process as a limitation upon the police power
of the state and of the concept that the reserved powers of the

state limit the commerce power of the national government. Cooley
and Dillon contributed to the development of the public purpose
maxim as a restriction upon the taxing and spending powers of
state and local governments.

Johnson, Allen, ed. READINGS IN AMERICAN CONSTITUTIONAL HISTORY,
1776-1876. Boston: Houghton Mifflin Co., 1912.

This turn-of-the-century collection of readings contains documents
ranging from colonial charters through the credentials of delegates
to the First Continental Congress to congressional debates on
and judicial interpretation of the Fifteenth Amendment.

Kent, James. COMMENTARIES ON AMERICAN LAW. 4 vols. 1826. Reprint. New York: Da Capo Press, 1971.

These volumes are revisions of Kent's lectures at Columbia and
cover in some detail a variety of common, statutory, and constitutional law problems.

Kerber, Linda K. FEDERALISTS IN DISSENT: IMAGERY AND IDEO-
LOGY IN JEFFERSONIAN AMERICA. Ithaca, N.Y.: Cornell University
Press, 1970.

With the Jeffersonian sweep of elective offices in 1800, the Federalist party moved from power to dissent until its demise. This
is a study of the Federalist criticism of the perceived instability
of popular democracy in the Jeffersonian era.

Konefsky, Samuel J. JOHN MARSHALL AND ALEXANDER HAMILTON:
ARCHITECTS OF THE AMERICAN CONSTITUTION. New York: Macmillan, 1967.

This is an examination of the contributions of Marshall as Chief
Justice and of Hamilton as party leader and member of the Washington cabinet to the evolution of the Constitution in its early
formative years. Because each initiated what came to be widely
accepted approaches to constitutional interpretation, each became
"prototypes of the interpreter-statesman demanded by the American
system of constitutional government."

Kurland, Philip B., ed. SUPREME COURT REVIEW. Chicago: University
of Chicago Press, 1960--. Annual.

This volume contains original essays on controversies dealt with
by the Supreme Court during the previous term.

Latham, Earl, ed. THE DECLARATION OF INDEPENDENCE AND THE
CONSTITUTION. 3d ed. Lexington, Mass.: D.C. Heath, 1976.

This is a collection of brief excerpts from the works of such
constitutional scholars as Bernard Bailyn (on the ideological
origins of the American Revolution), Andrew C. McLaughlin (on
the confederate period and the Constitution), Merrill Jensen (on
the Articles of Confederation), and Charles A. Beard, Robert
E. Brown, and Forrest McDonald (on the role of economic factors in the framing and ratification of the Constitution).

Lee, Charles R. THE CONFEDERATE CONSTITUTIONS. Chapel Hill: University of North Carolina Press, 1963.

> This is an analysis of the constitutional system of the Confederacy established by the southern states which seceded from the Union and of the similarities and differences between the two Confederate Constitutions—provisional and permanent—and the United States Constitution. The principal difference between the Confederate and national constitution was over the principle which in part led to the Civil War—the location of governmental sovereignty in the center or in the parts.

Lee, Richard Henry. LETTERS OF THE FEDERAL FARMER. OBSERVATIONS LEADING TO A FAIR EXAMINATION OF THE SYSTEM OF GOVERNMENT PROPOSED BY THE LATE CONVENTION. 1787. Reprint. Louisville, Ky.: Lost Cause Press, 1972. Microfilm.

> In contrast to the numerous editions of the FEDERALIST PAPERS, this collection of letters defending the Articles of Confederation and criticizing the Constitution is not so readily available, a not unexpected fate for the losing side. Lee's letters may also be found in EMPIRE AND NATION: LETTERS FROM A FARMER IN PENNSYLVANIA, JOHN DICKINSON. LETTERS FROM THE FARMER, RICHARD HENRY LEE, introduction by Forrest McDonald. (Englewood Cliffs, N.J.: Prentice-Hall, 1962). Letters numbers 6–18, dated 25 December 1787 to 25 June 1788 are also published by Quadrangle Press, Chicago, 1962. Richard Henry Lee. THE LETTERS OF RICHARD HENRY LEE, collected and edited by James Curtis Ballagh (New York: Macmillan, 1911–14). A 1978 edition entitled LETTERS FROM THE FARMER TO THE REPUBLICAN was published by the University of Alabama Press.

Lerner, Max. "Constitution and Court as Symbols." YALE LAW JOURNAL 46 (June 1937): 1290–1319.

> Later published as chapter 1 of THE DIVINE RIGHTS OF KINGS: A STUDY IN THE AMERICAN SUPREME COURT by Viking Press, this article agrees with other analysts that shortly after its ratification the Constitution became not merely an instrument of government but an object of worship. Written at the height of liberal disenchantment with a conservative Court, Lerner goes on to argue that by the post–Civil War period, the three principal elements in a pattern of divine right had been established, the three principles being fetishism of the Constitution, the Court's claim to exclusive guardianship of the Constitution and the tradition of judicial neutrality.

Levy, Leonard. JUDGMENTS: ESSAYS ON AMERICAN CONSTITUTIONAL HISTORY. Chicago: Quadrangle Books, 1972.

> This is a series of independent but interrelated essays. Part 1, entitled "Supreme Law and Its Expounders," deals with such broad topics as judicial review, the Fourteenth Amendment, the Bill of Rights and judicial biographies. Part 2 contains essays dealing with First Amendment issues. Part 3 deals with other civil rights issues such as self-incrimination, the fugitive slave law, and the origins of the separate but equal doctrine.

_____, ed. AMERICAN CONSTITUTIONAL LAW: HISTORICAL ESSAYS. New York: Harper and Row, 1966.

This is a collection of seven essays, each with a critical introductory note by the editor, dealing with various facets of constitutional law. The essays include John P. Roche's "The Founding Fathers: A Reform Caucus in Action," Max Lerner's "John Marshall and the Campaign of History," Robert J. Harris's "Chief Justice Taney: Prophet of Reform and Reaction," Walton H. Hamilton's "The Path of Due Process of Law," Robert G. McCloskey's "Economic Due Process and the Supreme Court: An Exhumation and Reburial," Robert L. Stern's "The Problems of Yesteryear—Commerce and Due Process," and Alpheus Mason's "The Supreme Court: Temple and Forum."

_____. THE SUPREME COURT UNDER EARL WARREN. New York: New Viewpoints, 1972.

This is a series of essays analyzing the role of the Supreme Court under Warren.

Lewis, Leon R. DEMOCRACY AND THE LAW. Washington, D.C.: Public Affairs Press, 1963.

In dealing with the question of whether the American political system as presently governed can cope with emergencies and maintain democracy and respect for individual rights and human freedom, the author in essence concludes that a move toward a parliamentary form of government would more effectively secure these ends. His examination of the Philadelphia convention, the early formative years under the Constitution, and the rise of political parties leads him to suggest that the Constitution, particularly the separation of powers doctrine, warped political parties. He suggests that Article V be amended to make it easier to amend the Constitution and that the House of Representatives be given the power to amend the Constitution "after it has won a majority vote in three successive sessions," a change which would have the effect of taking the Supreme Court out of politics and restoring the use of stare decisis. He further suggests that party members in the House choose presidential nominees and that legislative power be given to the House alone with the Senate authorized only to delay legislation.

McDonald, Forrest. E PLURIBUS UNUM: THE FORMATION OF THE AMERICAN REPUBLIC, 1776-1790. Boston: Houghton Mifflin Co., 1965.

This is an analysis of the process by which eighteenth-century Americans dealt with questions of unity and separation. During the revolutionary era the question of unity with or separation from Great Britain dominated political debate. From the Declaration of Independence to the adoption of the Constitution the question of the degree of unity and separation that would characterize the relationship between the states dominated political debate. The Articles of Confederation and the Constitution answered the question differently.

_____. WE THE PEOPLE: THE ECONOMIC ORIGINS OF THE CONSTITUTION. Chicago: University of Chicago Press, 1958.

This is a critical analysis and rejection of the Beard thesis on
the basis of incompatibility of that thesis with the economic and
political background and behavior of the framers. McDonald
argues that a fourth of the delegates had voted for paper money
and/or a debtor relief measure in their state legislatures and
were adversely affected by the Constitution. Further, the delegates were basically agricultural landholders rather than holders
of other forms of wealth as Beard had asserted and did not
generally act as a unified economic group. He concludes that
the framers represented the country as a whole rather than
a class or section and that both Federalists and anti-Federalists
represented the same groups.

McLaughlin, Andrew C. THE CONFEDERATION AND THE CONSTITUTION.
1905. Reissue. Foreword by Henry Steele Commager. New York: Collier
Books, 1962.

This is a history of the period under the Articles of Confederation and the period during which the Constitution was written and
adopted. It is an analysis of the development of the colonists
into a nation, of the inventiveness of the Northwest Ordinance
philosophy of treating territories as potential partners rather
than as colonists to be exploited, and of the invention of federalism after an experiment with confederation.

_____. A CONSTITUTIONAL HISTORY OF THE UNITED STATES. New
York: Appleton-Century Co., 1935.

A history of American constitutionalism from the colonial period
to the late nineteenth century when the judiciary transformed the
Fourteenth Amendment from an egalitarian measure to a laissez-
faire amendment.

_____. THE FOUNDATIONS OF AMERICAN CONSTITUTIONALISM. New
York: Peter Smith, 1932.

This was originally delivered as the 1932 Anson G. Phelps Lecture on early American, particularly New England, history at
New York University. McLaughlin focuses upon the relationship
between the political philosophy of New England puritanism and
American constitutional principles.

Main, Jackson Turner. THE SOVEREIGN STATES, 1775-1783. New York:
New Viewpoints, 1973.

Using contemporary newspapers, journals, and documents as a
basis for his analysis, Professor Main examines the internal
conflicts and changes during the revolutionary period when the
colonies were transformed into sovereign states and wrote and
adopted their first constitutions.

MAJOR STUDIES OF THE CONGRESSIONAL RESEARCH SERVICE: 1975-
76 SUPPLEMENT. Washington, D.C.: University Publications of America,
1976. Microfilm.

This is a supplement to the 1975 MAJOR STUDIES OF THE LEG-
ISLATIVE REFERENCE SERVICE/CONGRESSIONAL RESEARCH
SERVICE (1916-1974). It contains 165 studies prepared by the
Congressional Research Service including such studies as "Right

to Counsel in Criminal Proceedings: Federal and State Courts,"
"Executive Privilege: Withholding Information from the Congress,"
and "The Equal Employment Opportunity Act of 1972: Legislative
History." There is a title and subject guide.

MAJOR STUDIES OF THE LEGISLATIVE REFERENCE SERVICE/CON-
GRESSIONAL RESEARCH SERVICE (1916-1974). Washington, D.C.:
University Publications of America, 1975. Microfilm.

This is a compilation on 35mm microfilm of 242 studies done
for Congress by the Legislative Reference Service/Congressional
Research Service from 1916 to 1974. It includes such studies
as those on "The Abortion Controversy: Legislative and Judicial
Actions Following the Supreme Court's Invalidation of Restrictions
Upon Access to Abortions," "Wiretapping and Electronic Sur-
veillance: Federal and State Statutes," "Proposals to Reform
Our Presidential Electoral System," "The Power of Congress to
Prohibit Racial Discrimination in the Rental, Sale, Use and
Occupancy of Private Housing," and "Congressional Power of
Investigation."

Mason, Alpheus T., and Garvey, Gerald. AMERICAN CONSTITUTIONAL
HISTORY: ESSAYS BY EDWARD S. CORWIN. Gloucester, Mass.: Peter
Smith, 1970.

This contains abridged versions of twelve of Corwin's "best"
works. It also includes a section on reviews of his publications.

Morgan, Edmund S. THE BIRTH OF THE REPUBLIC, 1763-1789. Chicago:
University of Chicago Press, 1956.

This slim volume is an account of the period from the Revolutionary War to the ratification of the Constitution with emphasis upon
the basic agreements rather than the conflicts among those who
declared independence, prosecuted the war and wrote two constitutions.

Mosteller, Frederick, and Wallace, David L. INFERENCE AND DISPUTED
AUTHORSHIP: THE FEDERALIST. Reading, Mass.: Addison-Wesley
Publishing Co., 1964.

This application of statistical tools--Bayes' theorem--to the
question of authorship of some of the disputed FEDERALIST
PAPERS awards authorship to Madison.

Murphy, Paul L. THE CONSTITUTION IN CRISIS TIME, 1918-1969. New
American Nation Series, vol. 2, edited by Henry Steele Commager and
Richard B. Morris. New York: Harper and Row, 1972.

This work covers the period from the end of the first World War
to the end of the Warren era. It thus deals with the economic
conservatism of the Court in the 1920s and 1930s, the Constitutional Revolution of 1937 whereby the Court legitimized the New
Deal and governmental intervention into the economic order, the
impact of "total war" and the cold war upon constitutional interpretation and the emphasis upon individual rights by the Warren
Court.

Paul, Arnold M. CONSERVATIVE CRISIS AND THE RULE OF LAW, 1887–
1895. Ithaca, N.Y.: Cornell University Press, 1960.

Published for the American Historical Association, this is an
examination of conservative legal doctrines, such as substantive
due process, used to protect private property against public
demands for regulation and protection; judicial evolution of
these constitutional theories; and the changes in the attitudes
of lawyers and judges from the dominant egalitarianism and anti-
monopolism remaining from the Jacksonian era to the economic
conservatism of the last quarter of the nineteenth century. In
analyzing the changing attitudes of lawyers and judges from 1887
to 1895 when judicial reaction against populism reached its
height in the Pollock and Knight cases, the author argues that
it was the movement to the right within traditional conservatism
rather than the new Spencerian, laissez-faire forces standing
alone that accounted for judicial activism on the side of business
and against agrarian, labor, and progressive interests.

Pollak, Louis H., ed. THE CONSTITUTION AND THE SUPREME COURT:
A DOCUMENTARY HISTORY. 2 vols. Cleveland and New York: World
Publishing Co., 1966.

This is an extensive collection of materials ranging from official
documents, letters, and essays to Supreme Court opinions, many
of which are woven into essays and commentaries by the editor.
Volume 1 covers the revolutionary period through the ratification
of the Constitution and includes excerpts from such materials as
Paine's COMMON SENSE and John Adams's appraisal of COMMON
SENSE to Charles A. Beard's ECONOMIC INTERPRETATION
OF THE CONSTITUTION (see p. 36). Volume 2 focuses upon
democratic restraints on the power to govern and includes ex-
cerpts from materials ranging from Milton's AREOPAGITICA to
President Johnson's address to Congress on voting rights and
Supreme Court opinions on individual rights.

Powell, Thomas Reed. VAGARIES AND VARIETIES IN CONSTITUTIONAL
INTERPRETATION. New York: Columbia University Press, 1956.

Of these six essays, originally delivered as the James S. Carpentier Lectures at Columbia University shortly before Professor
Powell's death, two deal with the establishment and operation
of the Court's power of judicial review. The others deal with
congressional power to regulate commerce and with various
facets of federalism such as the effect of the states' police and
taxing powers on the national economy.

Randall, James G. CONSTITUTIONAL PROBLEMS UNDER LINCOLN. Rev.
ed. Urbana: University of Illinois Press, 1951.

Originally published in 1926, this analysis of constitutional issues
during the Civil War deals with such matters as the war powers
under the Constitution, the legal nature of the Civil War, the law
of treason, the power to suspend the writ of habeas corpus, the
constitutionality of military rule of civilians, the partition of
Virginia and the emancipation of slaves.

Rawle, William. A VIEW OF THE CONSTITUTION OF THE UNITED STATES OF AMERICA. New York: Da Capo Press, 1970.

> Originally published in 1829, this is an analysis of constitutionalism in general and of the major features of the American Constitution with emphasis upon such nineteenth-century concerns as the organization, structure, powers, and relationships between the three branches of the national government.

Read, Conyers, ed. THE CONSTITUTION RECONSIDERED. New York: Columbia University Press, 1938.

> This is a collection of papers read at the 1937 American Historical Association meeting on the occasion of the sesquicentennial anniversary of the United States. It contains eleven essays dealing with the background of the political, economic and social ideas behind the Constitution; six of which focus on the influence of the Constitution upon American thought, and nine which analyze the effects of the Constitution on other countries.

Rossiter, Clinton. ALEXANDER HAMILTON AND THE CONSTITUTION. New York: Harcourt, Brace and World, 1964.

> This is an examination of Hamilton's constitutional theory, his influence on the adoption and growth of the Constitution and his two victorious constitutional battles with Jefferson. Hamilton's contribution is examined within the context of five stages of the early history of constitutional development: the six or seven years that led to the Convention; the four months that led to its signing; the battle over ratification; the first years of Washington's administration; and the years of consolidation of the achievements of Washington and Hamilton, first under Adams and then under Jefferson, years in which Hamilton served as a young and discontented elder statesmen.

_____. THE AMERICAN QUEST, 1790-1860: AN EMERGING NATION IN SEARCH OF IDENTITY, UNITY AND MODERNITY. New York: Harcourt Brace Jovanovich, 1971.

> This is an analysis of the broad national developments in the seven decades between the revolution and the Civil War viewed as a national search for progress and modernization.

Rottschaefer, Henry. THE CONSTITUTION AND SOCIO-ECONOMIC CHANGE. FIVE LECTURES DELIVERED AT THE UNIVERSITY OF MICHIGAN, MARCH 24, 25, 26, 27 AND 28, 1947. Reprint. Foreword by E. Blythe Stason. New York: Da Capo Press, 1972.

> Originally delivered as the first Thomas M. Cooley Lectures, this is an analysis of the process by which the Constitution adapted to and accomodated the expansion of federal power prior to 1933 and the expansion of both federal and state powers to regulate in the socioeconomic area after 1933.

Rumble, Wilfred E. AMERICAN LEGAL REALISM: SKEPTICISM, REFORM AND THE JUDICIAL PROCESS. Ithaca, N.Y.: Cornell University Press, 1968.

This is an analysis of the contributions and impact on constitutional law of the realist movement which began to challenge
traditional legal reasoning, logic, and reliance on precedent in
the early part of the century.

Schofield, Henry. ESSAYS ON CONSTITUTIONAL LAW AND EQUITY AND
OTHER SUBJECTS. 2 vols. New York: Da Capo Press, 1972.

Originally published in 1921, these essays by Professor Schofield, collected after his death, examine a variety of constitutional topics such as the relationship between state and federal
courts, the full faith and credit clause, trial by jury, interstate
commerce, the contract clause, due process, cruel and unusual
punishment, religious freedom, and freedom of the press. There
are also essays devoted to various aspects of equity.

Schouler, James. CONSTITUTIONAL STUDIES, FEDERAL AND STATE.
New York: Dodd, Mead and Co., 1897. Reprint. New York: Da Capo
Press, 1971.

This is a study of colonial charters and early state constitutions,
the Continental Congress, the Articles of Confederation, and the
writing of the Constitution. It is also an analysis of key constitutional powers of the Congress, the president and courts, and
of such constitutional problems as the relation between state and
nation. One major section is devoted to state constitutions since
1789.

Schwartz, Bernard. A BASIC HISTORY OF THE UNITED STATES SU-
PREME COURT. Princeton, N.J.: D. Van Nostrand Co., 1968.

Part 1 of this brief overview of the Supreme Court from the
Judiciary Act of 1789 and the first Court to the mid-1960s and
the Warren Court is an account of the major distinguishing fea-
tures of each court and the constitutional trends of each era.
Part 2 is a collection of documents, letters, Supreme Court
opinions, presidential messages and vetoes and other commentaries
on the Court.

_____. FROM CONFEDERATION TO NATION: THE AMERICAN CONSTITU-
TION, 1835-1877. Baltimore: Johns Hopkins Press, 1973.

This is a constitutional history from the death of Chief Justice
John Marshall and the beginning of the Taney Court to the end
of Reconstruction with the compromise settling the disputed
presidential election of 1876. The author views this period as
a continuing constitutional convention which produced a major
shift away from judicial concern with drawing the line between
the national and state governments to concern with protecting
individual rights against both national and state governments.

_____. THE REINS OF POWER: A CONSTITUTIONAL HISTORY OF THE
UNITED STATES. New York: Hill and Wang, 1963.

This is a brief overview of such major aspects of constitutional
development as its theoretical debt to English political theory

and practice, the adoption of the Constitution, the early conflicts between nation and state, the supremacy of the Congress during Reconstruction, the proper role of the military in a republic, the judicial use of due process to protect laissez-faire economic theory, the Constitutional Revolution of 1937 and the status of constitutional theory in the 1950s.

Small, Norman, ed. THE CONSTITUTION OF THE UNITED STATES OF AMERICA: ANALYSIS AND INTERPRETATION. Washington, D.C.: Government Printing Office, 1964.

> Generally referred to as THE CONSTITUTION ANNOTATED, this revision of the 1952 version edited by Edward S. Corwin is the most widely used guide to judicial decisions interpreting the Constitution. Organized on the basis of the provisions of the Constitution, this volume briefly discusses Supreme Court opinions interpreting each provision. Prepared by the Legislative Reference Service of the Library of Congress.

Smith, James Morton, and Murphy, Paul L., eds. LIBERTY AND JUSTICE: A HISTORICAL RECORD OF AMERICAN CONSTITUTIONAL DEVELOPMENT. 2 vols. Rev. ed. New York: Knopf, 1965.

> With a short essay introducing each of the twenty-eight chapters, these volumes include excerpts from the public papers and speeches of public figures, public documents such as congressional legislation, resolutions and constitutional amendments, and judicial opinions related to the development of representative government and individual freedom. Volume 1 contains documents relevant to representative government beginning with the Charter of Virginia of 1606 to 1869. Volume 2 covers the period to 1956 and the Southern Manifesto.

Story, Joseph. COMMENTARIES ON THE CONSTITUTION OF THE UNITED STATES WITH A PRELIMINARY REVIEW OF THE CONSTITUTIONAL HISTORY OF THE COLONIES AND THE STATES BEFORE THE ADOPTION OF THE CONSTITUTION. 3 vols. Boston: Hilliard Gray, 1833. Reprint. Introduction by Arthur E. Sutherland. New York: Da Capo Press, 1970.

> This is a reprint of a classic work which was a standard text in law schools until the turn of the century when the case method began to be used. Story, who served simultaneously as a Supreme Court justice and as a Harvard law school professor from 1811 until his death in 1845 and who had participated in the development of the Constitution as a state legislator and as a lawyer arguing the first case (Fletcher v. Peck) in which a state law was declared unconstitutional, began his political career as a Jeffersonian and became a chief spokesman for the Marshallian concept of a strong central government. Volume I is devoted to a history of each of the colonies, of the revolutionary and confederate periods and the adoption and early controversies over the nature of the Constitution. Volume 2 is an analysis of the distribution of power among the three branches of the national government and the powers of Congress. Volume 3 continues the analysis of congressional power as well as executive and judicial powers.

Sutherland, Arthur E. CONSTITUTIONALISM IN AMERICA: ORIGIN AND EVOLUTION OF ITS FUNDAMENTAL IDEAS. New York: Blaisdell Publishing Co., 1965.

This is a history of the origins and development of five major constitutional theories in the United States--majority rule, justice, equality, division of governmental powers, and written constitutions.

_____, ed. GOVERNMENT UNDER LAW. Cambridge, Mass.: Harvard University Press, 1956.

This work contains eighteen papers delivered by American and foreign scholars and judges--each followed by comments and discussion by panelists--at a conference held at Harvard Law School in celebration of the bicentennial of John Marshall's birth. Among the papers are: Felix Frankfurter on "John Marshall and the Judicial Function," Francis Shackelford on "The Separation of Powers in Times of Crisis," Patrick Kerwin, Chief Justice of Canada, on "Constitutionalism in Canada," and Charles Fairman on "Government Under Law in Times of Crisis."

Swinder, William F. COURT AND CONSTITUTION IN THE TWENTIETH CENTURY. 3 vols. Indianapolis: Bobbs-Merrill, 1969, 1970, 1974.

This is an examination of the development of the Constitution in terms of what the author views as the first four crises of twentieth-century change--the Populist movement, the attempted reforms of Wilson's New Freedom, the Depression of the 1930s, and the period after the Second World War. Volume 1, subtitled THE OLD LEGALITY, 1889-1932, begins with the end of the first century of the Constitution and goes to the Depression. Volume 2, subtitled THE NEW LEGALITY, deals with the period from 1932 to 1968. It examines the clash between the old constitutional concept of laissez-faire and the new need for governmental intervention, the emerging activism and restraints forces in the Stone and Vinson courts, and the development of a new concept of federalism in which the relationship between the individual citizen and the national government changed. Part 1 of volume 3, subtitled A MODERN INTERPRETATION, consists of the original Constitution, the first ten amendments, the Civil War amendments and the amendments adopted through 1970 with brief comments on some of the provisions of each. The second part of the work is a clause-by-clause analysis of the Constitution with commentaries on relevant Supreme Court decisions, with major emphasis given to the Court's decisions since 1947.

Swisher, Carl B. AMERICAN CONSTITUTIONAL DEVELOPMENT. Rev. ed. Boston: Houghton Mifflin Co., 1954.

Written in the 1940s before the Court turned its attention to issues of individual rights, this work is especially useful for its analysis of the conflicts over nationalism and states' rights which dominated much of the nineteenth century. Its examination of the controversies over the proper role of government in the socioeconomic order, which dominated much of constitutional law from the late nineteenth century until the judicial triumph of the New Deal in the late 1930s, is equally helpful.

Taylor, John. CONSTRUCTION CONSTRUED AND CONSTITUTIONS VINDICATED. 1820. Reprint. New York: Da Capo Press, 1970.

This is an attack by Taylor of Virginia upon the expansion of national power by federal courts, Congress and presidents, an expansion viewed by the author as an intrusion into the powers constitutionally reserved for the states. This constitutional analysis was prompted in part by the Missouri Compromise, by Marshall's opinion in McCulloch v. Maryland, by the attempts to impose a national tariff and to inject the federal government into the construction of roads and canals.

Thorpe, Francis Newton. THE CONSTITUTIONAL HISTORY OF THE UNITED STATES, 1765-1895. 3 vols. New York: Da Capo Press, 1970.

Originally published in 1901. Volume 1 of this "biography of the national system" begins with the end of the French and Indian War and the enactment of the Stamp Act and ends with the writing of the Constitution, a period which to the author reveals that the national system evolved from colonial experience. Volume 2 covers the period from 1788 and the adoption of the Constitution to 1861 and the beginning of the Civil War. Volume 3 is an analysis of the constitutional developments from 1861 to 1895 and the changes wrought by the Civil War and the rise of business.

Tugwell, Rexford G. THE COMPROMISING OF THE CONSTITUTION: EARLY DEPARTURES. Notre Dame, Ind.: University of Notre Dame, n.d.

Written sometime in the late 1960s and perhaps a prelude to his MODEL CONSTITUTION (below) suggested by the Center for Democratic Institutions, this is an examination of the practices of the judiciary, the executive, and the legislative branches which depart from and thus changed the Constitution as originally written, as well as of the changes wrought by constitutional amendment, along with an argument that the Constitution needs to be replaced.

_____. A MODEL CONSTITUTION FOR A UNITED REPUBLICS OF AMERICA. Introduction by Harry S. Ashmore. Santa Barbara, Calif.: Center for the Study of Democratic Institutions, 1970.

This is a copy of the alternate constitution drafted at the Center which originally appeared in THE CENTER MAGAZINE in 1970, along with an explanatory note by Tugwell. Copies of the Declaration of Independence, the Articles of Confederation, and the Constitution, each with notes by Tugwell, are included in this edition of the MODEL CONSTITUTION.

Twiss, Benjamin R. LAWYERS AND THE CONSTITUTION: HOW LAISSEZ-FAIRE CAME TO THE SUPREME COURT. Princeton, N.J.: Princeton University Press, 1942.

This is an examination of the social and economic attitudes and
influence of lawyers in the late nineteenth century which led the
Supreme Court to read conservative economic theory into the
Constitution in the late nineteenth and early twentieth centuries.

Upshur, Abel P.   A BRIEF ENQUIRY INTO THE TRUE NATURE AND
CHARTER OF OUR FEDERAL GOVERNMENT: BEING A REVIEW OF
JUDGE STORY'S COMMENTARIES ON THE CONSTITUTION OF THE
UNITED STATES.   New York: Da Capo Press, 1971.

Originally published in 1840, this brief work is a criticism of
the central themes of Story's COMMENTARIES (see p. 53),
particularly the latter's emphasis upon Americans as "one people"
from the American Revolution on through the adoption of the
Constitution, his national supremacy views and his Federalist
concept of the role of the Supreme Court.

Whiting, William.   THE WAR POWERS OF THE PRESIDENT AND THE
LEGISLATIVE POWERS OF CONGRESS IN RELATION TO REBELLION,
TREASON AND SLAVERY.   1863.   Reprint.   New York: Da Capo Press,
1971.

Written before the Emancipation Proclamation and circulated
gratuitously by the Emancipation League, this is an argument in
support of a broad interpretation of the war powers of the president and of the Congress.   The author construes the war powers
to include the powers to define treason, to punish for rebellion
and to abolish slavery.

Chapter 5

BASIC PRINCIPLES OF

THE AMERICAN CONSTITUTIONAL SYSTEM

FEDERALISM

Adams, Henry, ed. DOCUMENTS RELATING TO NEW ENGLAND FEDER-
ALISM, 1800–1815. 1905. Reprint. New York: Burt Franklin, 1964.

> This is a collection of basic source materials relating to New
> England's hostility to national administrative policies, a hostility
> which led to the invocation of the doctrine of interposition and
> to the Hartford convention.

Ames, Herman V., ed. STATE DOCUMENTS ON FEDERAL RELATIONS:
THE STATES AND THE UNITED STATES. [c. 1900]. Reprint. New
York: Da Capo Press, 1970.

> This work contains 155 official documents, each with an intro-
> ductory note by the editor, in which state officials express their
> views of the federal–state relationship in resolutions and messages.
> They are organized under the following headings: "Interpretation
> of the Constitution During the First Two Decades of Its History,
> 1789–1809"; "States Rights and the War of 1812 (1809–1815)";
> "The Reserved Rights of the States and the Jurisdiction of the
> Federal Courts, 1819–1832"; "Tariff and Nullification, 1820–
> 1833"; "Slavery and the Constitution, 1789–1845"; and "Slavery
> and the Union, 1845–1861." Included are such documents as a
> Virginia Resolution sent to Congress on the assumption of state
> debts in 1790, a 1790 message of Georgia's governor rejecting
> Supreme Court authority to hear Chisholm v. Georgia, the
> resolution of the Hartford convention and a Virginia resolution
> opposing the second United States Bank.

Association of American Law Schools. SELECTED ESSAYS ON CONSTITU-
TIONAL LAW. 4 vols. Chicago: Foundation Press, 1938.

> Volume 3 of this work, entitled THE NATION AND THE STATE,
> contains eighty-nine essays on various facets of the federal–
> state relations.

Beck, James M. THE VANISHING RIGHTS OF THE STATES: A DIS-
CUSSION OF THE RIGHT OF THE SENATE TO NULLIFY THE ACTION
OF A SOVEREIGN STATE IN THE SELECTION OF ITS REPRESENTATIVES
IN THE SENATE. New York: George H. Doran Co., 1926.

This slim volume by a former solicitor general of the United
States examines the authority of Congress to refuse to seat or
to expel national legislators whose elections are certified by
the state. Written in response to the possibility that the Senate
would examine the qualifications of two Republican nominees and
winners of general elections in the 1926 elections in Pennsylvania
and Illinois, Beck examines English precedents on the matter of
expulsion, the debates at the Philadelphia convention, the division
of power between nation and state in conducting elections and
concludes that the question of the legitimacy of an election for
a member of the Congress is a matter for the state, not the
national government, to answer.

Bennett, Walter H. AMERICAN THEORIES OF FEDERALISM. University:
University of Alabama Press, 1964.

This is an analysis of the varying interpretations and theories
of federalism which have been advanced and adopted in the
United States from time to time and the role which these varying
understandings of federalism played in political conflicts.

Boucher, Chauncey S. THE NULLIFICATION CONTROVERSY IN SOUTH
CAROLINA. Chicago: University of Chicago Press, 1916.

This is a study of the broad conflict between the views of the
nationalists and liberal constructionists on the one hand and the
state sovereignists and strict constructionists on the other within South Carolina and within the nation during the Adams and
Jackson administrations. In an attempt to "delineate various
shades of party beliefs at all stages of the controversy," this
work examines the evolution of the nullification theory in the
late 1820s and the 1830s culminating in 1833 with the suspension
of nullification and adoption of a compromise tariff law and a
force bill.

Calhoun, John C. A DISQUISITION ON GOVERNMENT. 1853. Reprint.
New York: Poli Sci Classics, 1947.

This contains Calhoun's classic enunciation of the "concurrent
majority" theory.

Clark, Jane P. THE RISE OF A NEW FEDERALISM. New York: Columbia
University Press, 1938.

This is one of the early works which focused not upon the conflict between nation and state but upon the cooperation between
the two partners as illustrated by, for example, the extensive
participation by the state's administrative apparatus in carrying
out federal laws such as the selective service act.

Conference of Chief Justices. REPORT OF THE COMMITTEE ON FEDERAL-
STATE RELATIONSHIPS AS AFFECTED BY JUDICIAL DECISIONS,
AUGUST, 1958. Richmond: Virginia Commission on Constitutional Govern-
ment, 1958.

This report of the 1958 conference of the state chief justices is critical of the increasingly active role of the Supreme Court in the 1950s in acting as a superlegislature and in expanding national power at the expense of state power. The chief justices express alarm at the erosion of the traditional boundaries between state and national power. They are especially criticial of the application and expansion of the preemption doctrine in such cases as Pennsylvania v. Nelson , the invalidation of state legislation on the grounds that it is a regulation of interstate commerce, the narrowing of state immunity from national taxation, and the use of the Fourteenth Amendment to limit state authority in a variety of areas.

Corwin, Edward S. THE COMMERCE POWER VERSUS STATE POWER. Princeton, N.J.: Princeton University Press, 1936.

Written during the period when the Court was invalidating New Deal legislation enacted on the basis of the commerce clause on the grounds that it invaded the reserved powers of the states, Corwin argues for a broad construction of the commerce clause. In concluding that the intentions of the framers of the Constitution and precedent require a broad construction, Corwin examines judicial opinions such as Gibbons v. Ogden which broadly construed national power and the early Madisonian concept of broad construction. He also traces the development of such narrowing concepts as the concept that the power to regulate commerce does not include the power to prohibit, the concept that the reserved powers of the states constitute a limitation upon the delegated powers of Congress, and that manufacturing or production is distinct from commerce and is therefore within the reserved powers of the states.

_____. CONSTITUTIONAL REVOLUTION, LTD. Claremont, Calif.: Associated College, 1941.

This is a series of lectures delivered at Claremont College in which the author deals with the Supreme Court's acceptance of the New Deal in the late 1930s and with the "dissolving concepts" of dual federalism and laissez-faire.

_____. NATIONAL SUPREMACY: TREATY POWER AND STATE POWER. New York: Henry Holt and Co., 1913.

This study of the relationship between the national government's treaty-making power and the state's police power examines such matters as the scope of the treaty-making power, the supremacy of national power, the original view of the treaty-making power and the problem of national enforcement of treaties.

_____. "The Passing of Dual Federalism." VIRGINIA LAW REVIEW 36 (February 1950): 1-26.

This is an analysis of the change in judicial interpretation of the federal relationship in the late 1930s and early 1940s, changes which had the effect of allowing the expansion of national power. Corwin examines judicial development of the four postulates of what he calls dual federalism and demonstrates how each was

changed in favor of an interpretation conducive to centralization.
The four judicially constructed principles examined are: the
national government is one of enumerated powers only; the
purposes which it may constitutionally promote are few; within
their respective spheres the two governments are "sovereign"
and "equal"; and the relationship between the federal partners
is one of tension rather than cooperation. This article is reprinted in several collections of essays on constitutional law
including ESSAYS IN CONSTITUTIONAL LAW edited by Robert
G. McCloskey (see p. 83).

de Grazia, Alfred. ESSAYS ON APPORTIONMENT AND REPRESENTATIVE
GOVERNMENT. Washington, D.C.: American Enterprise Institute, 1963.

This is an examination of different theories of representation,
including the "egalitarian–majoritarian" theory embodied in Supreme Court apportionment opinions since Baker v. Carr, a
theory which the author views as a threat to the federal system.

Dwight, Theodore. HISTORY OF THE HARTFORD CONVENTION, WITH A
REVIEW OF THE POLICY OF THE UNITED STATES GOVERNMENT WHICH
LED TO THE WAR OF 1812. 1833. Reprint. New York: Da Capo Press,
1970.

This work focuses upon the adoption by New Englanders of the
interposition or nullification theory advanced by southerners in
the Virginia and Kentucky Resolutions and contains copies of
the resolutions adopted by the Hartford convention.

Earle, Valerie, ed. FEDERALISM: INFINITE VARIETY IN THEORY AND
PRACTICE. Itasca, Ill.: F.E. Peacock Publishers, 1968.

Of the seven essays dealing with federalism, three examine various aspects of American federalism. The essay by Alpheus T.
Mason looks at the role of the Court.

Elazar, Daniel J. AMERICAN FEDERALISM: A VIEW FROM THE STATES.
New York: Crowell, 1966.

Focusing upon the states, which he views as "the keystone of the
American government arch," rather than upon the national government, Elazar views the states' political and constitutional relationship to both the national government and to local government
and argues that the states are both well-integrated parts of the
national civil society and separate civil societies in their own
right and that the states have preserved their integrity not
through sharp separation from the national system but by tying
all levels of government together.

_____. AMERICAN PARTNERSHIP: INTERGOVERNMENTAL COOPERATION
IN THE NINETEENTH CENTURY UNITED STATES. Chicago: University
of Chicago Press, 1962.

This history of nineteenth-century constitutional theories and
practices of federalism emphasized cooperation and interdependence rather than conflict and independence.

Engdahl, David E. CONSTITUTIONAL POWER: FEDERAL AND STATE IN A NUTSHELL. Nutshell Series. St. Paul, Minn.: West Publishing Co., 1974.

> This is a summary of the constitutional law of federalism. The topics include the doctrines of enumerated national power and reserved state power, the necessary and proper clause and the implied powers doctrine, congressional powers to regulate commerce and to tax and spend, national control of state power, and intergovernmental cooperation and interstate compacts.

Fellman, David. "Ten Years of the Supreme Court—1937-1947: Federalism." AMERICAN POLITICAL SCIENCE REVIEW 40 (December 1947): 1142-60.

> This is a review of Supreme Court decisions in the decisive decade following the "constitutional revolution of 1937" when the Court began the process of redefining the federal-state relationship, allowing each partner in that relationship greater latitude in determining socioeconomic policy, facilitating cooperation between the two and reasserting national supremacy.

Frankfurter, Felix. THE COMMERCE CLAUSE UNDER MARSHALL, TANEY, AND WAITE. Chapel Hill: University of North Carolina Press, 1937.

> Originally delivered as the Weil Lectures at the University of North Carolina in 1936, each of the three essays deals with the manner in which the Court under the Chief Justiceship of Marshall, then Taney and finally Waite (omitting the period of the Chase Court which came between the Taney and Waite courts) construed the power of Congress to regulate commerce among the states and the effect of the different constructions upon the states and upon the federal relationship.

Goldwin, Richard A., ed. A NATION OF STATES. Chicago: Rand McNally, 1963.

> This collection of seven original essays examines various facets of the American federal system. Included are Morton Grodzins' "Centralization and Decentralization in the American Federal System," Martin Diamond's "What the Framers Meant by Federalism," Russell Kirk's "The Prospects for Territorial Democracy in America," Herbert T. Storin's "The Problems of Big Government," James J. Kilpatrick's "The Case for States' Rights," Henry Jaffa's "The Case for a Stronger National Government," and Walter Berns's "The Meaning of the Tenth Amendment."

Hutchison, William T. "Unite to Divide; Divide to Unite: The Shaping of American Federalism." MISSISSIPPI VALLEY HISTORICAL REVIEW 46 (June 1959): 3-18.

> Originally delivered as the presidential address at the 1959 meeting of the Mississippi Valley Historical Association, this article argues that the acquisition and administration of the West and the process of admitting those territories into the Union as states was a major centralizing force in American

federalism, aided in preserving an equilibrium between nationalism and states' rights and allowed American federalism to span
a continent with little violence.

Kallenbach, Joseph E. FEDERAL COOPERATION WITH THE STATES UN-
DER THE COMMERCE CLAUSE. Ann Arbor: University of Michigan Press,
1942.

This examination of the relationship between the federal and
state governments in the regulation of foreign and interstate
commerce focuses upon the constitutional developments in congressional use of its commerce power to supplement and support
state action. Because the congressional power to regulate commerce among the states is both concurrent and exclusive and although the Congress cannot constitutionally delegate its legislative powers to the states, Congress has devised, and the federal courts have upheld, various means by which the national
government permits, supports, and reinforces state regulation
of various facets of interstate commerce upon which Congress is
silent. Kallenbach analyzes such congressional actions as di-
vestment of the interstate character of goods, national prohibitions of the movement of goods into a state prohibiting such
goods, federal regulation of commerce for the protection of the
sending states, federal adoption of state laws as well as divest-
ment by constitutional amendment as in the Twenty-First Amendment.

Koch, Adrienne, and Ammon, Harry. "The Virginia and Kentucky Resolutions: An Episode in Jefferson's and Madison's Defense of Civil Liberties."
WILLIAM AND MARY QUARTERLY 5 (April 1948): 145-76.

Written during the resurgence of a states' rights movement in
the South in the late 1940s but before the invocation of the interposition theory following the Public School Segregation Cases in
1954, this is an account of the secret roles of Jefferson and
Madison in formulating the resolutions introduced in the Kentucky
legislature by John Breckinridge and in the Virginia legislature
by John Taylor and the later elaboration of the nullification
theory by the original authors. The article examines the differences, as well as the similarities, between the Madisonian and
the Jeffersonian views on the nature of the Union and the nature
and extent of the state's power to challenge the constitutionality
of national legislation interfering with basic human rights. The
authors emphasize the civil libertarian nature of the original
theory and its use in protesting the Alien and Sedition Acts.

Larsen, Charles E. "Nationalism and States' Rights in Commentaries on
the Constitution after the Civil War." AMERICAN JOURNAL OF LEGAL
HISTORY 3 (October 1959): 360-69.

This brief article examines the disagreements over the nature
of the Union and the location of sovereignty and/or the right of
secession among immediate post-Civil War commentators, such as
the nationalists John Norton Pomeroy and Thomas M. Cooley and
the states' rights advocates such as Roger Sherman, Baldwin

Foster and John Randolph Tucker. Noting that all emphasized
the importance of local self-government, Larsen suggests that
their common devotion to laissez-faire tied them to a static concept of federalism and precluded a dynamic role for either the
state or the national government.

Leach, Richard H. AMERICAN FEDERALISM. New York: W.W. Norton,
1970.

This is a constitutional, political, and administrative analysis
of the relationship between the national government and the states
and the problem of metropolitan areas which cross local and
sometimes state lines.

McGowan, Carl. THE ORGANIZATION OF JUDICIAL POWER IN THE
UNITED STATES. Evanston, Ill.: Northwestern University Press, 1969.

These 1967 Rosenthal Lectures at Northwestern University School
of Law examine the organization, functioning and sharing of judicial power between state and national courts, the "stresses of
coexistence" between the national and state judicial systems, and
the "quest for accommodation" between the two.

MacMahan, Arthur W., ed. FEDERALISM: MATURE AND EMERGENT. New
York: Macmillan, 1955.

This is a collection of essays on various aspects of federalism
(principally American but some foreign) and on the question of
whether this form of geographic entity may serve to unify Europe
and the developing nations.

Mason, Alpheus T. THE STATES RIGHTS DEBATE: THE ANTIFEDERA-
LISTS AND THE CONSTITUTION. Englewood Cliffs, N.J.: Prentice-Hall,
Spectrum, 1964.

This is an analysis of the position of the state sovereignists and
their losing battle with the nationalists both at the Philadelphia
convention and in the ratification process. There are excerpts
from the various plans and compromises of and between the two
sides and from the writings of the anti-Federalists.

Mogi, Soebei. THE PROBLEM OF FEDERALISM: A STUDY IN THE HIS-
TORY OF POLITICAL THEORY. Preface by Harold Laski. 2 vols. New
York: Macmillan, 1931.

This is an extensive analysis of the history of the federal theory.
Part 1, which deals with the history of the federal idea in the
United States, traces the origin of the American theory to
Aristotle and examines its adoption and adaptation in the American
Constitution. In looking at the theory from its adoption to the
late 1920s, the author discusses the interpretations of such
American commentators as Kent, Calhoun, and Webster. The
history of the theory in other countries is also studied.

Morley, Felix. FREEDOM AND FEDERALISM. Chicago: Henry Regnery
Co., 1959.

This is an examination of those forces moving American federalism away from what the author views as its original concept
and closer to a centralized, unitary system. The author argues
that as conceived by the framers of the Constitution, decentralized, nonmajoritarian federalism was designed to assure freedom
and social democracy by blocking political democracy and the
kind of majority rule embodied in Rousseau's "general will."
The forces which he sees as pushing federalism away from the
original concept are such forces as the Fourteenth Amendment
and judicial interpretation of that amendment, the New Deal, and
nationalization through foreign policy.

Murphy, William P. THE TRIUMPH OF NATIONALISM: STATE SOVER-
EIGNTY, THE FOUNDING FATHERS AND THE MAKING OF THE CONSTITU-
TION. Chicago: Quadrangle Books, 1967.

Written in response to the state sovereignty interposition theories
relied upon by the southern states as legal justification for massive resistance to judicially ordered school desegregation, this
is an analysis of the victory of nationalist over state sovereignty
forces from 1776 to 1789 which focuses upon the constitutional
convention and the ratification conventions. Caught up personally
in the conflict of the late 1950s and the early 1960s as a target
of the segregationist forces in Mississippi, the author takes a
strong pronationalist view of the eighteenth-century conflict.

Pound, Roscoe, ed. FEDERALISM AS A DEMOCRATIC PROCESS. New
Brunswick, N.J.: Rutgers University Press, 1942.

With commentaries by Edward S. Corwin and F.W. Coker, this
is a collection of three essays: "Law and the Federal Government," by Roscoe Pound; "Historical Background of the Federal
Government," by Charles H. McIlwain; and "Federalism and
Democracy," by Roy F. Nichols.

REPORT OF THE COMMITTEE ON INTERGOVERNMENTAL RELATIONS.
16 vols. Washington, D.C.: Government Printing Office, 1955.

This is the report of the Kestenbaum Commission appointed by
President Eisenhower to do a complete study of the American
federal system.

REPORTS OF THE JOINT COMMITTEE ON INTERGOVERNMENTAL RELA-
TIONS. Washington, D.C.: Government Printing Office, 1958-59.

These are the reports of the second committee appointed by
President Eisenhower to study American federalism. Whereas
the purpose of the first committee, which issued its report in
1955, was to do a general study of the operation of the federal
system, the purpose of this second committee was to study ways
in which functions could be returned to the states.

Rice, William G. A TALE OF TWO COURTS. JUDICIAL SETTLEMENT
OF CONTROVERSIES BETWEEN THE STATES OF THE SWISS AND
AMERICAN FEDERATIONS. Madison: University of Wisconsin Press,
1967.

This is an analysis of the similarities and differences in the manner in which two systems of federalism handle the basic problems of settling disputes between its constituent parts.

Riker, William H. FEDERALISM: ORIGIN, OPERATION AND SIGNIFI-
CANCE. Boston: Little, Brown, 1964.

This is a basic study of federalism in general, and American federalism in particular, in terms of its theory, its origin and purpose, and the institutions (such as the Senate, the president, the Courts, and the party systems) by which it is maintained.

Roettinger, Ruth L. THE SUPREME COURT AND STATE POLICE POWER:
A STUDY IN FEDERALISM. Washington, D.C.: Public Affairs Press, 1957.

This is an examination of judicial decisions relating to the nature and extent of the state's police powers. Emphasis is upon the period from 1930 to 1956, with a brief review of the cases and principles prior to 1930.

Schmidhauser, John R. THE SUPREME COURT AS FINAL ARBITER IN
FEDERAL-STATE RELATIONS, 1789-1957. Chapel Hill: University of
North Carolina Press, 1958.

This is an analysis of the role of the Supreme Court in deter-
mining the boundaries between national and state authority, in settling conflicts between these two levels of government and in asserting and protecting national supremacy.

Shuman, Samuel I., comp. THE FUTURE OF FEDERALISM. Detroit:
Wayne State University Press, 1968.

These five essays, originally delivered at the Wayne State Law School, deal with various aspects of the federal relationship. The essays included are: Robert C. Weaver, former secretary of HUD, on "Federal Executive Action and States Rights," Paul A. Freund on "The Supreme Court and the Future of Federalism," J. Skelly Wright, a federal Court of Appeals judge, on "The Federal Courts and the Nature and Quality of State Law-- from the Point of View of a Federal Judge," Charles S. Desmond, a former judge of the New York state Court of Appeals on "The Federal Courts and the Nature and Quality of State Law--From the Point of View of a State Judge," and Thomas A. Kuchel, United States senator from California, on "The Role of the Congress and the Political Vitality of State Government."

STATE PAPERS ON NULLIFICATION INCLUDING THE PUBLIC ACTS
OF THE CONVENTION OF THE PEOPLE OF SOUTH CAROLINA (1832-34);
THE PROCLAMATION OF THE PRESIDENT OF THE UNITED STATES;
AND THE PROCEEDINGS OF THE SEVERAL STATE LEGISLATURES
WHICH HAVE ACTED ON THE SUBJECT. 1834. Reprint. New York:
Da Capo Press, 1970.

This is a collection of official documents concerning South Caro-
lina's ordinance nullifying the national tariff and prohibiting its enforcement published by order of the General Court of Massachusetts. Included are all of the relevant official materials

emanating from South Carolina and from the president in reaction to the nullification attempt as well as the resolutions of other state legislatures in response to South Carolina's request for support in its fight with the national government.

Upshur, Abel P. A BRIEF ENQUIRY INTO THE TRUE NATURE AND CHARACTER OF OUR FEDERAL GOVERNMENT, BEING A REVIEW OF JUDGE STORY'S COMMENTARIES ON THE CONSTITUTION OF THE UNITED STATES. New York: Da Capo Press, 1971.

Originally published in Virginia in 1840 this analysis of the nature of the federal relationship is critical of Story's nationalism and supportive of a states' rights, decentralized theory.

Virginia Commission on Constitutional Government. WE THE STATES: AN ANTHOLOGY OF HISTORIC DOCUMENTS AND COMMENTARIES THEREON, EXPOUNDING THE STATE AND FEDERAL RELATIONSHIP. Richmond: William Byrd Press, 1964.

The Virginia Commission on Constitutional Government was established in reaction to the Supreme Court's 1954 Public School Segregation Cases for the purpose of challenging the legitimacy of national judicial interference with functions, education in particular, traditionally performed by the states. The documents in this publication support the state sovereignist position of the southern states in this period. It includes such materials as the Virginia Declaration of Rights, the Virginia and Kentucky Resolutions of 1798 and Jefferson's letters arguing against the constitutionality of the United States Bank.

THE VIRGINIA REPORT OF 1799–1800 TOUCHING THE ALIEN AND SEDITION LAWS: TOGETHER WITH THE VIRGINIA RESOLUTIONS OF DECEMBER 21, 1798. 1850. Reprint. Da Capo Press, 1970.

This is a collection of materials relating to Virginia's early nullification efforts. It contains such materials as the Alien and Sedition Acts, the Resolution of 1798 and the legislative debate on that resolution, the Kentucky Resolutions, the resolutions of other states in response to the Virginia and Kentucky Resolutions, the Report of 1799, the instructions to Virginia senators in 1800 as well as three letters written by Madison on the subject of nullification.

Warfield, Ethelbert. THE KENTUCKY RESOLUTIONS OF 1798: AN HISTORICAL STUDY. New York: G.P. Putnam's Sons, 1887.

This is a history of the nullification movement in Kentucky which examines the factors contributing to Kentucky's movement toward nullification, the adoption of the resolutions in 1798, the reactions toward the resolutions in the other states and in the Congress, the authorship of the resolutions and the doctrine of nullification and its effects.

Warren, Charles. THE SUPREME COURT AND THE SOVEREIGN STATES. Princeton, N.J.: Princeton University Press, 1924.

This work focuses upon the status of the states as sovereign
entities and the relationship, actual and potential, between the
Supreme Court and these sovereign units. Article III gives
to the Supreme Court jurisdiction over cases involving two
states. To the extent that a state is made a defendant before
a national tribunal, its sovereignty is diminished. When the
states turned to the interstate compact, rather than to litigation,
to settle disputes and to deal with common problems, a potential
new class of conflicts threatened to confront the Court--those
involving a breach of the interstate compact. Judicial enforcement of these compacts--agreements which Warren views as
"voluntary surrenders" of sovereignty--further threatens state
sovereignty and intensifies the problem of national enforcement
of judicial decrees against a state. Included in the appendix
are lists of interstate compacts in existence in the 1920s, lists
of acts giving congressional consent to such compacts, and the
debates in the state ratifying conventions which illustrate the
delegates' concern over the potential loss of state sovereignty.

Wendell, Mitchell. RELATIONS BETWEEN FEDERAL AND STATE COURTS.
New York: Columbia University Press, 1949.

This study of judicial federalism deals with the jurisdictional
boundaries and overlapping between the two court systems in the
dual American structure. There is an in-depth analysis of
Swift v. Tyson, which Wendell labels "an experiment in nation-
wide uniformity," and of Erie v. Tompkins which he views as
"a more modest uniformity."

Wheare, Kenneth C. FEDERAL GOVERNMENT. New York: Oxford University Press, 1946.

This is a survey of modern federal government. Wheare deals
with such questions as what federal government is, when it is
appropriate, how it is organized and how it works.

Wildavsky, Aaron, ed. AMERICAN FEDERALISM IN PERSPECTIVE.
Boston: Little, Brown, 1967.

This book of readings includes thirteen essays and excerpts on
various facets of American federalism--an analysis of the basic
concept, its origins, the relationship between federalism and
the party system and a comparison of the American system with
other federal systems.

SEPARATION OF POWERS

Andrews, William G., ed. COORDINATE MAGISTRATES: CONSTITU-
TIONAL LAW BY CONGRESS AND PRESIDENT. New York: Van Nostrand
Reinhold Co., 1969.

Although the Supreme Court is the final interpreter of the Constitution when it considers constitutional questions in the cases
and controversies coming before it, the other branches of government also consider and resolve constitutional questions. This

work, intended primarily for undergraduate students, is a collection of excerpts ranging from Lincoln's remarks on slavery in the Lincoln-Douglas debates to Senator Sam Ervin on the constitutionality of the 1964 Civil Rights Act in which congressmen and presidents present their arguments on the constitutional questions before them.

Barber, Sotirios A. THE CONSTITUTION AND THE DELEGATION OF CONGRESSIONAL POWER. Chicago: University of Chicago Press, 1975.

Originally a Ph.D. dissertation, this is an analysis of the basis of and necessity for the traditional rule that Congress may not redelegate the law-making power which the Constitution delegates to it. Although the Supreme Court's application of the rule has been increasingly flexible since Schechter, the author argues that congressional abdication of its powers to the president would betray the expectation, derived from the constituent act of establishing government, that government not change the basic arrangement of powers.

Binkley, Wilfred E. THE POWERS OF THE PRESIDENT: PROBLEMS OF AMERICAN DEMOCRACY. Garden City, N.Y.: Doubleday, Doran and Co., 1937.

This study of the evolution of the relationship between the president and Congress from the Philadelphia convention and the first Congress to the administration of Wilson traces the recurring shift of power from president to Congress, from Congress to president with presidential government replacing congressional government in the Wilson administration.

_____. PRESIDENT AND CONGRESS. New York: Knopf, 1947.

This is a historical analysis of the relationship between the president and the Congress.

Black, Henry C. THE RELATION OF THE EXECUTIVE POWER TO LEGISLATION. Princeton, N.J.: Princeton University Press, 1919.

Written in the World War I period, this is a study of the expansion of presidential power at the expense of the power of the Congress, an expansion which the author views as in conflict with the separation of powers doctrine and the intention of the framers of the Constitution and as a threat to individual liberties. He argues that those extralegal presidential powers which are found acceptable should be formally acknowledged by procedural changes rather than exercised without full public knowledge of the role of the president in the legislative process.

Braden, Stephen B. "Constitutional Law—Separation of Powers—Mandatory Injunction to the President." WISCONSIN LAW REVIEW 12 (1974): 198-211.

This is an examination of the 1973 case of Minnesota Chippewa Tribe v. Carlucci in which a district court held that it had the authority to issue a mandatory injunction to the president to perform a nondiscretionary official act. The author sees the case as one necessitating a balancing of the competing principles of separation of powers and the supremacy of law. He concludes that the district court, which discussed neither principle, reached a conclusion consistent with the modern trend toward increased judicial review over the executive branch.

Breckenridge, Adam C. CONGRESS AGAINST THE COURT. Lincoln: University of Nebraska Press, 1970.

> Warren Court decisions in such cases as <u>Mallory</u>, <u>Miranda</u>, and <u>Wade</u> which tightened the standards for the admissibility of confessions, along with other decisions designed to protect the procedural guarantees of persons accused of crime, led to the criticism that the Court was handcuffing law enforcement agencies. This work is an analysis of these judicial opinions and of the attempts by the 90th Congress in 1967-68 to overrule them by legislation. The author argues that Title II of the Omnibus Crime Act of 1968 which provides standards for determining the "voluntariness" of confessions is in conflict with <u>Miranda</u>.

Cheever, Daniel S., and Haviland, H. Field, Jr. AMERICAN FOREIGN POLICY AND THE SEPARATION OF POWERS. Cambridge, Mass.: Harvard University Press, 1952.

> This work studies the relationship between the president and the Congress in the formulation of foreign policy, the interbranch conflict inherent in the separation of powers doctrine and an argument in favor of greater bipartisan cooperation between the two branches. The authors examine the constitutional and organizational framework within which foreign affairs are conducted, the preeminence of the president from 1789-1829, the reversal of roles with Congress dominating foreign policy until the end of the nineteenth century, the resurgence of presidential power in the twentieth century, and the increased complexity of modern relations with foreign governments which makes change desirable.

Choper, Jesse H. "The Supreme Court and the Political Branches: Democratic Theory and Practice." UNIVERSITY OF PENNSYLVANIA LAW REVIEW 122 (April 1974): 810-58.

> In this study of the presumed conflict between majoritarian democracy and judicial review, Choper notes that all three branches have certain antimajoritarian features and that the Court has political checks upon its exercise of power just as the other two branches have checks upon their power but agrees that the Court is nonetheless more antimajoritarian than the other two branches. However, he argues that because the function of the Court and the essential role of judicial review is to guard against constitutional transgressions by popular majorities, the Court must know how to reject majority will when it must without endangering either its critical role or its other duties.

"Congressional Standing to Challenge Executive Action." UNIVERSITY OF PENNSYLVANIA LAW REVIEW 122 (April 1974): 1366-82.

Noting that one of the new weapons that Congress had developed
in an effort to curb executive power is litigation, this comment
examines four cases brought by members of Congress against
the executive branch and analyzes congressional standing in
light of the latest Supreme Court standing requirements. New
legislation authorizing suit by any citizen to vindicate the public
interest is urged.

Cope, Alfred H., and Krinsky, Fred, eds. FRANKLIN D. ROOSEVELT
AND THE SUPREME COURT. Problems in American Government Series.
Rev. ed. Boston: D.C. Heath, 1969.

This volume contains the text of the proposal submitted by F.D.R.
in 1937 to enlarge the Supreme Court as well as excerpts from
senate debate and from editorial comments on the proposal and
brief excerpts from scholarly works dealing with the policy-
making role of the Court and the reorganization of the judiciary.

Cox, Archibald. "Executive Privilege." UNIVERSITY OF PENNSYLVANIA
LAW REVIEW 122 (June 1974): 1383-1438.

In this study of the right of the executive branch to withhold
information from the courts and from Congress, Cox examines
the origins and constitutional base of the doctrine, judicial and
legislative reactions to its invocation, and the legitimacy of its
use. Generally unsympathetic to its use, Cox argues that the
increased power of the executive necessitates expansion of judicial enforcement powers to guard against executive abuse of
power.

Duff, Patrick W., and Whitewise, Horace D. "Delegata Potestas Non Potest
Delegari: A Maxim of American Constitutional Law." CORNELL LAW QUAR-
TERLY 14 (Fall 1929): 168-94.

Although the prohibition against congressional delegation of its
legislative power is primarily a function of the separation of
powers doctrine, the common law maxim that "delegated power
can not be delegated" is sometimes invoked as additional support
for the rule. The authors' analysis of early case law involving
delegation leads them to conclude that this maxim "insofar as it
is asserted to be a principle of constitutional law, is built upon
the thinnest of implications, or is the product of the unwritten
superconstitution." This article is reprinted in volume 4 of
SELECTED ESSAYS ON CONSTITUTIONAL LAW (see p. 79).

Eagleton, Thomas F. WAR AND PRESIDENTIAL POWER: A CHRONICLE
OF CONGRESSIONAL SURRENDER. New York: Liveright, 1974.

This is a study of the expansion of the war-making powers of
the president in general, the role of the chief executive in
Vietnam in particular, and congressional attempts to limit the
president's power. Senator Eagleton argues that the Constitution confers upon Congress the power to make the decision
to go to war and thus views the War Powers Resolution as a
surrender of congressional power because it permits unilateral
presidential action for ninety days.

Eisenberg, Theodore. "Congressional Authority to Restrict Lower Federal Court Jurisdiction." YALE LAW JOURNAL 83 (January 1974): 498-533.

> Noting that much of the validity of arguments in support of congressional authority to control lower court jurisdiction rests upon the assumption that Congress has the discretionary authority to create, and therefore to abolish, lower court, Eisenberg argues that Congress is constitutionally required to create lower courts and cannot abolish them. Further, he argues that congressional control over lower court jurisdiction extends only to that kind of control designed to prevent case overload and to promote efficiency. Thus, Congress cannot deny lower court jurisdiction to hear cases in which constitutional rights are at stake nor withdraw jurisdiction to grant constitutionally required remedies, such as the judicially devised remedy of busing to remedy the constitutional wrong of educational segregation.

Ervin, Sam, Jr. "Separation of Powers: Judicial Independence." LAW AND CONTEMPORARY PROBLEMS 35 (Winter 1970): 108-28.

> Originally delivered as part of a discussion of the respective roles of the legislative and judicial branches in controlling judicial behavior, this essay discusses the origins of the separation of powers doctrine in Aristotle's POLITICS, its reappearance in Locke's TWO TREATISES, its expansion in Montesquieu's SPIRIT OF THE LAWS, and its influence at the constitutional convention. Arguing that "judicial independence is the strongest safeguard against the exercise of power by men who want to live above the law rather than under it," Senator Ervin suggests that the framers of the Constitution knew that the activities of a few judges might handicap the operation of the system, but at the same time they realized that individual liberty is best protected by an independent judiciary.

"Executive Privilege--The President Does Not Have An Absolute Right to Withhold Evidence from a Grand Jury--Nixon v. Sirica." HARVARD LAW REVIEW 87 (May 1974): 1557-68.

> This is a brief analysis of a 1973 opinion of the Court of Appeals for the District of Columbia in which the district court order requiring the president to turn over tapes and documents for in camera inspection was upheld, thus rejecting President Nixon's broad claim of both unqualified immunity from judicial processes and absolute executive privilege.

Field, Oliver P. "Ten Years of the Supreme Court, 1937-1947: Separation and Delegation of Powers." AMERICAN POLITICAL SCIENCE REVIEW 61 (December 1947): 1161-70.

> This is a brief review of Supreme Court cases, such as Schechter, Panama Refining, Colegrove v. Green and Coleman v. Miller, involving the separation of powers doctrine decided from 1936 to 1947.

Fisher, Louis. PRESIDENT AND CONGRESS: POWER AND POLICY. New York: Free Press, 1972.

This work focuses upon the conflicts between the executive and legislative branches in exercising and sharing power in the making of policy in four major areas—legislative power, the spending power, the taxing power, and the war power. The emphasis is upon power and policy rather than process.

Giunta, Joseph J. "Standing, Separation of Powers, and the Demise of the Public Citizen." AMERICAN UNIVERSITY LAW REVIEW 24 (Spring 1975): 835-76.

This is a discussion of the existing law of standing in light of two Burger Court decisions rejecting standing, Schlesinger v. Reservists Committee to Stop the War and United States v. Richardson. The author argues that the opinions in these cases make it apparent that in nonstatutory cases the major obstacle to standing is the Court's concern with the separation of powers doctrine. He concludes that the Court has, by virtue of its standing requirements, written a large segment of the Constitution out of the reach of judicial protection and has allowed Congress to ignore some provisions of the Constitution.

Goodnow, Frank J. SOCIAL REFORM AND THE CONSTITUTION. New York: Macmillan, 1911.

Goodnow's examination of judicial decisions hostile to reform during the progressive era leads him to suggest that the only effective means of changing judicial policy would be a constitutional amendment limiting the tenure of judges and the independence of the judiciary. Because amending the Constitution is so difficult, he looks at other means by which the political branches can control the judicial branch—means such as regulation of the size of the Court and its jurisdiction, the abolition of lower courts and, most importantly as a practical means of influence, criticism of judicial decisions by the political branches. He suggests that even if Congress cannot constitutionally require a majority vote to invalidate legislation, it should nonetheless enact such legislation as an expression of dissatisfaction and criticism.

Gwyn, William B. THE MEANING OF THE SEPARATION OF POWERS: AN ANALYSIS OF THE DOCTRINE FROM ITS ORIGINS TO THE ADOPTION OF THE CONSTITUTION. Tulane Studies in Political Science Series, vol. 9. New Orleans: Tulane University, 1965.

This slim volume is primarily concerned with the one hundred-year period between the origin of the separation of powers doctrine in England during the mid-seventeenth century and its re-statement by Montesquieu in the mid-eighteenth century. The author examines five arguments that were put forth to justify separating the powers of government: efficiency, common interest, rule of law, accountability, and balancing.

Harris, Richard. DECISION. New York: E.P. Dutton and Co., 1971.

Designed for the general reader, and thus without footnotes or
bibliography, this is an account of the Senate rejection of the
nomination by President Nixon of G. Harrold Carswell to fill
the vacancy created by the resignation of Justice Abe Fortas.

Hart, James. THE ORDINANCE MAKING POWERS OF THE PRESIDENT
OF THE UNITED STATES. Johns Hopkins University Studies in Historical
and Political Science, vol. 43. Baltimore, Md.: Johns Hopkins University
Press, 1925. Reprint. New York: Da Capo Press, 1970.

This is an analysis of the constitutional construction and practice
of the rule-making, or legislative powers exercised by the president largely, though not soley, as a result of congressional dele-
gations of authority to the executive branch.

Henkin, Louis. FOREIGN AFFAIRS AND THE CONSTITUTION. New
York: W.W. Norton, 1972.

With approximately one-half of its 500 pages devoted to footnotes,
this scholarly work deals with the question of the extent to which
the Constitution governs foreign affairs. It examines the constitutional distribution of power between Congress and the president in foreign affairs and the role of the separation of powers
doctrine as well as the relevance of the federalism doctrine to
foreign affairs. It also examines the role of the judiciary in
this area and the limits which individual rights place upon
governmental authority to conduct foreign policy. There is also
a paperback edition published by Foundation Press.

Lehman, John. THE EXECUTIVE, CONGRESS, AND FOREIGN POLICY:
STUDIES OF THE NIXON ADMINISTRATION. New York: Praeger Publishers, 1976.

This review by a Deputy Director of the U.S. Arms Control and
Disarmament Agency of the origins and development of the congressional-executive relationship in foreign policy and analysis
of executive-congressional conflict between 1969-72 concludes
that the historic and contemporary dominance of the executive
is a result of the basic structure of the two branches.

Lippmann, Walter. THE SUPREME COURT, INDEPENDENT OR CONTROLLED?
New York: Harper and Brothers, 1937.

This contains several of Lippmann's columns originally published
in the New York HERALD TRIBUNE in 1937 dealing with the
conflict between the political branches and the Supreme Court
over New Deal legislation and with Franklin D. Roosevelt's
"court-packing" plan.

Mansfield, Harvey C., Jr., ed. CONGRESS AGAINST THE PRESIDENT.
New York: Praeger, 1975.

This is a collection of essays examining congressional attempts
in the Nixon era to reassert control through such measures as
the War Powers Act, budgetary reform and committee reorganization, attempts that seem to support the Madisonian view that
republican governments tend to aggrandize legislative power at

the expense of executive and judicial powers.

Morgan, Donald G. CONGRESS AND THE CONSTITUTION: A STUDY OF RESPONSIBILITY. Cambridge, Mass.: Belknap Press, Harvard University Press, 1966.

This is a study of the role Congress plays in constitutional interpretation. One section deals with congressional practice in the nineteenth century and the conflict between the Jefferson and the Marshall views on the respective roles of the three branches in constitutional interpretation, and one section focuses upon modern practice and congressional abdication of its responsibility to make constitutional decisions. The appendix includes a copy of the questionnaire sent to members of the 86th Congress and an analysis of the returns.

Morley, Felix. TREATY LAW AND THE CONSTITUTION: A STUDY OF THE BRICKER AMENDMENT. New York: American Enterprise Association, 1953.

This is a brief study of the expanding presidential role in making treaties and executive agreements and the attempt to amend the Constitution to limit presidential treaty-making power and to enlarge the congressional role in making international commitments.

Nichols, Egbert R., ed. CONGRESS OR THE SUPREME COURT: WHICH SHALL RULE AMERICA? New York: Noble and Noble, 1935.

The conflict between the social and economic philosophies of the political branches and the judicial branch reached crisis proportions in the mid-1930s as the Supreme Court invalidated New Deal legislation. Various proposals to curb the Court's power were debated. This work is a compilation of the major argument on both sides of the proposition "Resolved that Congress should have the power, by a 2/3 majority vote, to overrule decisions of the Supreme Court declaring congressional laws unconstitutional."

Parker, Reginald. "Separation of Powers Revisited: Its Meaning to Administrative Law." MICHIGAN LAW REVIEW 49 (May 1951): 1009-39.

This article challenges the notion that the separation of powers doctrine is a basic constitutional principle. Parker sees it as an expedient of governmental procedure—as a matter of form rather than substance.

Polsby, Nelson W. CONGRESS AND THE PRESIDENCY. Englewood Cliffs, N.J.: Prentice-Hall, 1964.

This is a brief overview of the relationship between the executive and congressional branches.

Pritchett, C. Herman. CONGRESS VERSUS THE SUPREME COURT, 1957-1960. Minneapolis: University of Minnesota Press, 1961.

Reaction against Supreme Court decisions in the 1950s--princi-
pally the Public School Segregation case and the Watkins case
questioning the authority of the House Un-American Activities
Committee--led to congressional attempts to limit the authority
of the Supreme Court. Pritchett examines the efforts of some
congressmen in the 85th and 86th congresses to curb the Court
and the near success of some of these attempts.

Randolph, Robert C., and Smith, Daniel C. "Executive Privilege and the
Congressional Right of Inquiry." HARVARD JOURNAL OF LEGISLATION
10 (June 1973): 621-72.

Viewing executive privilege as a grave threat to equilibrium
among the branches, this note discusses the problem stemming
from executive control of congressional sources of information,
analyzes the doctrine of executive privilege with emphasis upon
the effects of that doctrine in the area of foreign affairs, and
examines the political sanctions available to Congress in combatting executive refusal to supply information.

Reinstein, Robert, and Silvergate, Harvey. "Legislative Privilege and
the Separation of Powers." HARVARD LAW REVIEW 86 (May 1973): 1113-
83.

Written by the attorneys for Senator Gravel in defending his
decision to release classified documents, this article traces the
development of the speech and debate clause of Article I, section
6 as a means of preserving the separation of powers doctrine
by protecting the independence of the legislative branch. They
argue for a broad interpretation of the clause when congressmen
are the target of executive action. They believe that such a
construction is necessary both to protect the independence of the
legislative branch and to preserve the political neutrality of the
judicial branch. In contrast, they suggest that the clause should
be more narrowly construed in civil suits instituted by individuals
seeking to protect private, particularly constitutional, rights.
Because the Supreme Court, in the authors' view, has not given
to the clause the broad interpretation they urge, they examine
other means by which congressional independence within the
separation of powers system can be preserved.

Rogers, James G. WORLD POLITICS AND THE CONSTITUTION: AN
ENQUIRY INTO THE POWERS OF THE PRESIDENT AND CONGRESS,
NINE WARS AND A HUNDRED MILITARY OPERATIONS, 1789-1945. Bos-
ton: World Peace Foundation, 1945.

Written during the Dumbarton Oaks discussion leading to the
establishment of the United Nations, this brief work examines
the question of the constitutional placement of the authority to
meet an American obligation to carry out a Security Council
decision to use force. The author examines such questions as
whether each use of American troops under the United Nations
banner would require congressional action or whether such power
could constitutionally be exercised by the president alone.

Scigliano, Robert. THE SUPREME COURT AND THE PRESIDENCY. New
York: Free Press, 1971.

This is a study of the "special relationship" which the Supreme Court and the president have to each other which neither has to Congress. The author argues that "these two institutions were intended by the framers of the Constitution to act, for certain purposes, as an informal and limited alliance against Congress, and that they have in fact done so. The purposes of the alliance were to counterbalance the power of Congress, particularly the House of Representatives, and, to a lesser extent, to counterbalance the political principles of class interest which Congress was seen to embody." Rather than a study of judicial opinions dealing with the president, this is a study of the relationship between the two branches including such informal relationships as presidential consultation with justices on judicial appointments and presidential use of Supreme Court Justices for such nonjudicial functions as that performed by Justice Roberts at the Nuremberg trials and of Chief Justice Warren in the Kennedy assassination investigation.

Sharp, Malcolm P. "The Classical American Doctrine of Separation of Powers." UNIVERSITY OF CHICAGO LAW REVIEW 2 (April 1935): 385-436.

This is an analysis of the development of the idea of separating government powers as a guard against abuse from Aristotle to Locke and the working out of the implications of that idea in the American constitutional system by such men as John Adams, James Wilson, the varying gradations of flexibility and rigidity in the doctrine as envisaged by its early American advocates, and its adoption and application in early state constitutions and then in the national Constitution. This article is reprinted in volume 4 of SELECTED ESSAYS ON CONSTITUTIONAL LAW, see p. 79.

Shipley, Carl L. "Legislative Control of Judicial Behavior." LAW AND CONTEMPORARY PROBLEMS 35 (1970): 178-201.

Noting that the framers of the Constitution rejected all attempts to allow the legislative and executive branches to control judges and rejected all proposals to subordinate judges to the administrative control of other judges, this article argues that impeachment is the sole means of removal of judges and that Congress has no constitutional authority to provide for oversight of the judiciary. The article summarizes existing statutes supplementing impeachment as a means of protecting against unfit judges, such as appeal from court rulings, affidavits of personal prejudice, judges being subject to criminal statutes and the requirement that judges disqualify themselves if personally involved in a conflict, and suggests that these are sufficient to protect litigants against unfit judges.

Sofaer, Abraham D. WAR, FOREIGN AFFAIRS AND CONSTITUTIONAL POWER. Cambridge, Mass.: Ballinger Publishing Co., 1976-- .

This projected three-volume work is an analysis of the development of the respective powers of the president and of the Congress to begin and conduct war. The first volume deals with the English, colonial and state experiences prior to the adoption

of the Constitution, the origins of the war power at the constitutional convention and the ratifying conventions, and its interpretation and development in the administrations of Washington, John
Adams and Jefferson and an overview of the post-Jeffersonian
developments.

"Symposium: Separation of Powers." INDIANA LAW REVIEW 52 (Winter
1977): 311-447.

This symposium consists of six papers dealing with various facets
of the separation of powers doctrine: Wallace Mendelson on
judicial activism, Sen. James Abourezk on the congressional
veto, William H. Taft IV on social welfare law, Arthur Miller
and George M. Knapp on the congressional veto, Arthur W.
Rovine on international executive agreements and Sen. James
Sparkman on American foreign policy.

Tapia, Raul R.; James, John P.; and Levine, Robert. "Congress versus
the Executive: The Role of the Courts." HARVARD JOURNAL OF LEGIS-
LATION 11 (February 1974): 352-413.

Noting the increased use of the courts by Congress to challenge
executive actions and inactions and to protect the collective and
personal prerogatives of the legislative branch and its members,
this article looks at the reasons for such congressional use of
the judiciary and at judicial reactions to hearing such suits and
deciding a case on its merits--such problems as jurisdiction,
standing, and the political question doctrine.

U.S. Congress. Senate. EXECUTIVE PRIVILEGE: THE WITHHOLDING
OF INFORMATION BY THE EXECUTIVE, HEARINGS BEFORE THE SUB-
COMMITTEE ON SEPARATIONS OF POWERS OF THE COMMITTEE ON THE
JUDICIARY. 92d Cong., 1st sess., 1971. Washington, D.C.: Government
Printing Office, 1971.

In the late 1960s, the Congress began to assert a larger role
in foreign policy vis-a-vis the president, an attempt impeded in
congressional eyes by the refusal of the executive to share information with the legislative branch. These hearings into the
constitutionality of the executive privilege doctrine were probably
occasioned by President Nixon's reliance on that doctrine to refuse to turn over to Sen. Fulbright's Foreign Relations Committee
information concerning the military assistance program. Generally,
however, the hearings were a response to the intensified constitutional struggle between the president and the Congress over the
war powers in general and the American military role in Vietnam
in particular.

U.S. Congress. Senate. Library. PRESIDENTIAL VETOES: LIST OF
BILLS VETOED AND ACTIONS TAKEN THEREON BY THE SENATE AND
HOUSE OF REPRESENTATIVES, FIRST CONGRESS THROUGH THE
EIGHTY-SIXTH CONGRESSES, 1789-1968. Washington, D.C.: Government
Printing Office, 1969.

This compilation is arranged chronologically by congress and by
bill number.

Vanderbilt, Arthur T. THE DOCTRINE OF THE SEPARATION OF POWERS AND ITS PRESENT DAY SIGNIFICANCE. Lincoln: University of Nebraska Press, 1963.

> This work discusses the operation of the separation of powers doctrine not simply in the United States but in other countries which adopted the principle. The author sees the doctrine as an important means of curbing governmental power and protecting individual liberties.

Velvel, Lawrence. UNDECLARED WAR AND CIVIL DISOBEDIENCE: THE AMERICAN SYSTEM IN CRISIS. New York: Dunellen Publishing Co., 1970.

> Sponsored by the Lawyers Committee on American Policy towards Vietnam and written prior to the Cambodian incursion, this is an argument against the constitutionality of presidential wars and in support of the proposition that the framers of the Constitution intended the war-making power be shared by the president and the Congress rather than concentrated in presidential hands. Viewing the Vietnam War as just one phase in the process of concentration of power in the presidency, this work is also an indictment of Congress and the courts for abdicating their re- sponsibilities and allowing presidential preeminence. It includes suggestions for dealing with the "crisis of legitimacy" caused by the war and for rehabilitating constitutional democracy through such devices as civil disobedience and jury nullification.

Vile, M.J.C. CONSTITUTIONALISM AND THE SEPARATION OF POWERS. London: Oxford University Press, 1967.

> This is a study of the history of the theory of the separation of powers doctrine as a means of limiting governmental powers from its birth as a coherent theory of government in seventeenth-century England to its place in the political thought of England, France and the United States in the twentieth century. In addition to examining the connection between the doctrine and the theory of parliamentary government in England and France, the author looks at the use of the doctrine in American state constitutions beginning with Virginia in 1776 and its embodiment in the national Constitution in 1787.

Wilcox, Francis O. CONGRESS, THE EXECUTIVE AND FOREIGN POLICY. New York: Harper and Row for the Council on Foreign Relations, 1971.

> This is an analysis of the struggle between the president and the Congress over control of foreign policy, a conflict which reached its height in the Vietnam era. The author examines the struggle within the context of the three major constitutional powers of the Congress (its legislative power, its money power and the senate's authority over treaties and nominations) by which it may exercise control in foreign affairs. He also deals with two of the major questions concerning presidential power which were central to the conflict between the two branches: what kind of action can a president take in the absence of con- gressional delegation, and what kinds of international agree- ments can he make without senatorial approval?

Wilcox, Francis O., and Frank, Richard A., eds. THE CONSTITUTION AND THE CONDUCT OF FOREIGN POLICY. New York: Praeger Publishers, 1976.

> This collection of readings focuses on four substantive areas of presidential-congressional relationships in the area of foreign policy: the management of information about foreign policy, the role of the public in foreign policy making, the war power and the president's power to enter into agreements with foreign governments.

Wright, Quincy. THE CONTROL OF AMERICAN FOREIGN RELATIONS. New York: Macmillan, 1922.

> Written in the post-World War I period when the United States first came of age in international affairs, this work examines the legal and constitutional problems confronting American foreign policy makers which stem from what the author views as the twin sources of responsibility and authority; that is, the responsibilities of foreign policy makers are defined by international law whereas their powers are defined in the United States by constitutional law. In dealing with the constitutional limitations imposed upon American foreign policy agents, Wright examines the limitations imposed upon national policy makers by states' rights and private rights and the limitations imposed by the separation of powers doctrine.

JUDICIAL REVIEW

Alfange, Dean. THE SUPREME COURT AND THE NATIONAL WILL. 1937. Reprint. Port Washington, N.Y.: Kennikat Press, 1964.

> Written before Roosevelt's "court-packing" plan and the Supreme Court's acceptance of the New Deal, this examination of the relationship between the executive and legislative branches and the judicial branch was prompted by the author's conflicting loyalties: a belief in judicial review on the one hand and the belief that the manner in which the New Deal was invalidated was undemocratic on the other.

Association of American Law Schools. SELECTED ESSAYS ON CONSTITUTIONAL LAW. 4 vols. Chicago: Foundation Press, 1938.

> Volume 1, entitled THE NATURE OF THE JUDICIAL PROCESS IN CONSTITUTIONAL CASES, contains thirty-nine essays dealing with various facets of judicial review from an analysis of its origins to an appraisal of its exercise. Four essays by Edward S. Corwin on judicial review and judicial supremacy are included: " 'Higher Law' Background of Constitutional Law," "The Basic Doctrine of American Constitutional Law," "Marbury v. Madison and Judicial Review," and "Due Process Before the Civil War." It also includes such basic works as James Bradley Thayer's "The Origin and Scope of the American Doctrine of Constitutional Law," Oliver Field's "Judicial Review as an Instrument of Government," Howard J. Graham's "The Conspiracy Theory of the Fourteenth Amendment," and Thomas Reed Powell's "The Logic and Rhetoric of Constitutional Law."

Beard, Charles A. THE SUPREME COURT AND THE CONSTITUTION.
1912. Reprint. Introduction by Alan F. Westin. Englewood Cliffs, N.J.:
Prentice-Hall, 1952.

> This influential work argues that the framers intended the courts
> to exercise the power of judicial review. In this reissue,
> Westin's lengthy introduction sets forth the basic arguments in
> support of and in opposition to judicial review, examines the
> sources of the conflict, and presents criticisms of Beard's
> views. It also contains a bibliography which focuses on those
> works which deal with the legal and public debate over the
> Court's power in certain major periods: 1870–1880, 1880–
> 1920, and 1920–61.

Berger, Raoul. CONGRESS VERSUS THE SUPREME COURT. Cambridge,
Mass.: Harvard University Press, 1969.

> This is an examination of the questions of whether judicial review
> was conferred or usurped and, if conferred, what the framers of
> the Constitution envisaged as its scope--can Congress, under its
> Article III powers to regulate the appellate jurisdiction of the
> Supreme Court, deprive the Court of authority to exercise appel-
> late jurisdiction and thus limit the Court's power of judicial re-
> view? Berger concludes that judicial review was designed to
> check congressional excesses and to protect individual rights.

Black, Charles L., Jr. THE PEOPLE AND THE COURT: JUDICIAL REVIEW
IN A DEMOCRACY. New York: Macmillan, 1960.

> This is a defense of the role of judicial review in a democracy.

Cappelletti, Mauro. "Judicial Review in Comparative Perspective." CALI-
FORNIA LAW REVIEW 58 (October 1970): 1017-53.

> Viewing judicial review as one phase of the concept that legis-
> lation should be subordinate to some more permanent principles,
> the author examines the origins and development of this notion
> of higher law and the manner in which European and American
> democracies embodied this notion in their constitutional systems.

_____. JUDICIAL REVIEW IN THE CONTEMPORARY WORLD. Indianapolis:
Bobbs-Merrill, 1971.

> This slim volume is a comparative study of judicial review in
> France, Italy, Russia, Austria, England, and the United States
> with emphasis upon the latter.

Carr, Robert K. THE SUPREME COURT AND JUDICIAL REVIEW. New
York: Farrar and Rinehart, 1942.

> Looking at the Supreme Court "as a political agency, sharing
> power with the President and Congress" rather than as a judi-
> cial body applying legal rules to constitutional questions, Carr
> examines the origins of judicial supremacy in federal and state
> constitutional conventions and in Marbury v. Madison, the exer-
> cise of power by the Supreme Court in commerce and due process
> cases and the limitations imposed upon the exercise of the power
> of judicial review.

Corwin, Edward S. COURT OVER CONSTITUTION: A STUDY OF JUDI-
CIAL REVIEW AS AN INSTRUMENT OF POPULAR GOVERNMENT. Princeton, N.J.: Princeton University Press, 1938.

> Noting that the question of whether the framers intended the courts
> to have the power of judicial review has long been debated with
> no conclusive answer, Corwin turns to examine the question of
> what kind of judicial review was intended; that is, the scope of
> the power and the effect or finality of its exercise. Written
> after the "constitutional revolution of 1937," this work emphasizes
> judicial review as an instrument of popular government. Corwin
> sees judicial review as playing a role somewhat similar to that
> of the common law: a device for conserving the old in the con-
> text of the new. Further, it provides another step for discussion
> of public policies. He uses the Pollock case as an example of
> judicial misuse of its power by ceasing to be a part of the demo-
> cratic process and serving as a superlegislature.

_____. THE DOCTRINE OF JUDICIAL REVIEW: ITS LEGAL AND HIS-
TORICAL BASIS AND OTHER ESSAYS. Gloucester, Mass.: Peter Smith,
1963.

> Originally published in 1914, this is a collection of five essays,
> four on judicial review and one on the treaty-making power. In
> the leading essay, Corwin deals with Marbury v. Madison and
> the origins of judicial review. In his analysis of this case and
> the legal basis of the power of the judiciary to invalidate legis-
> lative actions, he argues that the courts, rather than the legis-
> lative branch, were given final authority over questions of con-
> stitutionality because early state legislatures so abused their
> power that the framers of the Constitution designed a system to
> curb such abuse by the national legislatures. In the other
> essays, Corwin deals with the Dred Scott case and the origins
> of judicial supremacy and the controversy over secession and
> nullification.

Coxe, Brinton. AN ESSAY ON JUDICIAL POWER AND UNCONSTITUTIONAL
LEGISLATION: BEING A COMMENTARY ON PARTS OF THE CONSTITUTION
OF THE UNITED STATES. New York: Da Capo Press, 1970.

> Originally published in 1893 this work is an argument in support
> of the doctrine of judicial review on the grounds that the Con-
> stitution expressly provides for such a power, that the framers
> of the Constitution intended to confer the power and that the
> exercise of such power in the United States predated the Con-
> stitution.

Davis, Horace. THE JUDICIAL VETO. New York: Da Capo Press, 1971.

> Originally published in 1914 this work consists of three essays
> critical of judicial invalidation of legislation in private litigation.
> Davis argues that because the constitutionality of a state statute
> is a political, not a legal, function, a law should be subject to
> judicial invalidation only in a suit against government.

Dean, Howard E. JUDICIAL REVIEW AND DEMOCRACY. New York: Random House, 1967.

This is an analysis of the establisment of the doctrine of judicial review in Marbury v. Madison, of some of the problems produced by judicial exercise of the power, of the Court's policy-
making role in such areas as property rights and civil liberties,
of the limitations of the self-restraint doctrine and of the compatibility of judicial review and American democratic theory.

Dewey, Donald. MARSHALL VERSUS JEFFERSON: THE POLITICAL BACK-
GROUND OF MARBURY VERSUS MADISON. New York: Knopf, 1970.

This is an analysis of judicial review in terms of the conflicts
between the Republicans and the Federalists that led the Jefferson administration to block delivery of the commissions of the
judicial appointees of the Adams administration and an examination of Marshall's opinion in Marbury. Dewey traces subsequent
attacks by a Republican Congress and by Jefferson upon the
federal judiciary as a result not only of Marbury but of Marshall's
opinions in such cases as McCulloch v. Maryland and Cohens v.
Virginia and the continuing and long-term conflicts between
Marshall and Jefferson growing out of such events as the circumstances surrounding the Burr treason trial and Marshall's publication of a five-volume LIFE OF WASHINGTON, which offended
Jefferson. Dewey suggests that even after Jefferson's death and
shortly before Marshall's death, the Chief Justice blamed Jefferson and his states' rights theories for the nullification crisis
in South Carolina in the 1830s over the tariff issue.

Ellis, Richard E. THE JEFFERSONIAN CRISIS: COURTS AND POLITICS
IN THE YOUNG REPUBLIC. New York: Oxford University Press, 1971.

This is an examination of the manner in which late eighteenth-
and early nineteenth-century Americans avoided, fought over and
resolved the question of the proper role of the judiciary in a
republic and its relationship to the other branches of government.
Ellis argues that disputes over the judicial issue and the implications of that issue was the overriding domestic issue of Jefferson's
first administration and was the issue around which the meaning
of the revolution of 1800 was to be defined.

Field, Oliver P. THE EFFECT OF AN UNCONSTITUTIONAL STATUTE.
Minneapolis: University of Minnesota Press, 1935. Reprint. New York:
Da Capo Press, 1971.

This study examines the three major effects of a judicial declaration that a statute is unconstitutional: the void ab initio theory
(the statute is null and void), the presumption of validity theory
(the law is to be given some effect, thus an election may be
valid even though the law under which it was conducted is unconstitutional), and the case-to-case theory (the statute is constitutional under some circumstances, unconstitutional under
others). The author looks at such questions as the status of
private corporations and municipal corporations organized under
unconstitutional statutes, the effect of an unconstitutional statute
on the status of public officials, the liability of public officials
for actions or nonaction and the recovery of unconstitutional taxes
and discusses the defects in the operation of judicial review.

Haines, Charles G. AMERICAN DOCTRINE OF JUDICIAL SUPREMACY.
New York: Macmillan Co., 1914. Rev. ed. Berkeley: University of
California Press, 1932. Reprint. New York: Da Capo Press, 1973.

> This is an analysis of the origins and scope of judicial review
> by state and national courts in the United States. Haines focuses
> primarily on the Supreme Court's review of national and state
> legislation and proposals made from time to time to restrict the
> Court's power. He examines such proposals as those requiring
> an extraordinary majority to invalidate legislation, permitting re-
> call of judges and of judicial decisions and providing for the
> abolition of judicial review.

Levy, Leonard W., ed. JUDICIAL REVIEW AND THE SUPREME COURT:
SELECTED ESSAYS. New York: Harper and Row, 1967.

> This is a selection of nine essays dealing with the question of
> judicial review with an introductory analysis by Levy of the
> major arguments over the legitimacy of the judiciary to invalidate
> legislation. The essays include such works as James Bradley
> Thayer's "The Origin and Scope of the American Doctrine of
> Judicial Review," and Eugene Rostow's "The Democratic Charac-
> ter of Judicial Review."

McCloskey, Robert G., ed. ESSAYS IN CONSTITUTIONAL LAW. New
York: Vintage Books, 1957.

> Part 1 of this collection contains five essays on judicial review:
> Charles A. Beard's "The Supreme Court--Usurper of Grantee,"
> James Bradley Thayer's "The Origin and Scope of the American
> Doctrine of Constitutional Law," Thomas Reed Powell's "The
> Logic and Rhetoric of Constitutional Law," and Max Lerner's
> "The Supreme Court and American Capitalism." The other nine
> essays and judicial opinions deal with other facets of constitu-
> tional interpretation.

Mace, George. "Anti-Democratic Character of Judicial Review." CALI-
FORNIA LAW REVIEW 60 (June 1972): 1140-49.

> In this brief article, Mace challenges the validity of the Hamil-
> tonian argument in "Federalist No. 78," that the Court "can
> exercise neither Force nor Will, but merely judgment," and of
> Eugene V. Rostow's efforts to demonstrate the essentially demo-
> cratic nature of judicial review. Mace argues that judicial re-
> view is essentially antidemocratic, that it draws courts into
> wholly political matters and prevents judicial detachment from
> the legislative process and that so long as the judicial part of
> the American system is undemocratic, the entire system will be
> undemocratic.

Meigs, William M. THE RELATION OF THE JUDICIARY TO THE CONSTITU-
TION. New York: Da Capo Press, 1971.

> Originally published in 1919, this is an examination of the con-
> stitutional role of the judiciary from the colonial era to the
> Philadelphia convention, an account of those instances in the
> pre- and postrevolutionary periods in which legislative enactments

were set aside by higher English and American authorities on constitutional grounds, and an analysis of the question of whether judicial review constitutes "judicial power" or "judicial suprem- acy."

Mendelson, Wallace. "Judicial Review and Party Politics." VANDERBILT LAW REVIEW 12 (March 1959): 447–57.

In this exploration of and support for the theory that "court intrusion upon national policy has thrived only in periods of unusual party weakness," Mendelson contrasts judicial retreat from national policy making when faced with a strong party sys- tem under Jefferson, Jackson, Lincoln, and Franklin Roosevelt with judicial triumph in making policy in the period from the late nineteenth century to 1937 when the party system was weak.

Nelson, William. "Changing Conceptions of Judicial Review: The Evolution of Constitutional Theory in the States: 1790–1860." UNIVERSITY OF PENNSYLVANIA LAW REVIEW 120 (June 1972): 1166–85.

This article argues that judicial review, originally perceived as a mechanism to protect the people against bad legislation, became a means by which judges were authorized to make law in the course of settling disputes between interest groups. Noting that neither Julius Goebel in his volume of the OLIVER WENDELL HOLMES DEVISE HISTORY OF THE SUPREME COURT OF THE UNITED STATES (see p. 182), which covered the period up to 1801, nor Charles Fairman in his volume (see p. 179), which covered the period from 1864 to 1888, discusses the Dred Scott case and that neither asks why or when judicial review became "an unchallenged dogma of constitutional law" although both indicate that it achieved this status somewhere between the 1790s and the 1860s, Nelson examines this question. He concludes that in the 1840s and the 1850s, judicial review became established in state courts on a new basis. It became a means by which interest groups, lacking control of the legislature, obtained a reconsideration and reevaluation of legislative policy by the judiciary. Thus, contrary to its initial conception, judicial review became a mechanism for protecting the people against themselves.

Rostow, Eugene V. "The Democratic Character of Judicial Review." HAR- VARD LAW REVIEW 66 (December 1952): 193–224.

Written in a period of relative judicial self-restraint of which he disapproves, Rostow rejects the argument of James Bradley Thayer and others who saw antidemocratic and debilitating influences stemming from judicial review and from the consequent legislative and popular dependence upon court to protect against unconstitu- tional governmental actions. Pointing to the democratic advances made by the Court in protecting against racial discrimination in education and voting cases in the 1940s and early 1950s and the undemocratic results of its refusal to exercise its full power in such cases as Dennis, Rostow argues that judicial review does not inhibit but rather releases democratic energies.

Thayer, James B[radley]. "The Origin and Scope of the American Doctrine of Constitutional Law." HARVARD LAW REVIEW 7 (October 1893): 129-56.

> In this classic analysis of the doctrine of judicial review, Thayer sees it in part as a consequence, though not a necessary one, of the colonial experience of being governed by written charters given by the Crown which had the force and effect of law. Noting the absence of such a doctrine in early state practices and the gradualism of its use and spread, he emphasizes the limited scope of the authority conferred on the judiciary and the danger of confusing what is constitutional and legal with what is just, right or moral which may stem from legislative and popular reliance upon the judiciary to protect against legislative abuse of power. This article is reprinted in volume 1 of SELECTED ESSAYS ON CONSTITUTIONAL LAW (see p. 79) and in Leonard W. Levy's JUDICIAL REVIEW AND THE SUPREME COURT: SELECTED ESSAYS (see p. 83) and indeed in virtually every major collection of essays focusing on judicial review.

Van Alstyne, William W. "A Criticial Guide to Marbury v. Madison." DUKE LAW JOURNAL, January 1969, pp. 1-47.

> This "guide" looks at the analyses of various constitutional scholars who view judicial review as it emerges from Marbury as an instrument of judicial self-defense designed to protect the status of the judiciary as a coordinate branch rather than to accord supremacy and includes materials on judicial review from other sources such as "Federalist Nos. 78 and 81," anti-Federalist writings, Marshall's speeches at the Virginia constitutional convention, and debates at various state ratifying conventions.

Von Moschzisker, Robert. JUDICIAL REVIEW OF LEGISLATION. A CONSIDERATION OF THE WARRANTS FOR AND MERITS OF OUR SYSTEM OF JUDICIALLY REVIEWING LEGISLATION TO ASCERTAIN ITS CONSTITUTIONAL VALIDITY. New York: Da Capo Press, 1971.

> Originally published in 1923, this work consists of two lectures delivered at the University of Pennsylvania Law School examining ancient, colonial and state precedents for judicial review, its support by framers of the Constitution, its enunciation in Marbury v. Madison, and its legitimacy. The appendix includes lists of Supreme Court decisions invalidating federal, state, and local legislation.

Warren, Charles. CONGRESS, THE CONSTITUTION, AND THE SUPREME COURT. Rev. ed. Boston: Little, Brown, 1935.

> First published in 1925, this work focuses upon those cases in which the Supreme Court invalidated congressional legislation.

Wright, Benjamin F. THE GROWTH OF AMERICAN CONSTITUTIONAL LAW. 1942. Reprint. Introduction by Robert G. McCloskey. The Court and the Constitution Series, edited by Phillip B. Kurland. Chicago: University of Chicago Press, 1967.

This work focuses on the doctrine of judicial review and examines those Supreme Court decisions which deal with the question of the constitutionality of state or national legislation. After a brief introductory chapter dealing with the relationship between democracy and judicial power, it examines the origin of judicial review and traces the use of that power through the late 1930s and early 1940s when the Court retreated from its attack upon the New Deal.

Chapter 6

ARTICLE I: CONGRESS
Powers, Structure, Obligations and Procedures.
Limitations on State Powers

American Assembly. Columbia University. THE CONGRESS AND AMERICA'S
FUTURE. Edited by and with an introduction by David B. Truman. 2d ed.
Englewood Cliffs, N.J.: Prentice-Hall, 1973.

> This collection of eight essays examines various constitutional,
> political, structural and procedural factors which influence the
> role of Congress. Such substantive issues as economic and
> national security policies and the prospects for change in the
> functioning of Congress are also discussed.

Bailey, Stephen K. CONGRESS IN THE SEVENTIES. New York: St.
Martin's Press, 1970.

> This brief overview of the place of Congress in the American
> political and constitutional system, a revision and updating of
> THE NEW CONGRESS, examines what the author views as
> dramatic changes in the influences upon and the policy orientation
> of Congress in the 1960s. It is primarily concerned with the
> extraconstitutional forces which influence the structure and
> functioning of Congress.

_____. THE NEW CONGRESS. New York: St. Martin's Press, 1966.

> This is an examination of various events from the mid-1950s to
> the mid-1960s--such as the Supreme Court's race relations and
> reapportionment decisions, the enlargement of the Rules Committee
> in 1961, and the invocation of cloture to defeat filibusters against
> civil rights legislation in the 1960s--which in the author's view
> revolutionized the internal structure, power relationships and
> role of Congress.

Barnett, William M., Jr. "Ten Years of the Supreme Court, 1937-1947:
The Power to Regulate Commerce." AMERICAN POLITICAL SCIENCE RE-
VIEW 61 (December 1947): 1170-81.

> A brief review of Supreme Court interpretation of the commerce
> clause both as a source of national power and as an implied
> limitation upon state power, with principal focus upon judicial
> expansion of national power in such cases as National Labor
> Relations Board v. Jones and Laughlin and U.S. v. Darby.

Barth, Alan. GOVERNMENT BY INVESTIGATION. New York: Viking Press, 1955.

> Written in reaction to what the author considers to be the abuses of the House Un-American Activities Committee and the Senate Internal Security Committee in the 1950s, this work is an analysis of the dangers to individual rights stemming from congressional investigations.

Beck, Carl. CONTEMPT OF CONGRESS: A STUDY OF THE PROSECUTIONS INITIATED BY THE COMMITTEE ON UN-AMERICAN ACTIVITIES, 1945-1957. New Orleans: Hauser Press, 1959. Reprint. New York: Da Capo Press, 1974.

> Although Congress had long assumed the power to employ the compulsory processes of the law to compel witnesses to appear and to testify before its investigative committees, it was not until the 1940s and 1950s that employment of these techniques led to major political and constitutional controversies. This work focuses upon the use of the contempt power by the most controversial of the congressional investigative committees. Although it focuses on The House Un-American Activities Committee, this historical-legal study of the power of Congress to force witnesses to appear and to testify under penalty of contempt looks at the development of the contempt power in the English Parliament, in colonial assemblies, in early congressional statutes and practices, and at judicial opinions prior to the 1940s and the Watkins and Barenblatt decisions in the 1950s. Included in the appendix are synopses of contempt citations from 1787 to 1943 and from 1944 to 1958 and statistical analysis of contempt citations in the two periods.

Beck, James M. "Nullification by Indirection." HARVARD LAW REVIEW 23 (April 1910): 441-55.

> Although Beck had earlier as solicitor general defended the authority of Congress to prohibit the shipment of lottery tickets in interstate commerce and would later defend the child labor tax before the Supreme Court in Bailey v. Drexel Furniture, as a private citizen he argues in this article against the constitutionality of congressional use of its commerce power as a means of accomplishing the illegitimate end of regulating that which is within the police powers of the state. He here opposes on constitutional grounds Sen. Beveridge's Child Labor Bill which prohibited the shipment in interstate commerce of goods produced at factories employing children. He argues that because the purpose was to regulate child labor, a power within the reserved powers of the states, and not to regulate commerce, it exceeded the commerce power of the Congress, an argument used by the Court in 1918 in Hammer v. Dagenhart. This article is reprinted in volume 3 of SELECTED ESSAYS ON CONSTITUTIONAL LAW.

Bentley, Eric R., ed. THIRTY YEARS OF TREASON: EXCERPTS FROM HEARINGS BEFORE THE HOUSE COMMITTEE ON UNAMERICAN ACTIVITIES, 1938-1968. New York: Viking Press, 1971.

Arranged chronologically and with commentaries and explanatory
notes by the editor, this extensive collection of materials culled
from the hearings of the House Un-American Activites Committee
focuses primarily on the testimony and questioning of playwrights,
screenwriters, actors, producers and others from the motion
picture and entertainment industries. Also included are materials
from contemporary newspaper and magazine accounts of and commentaries on the committee and its work. Included in the appendix are a list of committee members from 1938-70, the committee's
translation of a work by Bertolt Brecht and Hanso Eisler entitled
Die Massnahme [The rule or the doctrine] and a statement of
Paul Robeson which had not been available for insertion in the
proper place in the main body of the work.

Benton, Thomas H., ed. ABRIDGMENT OF DEBATES OF CONGRESS,
1789-1856. 16 vols. 1857. Reprint. New York: Viking Press, 1970.

This is an abridgment of congressional debates from 1789 to
1856 from the ANNALS OF CONGRESS published by Gales and
Seaton (see U.S. Congress, THE DEBATES AND PROCEEDINGS,
p. 111).

Berger, Raoul. IMPEACHMENT: THE CONSTITUTIONAL PROBLEM.
Cambridge, Mass.: Harvard University Press, 1973.

Although the impeachment power in the United States has been
used primarily to remove judges, Berger's analysis of the
origins and use of this power in England and the United States
leads him to conclude that parliamentary impeachment of the
king's ministers was a prime means of transferring power from
an absolute monarch to a supreme parliament and that the framers
of the Constitution intended that it be used by Congress principally to check presidential abuse of power. Thus, a president
may be impeached for nonindictable offenses. He argues for a
broad, though not unlimited, interpretation of this congressional
check on the other two branches.

Berman, Daniel M. IN CONGRESS ASSEMBLED: THE LEGISLATIVE
PROCESS IN THE NATIONAL GOVERNMENT. New York: Macmillan, 1964.

This analysis of the legislative process and the role of Congress,
which the author sees as different from that envisaged by the
framers as is the role and process of the other two branches,
examines congressional elections, the relationship between congressmen and their constituents, the relationship with the president, the role of committees and committee chairmen and staffs,
the role of the party system, as well as the appropriations process, the senatorial role in appointments and treaties and the
relationship between Congress and the Courts.

Black, Charles L., Jr. IMPEACHMENT: A HANDBOOK. New Haven,
Conn.: Yale University Press, 1974.

This slim volume, designed for the general reader, sets forth
the procedures for impeachment, the role of the House and of
the Senate and the kinds of offenses that are impeachable. It
also deals with the question of the role of the courts in the process.

Blough, Roy. THE FEDERAL TAXING PROCESS. New York: Prentice-Hall, 1952.

> This is a study of the process of making tax policy with emphasis upon the role of Congress, the executive, and, to a lesser extent, the judiciary. Because constitutional challenges to congressional taxing power have been relatively infrequent since the 1930s and thus of little importance in recent tax policy, little attention is paid to judicial interpretation of the constitutional power of Congress to tax and spend.

Brant, Irving. IMPEACHMENT: TRIALS AND ERRORS. New York: Knopf, 1972.

> An analysis of the origins and history of the impeachment powers of Congress leading to the conclusion that this power should be narrowly construed.

Brock, W.R. AN AMERICAN CRISIS: CONGRESS AND RECONSTRUCTION, 1865–1867. New York: St. Martin's Press, 1963.

> This work by an English author who writes "from the Northern point of view" focuses upon Congress in the crisis-ridden period following the Civil War in which Congress both dictated Reconstruction policy and dominated the executive and judicial branches. Pointing to the extraordinary majority by which Reconstruction legislation was adopted, the author argues that Reconstruction was not imposed by a minority but was a result of the democratic process and majority rule.

Buckley, William F. THE COMMITTEE AND ITS CRITICS: A CALM RE-VIEW OF THE HOUSE ON UN-AMERICAN ACTIVITIES. New York: G.P. Putnam's Sons, 1962.

> A collection of essays supporting the authority of government to investigate and expose the activities of subversive organizations.

Burnham, James. CONGRESS AND THE AMERICAN TRADITION. Chicago: Henry Regnery Co., 1959.

> This is a comprehensive examination of the historic and contemporary status and functioning of Congress within the broad framework of the philosophies of government advanced by the political practitioners and theorists of the generation that declared independence, wrote a Constitution, and established a government. Divided into three major sections--the basic political philosophy and ideology of the American system of government, the present position of Congress, and the future of Congress--the book examines the high status accorded Congress from the early formative years through much of the nineteenth century and its dominant power position during much of the period before its final fall during the New Deal when Congress became "a mere junior partner" rather than a peer of the other two branches. Looking at the manner in which the modern Congress through the 1950s exercised its law-making, money, treaty and investigatory powers, Burnham concludes that the fall of Congress is as much a result of abdication as of outside aggression. He argues that unless

Congress remains a coordinate branch "plebiscitary despotism"
will replace constitutional government and spell the end of
political liberty.

Burns, James MacGregor. CONGRESS ON TRIAL: THE LEGISLATIVE
PROCESS AND THE ADMINISTRATIVE STATE. New York: Harper and
Brothers, 1949.

In this criticism of congressional inability to meet the demands
of the modern "administrative" or social service state, Burns
examines and rejects proposals to energize Congress by a constitutional change to a cabinet form of government and advocates
the extra-constitutional reform of responsible party government.

Cannon, Clarence A., comp. CANNON'S PRECEDENTS OF THE HOUSE
OF REPRESENTATIVES OF THE UNITED STATES, INCLUDING REFER-
ENCE TO PROVISIONS OF THE CONSTITUTION, THE LAWS, AND
DECISIONS OF THE UNITED STATES SENATE. 11 vols. Washington,
D.C.: Government Printing Office, 1935-41.

Commonly referred to as CANNON'S PRECEDENTS, this covers
the period from 1917 to 1935 and continues HINDS' PRECEDENTS
which was published in 1907 and 1908 and which are here reprinted (see p. 100). Like its predecessor, CANNON'S PRECE-
DENTS is a compilation of House actions which serve as precedents for that body. Volumes 9-11 are an index-digest of the
complete work.

_____. CANNON'S PROCEDURES IN THE HOUSE OF REPRESENTATIVES.
Washington, D.C.: Government Printing Office, 1953.

This is a compilation of the procedures employed by the House
by the compiler of CANNON'S PRECEDENTS.

Carroll, Holbert N. THE HOUSE OF REPRESENTATIVES AND FOREIGN
AFFAIRS. Rev. ed. Boston: Little, Brown, 1966.

The Constitution assigns to the president and to the Senate the
preeminent role in international relations. Although the House
is assigned no specific foreign policy role by the Constitution,
it is nonetheless a significant factor in the conduct of American
foreign policy. This work focuses upon the role of the lower
house. It examines the increased influence of the House in the
period beginning in the later part of World War II and extending
through the "postwar years" of the late 1950s.

Chamberlain, Joseph P. LEGISLATIVE PROCESSES: NATIONAL AND
STATE. New York: Appleton-Century-Crofts, 1936.

This is an extensive descriptive study of the legislative process
at the national and state levels with emphasis upon the former.
It deals with the procedure by which legislation is enacted from
the stage of introduction to adoption, as well as with such matters
as the relationship between Congress and the other two branches,
the organization of Congress and the relationships between congressmen and their constituents and their parties. Thus, there

are articles by both defenders and critics of the role of the rules committee in the 1950s in particular, of the seniority system, of the committee assignment method, and the slowness and deliberateness of Congress. There are articles by supporters of the status quo and by advocates of minimal reform as well as more drastic change.

Clark, Joseph. CONGRESS: THE SAPLESS BRANCH. New York: Harper and Row, 1964.

This criticism by Senator Clark is directed at the unresponsiveness and obstructionism of Congress which he attributes largely to the committee and seniority systems which rendered majority rule virtually meaningless until the mid-1960s when various reforms began to change the internal functioning of both houses.

_____, ed. CONGRESSIONAL REFORM: PROBLEMS AND PROSPECTS. New York: Thomas Y. Crowell, 1965.

This is a collection of essays, articles, and excerpts from the works of leading scholars and of members of Congress dealing with various facets of congressional reform: whether reform is needed and, if so, what kind of reform.

Colegrove, Kenneth W. THE AMERICAN SENATE AND WORLD PEACE. New York: Vanguard Press, 1944.

This is a criticism of the Senate's "treaty-wrecking" habits and an argument in favor of amending the Constitution to provide for a more democratic process. Noting that a minority of one house of Congress can block a treaty, Colegrove suggests that the process be changed to vest ratification power in a majority of the members of both houses present and voting.

Congressional Quarterly. CONGRESS AND THE NATION: A REVIEW OF GOVERNMENT AND POLITICS IN THE POST-WAR YEARS. 4 vols. Washington, D.C.: 1965-76.

A comprehensive review of congressional actions since 1945 organized on the basis of major substantive areas such as civil liberties and internal security. It includes relevant nonlegislative materials as well--the review of congressional civil rights actions, for example, includes the controversial Moynihan Report on the Negro Family. Volume 1 covers the period from 1945-64; volume 2, 1965-68; volume 3, 1969-72; and volume 4, 1973-76.

_____. GUIDE TO THE CONGRESS OF THE UNITED STATES: ORIGINS, HISTORY, PROCEDURES. Washington, D.C.: 1971.

This extensive factual study of Congress is a history of colonial precedents and of American legislative procedures, party leaders, and committee systems. It treats in detail the various powers of Congress such as its fiscal powers, its role in foreign affairs and in nominations and its investigative powers. It has separate chapters on such matters as campaign financing, reapportionment. lobbying and congressional ethics.

_____. IMPEACHMENT AND THE U.S. CONGRESS. Washington, D.C.:
1974.

>Published during the crisis over the question of the impeachment
>of President Nixon, this work contains the debates at the con-
>stitutional convention on the impeachment problem, information
>about the thirteen impeachments in the past, the arguments over
>impeachment advanced by James St. Clair, President Nixon's
>lawyer, and John M. Doar, the House Judiciary Committee's
>lawyer, as well as the backgrounds of the members of the House
>Judiciary Committee which considered the impeachment of Nixon;
>also contains a bibliography.

_____. ORIGINS AND DEVELOPMENT OF CONGRESS. Washington, D.C.:
1976.

>This basic text is a history of Congress from its origins in the
>colonial period through the 1970s. Part 1 deals with the relation-
>ship between colonial governors and colonial assemblies, the
>Continental Congress, Congress under the Articles of Confedera-
>tion, and the debates at the Philadelphia convention over the
>powers of Congress. Part 2 deals with the House and the
>Senate from the adoption of the Constitution to the present.

_____. POWERS OF CONGRESS. Washington, D.C.: 1976.

>This basic text is an analysis of the origins, development and
>present status of the basic constitutional powers of Congress:
>the powers to tax and spend, to make war, to approve treaties,
>to impeach, to regulate foreign and interstate commerce, to
>investigate, to confirm appointments and to amend the Constitution.

CONGRESSIONAL QUARTERLY ALMANAC. Washington, D.C.: Congressional
Quarterly, 1945-- . Annual.

>Organized on the basis of subject matter, this is a compilation
>of materials on congressional activities during the preceding year
>originally reported in the CONGRESSIONAL QUARTERLY WEEKLY
>REPORTS.

CONGRESSIONAL QUARTERLY WEEKLY REPORT. Washington, D.C.:
1942-- .

>This weekly publication presents summaries of congressional
>activities and congressional-presidential activities for the past
>week: roll-call votes, the status of bills and other congressional
>matters, including elections. The CONGRESSIONAL QUARTERLY
>ALMANAC is an annual compilation of the material.

Corwin, Edward S. "The Basic Doctrine of American Constitutional Law."
MICHIGAN LAW REVIEW 12 (February 1914): 247-74.

>This is an analysis of judicial development of the doctrine of
>vested rights, a doctrine which is based upon the assumption
>that property is a fundamental right and which treats any law
>impairing vested rights as void. Corwin maintains that this
>doctrine represents the first great achievement of the courts

after the establishment of judicial review and that it represents
the essential spirit and point of view of the founders of the Constitution who wrestled with the problem of how to harmonize
majority rule with minority rights and how to construct representative institutions while protecting the security of property.
This article is reprinted in volume 1 of SELECTED ESSAYS ON
CONSTITUTIONAL LAW (see p. 79).

_____. "The Power of Congress to Prohibit Commerce." CORNELL LAW
QUARTERLY 18 (1933): 477–513.

Written before the final rejection of such reasoning in Darby,
this is a criticism of the Supreme Court's holding in such cases
as Hammer v. Dagenhart that the power to regulate commerce
does not include the power to prohibit the movement of goods in
interstate commerce unless such goods are harmful. On the
basis of his analysis of the intention of the framers of the Constitution and of judicial, presidential and congressional precedent.
Corwin argues that the power to prohibit commerce is embraced
within the power to regulate commerce. This article is reprinted
in volume 3 of SELECTED ESSAYS ON CONSTITUTIONAL LAW
(see p. 79).

Cushman, Robert E. "The National Police Power Under the Commerce
Clause of the Constitution." MINNESOTA LAW REVIEW 3 (1919): 289–315,
381–410, and 452–79.

Although written before the explosion of "police power" measures
enacted by the national government since the New Deal, this is a
still-valid analysis of the constitutional technique by which Congress in effect exercises police power by indirection; that is,
it uses a delegated power as a constitutional peg upon which to
rest legislation designed to protect the national welfare—a national
police power. Cushman examines various pieces of national
legislation based upon the commerce clause and judicial reaction
to that technique up through the Progressive era. The first two
installments of this article are reprinted in volume 3 of SELECTED
ESSAYS ON CONSTITUTIONAL LAW (see p. 79).

Dahl, Robert A. CONGRESS AND FOREIGN POLICY. New York: Harcourt, Brace and Co., 1950.

An analysis of the dilemma posed by the inability of Congress to
participate wisely in foreign policy on the one hand and the
necessity for participation by the people's representatives on
the other. Written during the Cold War amidst the general assumption that presidential control of foreign policy was essential, this
work attempts to prescribe means by which "Congress may be
relieved of all or part of its responsibility" in foreign affairs
so that the more efficient executive branch could have a freer
hand.

Dangerfield, Royden J. IN DEFENSE OF THE SENATE: A STUDY IN
TREATY MAKING. Norman: University of Oklahoma Press, 1933. Reprint.
Ann Arbor, Mich.: University Microfilms, 1967. Microfilm-xerography.

Noting the avalanche of criticism directed toward the Senate
role and the two-thirds requirement in treaty-making, particularly
after an acrimonious fight such as that over the Treaty of Versailles, Dangerfield examines the evolution of the treaty-making
power from the Articles of Confederation and the debates at
Philadelphia through the late 1920s. Focusing upon the role of
the Senate and the Senate Foreign Relations Committee but considering also the executive branch, he analyzes the action taken
by the Senate on the 833 treaties submitted to it between 6 February 1778 and 6 February 1928 by isolating and subjecting to
statistical analysis those factors he believes influenced delay,
modification, rejection or ratification. On the question of the
two-thirds requirement, he concludes that most of the treaties
rejected would have suffered the same fate had a majority rule
been in effect. In addition to a number of graphs and tables
documenting such matters as the frequency distribution of delayed
treaties and the periods of delay in ratification by type of treaty,
by decades, by the president and by the secretary of state, there
is included in the appendix lists of the treaties negotiated prior
to the adoption of the Constitution, those negotiated between 1788
and 1928, those never submitted for ratification, those submitted
but withdrawn and other such relevant materials.

DePauw, Linda G., ed. DOCUMENTARY HISTORY OF THE FIRST FED-
ERAL CONGRESS, 1789-1791. 3 vols. Baltimore: Johns Hopkins University Press, 1972.

These three volumes contain the full record of the debates and
actions of the first Congress from 4 March 1789 to 3 March 1791.
Volume 1, SENATE LEGISLATIVE JOURNAL, contains the official
papers of the Senate. Volume 2, SENATE EXECUTIVE JOURNAL
AND RELATED DOCUMENTS, contains such unofficial materials
as letters to or from congressmen, newspaper accounts of congressional action, and diary entries. Volume 3, HOUSE OF
REPRESENTATIVES JOURNAL, contains records relating to
the Hours. There is an editorial note in the introduction to
each volume.

Dionisopoulous, P. Allan. REBELLION, RACISM, AND REPRESENTATION:
THE ADAM CLAYTON POWELL CASE AND ITS ANTECEDENTS. DeKalb:
Northern Illinois University Press, 1970.

The Constitution assigns to each house the authority to judge
the conduct of its members: they may exclude, expel and censure.
This work is an analysis of what the author views as the abuse
of this power by both houses which have refused to seat duly
elected and qualified persons because of disapproval of beliefs
or past conduct--exclusion of polygamists, socialists, pacifists
and those who participated in the southern effort to secede.

Dunne, Gerald T. MONETARY DECISIONS OF THE SUPREME COURT.
New Brunswick, N.J.: Rutgers University Press, 1960.

With a brief look at the pre-constitutional period and at the debates at Philadelphia on the Article I provision authorizing Congress to coin money and regulate the value thereof, this slim volume
examines a number of Supreme Court decisions involving national

power over money and banking. He looks at <u>McCulloch</u> v. <u>Maryland</u> which he labels the "false dawn of federal supremacy," at the resurgence of state authority in the 1830s and finally at the triumph of national constitutional power in the 1930s. The author concludes that although congressional policy favors coexistence in banking, the constitutional powers of Congress have so expanded that the Court won't even hear cases challenging the Federal Reserve System or the Federal Deposit Insurance Corporation or the impact of these institutions on state banks.

Eberling, Ernest J. CONGRESSIONAL INVESTIGATIONS: A STUDY OF THE ORIGIN AND DEVELOPMENT OF THE POWER OF CONGRESS TO INVESTIGATE AND PUNISH FOR CONTEMPT. 1928. Reprint. New York: Octagon, 1972.

This Columbia Ph.D. dissertation in political science, apparently published originally by the author, is an in-depth study of congressional investigatory power to the 1920s. Organized chronologically and topically, it examines the origins and development of the investigatory power prior to 1789, the exercise of the power by Congress under the Constitution to 1827, congressional procedures and practices between 1827 and the 1920s, the statutory evolution of the power, and judicial review of the power of both Congress and administrative agencies to compel testimony and to punish for contempt. Congressional statutes dealing with the investigatory power and the power to punish for contempt are included in the appendix.

Freund, Ernst. THE POLICE POWER: PUBLIC POLICY AND CONSTITUTIONAL RIGHTS. 1904. Reprint. New York: Arno Press, 1976.

This massive work examines the police power of the states in terms of its meaning ("to promote the public welfare by restraining the use of liberty and property"), its place among governmental powers, its operation in various substantive areas, and its relationship to national power, particularly congressional power to regulate commerce among the states.

_____. STANDARDS OF AMERICAN LEGISLATION: AN ESTIMATE OF RESTRICTIVE AND CONSTRUCTIVE FACTORS. Preface by Francis A. Allen. 1917. 2d ed. Reprint. Chicago: University of Chicago Press, 1965.

This is an expanded version of a series of lectures delivered at Johns Hopkins University in 1915 in which Freund's exploration of a policy-making process guided by judicially constructed constitutional concepts leads him to conclude that such concepts are inadequate guides to law making. He argues that policy in the socioeconomic area should be made by legislative, not judicial, agents and attempts to discern some principles to guide legislative law making. Taking the position that there is confusion between what the Constitution permits and what is good or just public policy, he suggests that legislation should be guided by two basic principles: correlation or the interdependence of rights and obligations and standardization or avoidance of inconsistency and caprice.

Gallagher, Hugh G. ADVISE AND OBSTRUCT: THE ROLE OF THE
UNITED STATES SENATE IN FOREIGN POLICY DECISIONS. Foreword
by Sen. Philip A. Hart. New York: Delacorte Press, 1969.

> Designed for the general audience, this work by a former adminis-
> trative assistant to Senator Robert Bartlett of Alaska is a study
> of the internal politics of senatorial participation in various
> foreign affairs matters from the conflict over Jay's Treaty in
> the Washington administration to the Vietnam War in the Johnson
> administration.

Galloway, George B. CONGRESSIONAL REORGANIZATION REVISITED.
College Park: Bureau of Governmental Research, University of Maryland,
1956.

> This is a brief sketch of major developments in the committee
> structure, operations and staffing and in such areas as fiscal
> controls and lobbying in the first decade following the Legis-
> lative Reorganization Act of 1946.

_____. THE LEGISLATIVE PROCESS IN CONGRESS. New York: Thomas
Y. Crowell, 1953.

> This descriptive study of the legislative process covers such
> matters as the constitutional powers of Congress (expressly
> delegated, expressly prohibited, and implied), the original de-
> sign of congressional powers and functions in comparison to
> the present pattern, the procedure for enacting a law, the
> administrative supervision role of Congress, the role of various
> participants in the legislative process and the Reorganization
> Act of 1946.

Gavit, Bernard C. THE COMMERCE CLAUSE OF THE UNITED STATES
CONSTITUTION. Bloomington, Ind.: Principia Press, 1932. Reprint.
New York: AMS Press, 1970.

> This is an in-depth analysis of all major Supreme Court decisions
> from the early nineteenth century to the late 1920s involving a
> constitutional challenge to state or national legislation in which
> the commerce clause was the basis of the challenge. It thus
> deals with such basic questions as the meaning of "commerce"
> and "among the states," and the scope of national power derived
> from the commerce clause as well as with the basic question of
> whether national commerce power is exclusive or concurrent.
> Included in the appendix are a chronological list of Supreme
> Court commerce cases with a brief indication of the Court's
> holdings in each, a list of cases in which congressional regula-
> tion was not upheld, a list of cases in which state regulation was
> upheld, and a list of cases in which the state regulation was not
> upheld.

Goodman, Walter. THE COMMITTEE: THE EXTRAORDINARY CAREER
OF THE HOUSE COMMITTEE ON UN-AMERICAN ACTIVITIES. Foreword
by Richard A. Rovere. New York: Farrar, Straus and Giroux, 1968.

This is an account of the thirty-year career of one of the most controversial investigating committees ever created and nurtured by Congress.

Goodnow, Frank J. SOCIAL REFORM AND THE CONSTITUTION. New York: Burt Franklin, 1911.

This is an analysis of the constitutional authority of the national government to regulate in the socioeconomic order written when a narrow construction of Congress's commerce power vied with and was frequently victorious over the broad construction prevalent today. It deals with such matters as the power of Congress to regulate navigation, to prohibit commerce, to prohibit the sale of articles, and constitutionality of governmental regulation of law, of taxation and of various forms of government aid such as care of the aged.

Goodwin, George, Jr. CONGRESS: ANVIL OF AMERICAN DEMOCRACY. Glenview, Ill.: Scott, Foresman, 1967.

This book of readings covers such topics as the procedure for enacting legislation, the oversight function of Congress, the roles of pressure groups, political parties and constituents in the congressional decision-making process and congressional reform.

Griffith, Ernest S., and Valeo, Francis R. CONGRESS: ITS CONTEM-PORARY ROLE. 5th ed. New York: New York University Press, 1975.

Updated after Watergate and the end of the Vietnam War, events which in the authors' view led Congress to attempt to reacquire its constitutional powers, this is a study of the formal constitutional status of Congress, its internal organization and operations, and its role in modern society. They conclude that even though the formal constitutional powers of Congress have changed little either by formal constitutional amendment or by judicial interpretation and even though in the 1970s it restored equilibrium by becoming more assertive, it is unlikely that it could again play the dominant role criticized by Wilson in his CONGRESSIONAL GOVERNMENT (see p. 114).

Groennings, Sven, and Hawley, Jonathan, eds. TO BE A CONGRESSMAN: THE PROMISE AND THE POWER. Preface by Evron M. Kirkpatrick. Prologue by Rep. William Steiger. Introduction by Sen. Hubert H. Humphrey. Washington, D.C.: Acropolis Books, 1973.

These eleven essays, each written by a "participant observer" under the Congressional Fellowship Program sponsored by the American Political Science Association, deal with various elements of congressional life from campaigns and committee assignment politics to senatorial leadership and congressional relations with the press.

Gunther, Gerald, ed. JOHN MARSHALL'S DEFENSE OF McCULLOCH V. MARYLAND. Stanford, Calif.: Stanford University Press, 1969.

With an introductory essay by the editor, author of two forth-
coming volumes on the Marshall Court in the OLIVER WENDELL
HOLMES DEVISE HISTORY OF THE SUPREME COURT, this
is an exchange of pseudonymous essays between states' rights
advocates and Marshall. Shortly after McCulloch v. Marshall,
the RICHMOND ENQUIRER, a states' rights newspaper, began
publishing a series of articles attacking Marshall's opinion in
that case. The first two essays signed "Amphictyon" and probably written by Judge William Brockenbrough prompted a response
by Marshall in an essay signed "A Friend of the Court" and
published in the PHILADELPHIA UNION, a nationalist newspaper.
The ENQUIRER then published four essays signed "Hampden"
and written by Judge Spencer Roane. Marshall again responded
under the same pseudonym with a nine-part reply to "Hampden."

Hacker, Andrew. CONGRESSIONAL DISTRICTING: THE ISSUE OF
EQUAL REPRESENTATION. Rev. ed. Washington, D.C.: Brookings Institution, 1964.

Written shortly after Baker v. Carr, with a revised edition prepared after Wesberry and Reynolds, this is a study of the possible efforts of the Court's reapportionment decisions upon congressional districting. Hacker examines the constitutional and
historical background of congressional districting, the Court's
reaction to various challenges to malapportioned state legislatures from Colegrove to Baker and the extent and consequences
of inequalities in the House of Representatives.

Hamilton, James. THE POWER TO PROBE: A STUDY OF CONGRESSIONAL
INVESTIGATIONS. Introduction by Sen. Sam J. Ervin. New York: Random House, 1976.

This work by an assistant chief counsel to the Senate Select
Committee on Presidential Campaign Activities, which conducted
an investigation of the Watergate affair, deals with some of the
general problems encountered by congressional committee investigations of the executive branch (how to maintain the integrity of
the separation of power doctrine) as well as problems encountered
by any committee investigating an area of intense public concern
(how to prevent leaks to the press). Hamilton traces the legal
history of congressional investigations from the postrevolutionary
period to the present.

Hamilton, Walton H., and Adair, Douglass. THE POWER TO GOVERN:
THE CONSTITUTION THEN AND NOW. New York: W.W. Norton, 1937.
Reprint. New York: Da Capo Press, 1972.

Written at the height of narrow judicial construction of congressional
power to regulate in the socioeconomic area, this work is a
criticism of the narrow interpretation of the commerce clause
which became the pattern at the same time that industry became
more and more interstate in character. It is an analysis of the
paradox by which "a constitution which was an embodiment of
mercantilist doctrine has become an expression of economic in-
dividualism."

Article I

Harris, Joseph H. THE ADVICE AND CONSENT OF THE SENATE. Berkeley and Los Angeles: University of California Press, 1953.

An analysis of the role of the Senate in the process of appointment. Set against the background of the debates over the appointment power at the constitutional convention, Harris examines the early history of senatorial confirmation and the battles between presidents and the Senate over the proper role of the Senate as well as the fight over particular confirmations such as that of Brandeis.

Harris, Joseph P. CONGRESSIONAL CONTROL OF ADMINISTRATION. Washington, D.C.: Brookings Institution, 1964.

Although the prime constitutional function of Congress is to legislate, it also has the power of administrative oversight. After a brief introductory section placing the problem of oversight within its constitutional and political setting, this work examines the various means by which Congress attempts to exercise control over the executive branch. It examines congressional control of executive organization, the budget process in various periods before 1921, the enactment of the Budget Control Act of 1921 and subsequent use of the budget as an instrument of control, the appropriations process, control through auditing and the General Accounting Office. It also looks at the use of investigation as a means of control as well as the use of the legislative veto by resolution and by committee and the constitutional issue raised by the veto technique.

Hinds, Asher C., comp. PRECEDENTS OF THE HOUSE OF REPRESENTATIVES. 5 vols. Washington, D.C.: Government Printing Office, 1907-8.

Generally referred to as HINDS' PRECEDENTS, this is a compilation of House actions which serve as precedents for the House of Representatives. Compiled by the clerk at the speaker's table, these precedents are organized on the basis of major substantive areas of congressional actions such as general election cases, removal of officers, investigative powers, impeachment powers and the general conduct of House business. This compilation, begun by Hinds, is continued in Clarence Cannon, PRECEDENTS OF THE HOUSE OF REPRESENTATIVES (see p. 91), commonly referred to as CANNON'S PRECEDENTS. HINDS' PRECEDENTS constitute the first five volumes of House precedents and CANNON'S PRECEDENTS constitute the remainder of the eleven-volume series. Volumes 9 through 11 are an index and digest of the complete work.

Holt, William S. TREATIES DEFEATED BY THE SENATE: A STUDY OF THE STRUGGLE BETWEEN PRESIDENT AND SENATE OVER THE CONDUCT OF FOREIGN RELATIONS. Baltimore: Johns Hopkins Press, 1933. Reprint. Gloucester, Mass.: Peter Smith, 1964.

In this analysis of the circumstances surrounding senatorial rejection of each treaty from 1789 to 1919, the author looks at the reasons for the action to determine whether the defeat was one phase of the general struggle between the President and Congress for control over foreign policy or whether it was a result of domestic politics. Organized topically and chronologically, this work first examines the debates at the constitutional convention over the question of the location of power over foreign affairs in general and the treaty-making power in particular and then looks at the early contests and precedents in the period between 1789 and 1815 and at each subsequent contest through the Versailles Treaty.

Huitt, Ralph K., and Peabody, Robert L. CONGRESS: TWO DECADES OF ANALYSIS. New York: Harper and Row, 1969.

The first one-half of the book is a long essay by Peabody on research on Congress. The second one-half is a collection of six of Huitt's essays on such matters as executive-legislative relations, leadership in the Senate, the internal distribution of influence in the Senate and a case study of congressional committees.

Hurst, James Willard. A LEGAL HISTORY OF MONEY IN THE UNITED STATES, 1774-1970. Lincoln: University of Nebraska Press, 1973.

In this history of the evolution of constitutional and political control of money matters from the pre-Revolutionary period to 1970, Hurst suggests that the basic foundations of monetary policy were laid between 1774 and 1788 and that the framers of the Constitution spent little time with national money provisions because they agreed on the key issues and focused attention therefore on limiting state authority over money supply by such constitutional devices as prohibiting states from emitting bills of credit or making anything other than gold or silver legal tender. In the constitutional period, the contending agents for control and influence varied. Between 1787-1860, the key issues of monetary policy involved the distribution of power over money between nation and state and between legal and market processes. Between 1860 and 1908, federalism ceased to be a major issue and control was more centralized although in practice Congress allowed state-chartered commercial banks to influence money supply. Between 1908 and 1970, monetary policy was firmly centralized but a new struggle for control emerged with the White House, the Federal Reserve System, and the Treasury Department in competition. With the enactment of the Employment Act of 1946 and the creation of the Council of Economic Advisers, presidential authority increased and by 1970 monetary policy emerged as a result of an interplay between the Federal Reserve System and the White House.

Jacobs, Andrew. THE POWELL AFFAIR: FREEDOM MINUS ONE. Indianapolis: Bobbs-Merrill, 1973.

This is an account, by a member of the Select Committee appointed to consider the Adam Clayton Powell case, of the day to day work of that nine member committee. On the basis of its understanding of the relevant constitutional provisions—particularly section 2, clause 2 specifying the qualifications of members of the House (25 years of age, a U.S. citizen for seven years and an inhabitant of the state represented) and of section 5, clause 2 (that members can be expelled only by a two-thirds vote)—the Committee recommended that Powell be censured and fined but not denied his seat. The full House rejected and went beyond this recommendation; by a vote of 222 to 202 it voted not to seat Powell. Thus, in the words of the title, the House was "minus one." In 1969, the Supreme Court agreed with the committee's constitutional interpretation and held that the House had violated the Constitution in excluding Powell. Powell was fined $5,000 and seated. Reelected the following year, he was later defeated in a bid for reelection. Included in the appendix are the House resolution creating the committee, the relevant constitutional provisions, various motions and communications between Powell and others and the committee, and the recommendations of the committee to the full House.

Johnsen, Julia E., comp. THE INVESTIGATING POWERS OF CONGRESS. New York: H.W. Wilson, 1951.

A collection of excerpts from such varied sources as mass circulation magazines and scholarly journals dealing with the general question of congressional investigatory authority. Although prompted by the controversy aroused by the House Un-American Activities Committee, this volume contains articles which deal not just with that committee but with such matters as the origin and necessity of legislative possession of this essentially non-legislative power.

_____. REORGANIZATION OF THE SUPREME COURT. New York: H.W. Wilson, 1937.

Confronted with judicial invalidation of New Deal legislation, Franklin D. Roosevelt inserted into a general governmental reorganization plan submitted to Congress a proposal to change the Court: he suggested an enlargement of the Court by adding a justice for each justice who remained on the court over six months after reaching the age of seventy. This work summarizes the major arguments in support of and in opposition to the plan and contains a series of essays in support of and in opposition to it.

Keller, Morton. IN DEFENSE OF YESTERDAY: JAMES M. BECK AND THE POLITICS OF CONSERVATISM, 1861-1936. New York: Coward-McCann, 1958.

Although a biography, this work serves primarily as a vehicle for an analysis of American socioeconomic conservatism in the fluctuating period of the movement from laissez-faire to the welfare state in the late nineteenth century until the triumph of the New Deal. As both a high ranking official in the Justice Department who defended progressive legislation and as a corporation lawyer and author who grew increasingly hostile toward the expanding role of government in the 1920s until his death in 1936, Beck participated in many of the constitutional controversies over the proper role of government in the socioeconomic arena. This work deals with those constitutional controversies.

Kutler, Stanley I. PRIVILEGE AND CREATIVE DESTRUCTION: THE CHARLES RIVER BRIDGE CASE. Philadelphia: J.B. Lippincott Co., 1971.

> This is an account of the background of the Charles River Bridge case, the public policy implications of that case and an analysis of the "constitutional revolution of 1837" when the Taney Court, though not rejecting the Marshall Court's concern for property, began the process of balancing public and private interests and enlarging the scope of the state's power to provide for the public welfare.

Landis, James McCauley. "Constitutional Limitations on the Congressional Power of Investigation." HARVARD LAW REVIEW 40 (December 1926): 153-221.

> Written long before the activities of the House Un-American Activities Committee gave rise to the idea that the specific prohibitions of the Bill of Rights limited congressional investigatory powers and indeed before the Bill of Rights became a major limitation on governmental powers, this is an analysis of, first, the origin and use of congressional power to compel witnesses to appear and to testify and, second, the origin of the idea that there are constitutional limitations on that power. Landis traces the origins of the power to the British Parliament and discusses its development and use in state legislatures and then in Congress from the St. Clair inquiry in 1793 to its uses through the early twentieth century. In dealing with the development of the idea of limitations, he examines the arguments of John Quincy Adams, the first major opponent of unlimited congressional power to investigate, who challenged the constitutional legitimacy of some aspects of the House hearings over the renewal of the charter of the Bank of the United States on the grounds that nonofficial conduct of a citizen is immune to congressional scrutiny, an argument resurrected by the Court in Kilbourn v. Thompson when it held that the House had exceeded its power because it had no legislative aim in mind.

Lee, R. Alton. HISTORY OF REGULATORY TAXATION. Lexington: University Press of Kentucky, 1973.

> This is an examination of congressional use of its taxing power to achieve regulatory ends, thus transforming this revenue raising authority into a national police power. In tracing this kind of use of the taxing clause chronologically, Lee looks at its use in regulating and/or prohibiting oleomargarine, impure foods, narcotics, firearms, gambling and child labor and the constitutional arguments advanced in Congress and in the courts on each of these measures by strict constructionists and liberal constructionists.

Lowi, Theodore, ed. LEGISLATIVE PROCESS, USA: CONGRESS AND THE FORCES THAT SHAPE IT. Boston: Little, Brown, 1962.

> This book of readings includes excerpts from a variety of works dealing with such matters as representative government in general, the powers, organization and processes of government, the party role in Congress, the relationship between the executive and legislative branches and congressional oversight of the adminis-

tration. Included are excerpts from Supreme Court opinions
(such as Wickard v. Filburn and the Civil Rights Cases), from
presidential commissions' studies (such as the report of Truman's
Civil Rights Commission), from works of scholars such as John
Stuart Mill (on representative government) and Woodrow Wilson
(on government by committee) and from other sources such as
the American Political Science Association's report on a responsible two-party system.

McCall, Samuel W. THE BUSINESS OF CONGRESS. New York: Columbia
University Press, 1911.

Originally delivered as eight lectures at Columbia in 1908, this
book outlines the basic powers of Congress and the formal and
informal procedures it employs in carrying out its law-making
authority.

McGeary, M. Nelson. THE DEVELOPMENT OF CONGRESSIONAL INVES-
TIGATIVE POWER. Columbia Studies in the Social Sciences Series. New
York: Columbia University Press, 1940.

This study of congressional inquiries conducted in pursuance of
a resolution or statute by congressional committees or subcom-
mittees (thus excluding those undertaken by standing committees
on their own initiative or those by select committees) examines
the purposes of investigations, the procedures employed, the
legal limitations on the activities of investigating committees and
Supreme Court decisions through the 1920s upholding congressional authority to investigate.

McKay, Robert. "Taxing and Spending for the General Welfare: A Reply
to Mr. Nilsson." AMERICAN BAR ASSOCIATION JOURNAL 48 (January
1962): 38-42.

In this reply to George W. Nilsson's support of a narrow construction of the general welfare clause (see p. 105), McKay argues
in support of the broad or Hamiltonian interpretation of that
clause.

Magrath, C. Peter. YAZOO--LAW AND POLITICS IN THE NEW REPUBLIC:
THE CASE OF FLETCHER V. PECK. Providence, R.I.: Brown University
Press, 1966.

Because Marshall read the doctrine of vested rights into the contract clause in Fletcher v. Peck, that clause became the principal basis for challenging state legislation regulating business until
the end of the nineteenth century and dominated constitutional
law until its replacement by the due process clause of the Fourteenth Amendment in the early twentieth century. This work is
a study of the background and repercussions of Fletcher v. Peck.
It examines the politics of public lands in Georgia, the relationship between Georgia lands and national politics, the use of constitutional politics to protect land speculators, the opinion in
Fletcher v. Peck, the effect of that opinion upon American constitutional law for the rest of the century, and judicial interpretation of the contract clause through Home Building and Loan
Association and the fall of the contract clause. About one-half

of the book consists of an appendix which includes, among other
things, Hamilton's legal opinion to the Yazoo land companies
which, Magrath says, is the first recorded suggestion that the
contract clause forbade not just state interference with private
contracts but state interference with public contracts, an interpretation used by Marshall first in Fletcher and then in Dartmouth.

Mansfield, Harvey C., ed. CONGRESS AGAINST THE PRESIDENT. New
York: Praeger Publishers, 1975.

This collection of thirteen essays dealing with various aspects
of congressional relations with the president considers such
matters as the dispersion of authority within Congress, the
fights over budgeting and the executive privilege doctrine, senatorial confirmation of executive appointments during the Nixon
era and the role of Congress in foreign affairs during the Nixon
administration.

Miller, Arthur S. "Constitutional Revolution Consolidated: The Rise of
the Positive State." GEORGE WASHINGTON LAW REVIEW 35 (December
1966): 172-90.

This is an analysis of the constitutional flexibility and expansion
of discretionary power of the political branches which followed
judicial abandonment of its involvement in socioeconomic policy
in 1937. It examines the acceptance of governmental responsibility for the economic well-being of the populace, an acceptance
epitomized by the enactment of the Employment Act of 1936, and
some of the problems, complexities and rearrangements of relationships arising out of the Positive State.

Moe, Ronald C., ed. CONGRESS AND THE PRESIDENT: ALLIES AND
ADVERSARIES. Pacific Palisades, Calif.: Goodyear, 1971.

This collection of twenty-one essays by various students of Congress and the presidency examines such major topics of congressional-executive relationships as their respective roles in foreign
affairs generally and in war-making in particular and in furnish-
ing legislative leadership.

Morrow, William L. CONGRESSIONAL COMMITTEES. New York: Charles
Scribner's Sons, 1969.

This is an analysis of the role of congressional committees, with
emphasis upon the standing committees, within a constitutional
and political system which disperses governmental power between
the center and the parts, between the two congressional houses,
among the three branches, and within each house.

Nilsson, George W. "There is No 'General Welfare Power' in the Constitution of the United States." AMERICAN BAR ASSOCIATION JOURNAL 47
(January 1961): 43-47.

In this brief examination of the general welfare clause and the
intention of the framers of the Constitution, Nilsson supports a

narrow or Madisonian construction and argues that the checks and balance system has been threatened by the concentration of power in the federal government and by the unwarranted broad construction of the general welfare clause.

Plous, Harold J., and Baker, Gordon. "McCulloch v. Maryland: Right Principle, Wrong Case." STANFORD LAW REVIEW 9 (1957): 710-31.

In this analysis of McCulloch, the authors suggest that Marshall used the case to expound his concepts of liberal interpretation, implied powers and nationalism even though the factual background of the case, particularly the private, profit-making nature of the bank, made it an inappropriate vehicle for the enunciation of these principles. In addition, the authors argue that the opinion's sweeping assertion that the power to tax is the power to destroy led to later unnecessary complications in determining the extent of intergovernmental tax immunity.

Powell, Thomas Reed. "The Child Labor Law, the Tenth Amendment and the Commerce Clause." SOUTHERN LAW QUARTERLY 3 (1918): 175-202.

This is a criticism of the narrow interpretation of the commerce clause used by the Court in Hammer v. Dagenhart in 1918 and an argument in favor of a return to a broad construction of the commerce clause. Powell argues that the regulation of child labor is a policy question to be answered by Congress and not by the courts. This article is reprinted in volume 3 of SELECTED ESSAYS ON CONSTITUTIONAL LAW (see p. 79).

Prentice, E. Parmalee, and Egan, John G. THE COMMERCE POWER AND THE FEDERAL CONSTITUTION. Chicago: 1898.

Since the late nineteenth century and particularly since the New Deal, the commerce clause has been primarily important as a source of national power to regulate the socioeconomic order. Until the late nineteenth century, however, the major constitutional controversies involving the commerce clause involved state, not national legislation. The focal point of this work is the commerce clause as a limitation on state power rather than a source of congressional power.

Radford, Robert S., ed. THE POWER OF CONGRESS (AS CONGRESS SEES IT): THE CONGRESSIONAL CORRESPONDENCE OF ROBERT LE FEVRE. Los Angeles: Pine Tree Press, 1976.

With an introduction by the editor, this is an exchange of over one hundred letters between LeFevre and the forty-six congressmen who responded to his question, addressed to all 435 members, concerning the compatibility between personal integrity and the representation of the diverse and conflicting interests of constituents. The letters also deal with a variety of issues other than the question of whether a congressman can be both representative and honest.

Rhode, William E. COMMITTEE CLEARANCE OF ADMINISTRATIVE DECISIONS. East Lansing: Bureau of Social and Political Research, Michigan State University, 1959.

Despite constitutional limitations on congressional delegation of
its power, more and more discretion is conferred on the administration. Because Congress found the traditional means of annual
budget review, periodic hearings by standing committees, and
setting up rigid standards and principles to guide the administration to be inadequate, it devised the supplementary tool of
committee clearance of administrative decisions prior to execu-
tion. This slim volume examines this technique, first used in
the late 1920s, and concludes that committee clearance, both
formal and informal, is an improper addition to the repertory
of instruments for control of administrative discretion.

Ribble, Frederick D. STATE AND NATIONAL POWER OVER COMMERCE.
Columbia Legal Studies Series. New York: Columbia University Press,
1937.

This is an analysis of changing judicial theories and approaches
to the constitutional question of the state's authority to regulate
interstate commerce from the early nineteenth century to the
1930s.

Riddick, Floyd M. CONGRESSIONAL PROCEDURE. Boston: Chapman and
Grimes, 1941.

This is a study of the way in which Congress organizes itself
to carry out its lawmaking function. After an introductory chapter devoted to congressional functions not immediately connected
with the legislative process (such as the qualifications of members
and their immunities, election of the president and vice-president
by Congress and the impeachment procedure), it examines the
organization and procedures of the House and contrasts them to
those of the Senate. It devotes separate chapters to the political organization of the House, the Speaker, the floor leaders,
the rules committee, the standing committees and the Committee
of the Whole.

Robinson, James A. CONGRESS AND FOREIGN POLICY-MAKING: A
STUDY IN LEGISLATIVE INFLUENCE AND INITIATIVE. Rev. ed. Homewood, Ill.: Dorsey, 1967.

Although the Constitution vests primary authority in foreign
affairs in the president, Robinson argues that the basic reasons
for the secondary role of Congress are extraconstitutional, not
constitutional. For various reasons, such as the changing character of information or intelligence in modern policy making,
Congress's role in foreign policy is primarily to legitimate and/
or to amend recommendations initiated by the executive and to
deal with situations usually identified by the executive.

Schlesinger, Arthur M., Jr., and Bruns, Roger, eds. CONGRESS INVESTI-
GATES: A DOCUMENTED HISTORY 1792-1974. 5 vols. Ann Arbor:
Chelsea House Publishers in association with R.R. Bowker, 1975.

Each of the twenty-nine original essays in this multivolume work
is a scholarly analysis of congressional investigations ranging
from the St. Clair investigation in 1792 to the investigation of
the Watergate Committee in 1973. Investigations covered include

Article I

those of James Wilkinson in 1810; the Burning of Washington,
1814; the Seminole War, 1818; Calhoun's Conduct as Secretary
of War, 1826; the Bank of the United States, 1812; frauds in
the Administration of Indian Affairs, 1832; the Attack on Charles
Sumner, 1856; the Harper's Ferry Inquiry, 1859; the Covode
Investigation, 1860; the Joint Select Committee on the Conduct
of the War, 1861; the Reconstruction Committee, 1865; the
impeachment investigation of Andrew Johnson, 1867; the Ku-
Klux Klan, 1871; the Ballinger-Pinchot affair, 1910; elections
of 1904, 1908 and 1912; Pujo Money Trust, 1912; Teapot Dome,
1924; Pecora Stock Exchange, 1934; the Dies Committee, 1938;
the Truman Committee on the National Defense Program, 1941;
Pearl Harbor, 1945; the Kefauver Committee on Organized Crime,
1950; the Joint Committee on Armed Services and Foreign Relations, 1954; and the TFX plane contract, 1963. There is also
an abridgment of the five-volume series which includes sixteen
of the original twenty-nine essays.

Schmeckebier, Laurence F. CONGRESSIONAL APPORTIONMENT. Washington, D.C.: Brookings Institution, 1941.

This is a historical analysis of congressional actions to carry
out the constitutional requirement of apportioning seats in the
House of Representatives among the states every ten years.

Simpson, Alexander. A TREATISE ON FEDERAL IMPEACHMENTS: WITH
AN APPENDIX CONTAINING, INTER ALIA, AN ABSTRACT OF THE ACTS
OF IMPEACHMENT IN ALL THE FEDERAL IMPEACHMENTS IN THIS
COUNTRY AND IN ENGLAND. Philadelphia: Law Association, 1917. Re-
print. Wilmington, Del.: Scholarly Resources, 1973.

Originally a lawyer's brief in 1916 in impeachment proceedings
against a judge, this work deals with some of the basic questions
raised in the controversy over President Nixon: can a public
official be impeached for other than an indictable offense, can
one be impeached after he has ceased to be a "civil officer of
the United States," and what are the offenses embraced within
the language "high crimes and misdemeanors?"

"Standing to Sue for Members of Congress." YALE LAW JOURNAL 83
(July 1974): 1665-88.

This is an argument for enlarging, to the point of abandoning,
the traditional understanding of "standing" in cases involving
congressional challenges to executive action as well as in other
situations. It is suggested that the interests of members of the
Congress in maintaining the effectiveness of their votes and in
obtaining information related to their duties are sufficient to
grant standing. Beyond this, it is argued that "the fact that a
plaintiff cares enough to bring the suit should be sufficient proof
of his stake in the matter to satisfy any Article III requirement."

Stennis, John C., and Fulbright, J. William. THE ROLE OF CONGRESS
IN FOREIGN AFFAIRS. Washington, D.C.: American Enterprise Institute
for Public Policy Research, 1971.

This is a debate between Senators Stennis and Fulbright on the question of the proper constitutional and political role of Congress in international relations. The book consists of a lecture by each senator, rebuttals, and a panel discussion with questions directed to the speakers by journalists and scholars.

Stern, Robert L. "The Commerce Clause and the National Economy, 1933–1946." HARVARD LAW REVIEW 59 (May 1946): 645–93; (July 1946): 884–947.

With a brief review of the leading precedents before the 1930s, this is an analysis, by a Justice Department participant in much of the New Deal litigation, of judicial interpretation of congressional power derived from the commerce clause from 1933 to 1946. It examines the background, enactment and operation of major New Deal legislation based on the commerce clause (the National Industrial Recovery Act, the Guffey Coal Act, the Wagner Act, the first and second Agricultural Adjustment Acts, the Fair Labor Standards Act and legislation regulating insurance), the arguments before the Supreme Court in defending and attacking the legislation, and Supreme Court decisions first invalidating and then upholding national power to deal with national social and economic problems.

Stites, Francis N. PRIVATE INTEREST AND PUBLIC GAIN: THE DARTMOUTH COLLEGE CASE, 1819. Amherst: University of Massachusetts Press, 1972.

This is an examination of the Dartmouth College case in terms of the history of Dartmouth, the religious and partisan clashes which gave rise to the case, the litigation at the state level, the Supreme Court's opinion and the consequences of that opinion for public and private colleges and universities.

Strong, Frank R. "Court v. Constitution: Disparate Distortions of the Indirect Limitations in the American Constitutional Framework." NORTH CAROLINA LAW REVIEW 54 (January 1976): 125–72.

This article suggests that there are dual limitations on the exercise of governmental power: direct limitations imposed by, for example, the prohibitions of the Bill of Rights and indirect limitations imposed by the separation of powers doctrine and the federal principle. Strong argues that the Court has either ignored or had difficulty understanding and applying these indirect limitations. Noting that, aside from the contract clause, constitutional review of indirect limitations was more common than that of direct limitations until the due process clause and then the prohibitions of the Bill of Rights came into use in the nineteenth century, he suggests that appreciation of the former has dulled. He is especially critical of the Warren Court and examines the opinions in South Carolina v. Katzenbach and Flast v. Cohen as examples of that Court's misunderstanding of the dualism of constitutional limitations on congressional power. He notes with approval the Douglas opinion in Doe v. McMillan as indicative of Douglas's growing appreciation of this dualism.

Despite the Darby assertion that the Tenth Amendment is but a truism and despite the Court's tendency to ignore the basic constitutional principle that Congress does not possess a power unless that power is given to it by the Constitution, Strong insists that the Tenth Amendment is not without significance as a limitation on national power.

Taylor, Telford. GRAND INQUEST: THE STORY OF CONGRESSIONAL INVESTIGATIONS. New York: Simon and Schuster, 1955. Reprint. New York: Da Capo Press, 1974.

This is a study of the origins and growth of congressional investigatory authority from the investigation of St. Clair's defeat in 1781 to the House Un-American Activities Committee investigations in the 1950s. Designed for the general reader, this work deals with such problems as the relationships between the investigatory powers and the separation of power doctrine and the conflicts between the legislative investigatory process and individual rights.

Tiedeman, Christopher G. LIMITATIONS ON POLICE POWER. St. Louis: F.H. Thomas, 1886.

This systematic exposition of laissez-faire conservatism is one of the late nineteenth century scholarly works that is assumed to have had some influence upon judicial development of constitutional restraints upon the states' power to regulate in the socioeconomic order.

Tompkins, Dorothy. CHANGES IN CONGRESS: PROPOSALS TO CHANGE CONGRESS, TERMS OF MEMBERS OF THE HOUSE: A BIBLIOGRAPHY. Berkeley: Institute of Governmental Studies, University of California, 1966.

This is a bibliography of about two hundred books, articles and documents relating to recommended changes in congressional structure, organization, and procedures since the 1946 Reorganization Act.

_____. CONGRESSIONAL INVESTIGATIONS OF LOBBYING: A SELECTED BIBLIOGRAPHY. Berkeley: Bureau of Public Administration, University of California, 1956.

This is a bibliography of works dealing with congressional inquiries concerning lobbying.

_____. INVESTIGATING PROCEDURES OF CONGRESSIONAL COMMITTEES: A BIBLIOGRAPHY. Berkeley: Bureau of Public Administration, University of California, 1954.

This is a bibliography of works dealing with the procedures employed by congressional committees undertaking investigations.

U.S. Congress. CONGRESSIONAL RECORD. Washington, D.C.: Government Printing Office, 1873-- . Daily.

This is a record of the delegates and proceedings on the floor of each house, messages to Congress, and the votes taken, published daily while Congress is in session. Members may edit their remarks as well as insert remarks not actually made on the floor. Biweekly indexes are published during each session and cumulative indexes are published each year. It also contains a section on the history of each bill arranged by the Bill Number.

_____. THE DEBATES AND PROCEEDINGS OF THE CONGRESS OF THE UNITED STATES WITH AN APPENDIX CONTAINING IMPORTANT STATE PAPERS AND PUBLIC DOCUMENTS AND ALL THE LAWS OF A PUBLIC NATURE, WITH A COPIOUS INDEX. Washington, D.C.: Gales and Seaton, 1834–55.

This record of congressional proceedings, commonly referred to as the ANNALS, covers the first through the sixteenth congresses.

_____. HEARINGS.

Verbatim report of the testimony taken in public hearings by the standing and select committees in both houses. Particular hearings may be located by consulting the following indexes:

U.S. Congress. Senate. Library. CUMULATIVE INDEX OF CONGRESSIONAL COMMITTEE HEARINGS (NOT CONFIDEN-TIAL IN CHARACTER) FROM THE 74TH CONGRESS (JAN. 3, 1935) THROUGH 85TH CONGRESS (JAN. 3, 1959) IN THE UNITED STATES SENATE LIBRARY. Washington, D.C.: Government Printing Office, 1959.

_____. INDEX OF CONGRESSIONAL COMMITTEE HEARINGS (NOT CONFIDENTIAL IN CHARACTER) PRIOR TO JAN. 3, 1935, IN THE UNITED STATES SENATE LIBRARY. Washing-ton, D.C.: Government Printing Office, 1935. Reprint. New York: Kraus, 1969.

_____. QUADRENNIAL SUPPLEMENT TO THE CUMULATIVE INDEX OF CONGRESSIONAL COMMITTEE HEARINGS (NOT CONFIDENTIAL IN CHARACTER) FROM THE 86TH CONGRESS (JAN. 7, 1959) THROUGH THE 87TH CONGRESS (JAN. 3, 1963) TOGETHER WITH SELECTED COMMITTEE PRINTS IN THE UNITED STATES SENATE LIBRARY. Washington, D.C.: 1963.

U.S. Congress. House of Representatives. Library. INDEX TO CONGRESSIONAL COMMITTEE HEARINGS IN THE LIBRARY OF THE UNITED STATES HOUSE OF REPRESENTATIVES PRIOR TO JAN. 1, 1951. Washington, D.C.: Government Printing Office, 1954.

_____. SUPPLEMENTAL INDEX TO CONGRESSIONAL COM-MITTEE HEARINGS, JAN. 3, 1949 TO JAN. 3, 1955; 81st, 82ND, AND 83RD CONGRESS, IN THE LIBRARY OF THE UNITED STATES HOUSE OF REPRESENTATIVES. Washington, D.C.: 1956.

The hearings are indexed by subject, by committee, and by bill number. Prior to 1909, hearings are indexed in the CHECK-LIST. The hearings since 1869, on microfiche, along with indexes and shelflists are also published by Greenwood Press, Westport, Connecticut. UNITED STATES CONGRESSIONAL HEARINGS: HOUSE, SENATE, JOINT, SELECTS AND SOCIAL COMMITTEE HEARINGS. Greenwood Press, Westport, Conn., 1967-71.

U.S. Congress. Senate. PUBLIC DOCUMENTS OF THE FIRST FOUR-TEEN CONGRESSES, 1789-1817: PAPERS RELATING TO EARLY CON-GRESSIONAL DOCUMENTS. Washington, D.C.: Government Printing Office, 1900.

This is a chronological arrangement of public documents which lists and describes the publications and notes the library location of each. A supplement was published in volume 1 of the ANNUAL REPORT of the American Historical Association.

U.S. Congress. Senate. Library. SENATE ELECTION, EXPULSION AND CENSURE CASES FROM 1793 TO 1972. Compiled by R.D. Hupman under the direction of Francis R. Valeo for the Subcommittee on Privileges and Elections of the Committee on Rules and Administration. Rev. ed. 92d Cong., 1st sess., Senate Document 72-7. Washington D.C.: Government Printing Office, 1972.

This revision of Senate Document number 71 of the 87th Congress is a study of all the Senate cases concerning elections, expulsions, and censure.

UNITED STATES CONGRESSIONAL COMMITTEE PRINTS. FROM THE FIRST ISSUES THROUGH 1969. PHASE I: 61ST-91ST CONGRESS IN THE UNITED STATES LIBRARY. Westport, Conn.: Greenwood Press, 1976. Microfiche.

Committee prints are reports by congressional committee staffs to the committee concerning matters which the committees are considering. They are unofficial working papers rather than official government documents. They are therefore not readily available nor are they listed along with official documents in such publications as the MONTHLY CATALOG. This microfiche collection assembles these studies. Greenwood Press also publishes a bibliography and index to the committee prints.

UNITED STATES CONGRESSIONAL HEARINGS: HOUSE, SENATE, JOINT, SELECT, AND SPECIAL COMMITTEE HEARINGS. Westport, Conn.: Greenwood Press, 1967-71. Microfiche.

Congressional hearings from 1869 to 1969 are produced on microfiche along with indexes and shelflists.

Wallace, Robert A. CONGRESSIONAL CONTROL OF FEDERAL SPENDING. Detroit: Wayne State University Press, 1960.

Although Congress is given the constitutional power to spend, it has been dependent upon the executive branch in this as in other areas requiring centralized leadership. Written before congressional reform of its taxing and spending procedures in the 1970s, reforms designed to furnish Congress with the means of reasserting its control of spending, this detailed guide through the maze of appropriations procedures by a former assistant to Sen. Paul Douglas is concerned not with the political or constitutional power of Congress but with techniques for congressional control of the appropriations function. It furnishes clues to congressional motivation for abdication of its constitutional role in spending.

Watson, H. Lee. "Congress Steps Out: A Look at Congressional Control of the Executive." CALIFORNIA LAW REVIEW 63 (July 1975): 983-1094.

This is an extensive analysis of the constitutional propriety of various extralegislative procedures by which Congress, its committees and/or its individual members exercise control over the executive branch after legislation has been passed. The author traces the development and increasing use since World War II of such techniques as the committee veto, by which the administration can exercise statutorily conferred power only with the approval of one or more committees, and the procedure of authorizing Congress by single or concurrent resolution to approve or disapprove statutorily conferred exercises of administrative power. He concludes that legislative control achieved by actions outside the constitutionally specified legislative process is potentially incompatible with the intention of the framers and should be limited. He argues that the committee veto is invalid per se and that the use of the single or concurrent resolution device in substantive categories other than presidential reorganization and control of nonstatutory administrative actions is invalid.

Weaver, Warren, Jr. BOTH YOUR HOUSES: THE TRUTH ABOUT CONGRESS. New York: Praeger Publishers, 1972.

Designed for the popular audience, this work examines the "most flagrant inadequacies" of Congress and the governmental crisis produced by these shortcomings.

Weeks, Kent M. ADAM CLAYTON POWELL AND THE SUPREME COURT. New York: Dunellen Publishing Co., 1971.

This is a study of the legal and political conflicts involved in Powell v. McCormack and of the Court's opinion in that case as well as congressional reaction to it.

Willoughby, William F. PRINCIPLES OF LEGISLATIVE ORGANIZATION AND ADMINISTRATION. Washington, D.C.: Brookings Institution, 1934.

This massive study of Congress examines at length its organization and procedure, its composition, its relations with the executive and judicial branches, and the various functions, such as legislative and electoral, it performs.

Wilmerding, Lucius. THE SPENDING POWER: A HISTORY OF THE EFFORTS OF CONGRESS TO CONTROL EXPENDITURES. New Haven, Conn.: Yale University Press, 1941.

This is an analysis of the means by which Congress attempts
to control expenditures after the money has been appropriated
and the ineffectiveness of such attempts to oversee the executive
branch.

Wilson, Woodrow. CONGRESSIONAL GOVERNMENT. Boston: Houghton
Mifflin Co., 1885.

This is a classic analysis of the nineteenth-century congressional
domination of the executive branch. There are a number of
editions of this work.

Wood, Stephen B. CONSTITUTIONAL POLITICS IN THE PROGRESSIVE
ERA: CHILD LABOR AND THE LAW. Chicago: University of Chicago
Press, 1968.

This is an analysis, within the framework of the conflict between
popular sovereignty and judicial supervision, of the early unsuccessful congressional attempts to regulate child labor first by
relying upon the commerce clause and then upon the taxing clause,
the first invalidated in Hammer v. Dagenhart and the second in
Bailey v. Drexel Furniture. The author traces the rise of the
child labor reform movement in the progressive era, the political
success in obtaining congressional enactment of such a law,
judicial invalidation of the law, the response to this invalidation,
the passage of a second piece of legislation, and judicial invalidation of this second attempt.

Wright, Benjamin F. CONTRACT CLAUSE OF THE CONSTITUTION. Cambridge, Mass.: Harvard University Press, 1938.

The contract clause was the major constitutional limitation upon
the power of the state until the late nineteenth and early twentieth century. Judicial construction of the due process clause
of the Fourteenth Amendment replaced the contract clause as the
chief means of constitutional control of the police power of the
state. This work is an analysis of the role and decline of the
contract clause as a restraint upon the power of the state.

Chapter 7

ARTICLE II: THE PRESIDENT, VICE-PRESIDENT,

AND THE EXECUTIVE BRANCH

Annual Chief Justice Earl Warren Conference on Advocacy in the United
States of America. FINAL REPORT: THE POWERS OF THE PRESIDENCY.
Cambridge, Mass.: Roscoe Pound–American Trial Lawyers Foundation, 1975.

> This final report of the June 1975 conference includes twenty-
> eight recommendations concerning the president's war powers,
> his powers in foreign affairs and his powers in domestic affairs.
> It also includes three background papers on these subjects:
> Raoul Berger, "Presidential War Powers," Louis Henkin, "Presi-
> dential Powers in Foreign Affairs," and Philip B. Kurland,
> "Toward a Responsible American Presidency." The appendix
> includes such materials as the 1975 Senate bill entitled "Water-
> gate Reorganization and Reform Act" and the 1973 "War Powers
> Resolution."

Bayh, Birch. ONE HEARTBEAT AWAY: PRESIDENTIAL DISABILITY
AND SUCCESSION. Preface by Dwight D. Eisenhower. Foreword by
Lyndon Johnson. Indianapolis: Bobbs-Merrill, 1968.

> This work by the principal force behind and author of the Twenty-
> Fifth Amendment documents the near crisis produced by the lack
> of a regularized procedure for coping with presidential disability.
> It traces the course of the amendment from its initiation in com-
> mittee to its ratification by Minnesota and Nevada on 10 February
> 1966 and the formal signing of the proclamation by President
> Johnson and the GSA administrator on 23 February 1966.

Benedict, Michael L. THE IMPEACHMENT AND TRIAL OF ANDREW JOHN-
SON. New York: W.W. Norton, 1973.

> This analysis of the events leading to the impeachment of John-
> son and of the votes in the House and Senate leads the author
> to the conclusion that it was not primarily the radical Republi-
> cans and a minority who sought to remove the president because
> of the latter's reconstruction policy but that the dissatisfaction
> with the president was widespread and deeply felt among members
> of both houses. He argues that the grounds for impeachment
> are not limited to criminal acts and that congressional postwar
> policy was advanced, not retarded, by the removal attempt.

Berger, Raoul. "Congressional Subpoenas to Executive Officials." COLUM-
BIA LAW REVIEW 75 (June 1975): 865-96.

> In this examination of the authority of Congress to issue sub-
> poenas to the president and to his subordinates and of the autho-

rity of the courts to enforce such subpoenas, Berger deals with some of the questions he believes the Court of Appeals (in Senate Select Committee v. Nixon in 1974) avoided when it rejected the Committee's request for judicial enforcement of its demand for tapes of White House conversations. Concerned about the "presumptively privileged" status of presidential communications, adopted by the Supreme Court in U.S. v. Nixon, Berger argues that Congress has the authority to issue such subpoenas and to enforce such subpoenas (by arrest of the offending party, by suits initiated by the involved committee, and by contempt citations).

_____. EXECUTIVE PRIVILEGE: A CONSTITUTIONAL MYTH. Cambridge, Mass.: Harvard University Press, 1974.

Since the administration of George Washington, presidents have asserted the authority to withhold from the other branches confidential communications within the executive branch. In United States v. Nixon, the Supreme Court dealt with this issue of executive privilege and held it to be a constitutional doctrine. In this study of the doctrine, Berger concludes that it is without historical foundation.

_____. "The Presidential Monopoly of Foreign Relations." MICHIGAN LAW REVIEW 71 (November 1972): 1-58.

In this examination of presidential power in foreign affairs, Berger focuses upon executive agreements and the question of whether the Senate may constitutionally be excluded from knowledge of and participation in negotiations with foreign nations. He examines and rejects various arguments in support of presidential "monopoly" in international affairs and concludes that neither executive agreements nor presidential monopoly of negotiations with foreign governments is warranted by the text of the Constitution and that the Constitution requires senatorial participation.

_____. "War-Making by the President." UNIVERSITY OF PENNSYLVANIA LAW REVIEW 121 (November 1972): 29-86.

In this attack upon the constitutionality of unilateral presidential action in Vietnam, Berger argues that virtually all war-making power belongs to Congress. Taking the position that the "cardinal index of constitutionality is the Constitution itself" rather than what has been said about it or what actions past presidents have taken, he insists that the framers of the Constitution intended the president's authority to use armed forces to be limited to repelling sudden attacks and concludes that congressional legislation so limiting presidential power is constitutionally unassailable.

Best, Judith. THE CASE AGAINST DIRECT ELECTION OF THE PRESIDENT: A DEFENSE OF THE ELECTORAL COLLEGE. Ithaca, N.Y.: Cornell University Press, 1971.

With the apparent increase in support for a constitutional amendment to abolish the electoral college, this study is a reminder
of the moderating and unifying influence of the presidential selection technique devised in 1789: reinforcement of the two-
party system, protection of minority influence and minimization
of factionalism. Best examines and rejects the major arguments
against the electoral college and in favor of direct election of
the president, such arguments as the possibility of a runnerup
president, of faithless electors and the inequality of individual
votes. She argues that the present system is both a known
quantity and meets all the requirements of a democratic and
American electoral process: it produces a definite and accepted
winner with no uncertainty, it preserves the prestige, power and
potential for leadership, it supports a nonideological two-party
system, it preserves federalism and it provides effective representation and political equality.

Binkley, Wilfred E. THE POWERS OF THE PRESIDENT: PROBLEMS OF
AMERICAN DEMOCRACY. Garden City, N.Y.: Doubleday, Dorans Co.,
1937.

This is an examination of the constitutional and political relationship between the president and Congress from the Philadelphia
convention to the first administration of Franklin D. Roosevelt.
It discusses the manner in which the constitutional convention
dealt with the problem, the varying solutions of the Federalist
party, of the Jeffersonians and of Jackson, the ascendancy of
the executive branch under Jackson and Lincoln, the reaction
against the executive and the establishment of congressional
government after Lincoln's death, and the attempts to reestablish
executive leadership under McKinley, Wilson, and the two Roosevelts.

Blackman, John L., Jr. PRESIDENTIAL SEIZURE AND LABOR DISPUTES.
Cambridge, Mass.: Harvard University Press, 1967.

This is an examination of the seventy-one instances of presidential seizure and operation of industries as a means of coping
with labor-management disputes which threatened to cut off an
essential service or product. The appendix includes lists of
seizures, of federal laws authorizing seizures, of disputes
settled during governmental possession and of those not so
settled.

Boyd, Julian P. "The Expanding Treaty-Making Power." NORTH CAROLINA
LAW REVIEW 6 (June 1928): 428-53.

This examination of the role of federalism in the treaty-making
power and of Missouri v. Holland argues that even before this
decision it was constitutionally settled that Congress had the
constitutional power to enact legislation enforcing treaties even
if such legislation would be an unconstitutional infringement upon
the powers of the states in the absence of a treaty. Boyd
suggests that the proper limitations on subject matter of treaties
have been and should continue to be determined by the political
process rather than by constitutional theory. This article is reprinted in volume 3 of SELECTED ESSAYS ON CONSTITUTIONAL
LAW (see p. 79).

Breckenridge, Adam C. THE EXECUTIVE PRIVILEGE: PRESIDENTIAL CONROL OVER INFORMATION. Lincoln: University of Nebraska Press, 1974.

> Written before the Supreme Court's decision in U.S. v. Nixon, this is a study of the development and constitutional base of the doctrine of executive privilege, its invocation by various presidents since Washington to refuse to comply with demands for information by the other branches, the conflicts between coequal branches that have led to and resulted from its use, its necessity in protecting executive privacy and the need for control to prevent its abuse.

Brown, Stuart G. THE AMERICAN PRESIDENCY: LEADERSHIP, PARTISANSHIP AND POPULARITY. New York: Macmillan, 1966.

> In this study of the relationship between presidential popularity, partisanship and leadership, the author argues that in the twentieth century, popularity is increasingly important. Although, in the nineteenth century, the two Adamses and Hayes, for example, were moderately effective, though not popular, in the twentieth century, popularity is important in order to be effective. He further argues that popular unpartisan presidents have, for the most part, either been unable or unwilling to make use of their popularity as a means of leadership while partisan presidents, for the most part, have been both willing and able to use their popularity to achieve their goals; on a controversial, divisive issue, partisan popularity is especially necessary while on a less divisive issue partisanship is less important. Chapter 3 is an analysis of the relationship between presidential popularity and constitutional issues. It examines Washington's support of Hamilton's bank proposal which depended upon a loose construction of the Constitution although the president as a matter of principle preferred Jefferson's strict construction; Jefferson's purchase of Louisiana; Monroe's role in supporting internal improvements and the Missouri Compromise; Jackson's destruction of Clay's American system, of Biddle's bank, and of Calhoun's nullification movement, Eisenhower's role in Little Rock and civil rights, and Franklin Roosevelt's confrontation with the Supreme Court.

Burns, Edward McNall. JAMES MADISON: PHILOSOPHER OF THE CONSTITUTION. 1935. Reprint. New York: Octagon, 1968.

> This is an analysis of the political theories of Madison and the influence of these theories in the formation of the Constitution.

Burrill, Richard L. CONTROVERSY OVER THE PRESIDENTIAL ELECTORAL SYSTEM. San Francisco: R & E Research Associates, 1975.

> This analysis of the presidential selection process examines the manner in which the electoral college system works, the criticisms of the electoral college system, and the relationship between the selection method and the two-party system. It also looks at federalism and the effects of the electoral college system on small and large states, on urban and rural areas, and on minority groups and the chances of election of a "minority" president.

The appendix includes copies of various proposals to amend the
Constitution to prove an alternative method of selecting the president, such as the various direct election and proportional election
schemes.

Byrd, Elbert M. TREATIES AND EXECUTIVE AGREEMENTS IN THE
UNITED STATES: THEIR SEPARATE ROLE AND LIMITATIONS. Foreword by Elmer Plischke. The Hague: Nijhoff, 1960.

This study of the types of international agreements to which the
United States is a party examines the constitutional limitations
upon and the government agencies involved in each. Byrd argues
that there are four types of international agreements (treaties,
congressional-executive agreements, presidential agreements, and
state compacts with foreign governments), that the choice of which
is appropriate depends upon both constitutional and political considerations, and that the treaty-making agency is a separate
branch of the federal government (the president and two-thirds
of the Senate). The appendix includes the major constitutional
provisions relating to international affairs, relevant excerpts
from the FEDERALIST PAPERS, and treaty decisions of the
Supreme Court.

Corwin, Edward S. THE PRESIDENT: OFFICE AND POWERS, 1787-1948:
HISTORY AND ANALYSIS OF PRACTICE AND OPINION. 3d rev. ed.
New York: New York University Press, 1957.

In this historical and legal analysis of the constitutional powers
and status of the president, the author concludes that in the
historic struggle between the constitutional concept that the president should be subordinate to Congress and the theory that he
should be independent, the latter view prevailed to such an extent that the office became highly personalized and power con-
centrated. He argues that a new type of cabinet composed of
members with independent power bases might offset the dangers
stemming from concentration.

_____. THE PRESIDENT'S CONTROL OF FOREIGN RELATIONS. Prince-
ton, N.J.: Princeton University Press, 1917. Reprint. Ann Arbor, Mich.:
University Microfilms, 1972. Microfilm-xerography.

This analysis of the theory that control of foreign affairs is in
nature an executive function which belongs to the president begins
with an examination of the debate carried on in Philadelphia newspapers between Hamilton, writing as "Pacificus," and Madison,
writing as "Helvidius," over the power of the president in the
diplomatic field, a debate prompted by Washington's Proclamation
of Neutrality. The work is primarily a historical study of the
president's constitutional power of recognition, of making treaties
and executive agreements, and of his war-making powers.

_____. "The Steel Seizure Case: A Judicial Brick Without Straw."
COLUMBIA LAW REVIEW 53 (January 1953): 53-66.

In this brief criticism of the various opinions in Youngstown v. Sawyer, Corwin concludes that congressional legislation that is comprehensive enough to apply to a variety of labor disputes and explicit enough to prevent presidential abuse is needed. The article is reprinted in Robert G. McCloskey's ESSAYS IN CON-STITUTIONAL LAW (see p. 83).

_____. "Tenure of Office and the Removal Power Under the Constitution." COLUMBIA LAW REVIEW 27 (April 1927): 353-404.

Written before the Humphrey case, this is an analysis of Myers v. United States which Corwin views not only as a "menacing challenge" to administrative organization but as "a positive in-stigation of strife between the President and the Congress." He criticizes Taft's reasoning and, on the basis of his analysis of the debates at the Philadelphia convention and at the first Congress, sets forth an alternative and more limited interpre-tation of the president's removal powers. This article is re-printed in volume 4 of SELECTED ESSAYS ON CONSTITUTIONAL LAW (see p. 79) under the title "The President's Removal Power Under the Constitution." It was also reprinted by the National League under this title in 1927.

Corwin, Edward S., and Koenig, Louis W. THE PRESIDENCY TODAY. New York: New York University Press, 1956.

Because the Second World War and postwar era demonstrated that "crisis and especially international crisis, has become a constant factor in national existence" and because "reliance on intermittent recourse to presidential dictatorship is no longer the answer," the authors of this short volume suggest that methods be devised for establishing closer working relations between Congress and the president so that legislative power can be more speedily available to respond to crises and to minimize presidential lawmaking. The second problem addressed is that of presidential disability.

Cowles, Willard B. TREATIES AND CONSTITUTIONAL LAW: PROPERTY INTERFERENCES AND DUE PROCESS OF LAW. Washington, D.C.: Ameri-can Council on Public Affairs, 1941.

This is an extensive analysis of judicial decisions involving treaties with a view toward determining whether the due process and just compensation clauses of the Fifth Amendment limit the domestic or internal application of treaties.

Cummings, Homer, and McFarland, Carl. FEDERAL JUSTICE: CHAPTERS IN THE HISTORY OF JUSTICE AND THE FEDERAL EXECUTIVE. New York: Macmillan, 1937.

Prompted by and a byproduct of the effort by Attorney General Cummings to collect and classify the papers, correspondence, and official documents of attorneys general since the Washington administration and of the Justice Department since its creation in 1870, this is a study of the role of attorneys general from Ed-mund Randolph and of the department from its establishment in issuing advisory opinions, in making decisions about prosecutions, in supervising investigations, in bringing suit in the name of the United States and its role in major Supreme Court decisions which affected public policy making up to the early 1930s.

Daniels, Walter M., comp. PRESIDENTIAL ELECTION REFORMS. New York: H.W. Wilson, 1953.

This collection of articles from a variety of popular periodicals deals with various facets of the presidential election process such as the development and structure of the political party system, nominations, campaigns and elections and the arguments for and against direct election of the president. The appendix includes the texts of various proposals introduced in Congress to alter the electoral college system.

Deutsch, Eberhard P. "The President as Commander in Chief." AMERICAN BAR ASSOCIATION JOURNAL 57 (January 1971): 27-32.

This brief article is a defense of the constitutionality of presidential war making. Deutsch argues that as commander in chief, the president has full power to conduct military operations during a war, whether declared or undeclared. Not only is the president constitutionally authorized to repel invasion, he is authorized to take military action in noninvasion situations and is not subject to a congressional order to remove troops.

_____. "The Treaty-Making Clause: A Decision for the People of America." AMERICAN BAR ASSOCIATION JOURNAL 37 (September 1951): 659-62; 712-14.

Deutsch argues that American participation in international human rights agreements could threaten the domestic protections of the Bill of Rights. Because the rights guaranteeed by such agreements fall short of constitutional guarantees and because treaties are self-executing and supreme, they may abridge constitutional rights.

Dewitt, David M. THE IMPEACHMENT TRIAL OF ANDREW JOHNSON, SEVENTEENTH PRESIDENT OF THE U.S.: A HISTORY. New York: Macmillan, 1903.

Viewing the conflict between Johnson and Congress over the Tenure of Office and the Reconstruction Acts as rooted in the latter's goal of "stripping the executive of its prerogative and the subjugation of the South," the author traces the conflict from the convening of the 39th Congress through the failure of the first impeachment attempt, the reinstatement of Stanton, and the impeachment to the acquittal of Johnson.

DIRECT ELECTION OF THE PRESIDENT. Washington, D.C.: American Enterprise Institute for Public Policy Research, 1977.

This brief monograph describes the historical development and operation of the present system by which the president is selected, mechanics of direct election in the most recently proposed constitutional amendment (S J Res. 1, H J Res. 138 and H R Res. 144) and the criticism of direct election.

Elliff, John T. CRIME, DISSENT AND THE ATTORNEY GENERAL: THE JUSTICE DEPARTMENT IN THE 1960S. Sage Series on Politics and the Legal Order. Beverly Hills, Calif.: Sage Publications, 1971.

> This is a study of the forces that determine Justice Department policy. It examines three areas of policy making in the 1960s—criminal justice, black militancy, and antiwar dissent—and the judicial, presidential and congressional decisions and actions in these areas that contributed to the nationalization of the criminal justice system and the centralization of law enforcement policy making.

Ellis, Richard E. THE JEFFERSONIAN CRISIS: COURTS AND POLITICS IN THE YOUNG REPUBLIC. New York: Oxford University Press, 1971.

> Viewing the judiciary issue "with its corresponding implications for constitutional change" as "the overriding domestic issue of Jefferson's first term" and "the issue around which the meaning of the 'revolution of 1800' was to be defined," this "revisionist" history argues that settlement of the unresolved dispute over the nature of the federal and state judicial systems was a result of a victory by the "moderates" of both the Republican and Federalist parties over the radical elements in both parties rather than a partisan triumph.

Feerick, John D. FROM FALLING HANDS: THE STORY OF PRESIDENTIAL SUCCESSION. Foreword by Paul A. Freund. New York: Fordham University Press, 1965.

> This is an account of the vice-presidency from John Adams to Lyndon Johnson by a member of a special committee of the American Bar Association created to consider the problems of presidential disability and succession. Because the basic recommendations of that committee were in large measure those embodied in the Twenty-Fifth Amendment, this analysis of the proposed solution sheds light on the intentions of that Amendment.

Fields, Howard. HIGH CRIMES AND MISDEMEANORS. New York: W.W. Norton, 1978.

> This is an account of the Nixon impeachment proceedings in the House Judiciary Committee.

Fisher, Louis. "Delegating Power to the President." JOURNAL OF PUBLIC LAW 19 (May 1973): 251-82.

> This is an explanation of why Congress delegates power to the president and an identification of the safeguards that prevent delegation from becoming abdication. Fisher suggests that the reasons for delegation (continuity in office, flexibility in timing, channel for foreign communication, speed in national emergencies, national symbol of unity) are relative; that is, it is not so much that the president has these qualities as it is that Congress lacks them. The safeguards he identifies (guidelines for policy, procedural requirements and oversight) are backed by congressional ability to take back that which it has given.

Fleming, William. "Danger to America: The Draft Covenant on Human Rights." AMERICAN BAR ASSOCIATION JOURNAL 37 (September–November 1951): 739–42; 794–99; 816–20; 855–60.

> The first part of this article emphasizes the dangers to economic, social, and cultural rights posed by the United Nations Human Rights Covenant. The second part focuses upon the civil and political provisions of the covenant and the threat of these provisions to these rights as protected by the American Constitution.

Friedman, Leon, and Neuborne, Burt. UNQUESTIONING OBEDIENCE TO THE PRESIDENT: THE ACLU CASE AGAINST THE LEGALITY OF THE WAR IN VIETNAM. Introduction by Sen. George McGovern. New York: W.W. Norton, 1972.

> This is a collection and analysis of the legal documents--briefs, oral arguments and judicial opinions of the district courts, the Courts of Appeal and the Supreme Court--in two separate cases brought by the American Civil Liberties Union in the name of Salvatore Orlando and Malcolm Beck challenging the constitutionality of the Vietnam War. The basic ACLU argument was that the president has no constitutional authority to initiate and prosecute a war independent of Congress, that the war in Vietnam was a presidential war and therefore a presidential usurpation of congressional power.

Frohnmayer, David B., and Stanton, Ellen M. ESSAYS ON EXECUTIVE PRIVILEGE. Chicago: American Bar Foundation, 1974.

> This work consists of two essays dealing with the question of the extent of congressional authority to obtain information from the executive branch and the question of the authority of the judiciary to enter the area of executive privilege. The authors were winners of the American Bar Foundation's 1973–74 essay competition.

Goldsmith, William M., ed. THE GROWTH OF PRESIDENTIAL POWER: A DOCUMENTED HISTORY. 3 vols. New York: Chelsea House Publishers, in association with R.R. Bowker, 1974.

> This is a collection of over one hundred documents dealing with the evolution of the presidency from the constitutional convention to the present.

Grundstein, Nathan. PRESIDENTIAL DELEGATION OF AUTHORITY IN WARTIME. Pittsburgh: University of Pittsburgh Press, 1961.

> In contrast to the more familiar constitutional problem of delegation of congressional authority to the president, this work deals with the question of subdelegation, that is, the delegation by the president to his subordinates of the extensive powers delegated to him by the Congress in times of war. The author examines the legacy of World War I and judicial decisions prior to the Second World War but focuses primarily on the subdelegation problems of the second war. The work was originally published as three articles in the GEORGE WASHINGTON LAW REVIEW, April 1947 and April and June 1948, volumes 15 and 16.

Article II

Haight, David E., and Johnston, Larry D., eds. THE PRESIDENT: ROLES AND POWERS. Chicago: Rand McNally, 1965.

> This book of readings contains brief excerpts from the views of a variety of presidents, scholars, politicians and political thinkers on such matters as the origin of the office of the president, the selection of the president and vice-president, presidential succession, the president's role as chief executive, chief administrator, chief legislator and commander in chief and his relationships with Congress, the public and his advisors.

Hardin, Charles M. PRESIDENTIAL POWER AND ACCOUNTABILITY: TOWARD A NEW CONSTITUTION. Chicago: University of Chicago Press, 1974.

> Although written in reaction to the Watergate era, the author views the "ills of 1973" not as isolated phenomena stemming from one administration's abuse of power but as "symptoms of deep, structural faults in the American Constitution and its operational theory." To remedy the wrongs of the system, this work advocates constitutional changes which would establish essentially a parliamentary form of government in which a cohesive opposition would play the role of watchdog and critic, a role that can be effectively filled neither by the sovereign people nor any other entity under the present constitutional system.

Harvey, James C. BLACK CIVIL RIGHTS DURING THE JOHNSON ADMINISTRATION. Jackson: University and College Press of Mississippi, 1973.

> This sequel to CIVIL RIGHTS DURING THE KENNEDY ADMINISTRATION describes the civil rights advances between 1963 and 1969 and the efforts of the Johnson administration to use national power to ameliorate the problems facing blacks. It analyzes the Civil Rights Act of 1964, the Voting Rights Act of 1965, the Civil Rights Act of 1968, and national action in the areas of housing, employment, voting, education, and health and welfare services.

Henkin, Louis. "The Constitution, Treaties and Human Rights." UNIVERSITY OF PENNSYLVANIA LAW REVIEW 116 (April 1968): 1012-32.

> This is a brief examination and rejection of the argument, used by opponents of American participation in international conventions on human rights, that the Constitution forbids involvements in such covenants. In rejecting the validity of the argument that the Constitution forbids the use of the treaty power for such purposes because the human rights of Americans are essentially a matter of domestic rather than international concern, Henkin examines the broad construction of the treaty-making power by the Court and concludes that the Constitution is no bar to such agreements. He suggests that the decision to enter such agreements must therefore be made on nonconstitutional grounds.

Hirschfield, Robert S., ed. THE POWER OF THE PRESIDENCY: CONCEPTS AND CONTROVERSY. New York: Atherton Press, 1968. Reprint. Chicago: Aldine, 1973.

This collection consists of excerpts from a variety of sources on the powers of the president ranging from Patrick Henry and the FEDERALIST PAPERS to presidential speeches and scholarly analyses. It includes such materials as the debates of "Pacificus" (Hamilton) and "Helvidius" (Madison) over Washington's Proclamation of Neutrality, Jackson's nullification speech, Lincoln's first inaugural address and his message to Congress on the war with the South, the writings and speeches of presidents from Theodore Roosevelt to Lyndon Johnson, Supreme Court decisions and works of Edward S. Corwin, Clinton Roositer and Richard Neustadt.

Holman, Frank E. "Treaty Law-Making: A Blank Check for Writing a New Constitution." AMERICAN BAR ASSOCIATION JOURNAL 36 (September 1950): 707-11, 787-90.

Holman argues that ratification of the United National Covenant on Human Rights would change domestic law and would transform the United States into a Socialist state. Because treaties are the supreme law of the land as specified in Article VI and because Missouri v. Holland removed limitations on the treaty-making power, even the Constitution could be amended by treaty in his view.

Humbert, Willard H. THE PARDONING POWER OF THE PRESIDENT. Washington, D.C.: American Council on Public Affairs, 1941.

This is an examination of the theory and practice of the pardoning power from the colonial period through the late 1930s. Major attention is given to the discussions of the power at the Philadelphia convention and to the constitutional and legal aspects of the power as interpreted by the judiciary. There is also an account of the procedures employed by the executive branch in using the power.

Israel, Fred L., ed. THE STATE OF THE UNION MESSAGES OF THE PRESIDENTS. Introduction by Arthur M. Schlesinger, Jr. 3 vols. New York: Chelsea House Publishers in association with R.R. Bowker, 1967.

Volume 1 includes the state of the union addresses from 1790-1860, volume 2 covers 1861-1904 and volume 3 covers the period from 1905-1966.

Jackson, Carlton. PRESIDENTIAL VETOES, 1792-1945. Athens: University of Georgia Press, 1967.

This is an examination of the veto power as a positive as well as a flexible instrument for presidential participation in the legislative process. The author traces the presidential use of the veto from Washington through Franklin D. Roosevelt's last term and concludes that the veto power has been positive because it has been used not just to kill legislation or to force a two-thirds vote but to force Congress to change a bill, thus giving the president a positive and powerful legislative role. In addition, the author suggests that the veto power is a flexible instrument because it makes compromise between the two branches possible. His study reveals that only Jackson and Andrew Johnson (and on occasion Franklin D. Roosevelt) failed to use the veto as a compromising agent.

Article II

Jenkins, Gerald L. "The War Powers Resolution: Statutory Limitations on the Commander-in-Chief." HARVARD JOURNAL ON LEGISLATION 11 (February 1974): 181-204.

This comment is an explanation of the factors which led Congress to pass the War Powers Resolution in 1973, asserting its power in war making, and an examination of how and if that resolution will enable Congress to enlarge its role in initiating and conducting war.

Johnsen, Julia A., comp. DIRECT ELECTION OF THE PRESIDENT. New York: H.W. Wilson, 1949.

This is a collection of brief selections from popular and scholarly periodicals which discuss the various proposals made in the 1940s to change the electoral college system, proposals ranging from abolition of the electoral college and institution of direct election to retaining the electoral votes and abolishing electors. Some of the selections advocate reform and some criticize the proposed reforms.

Kallenbach, Joseph E. THE AMERICAN CHIEF EXECUTIVE: THE PRESIDENCY AND THE GOVERNORSHIP. New York: Harper and Row, 1966.

Although this work deals with both the president and governors, it is principally a historical, institutional and functional analysis of the presidency.

_____. "The Presidency and the Constitution: A Look Ahead." LAW AND CONTEMPORARY PROBLEMS 35 (Summer 1970): 445-60.

Noting that five of the fifteen amendments added since the Bill of Rights (12th, 20th, 22nd, and 25th) changed structural aspects of the office of the presidency and that three others (15th, 19th, and 24th) further affected the presidency by broadening its popular base, Kallenbach assesses, within the framework of the built-in conflicts between the various roles played by the president, the prospects for a constitutional amendment changing the electoral college system.

Kurland, Philip B. WATERGATE AND THE CONSTITUTION. Chicago: University of Chicago Press, 1978.

In this examination of the constitutional issues raised by Watergate, Kurland suggests that the basic problem stemmed from the concentration of power in presidential hands and that a more balanced distribution of power between legislative and executive branches would tend to minimize constitutional abuse.

Learned, Henry B. THE PRESIDENT'S CABINET: STUDIES IN THE ORIGIN, FORMATION, AND STRUCTURE OF AN AMERICAN INSTITUTION. New Haven, Conn.: Yale University Press, 1912. Reprint. New York: Burt Franklin, 1972.

A study of the historical development of the cabinet from its English antecedents through congressional establishment in 1789

of the Departments of State, Treasury, War, and Justice and the
presidential use of the heads of these departments as an advisory
body to subsequent creation of additional departments and presidential use of the cabinet until the early twentieth century.

Lofgren, Charles A. "War-Making Under the Constitution: The Original
Understanding." YALE LAW JOURNAL 81 (March 1972): 672-702.

This article deals in general with the question of how Americans
in 1787-88 understood the war-making clause and in particular
with the question of the original understanding of the allocation
of war-making power and whether that power included undeclared
wars. Noting that the debate over the constitutional meaning of
the war-making power began with Hamilton's defense of the constitutionality of Washington's Neutrality Proclamation and that
undeclared war was not unknown in fact or in theory in the
eighteenth century, Lofgren argues that to "declare" war in the
Constitution meant to "commence" war, whether declared or undeclared. He concludes that while the early Congresses were
understood to have at least a coordinate and probably a dominant
role, the president became dominant and that the Vietnam War re-
newed debate on the question of the legitimate role of the president.

Lomask, Milton. ANDREW JACKSON: PRESIDENT ON TRIAL. New
York: Farrar, Strauss, 1960.

Designed for the general reader, this popular work looks at
the crises of the Reconstruction era, including the impeachment
and trial of Johnson, largely by examining the action of the major
public figures caught up in the controversy between the president
and the Congress.

Longley, Lawrence D., and Braun, Alan G. THE POLITICS OF ELECTORAL
COLLEGE REFORM. Foreword by Sen. Birch Bayh. New Haven, Conn.:
Yale University Press, 1972.

This is an examination of the operation of the electoral college
system and of various proposed reforms advocating adoption of a
constitutional amendment providing for direct election of the president.

Lord, Clifford, ed. PRESIDENTIAL EXECUTIVE ORDERS. 2 vols. New
York: Hastings House, 1944.

Volume 1 lists the executive orders chronologically beginning
with 20 October 1862 and going through 29 December 1938.
Volume 2 is an index to executive orders alphabetized by topic
or subject of the order.

Loss, Richard, ed. PRESIDENTIAL POWER AND THE CONSTITUTION:
ESSAYS BY EDWARD S. CORWIN. Ithaca, N.Y.: Cornell University
Press, 1976.

With an introduction by the editor, this is a collection of twelve
of Corwin's essays on presidential power from Wilson to Truman.
Three of the essays focus on Wilson and presidential power during

World War I, four examine presidential power during the Roosevelt administration and World War II, two deal with the Truman
period and the Steel Seizure Case and the others examine the
problems surrounding the growth of presidential power after the
constitutional revolution of the 1930s.

Lurie, Leonard. THE IMPEACHMENT OF RICHARD NIXON. New York:
Berkeley Publishing Co., 1973.

Written prior to the resignation of President Nixon, this paperback designed for the general reader is a review of Watergate-
related activities and a call for the impeachment of the president.

McClure, Wallace M. INTERNATIONAL EXECUTIVE AGREEMENTS: DEMO-
CRATIC PROCEDURES UNDER THE CONSTITUTION OF THE UNITED
STATES. New York: Columbia University Press, 1941.

This examination of the executive agreement as a replacement for
treaties and for "minority control" (meaning the ability of one-
third of the Senate to defeat a treaty) and as a means of exercising democratic control in international affairs deals with the
use of both devices from 1776 to 1941. It examines various
constitutional issues such as the president's general powers in
international affairs as well as his power to enter into executive
agreements and the role of Congress, of the House and congressional negotiators. The appendix includes copies of some 1940
executive agreements and a list of Supreme Court decisions
dealing with executive agreements. The bibliography includes
citations to executive agreements.

McCormick, Richard P. THE SECOND AMERICAN PARTY SYSTEM: PARTY
FORMATION IN THE JACKSONIAN ERA. Chapel Hill: University of North
Carolina Press, 1966.

The "second party system" of the title refers to the party system
of the 1830s as distinct from that of the 1790s and of the 1850s.
In this state-by-state analysis of the revival of the party system,
the author argues that this second party system--which resulted in
a competitive two-party system in each state as well as in the nation as a whole--had its origins in the successive contests for the
presidency between 1824 and 1840 and was conditioned by the changing constitutional and legal environment of the era. Whereas in
1800 each state had operated under a different set of rules, by 1840
the rules had become relatively uniform nationally and this uniformity in electoral rules conditioned the new party system.

McCoy, Donald R., and Ruetten, Richard T. QUEST AND RESPONSE:
MINORITY RIGHTS AND THE TRUMAN ADMINISTRATION. Lawrence:
University Press of Kansas, 1974.

Although the civil rights accomplishments of the Truman administration are dwarfed when compared to national policy in the 1960s,
it was during that administration that minority rights began to
receive more than token national attention. This work examines
and assesses the advances in minority rights from 1945 to 1953.

McDougal, Myres, and Lans, Asher. "Treaties and Congressional-Executive or Presidential Agreements: Interchangeable Instruments of National Policy." YALE LAW JOURNAL 54 (March 1945): 181-351; (June 1945): 534-615.

Written in the 1940s at the height of the popularity of presidential leadership in foreign affairs, this lengthy analysis of executive agreements and of congressional-presidential agreements argues in support of the constitutionality of these alternatives to treaties. The authors conclude that the practices of successive adminis- trations, supported by Congress and by judicial decisions, have made these agreements interchangeable with treaties entered into with the advice and consent of two-thirds of the Senate.

Mason, Edward Campbell. THE VETO POWER: ITS ORIGIN, DEVELOP- MENT AND FUNCTION IN THE GOVERNMENT OF THE UNITED STATES, 1789-1889. Harvard Historical Monographs, no. 1. Boston: Ginn, 1890. Reprint. New York: Russell and Russell, 1967.

In this study of the development and operation of the veto power, Mason traces the origin of the power to the Teutonic tribes and to the legislative relationship between the king and Parliament, and its appearance in the colonies, in early state constitutions, in the Articles and in the Constitution. He focuses on the use of that power by American presidents through the administration of Grover Cleveland. Organized primarily upon the basis of the subject matter of vetoed legislation, this work examines those vetoes affecting the form of government (such as Washington's veto of a bill providing for the apportionment of the members of the House), those affecting the distribution of the powers of government (such as Jackson's veto of the bill rechartering the Second Bank of the United States and subsequent protest against the Senate resolution of censure of the president for removal of federal funds from that bank), and those affecting the exercise of powers by the government (such as vetoes of public land grant bills by several presidents). In addition, one chapter is devoted to constitutional procedures and questions (such as the constitu- tionality of a pocket veto, whether a bill may be vetoed without stating the reason and whether a president can refuse to carry out a congressional act) and one looks at political developments in the use of the veto power (such as the reasons given for vetoes, the effect of the veto on political parties and on legislation). The appendix includes such materials as a chronological list of all 433 bills vetoed from 6 April 1789 to 4 March 1889, together with a brief legislative history of each bill.

Matthews, Craig. "The Constitutional Power of the President to Conclude International Agreements." YALE LAW JOURNAL 64 (January 1955): 345- 89.

In this examination of the extent to which the Constitution confers independent power upon the president to conclude international agreements, the author bases his answers primarily on prior practice because of the paucity of case law. He concludes that the president has far-reaching leadership authority generally in dealing with foreign governments and specifically in entering into international agreements. He argues that although such congres- sional powers as those to raise armies and money may be used to check presidential foreign affairs power, the basic power belongs to the president.

Matthews, Donald R., ed. PERSPECTIVES ON PRESIDENTIAL SELECTION. Studies in Presidential Selection Series. Washington, D.C.: Brookings Institution, 1973.

This is a collection of seven essays, plus an introduction by the editor, selected as the best manuscripts submitted in a Brookings Institution open competition for original scholarly papers on the subject of presidential selection. The essays include "Presidential and Prime Ministerial Selection" by Hugo Heclo, "Party and Convention Organization and Leadership Selection in Canada and the United States" by Carl and Ellen Baar, "Selection of French Presidents" by Elijah Ben-Zion Kaminsky, "Theory of Presidential Nominations—1968 Illustrations" by James P. Zais and John H. Kessel, "Delegate Turnover at National Party Conventions, 1944–1968" by Lock K. Johnson and Harlan Halin, "Biases of the Electoral College: Who is Really Disadvantaged" by John H. Yunker and Lawrence D. Longley, and "Logic and Legitimacy: On Understanding the Electoral College Controversy" by Max S. Power.

May, Ernest R., ed. THE ULTIMATE DECISION: THE PRESIDENT AS COMMANDER-IN-CHIEF. New York: George Braziller, 1960.

These nine essays, including four by the editor, focus on the constitutional role of the president as commander-in-chief, the reasons why the framers conferred this power on the president, and the manner in which individual presidents have played this role. There are separate essays dealing with the exercise of the commander-in-chief power during time of war by Madison, Polk, Lincoln, McKinley, Wilson, Franklin D. Roosevelt, Truman, and Eisenhower. The authors, in addition to the editor, are Marcus Cunliffe, Leonard D. White, T. Harry Williams, William R. Emerson, and Wilbur W. Hoare, Jr.

Michener, James A. PRESIDENTIAL LOTTERY: THE RECKLESS GAMBLE IN OUR ELECTORAL SYSTEM. New York: Random House, 1969.

Designed for the general audience and written shortly after what the author views as the "narrow escape from chaos" in the election of 1968, this work urges revision of the electoral college system at least to allow the states to report their electoral votes directly rather than through the intermediary of electors and to prevent the selection of the president by the House of Representatives. An extensive appendix includes those constitutional provisions relevant to presidential selection (Article II, Amendments 12, 20, 22, 23 and 25); copies of proposed amendments to the Constitution (the automatic, district, proportional and direct popular vote plans) and the Banzhaf studies of the four plans.

Moore, John Norton. "Contemporary Issues in an Ongoing Debate: The Roles of Congress and the President in Foreign Affairs." INTERNATIONAL LAWYER 7 (October 1973): 733–45.

Written in a period of conflict between Congress and President Nixon precipitated by continuation of the Vietnam War and during the debate over the War Powers bills to limit presidential power, this article examines the historic confrontations between the two branches, the constitutional powers of each in international affairs in general and in the areas of war and international agreements in particular. Moore argues for congressional moderation in attempting to limit the president's role in foreign affairs and for reconciliation between the two branches.

Morris, Richard B., ed. GREAT PRESIDENTIAL DECISIONS: STATE PAPERS THAT CHANGED THE COURSE OF HISTORY FROM WASHINGTON TO NIXON. Rev. ed. New York: Harper's Torchbook, 1973.

This is a compilation of the texts of forty presidential documents--speeches, proclamations, messages to Congress--with a brief introduction to each by the editor.

Mugridge, Donald H. THE PRESIDENTS OF THE UNITED STATES. 1789-1962: A SELECTED LIST OF REFERENCES. Washington, D.C.: Library of Congress, General Reference and Bibliography Division, 1963.

This is an annotated bibliography of writings by and biographies of each president from Washington to Kennedy plus an introductory section devoted to works dealing with the presidency, presidential elections, and the vice-presidency. There are subject indexes to presidential elections, first ladies, vice-presidents, and an index of authors, editors, and titles.

Nikolaieff, George A., ed. THE PRESIDENT AND THE CONSTITUTION. New York: H.W. Wilson, 1974.

With introductory comments by the author, this is a collection of newspaper and magazine columns and commentaries published during the Watergate era by a variety of scholars and journalists dealing with Watergate, the growth of presidential power, executive privilege and impoundment, the demands for President Nixon's impeachment or resignation, the beginning of the impeachment process by the House Judiciary Committee and the events surrounding the resignation of President Nixon.

Peirce, Neal R. THE PEOPLE'S PRESIDENT: THE ELECTORAL COLLEGE IN AMERICAN HISTORY AND THE DIRECT VOTE ALTERNATIVE. Foreword by Tom Wicker. New York: Simon and Schuster, 1968.

This is a history of the electoral college and an analysis of the major constitutional, political and social considerations involved in changing the method of election of the president. The author urges abolition of the electoral college and adoption of a direct election system. Included in the appendix are such materials as a list comparing the popular and electoral vote percentages from 1824 to 1964 and elections in which minor shifts could have changed the election; copies of proposed constitutional amendments to change the method of presidential selection; a list of allocation of electoral votes under existing and alternative systems for each election from 1864 to 1964; the findings of Gallup polls on instituting the direct election system, and the results of computer analysis of large versus small state power in the electoral college.

Phelps, Edith M., comp. A SINGLE SIX YEAR TERM FOR PRESIDENT. New York: H.W. Wilson, 1925.

This slim volume contains brief selections from arguments in support of and in opposition to a single six year term along with bibliographies of works both in support of and in opposition to such a constitutional amendment.

Pittman, Benn. THE ASSASSINATION OF PRESIDENT LINCOLN AND THE TRIAL OF THE CONSPIRATORS. Introduction by Philip Van Doren Stern. 1954. Reprint. Westport, Conn.: Greenwood Press, 1974.

This is the original courtroom testimony of the trial of those charged with the assassination of Lincoln.

"Presidential Impoundment: Constitutional Theories and Political Realities." GEORGETOWN LAW JOURNAL 61 (May 1973): 1295-1325.

In 1972, Congress enacted the Federal Impoundment and Information Act requiring the president to notify it of impoundment and to furnish it with relevant information. Written in the period of the conflict between President Nixon and Congress which gave rise to this legislation, this article is an analysis of the historical and theoretical underpinnings of the impoundments debate. It attempts to delineate various understandings of impoundment, to identify the sources of presidential power to refuse to spend appropriated funds and the possible legislative and judicial reactions to the presidential use of this power.

"The Presidential Veto Power: A Shallow Pocket." MICHIGAN LAW REVIEW 70 (November 1971): 148-54.

This discussion of the pocket veto examines the question of whether presidential refusal to sign or to veto a bill constitutes a veto if the Congress is in recess. This question arose in connection with the Family Practice of Medicine Act passed by both houses and sent to the president at the time of the 1970 Christmas recess. President Nixon neither signed nor returned the bill but maintained that it was vetoed because neither house was in session to receive it if it were returned. This note argues that there is no significant reason that the return of a disapproved bill cannot be made to the house of origin during a recess of any length; the ten-day period was designed to assure that the president would be afforded the time to examine the bill, not to limit congressional authority to override a veto.

PROCEEDING IN THE TRIAL OF ANDREW JOHNSON BEFORE THE UNITED STATES SENATE ON THE ARTICLES OF IMPEACHMENT EXHIBITED BY THE HOUSE OF REPRESENTATIVES, WITH AN APPENDIX. Washington, D.C.: F. and J. Rives and George A. Bailey, Reporters and Printers of the Debate of Congress, 1868.

This is the official transcript of the proceedings in the trial
and an official copy of the articles of impeachment and other
documents entered, in accordance with an act of the Congress,
in the Clerk's Office in the Supreme Court of the District of
Columbia in 1868. The appendix includes an alphabetized list of
the witnesses for the prosecution and for the defense together
with the subject of their argument and a copy of a number of
arguments presented on various legal points which were not a
part of the official proceedings, such as Charles Sumner's
argument upon the question of the right of the Chief Justice to
rule on questions of law and to vote, and briefs on the law of
impeachable crimes and offenses.

PROPOSALS FOR REVISION OF THE ELECTORAL COLLEGE SYSTEM.
Washington, D.C.: American Enterprise Institute for Public Policy Research,
1969.

This is a brief look at the present system for selecting presidents,
the principal objections to the present procedures, the proposals
for revisions and the arguments in support of and in opposition
to the various proposals: direct popular election, elimination of
the independence of electors, and district voting.

Randall, James G. CONSTITUTIONAL PROBLEMS UNDER LINCOLN. Rev.
ed. Urbana: University of Illinois Press, 1951.

This is a historical examination of those presidential actions
during the Civil War era which, in the author's view, gave rise
to significant constitutional problems, issues such as the use of
the war power in response to civil strife, the suspension of the
writ of habeas corpus, military governance of civilian populations,
the admission of a part of Virginia as a state and general problems
of the relationship between state and national governments.

Reznick, Lois. "Temporary Appointment Power of the President." UNIVER-
SITY OF CHICAGO LAW REVIEW 41 (Fall 1973): 146-63.

When President Nixon appointed an acting director of the Office
of Economic Opportunity in January of 1973 without senatorial
consent, the appointment was viewed by some as an attempt to
dismantle the agency and questions about the legitimacy of the
appointment were raised. This article examines executive and
judicial interpretation of the constitutional power of the President to make temporary appointments without senatorial confirmation, the statutory authorization for such appointments and the
procedures for challenging the legality of these appointments.

Rich, Bennett M. THE PRESIDENT AND CIVIL DISORDER. Washington,
D.C.: Brookings Institutions, 1941.

This is a study of each instance (with the exception of the Reconstruction era) in which the president used military force to
deal with domestic disturbances from the Whiskey Rebellion in
Washington's administration to a strike at North American Avia-
tion in Los Angeles in 1941. One chapter is devoted to the constitutional and legislative sources of presidential authority to use
forces to maintain domestic peace.

Roberts, Charles, ed. HAS THE PRESIDENT TOO MUCH POWER? New
York: Harper's Magazine Press, 1973.

> This is a collection of materials taken from the proceedings of
> the Washington Journalism Center's Conference of Journalists
> held in October 1973. Included among the sixteen essays are:
> Arthur S. Miller, "Executive Privilege: What Are the Limits?,"
> Theodore C. Sorenson, "The Case for a Strong Presidency,"
> Senator Howard Baker, "What Presidential Powers Should be
> Cut?," James L. Sundquist, "What Happened to Our Checks and
> Balances," Louis Fisher, "The President Versus Congress: Who
> Wins?," and James McGregor Burns, "Dictatorship--Could It
> Happen Here?"

Rodino, Peter W., Jr. IMPEACHMENT OF RICHARD M. NIXON, PRESI-
DENT OF THE UNITED STATES: THE FINAL REPORT OF THE COM-
MITTEE ON THE JUDICIARY HOUSE OF REPRESENTATIVES. Intro-
duction by R.W. Apple. New York: Bantam, 1975.

> Another commercial publication of the Government Printing Office's
> official committee report.

_____. THE IMPEACHMENT REPORT: A GUIDE TO CONGRESSIONAL
PROCEEDINGS IN THE CASE OF RICHARD M. NIXON. Compiled and
edited by the staffs of United Press International and World Almanac. Introduction by Helen Thomas. New York: Signet, 1974.

> This is a transcript of debate and votes on the Articles of Im-
> peachment in the House Judiciary Committee as well as back-
> ground information on the events leading to the impeachment
> hearings.

Rosenberg, Kenyon C., and Rosenberg, Judith K. WATERGATE: AN ANNO-
TATED BIBLIOGRAPHY. Littleton, Colo.: Libraries Unlimited, 1975.

> This is a bibliography of accounts, commentaries and analyses
> of the various facets of the constitutional crises embraced within
> the term "Watergate."

Ross, Edmund G. HISTORY OF THE IMPEACHMENT OF ANDREW JOHN-
SON, PRESIDENT OF THE UNITED STATES, BY THE HOUSE OF REP-
RESENTATIVES, AND HIS TRIAL BY THE SENATE, FOR HIGH CRIMES
AND MISDEMEANORS IN OFFICE, 1868. New York: Burt Franklin, 1896.

> Written by one of the seven Republican senators who voted for
> Johnson's acquittal, this is an analysis of Johnson's reconstruc-
> tion policy, which the author viewed as consistent with that of
> Lincoln, and of the conflict between Johnson and the Congress
> which led to the impeachment and trial and a brief account of
> the trial itself. The author argues that the real basis for the
> impeachment was an attempt by the Congress to control executive
> powers.

Rossiter, Clinton. THE AMERICAN PRESIDENCY. New York: Harcourt,
Brace and World, 1956.

This is an analysis of the myriad of constitutional and extraconstitutional roles of the American president--the ceremonial role
of chief of state, the supervisory role of chief executive, the
foreign role of chief diplomat and the constitutional role of chief
legislator as well as such extraconstitutional roles as chief of
party and voice of the people.

_____. THE SUPREME COURT AND THE COMMANDER IN CHIEF. Intro-
duction by Richard P. Longaker. Rev. ed. Ithaca, N.Y.: Cornell University Press, 1977.

This is an examination of judicial interpretation of the war powers
of the president derived from his constitutionally designated role
as commander in chief.

Scheiber, Harry N. THE WILSON ADMINISTRATION AND CIVIL LIBER-
TIES, 1917-1921. Ithaca, N.Y.: Cornell University Press, 1960.

Originally an M.A. thesis, this slim volume is an account of the
repression of individual liberties in the World War I period,
beginning with Wilson's prewar verbal attacks on opponents of
his war preparedness program. The author examines the president's role in the enactment of the Espionage and Sedition Acts
of 1917 and 1918, presidential delegation of broad discretionary
powers to the Justice and Post Office Departments to enforce
these acts both during and after the war and Wilson's refusal
until the last days of his administration to sign legislation re-
pealing the wartime statutes.

Schilling, Joan H., comp. THE WATERGATE INDEX: AN INDEX TO
"WATERGATE" MATERIAL AS REPORTED IN THE WASHINGTON POST
BETWEEN JUNE 16, 1972 AND JUNE 20, 1973. Wooster, Ohio: Microphoto
Division, Bell and Howell, 1975.

The WASHINGTON POST was the earliest and most persistent
pursuer of developments beginning with the break-in of Democratic national headquarters in June of 1972. This is an index
to Watergate-related articles appearing in the POST between
June of 1972 and June of 1973.

Schlesinger, Arthur M., Jr. THE IMPERIAL PRESIDENCY. New York:
Houghton Mifflin Co., 1973.

This work, which added a new slogan to the American political
vocabulary, is an examination of the shift in the constitutional
balance of power from the legislative to the executive branch.
Although this presidential "appropriation" of powers which, the
author believes, constitutionally belongs to the Congress occurred
in both the domestic and the international arenas and was the
result not only of presidential usurpation but of congressional
abdication, the major emphasis is upon presidential war-making
powers.

Schnapper, M.B., ed. PRESIDENTIAL IMPEACHMENT: A DOCUMENTARY
OVERVIEW. Introduction by Alan Barth. Washington, D.C.: Public Affairs
Press, 1974.

This collection of impeachment materials, gathered at the height
of the controversy over the impeachment of President Nixon,
includes excerpts from various sources such as a report on the
constitutional grounds for impeachment by the staff of the Judiciary
Committee, an analysis of constitutional standards for presidential
impeachment by President Nixon's attorneys, a report on the role
of Congress and the courts in impeachments by a committee of
the New York Bar Association, an argument in favor of impeachment of Nixon by the American Civil Liberties Union, a statement on the responsibilities of the House Judiciary Committee
by its chairman Peter Rodino and a report on the relationship
between executive privilege and presidential impeachment by the
Legal Counsel Office of the Justice Department.

Schubert, Glendon A. THE PRESIDENCY IN THE COURTS. Minneapolis:
University of Minnesota Press, 1957.

This is an examination of state and national judicial interpretation of presidential power between 1790 and 1956. Of the
eight hundred cases dealing with the issue of presidential power,
only thirty-eight held the presidential action invalid, and of this
number only fourteen were rulings of the United States Supreme
Court. Of this number, only two invalidated a major presidential
action: the steel seizure case in 1952 and Cole v. Young which
placed limitations upon the presidential loyalty program in the
1950s.

Schwartz, Bernard. A COMMENTARY ON THE CONSTITUTION OF THE
UNITED STATES. New York: Macmillan, 1963.

Judicial interpretation of presidential powers is covered in
volume 2.

Silva, Ruth C. PRESIDENTIAL SUCCESSION. Ann Arbor: University
of Michigan Press, 1951.

This is an examination of the constitutional and congressional
provisions for succession to the presidency in the event of the
death, resignation, or disability of the occupant.

Sindler, Allan P. UNCHOSEN PRESIDENTS: THE VICE-PRESIDENT
AND OTHER FRUSTRATIONS OF PRESIDENTIAL SUCCESSION. Berkeley
and Los Angeles: University of California Press, 1976.

Written after the "unanticipated" use of the Twenty-fifth Amendment with the Agnew and Nixon resignations and the presidential
and congressional selections of Ford and Rockefeller to fill the
vacancy in the vice-presidency, this slim volume focuses on the
"anomalous" office of vice-president, the varying constitutional
and congressional attempts to deal with the problem of successions
to the presidency and offers some additional options, one of which
is the suggestion of special elections to fill a presidential vacancy.

Smith, J. Malcolm, and Cotter, Cornelius P. POWERS OF THE PRESIDENT
DURING CRISES. Washington, D.C.: Public Affairs Press, 1960. Reprint.
New York: Da Capo Press, 1972.

This brief work focuses upon the invocation of emergency powers
by presidents from the early 1930s through the 1950s. The
authors argue that the use of emergency powers is compatible
with democracy, that the Constitution provides for its use and
that statutory laws exist for placing restraints in order to prevent abuse. In addition to examining the concept of emergency
power in democratic political thought and in American legislation,
they look at the specific ways in which such power has been invoked to regulate and/or control persons, property and communications, at statutory restraints upon the administration of emergency powers and at the varying attitudes of courts and individual
justices toward the degree of constitutional flexibility allowing or
disallowing presidential power from Ex Parte Milligan to the Steel
Seizure Case.

Sofaer, Abraham. "Executive Privilege: An Historical Note." COLUMBIA
LAW REVIEW 75 (November 1975): 1318-21.

This brief note relates three incidents in Washington's administration in which the president and his advisors discussed the
authority for and desirability of refusing to accede to congressional requests for information: a House committee request for
information on the St. Clair defeat, a House request for papers
relating to Jay's Treaty and the Senate request for correspondence between the State Department and the French government.

Spanier, John W. THE TRUMAN-MacARTHUR CONTROVERSY AND THE
KOREAN WAR. Cambridge: Belknap Press, Harvard University Press,
1959.

This is a study of the constitutional concept of civilian control
of the military assured by conference upon the president of the
commander-in-chief power as exemplified by the conflict between
President Truman and General MacArthur which resulted in the
firing of the general and political controversy.

Stanwood, Edward. A HISTORY OF THE PRESIDENCY FROM 1788 TO
1897. 2 vols. Boston: Houghton Mifflin Co., 1892-1926.

This nineteenth-century history is a narrative of presidential
campaigns and of the conduct of the office of the presidency from
Washington to Cleveland's second term.

Stein, Charles W. THE THIRD TERM TRADITION: ITS RISE AND
COLLAPSE IN AMERICAN POLITICS. 1943. Reprint. Westport, Conn.:
Greenwood Press, 1972.

Written before the adoption of the Twenty-second Amendment,
this is an analysis of the anti-third term tradition from 1787 to
the 1930s and an account of those instances in which presidents
were tempted to run for a third term, with particular emphasis
upon those who succumbed to that temptation. Substantially completed before Franklin D. Roosevelt's bid for a third term, the
book is skimpy on the first successful break with the two-term
tradition.

Stryker, Lloyd P. ANDREW JOHNSON: A STUDY IN COURAGE. New
York: Macmillan, 1936.

With a few chapters devoted to the early life and career of Johnson, this sympathetic biography focuses primarily on the tumul-
tous relationship between the president and Congress culminating
in impeachment by the House and acquittal by the Senate.

Sutherland, Arthur E., Jr. "Restricting the Treaty Power." HARVARD
LAW REVIEW 65 (1952): 1305-35.

In 1951, Sen. Bricker introduced a constitutional amendment
placing various limitations upon the powers to make treaties and
executive agreements. It prohibited a treaty or executive agreement which infringed upon individual rights, which vested in any
international organization or foreign government the constitutional
power of Congress, the executive or judicial branches, which
changed national or state law unless explicitly permitted by joint
resolution, forbade executive agreements "in lieu of" treaties
and placed other restrictions on executive agreements. In this
article, Sutherland examines the origins and development of the
treaty power and argues that the proposed amendment was both
unnecessary and unwise. He suggests that it was unnecessary
because the treaty power does not allow the national government
to take action forbidden by the Constitution and has not been used
to abuse power. He sees it as undesirable because executive
agreements are a necessary instrument in conducting increasingly
complex foreign policy, because the wording of the limitation "in
lieu of" treaties is too indefinite and because the amendment as
a whole was too rigid and specific in an area requiring flexibility.
This article is reprinted in Robert G. McCloskey's ESSAYS IN
CONSTITUTIONAL LAW (see p. 83).

Taft, William Howard. OUR CHIEF MAGISTRATE. New York: Columbia
University Press, 1916.

Written after his presidency, Taft here articulates his "Whig"
view of the president's powers. In contrast to Theodore Roosevelt's "steward of the people" view that the president possessed
any power necessary which was not prohibited, Taft argues that
the Constitution does not confer broad undefined power on the
president; rather his power is limited to those specifically or
by necessary implication granted to him by the Constitution and
by the Congress.

Thach, Charles C. THE CREATION OF THE PRESIDENCY, 1775-1789:
A STUDY IN CONSTITUTIONAL HISTORY. 1923. Baltimore: Johns
Hopkins Press, 1969.

With an introduction to the second printing by Herbert J. Storing,
this slim volume is a scholarly analysis of political attitudes toward
the question of the compatibility of executive power and representative principles prior to the constitutional convention, the national
and state experiences and experiments with executive power from
1776 to 1787, the movement toward a strong chief executive, the
debates of the constitutional convention and of the first session
of the First Congress on the presidency, on the organization of
the executive branch and on the authority of the chief executive
to remove subordinates. The author credits James Wilson, and to
a lesser extent Gouverneur Morris, with devising and gaining

acceptance for a strong chief executive responsible to the people.

Tompkins, Dorothy. THE OFFICE OF THE VICE-PRESIDENT: A SELECTED
BIBLIOGRAPHY. Berkeley: Bureau of Public Administration, University
of California, 1957.

This is a bibliography of works focusing upon the role of the vice-
presidency.

_____. PRESIDENTIAL SUCCESSION: A BIBLIOGRAPHY. 1964. Berke-
ley: Institute of Government Studies, University of California, 1965.

Compiled in response to the revived interest in presidential dis-
abilities brought about by the assassination of President Kennedy,
and published prior to the adoption of the Twenty-fifth Amendment,
this bibliography lists works dealing with the problems of succession to the presidency in the event of the death, disability or
resignation of its occupant, succession beyond the vice-presidency
and various proposals, including constitutional amendments for
changing the system.

_____. SELECTION OF THE VICE-PRESIDENT. Berkeley: Institute of
Government Studies, University of California, 1974.

A bibliography of materials dealing with the question of alternative
methods of choosing vice-presidents.

Tourtellot, Arthur B. THE PRESIDENTS ON THE PRESIDENCY. 1964.
New York: Russell and Russell, 1970.

This is a collection of excerpts from the writings, speeches and
other public documents of presidents from Washington to Kennedy.
Organized on the basis of subject matter, it includes presidential
statements on such matters as the president as national leader
and as administrator, his appointive, removal and commander in
chief powers, the relationships between the president and Congress
and the judiciary, and the limitations on the presidency. There
is a bibliography of published and unpublished presidential writings
and where each president's papers are deposited.

"Trial of Andrew Johnson." CONGRESSIONAL GLOBE. 40th Cong., 2d
sess., Supp. Washington, D.C.: Government Printing Office, 1868.

In 1868 President Johnson was impeached by the House, tried
by the Senate and acquitted by one vote short of the necessary
two-thirds majority on eleven counts of high crimes and misdemeanors. This official record of the first attempt to remove
a president through the impeachment process reveals the conflicts
between the two branches during the post-Civil War era over which
would dominate national governmental policy and over the differing
interpretations of the respective constitutional powers of the two
branches.

TRIAL OF ANDREW JOHNSON, PRESIDENT OF THE UNITED STATES,
BEFORE THE SENATE OF THE UNITED STATES, ON IMPEACHMENT
BY THE HOUSE OF REPRESENTATIVES FOR HIGH CRIMES AND MIS-
DEMEANORS. 2 vols. New York: Plenum Publishing Corp., 1970;

3 vols. New York: Da Capo Press, 1970.

> These are commercially published copies of the official 1868
> impeachment.

U.S. Congress. House of Representatives. IMPEACHMENT: SELECTED
MATERIALS ON PROCEDURE. 93d Cong., 2d sess. Washington, D.C.:
Government Printing Office, 1974.

> This report deals exclusively with procedural questions relating
> to impeachment. This second volume of IMPEACHMENT: SE -
> LECTED MATERIALS consists of materials from HINDS' PRE-
> CEDENTS (see p. 100) and CANNON'S PRECEDENTS (see p. 91).

U.S. Congress. House of Representatives. Committee on the Judiciary.
CONSTITUTIONAL GROUNDS FOR IMPEACHMENT. REPORT OF THE STAFF
OF THE IMPEACHMENT INQUIRY. 93d Cong., 2d sess., February 1974.
Washington, D.C.: Government Printing Office, 1974.

> This staff report on the constitutional grounds for impeachment
> examines the historical origins of impeachment in terms of
> English parliamentary practices, the intention of the framers
> of the Constitution and impeachment cases in the United States.
> The appendix includes relevant portions of the debates at the
> Philadelphia convention of 1787 and the records of impeachment
> cases involving senators and federal judges.

_____. THE FINAL REPORT OF THE COMMITTEE ON THE JUDICIARY,
HOUSE OF REPRESENTATIVES. Washington, D.C.: Government Printing
Office, 1974.

> This is the official version of the 528-page report of the Judiciary
> Committee on the question of the impeachment of President Nixon.
> There are also several publications of the REPORT, including
> the Signet and Bantam publications.

U.S. Congress. House of Representatives. Committee on the Judiciary.
Committee Print. IMPEACHMENT: SELECTED MATERIALS. Washington,
D.C.: Government Printing Office, 1973.

> This 700-page volume regarding the constitutional bases for im-
> peachment contains materials prepared for the committee consider-
> ing the impeachment of President Nixon. This committee print
> brings together scattered materials, some of which were out of
> print, such as excerpts from the debates at the constitutional
> convention and the proceedings of the trial of Andrew Johnson.

U.S. Congress. House of Representatives. Staff of the House Committee
on the Judiciary. CONSTITUTIONAL GROUNDS FOR PRESIDENTIAL IM-
PEACHMENT. 93d Cong., 2d sess. Washington, D.C.: Government Printing Office, 1974.

> Prepared for the committee considering the impeachment of Presi-
> dent Nixon, this report deals with the question of what constitutes
> an impeachable offense. The conclusion is that an impeachable
> offense need not be a criminal act.

U.S. Congress. Senate. ELECTION OF THE PRESIDENT OF THE
UNITED STATES BY THE HOUSE OF REPRESENTATIVES. Washington,
D.C.: Government Printing Office, 1925.

Prepared by George Schulz under the direction of H.H.B. Meyer,
Director of the Legislative Reference Service of the Library of
Congress, this history of presidential selection was designed to
point out some of the constitutional questions, such as presidential succession, not dealt with adequately by the Constitution.
It describes the debates at Philadelphia on presidential selection,
the method of counting electoral votes and the inadequacy of the
original constitutional provisions which failed to require separate
ballots for president and vice-president. It discusses the Burr-
Jefferson tie, the adoption of the Twelfth Amendment and subsequent congressional attempts to deal with presidential succession
and the inadequacy of these pre-1925 attempts.

Van Alstyne, William, W. "Congress, the President, and the Power to
Declare War: A Requiem for Vietnam." UNIVERSITY OF PENNSYLVANIA
LAW REVIEW 121 (November 1972): 1-28.

In this examination of presidential war-making authority, Van
Alstyne argues that while a president may repel a sudden invasion,
he may not constitutionally sustain use of military troops abroad
in the absence of a congressional declaration of war and that
even in a declared war, Congress retains review and control
power. On the question of the authority of Congress to delegate
its authority to declare war, he concludes that the treaty-making
power does not so permit. Further, even if such a delegation
is ever permissible either by treaty or by joint resolution, Van
Alstyne argues that in the case of Vietnam, presidential war action
after the repeal of the Gulf of Tonkin resolution on 12 January
1971 was illegal.

Wallace, Don. "The War-making Powers: A Constitutional Flaw?" CORNELL
LAW REVIEW 57 (May 1972): 719-76.

Rather than dealing with the explicit question of the constitutionality of presidential action in Vietnam, Wallace directs his attention to the broader question raised by that war; that is, does
the Constitution make proper provision for the undertaking of
war? He examines three factors he believes are overlooked in
most constitutional and legal arguments over the Vietnam war:
the flawed character of the separation of powers doctrine in
foreign affairs, the almost total refusal of the judiciary to get
involved in questions of war, and the reality of the international
system which is governed more by the law of the jungle than by
the rule of law.

Wells, John M., and Wilhelm, Maria, eds. THE PEOPLE VS. PRESIDENTIAL
WAR. Foreword by Sen. J. William Fullbright. New York: Kennikat Press,
Dunellen Books, 1970.

In the late 1960s, in response to a citizens' petition, the Massachusetts legislature enacted a law designed to challenge the constitutionality of the war in Vietnam. The Shea-Wells Act provided that no citizen of Massachusetts could be forced to serve

in a war outside the United States unless Congress declared
war. The attorney general of the state was to defend any Massachusetts citizen drafted. This slim volume, a collection of essays
written before Massachusetts attempted to test the constitutionality
of the law and the war before the Supreme Court, relates the
various stages in the process of enactment of the legislation.

Westin, Alan F. THE ANATOMY OF A CONSTITUTIONAL LAW CASE:
YOUNGSTOWN SHEET & TUBE CO. v. SAWYER: THE STEEL SEIZURE
DECISION. New York: Macmillan, 1958.

This is a study of the events leading up to President Truman's
seizure of the steel mills and the reactions to that decision. The
opinions of the lower courts and the Supreme Court are included.

Wharton, Francis. STATE TRIALS OF THE UNITED STATES DURING
THE ADMINISTRATION OF WASHINGTON AND ADAMS, WITH REFERENCES,
HISTORICAL AND PROFESSIONAL, AND PRELIMINARY NOTES ON THE
POLITICS OF THE TIME. 1849. Reprint. New York: Burt Franklin,
1970.

This contains the records of the twenty-one trials (for such
offenses as libel and sedition, as well as impeachment trials)
during the first twelve years under the Constitution. Each of
the trials here recorded had important repercussions for future
constitutional and political developments. As introductory essay
to each record places the trial in historic perspective. The
introductory chapter is an analysis of the role and activities of
federal judges in this critical period in constitutional development as well as biographical sketches of each of the judges and
lawyers involved in the trials.

Williams, Irving G. THE AMERICAN VICE PRESIDENCY: NEW LOOK.
Doubleday Short Studies Series. Garden City, N.Y.: Doubleday, 1954.

This slim volume is a history of the office of the vice-presidency,
the role of the vice-president as an officer of the Senate, his
relationship with the president, the manner in which the nature
of that office differs from that envisaged by the framers and the
problem of presidential succession.

Wilmerding, Lucius. THE ELECTORAL COLLEGE. New Brunswick, N.J.:
Rutgers University Press, 1958. Reprint. Boston: Beacon Press, 1964.

This is an examination of the construction of the electoral college
system at the Philadelphia convention, of the changes wrought by
the Twelfth Amendment, of the states' choice of means of appointing electors and of the procedures employed by the House of
Representatives when it is called upon to choose a president.
Wilmerding argues that the framers intended the president to be
chosen by the people of the nation as a whole. Because the
states are authorized to choose the method of selecting electors
and because they have chosen the winner-take-all system, the
intent of the framers has been defeated. Within the framework
of this interpretation, he examines three major changes proposed
in the late 1950s: the district system, direct national election,
and proportional voting.

Wolk, Allan. THE PRESIDENCY AND BLACK CIVIL RIGHTS. Cranbury,
N.J.: Fairleigh Dickinson University Press, 1971.

This study of civil rights from the administration of Eisenhower
to that of Nixon focuses upon the implementation of national
educational and voting policies in the Kennedy and Johnson administrations. He attributes what he views as the ineffectiveness
of national civil rights efforts partly to the absence of inter-
agency coordination and to the relative lack of presidential leadership.

Wormuth, Francis D. "The Nixon Theory of the War Power: A Critique."
CALIFORNIA LAW REVIEW 60 (May 1972): 623-704.

In this criticism of President Nixon's interpretation of the
commander-in-chief provision as the major basis for presidential
authority to conduct the war in Vietnam, the author argues that
"the words of the Constitution are quite clear" on the question
of unilateral presidential war action; that is, that the president
possesses no such power. He is particularly critical of the
Supreme Court's refusal to involve itself in the controversy over
Vietnam because while he thinks the Constitution quite clear on
the substantive issue, the only constitutional guardian is the
Court and unless it ruled presidential action unconstitutional, no
other authoritative agency could do so.

Young, Donald. AMERICAN ROULETTE: THE HISTORY AND DILEMMA OF
THE VICE-PRESIDENCY. New York: Holt, Rinehart and Winston, 1965.

Written after the assassination of President Kennedy and before
the adoption of the Twenty-fifth Amendment, this is an account
of the office of the vice-presidency, of each of the vice-presidents
from John Adams to Lyndon Johnson who became president whether
through the death of the president or subsequent election in his
own right and of some of the other vice-presidents whose per-
formances illustrate the importance and frustrations of the office.
The author also suggests means of dealing with the constitutional
problems of presidential succession and disability.

Yunker, John H., and Longley, Lawrence D. THE ELECTORAL COLLEGE:
ITS BIASES NEWLY MEASURED FOR THE 1960S AND 1970S. Sage
Professional Papers in American Politics Series. Beverly Hills: Sage
Publications, 1976.

This brief paper is an empirical analysis of the state, regional
and group biases in presidential elections from 1964 through
1980 under the electoral college system, the proportional plan,
the district plan and the direct vote plan.

Zeidenstein, Harvey. DIRECT ELECTION OF THE PRESIDENT. Lexington,
Mass.: Lexington Books, 1973.

Written after the Senate debate on Senate Resolution 1 proposing
a constitutional amendment to provide for direct election of the
president, this work examines the arguments advanced against
the proposal by such critics as Alexander Bickel and Richard
Goodwin, the arguments against the electoral college and outlines
the arguments in favor of direct election. After analyzing the

"predicted dysfunctional" consequences of direct election, the author argues for the abolition of the electoral college.

Zinn, Charles J. THE VETO POWER OF THE PRESIDENT. Washington, D.C.: Government Printing Office, 1951.

This committee print, prepared for the House Judiciary Committee, is a brief study of the background and nature of the veto power in ancient Rome, England, colonial America, and in the Constitution; of such problems as circumvention by use of a concurrent resolution; and of the pocket and item veto. The appendix includes a copy of a proposed bill to define more explicitly such aspects of veto procedure as the time alloted for its exercise.

PRESIDENTIAL PAPERS AND BIOGRAPHIES

Adams, John. THE ADAMS PAPERS: DIARY AND AUTOBIOGRAPHY OF JOHN ADAMS. Edited by Lyman Henry Butterfield, assisted by Leonard C. Falser and Wendell D. Garrett. 4 vols. Cambridge, Mass.: Belknap Press, Harvard University Press, 1961.

Volume 1 contains the diary from 1755 to 1770. Volume 2 contains the diary from 1771 to 1781. Volume 3 contains the diary from 1782 to 1804 and Adams's autobiography to October of 1776. Volume 4 contains the autobiography from 1777 to 1780. Butterfield, assisted by Wendell D. Garrett and Marjorie Sprague, is the original editor of THE ADAMS FAMILY CORRESPONDENCE (Belknap Press, 1963). Other John Adams papers published by Belknap are being edited by Robert J. Taylor (see p. 144) and two volumes of Series II, GENERAL CORRESPONDENCE AND OTHER PAPERS OF THE ADAMS STATESMEN, have thus far been pulbished as THE ADAMS PAPERS: PAPERS OF JOHN ADAMS and cover September 1755 to April 1775.

_____. THE ADAMS PAPERS: THE PAPERS OF JOHN ADAMS. Edited by Robert J. Taylor. 2 vols. to date. Cambridge, Mass.: Belknap Press, Harvard University Press, 1977-- .

The first two volumes of the John Adams papers cover from September 1755 to April 1775. Volume 1, covering September 1755 to October of 1773, includes an introduction by the editor in which he comments on the general status of the publication of THE ADAMS PAPERS, presents a general overview of Series III of the papers (GENERAL CORRESPONDENCE AND OTHER PAPERS OF THE ADAMS STATESMEN) and discusses the career of John Adams as public servant and as revolutionary. Volume 2, covering the period from December 1773 to April of 1775, includes such materials as Adams's essays in Massachusetts papers ("Novanglus" among others) in which he formulated a general theory of the relationship between the colonists and Great Britain. The publication of the other Adams papers, edited by Lyman Henry Butterfield (THE ADAMS FAMILY CORRESPONDENCE published in four volumes and covering the period to September 1782 and THE DIARY OF CHARLES FRANCIS ADAMS in six volumes and covering through June of 1836) is being held in abeyance by Belknap while work proceeds with the editing and publication of this series of the John Adams papers.

_____. THE FOUNDING FATHERS: JOHN ADAMS: A BIOGRAPHY IN HIS OWN WORDS. Edited by James Bishop Peabody. Founding Fathers Series. Introduction by L.H. Butterfield. New York: Newsweek, distributed by Harper and Row, n.d.

Published sometime in the early 1970s the materials included are extracted from THE DIARY AND AUTOBIOGRAPHY OF JOHN ADAMS, (see p. 144) and ADAMS FAMILY CORRESPONDENCE, 4 volumes published as of 1973.

_____. LEGAL PAPERS OF JOHN ADAMS. Edited by L.K. Wroth and H.B. Zobel. 3 vols. Cambridge, Mass.: Harvard University Press, 1965.

This is a collection of the legal cases in which John Adams was involved as a lawyer.

_____. THE WORKS OF JOHN ADAMS. Edited by Charles Francis Adams. 10 vols. Boston: Little, Brown, 1851.

This collection of the writings of John Adams, along with a bio-graphy by his grandson, is credited by one Adams biographer (Peter Shaw, THE CHARACTER OF JOHN ADAMS, published for the Institute of Early American History and Culture by the University of North Carolina, 1976) with creating a long accepted but false image of Adams as a judicious and prudent man rather than the passionate rebel of the Revolution and theoretician of government portrayed by later biographers. Volume 1 of this ten-volume work contains the biography. John Adams's diary and autobiography, along with some essays, are contained in volumes 2 and 3. The DEFENCE OF THE CONSTITUTIONS OF THE GOVERNMENTS OF THE UNITED STATES is contained in volumes 4,5, and 6, along with other political works and letters. The remaining volumes contain Adams's official correspondence and other letters.

Adams, John; Adams, Abigail; and Jefferson, Thomas. THE ADAMS-JEFFERSON LETTERS. Edited by Lester J. Cappon. 2 vols. Chapel Hill: University of North Carolina Press, 1959.

This is a collection of the correspondence between Jefferson and John and Abigail Adams. Volume 1 covers the period from 1777 to 1804. Volume 2 covers the period from 1812 until the deaths of Jefferson and Adams in 1826. There is a short one-volume abridgment of the correspondence between John Adams and Jefferson edited by Paul Wilstach and published by Capricorn Books and by Bobbs-Merrill.

Adams, John, and Adams, John Quincy. THE SELECTED WRITINGS OF JOHN AND JOHN QUINCY ADAMS. Edited by Adrienne Koch and William Peden. New York: Knopf, 1946.

With a biographical introduction by the editors, this one-volume selection of the writings of John and John Quincy Adams consists primarily of materials extracted from their diaries and their public and private correspondence.

Adams, John, and Jefferson, Thomas. CORRESPONDENCE OF JOHN ADAMS AND THOMAS JEFFERSON, 1812-1826. Edited by Paul Wilstach. Indiana-polis: Bobbs-Merrill, 1925.

> With an introduction and comments by the editor, this small volume is a collection of some of the letters exchanged between Adams and Jefferson after their presidential years and revival of their earlier friendship, a friendship disrupted by political disagreements and rivalries. There is also a Capricorn paper-back edition of this selection of letters.

Adams, John Quincy. THE DIARY OF JOHN QUINCY ADAMS, 1794-1845: AMERICAN POLITICAL, SOCIAL AND INTELLECTUAL LIFE FROM WASH-INGTON TO POLK. Edited by Allan Nevins. New York: Longmans, Green and Co., 1928.

> This diary consists of selections from THE MEMOIRS OF JOHN QUINCY ADAMS, COMPRISING PORTIONS OF HIS DIARY FROM 1795 TO 1848, a twelve-volume work published by Charles Francis Adams between 1874 and 1877. The selections are designed to present a portrait of major aspects of American life under the Constitution from the administration of the first president to the Mexican war.

_____. THE WRITINGS OF JOHN QUINCY ADAMS. Edited by C. Worthing-ton Ford. 7 vols. New York: Macmillan, 1913.

> This collection of the voluminous papers, letters to his parents, diplomatic communications and other writings of John Quincy Adams is arranged chronologically. Volume 1 covers 1779-96, volume 2 covers 1796-1801, volume 3 covers 1801-10, volume 4 covers 1811-13, volume 5 covers 1814-16, volume 6 covers 1816-19, and volume 7 covers 1820-23.

Arnold, Isaac W. THE LIFE OF ABRAHAM LINCOLN. 3d ed. Chicago: Jansen, McClurg, 1885.

> Taking the view that Lincoln was "as pure, as just, as patriotic as the father of his country" who "is his only peer," the author examines Lincoln's ancestry and early life but concentrates primarily on his political life as state legislator, congressman, and president.

Barre, W.L. THE LIFE AND PUBLIC SERVICES OF MILLARD FILLMORE. New York: Lenox Hill, 1956. Reprint. New York: Burt Franklin, 1971.

> This biography begins with Fillmore's birth and covers his education and his career as a lawyer and as a politician at the state level, in Congress and in the White House.

Barrett, Joseph H. THE LIFE OF ABRAHAM LINCOLN, PRESENTING HIS EARLY HISTORY, POLITICAL CAREER AND SPEECHES IN AND OUT OF CONGRESS; ALSO A GENERAL VIEW OF HIS POLICY AS PRESIDENT OF THE UNITED STATES WITH HIS MESSAGES, PROCLAMATION, LETTERS, ETC. AND A CONCISE HISTORY OF THE WAR. Cincinnati: Moore, Wil-stach and Baldwin, 1864.

Written during the Civil War and published prior to Lincoln's
assassination, this work concentrates on his public life and
ends with his appointment of Grant and the opening of the 1864
military campaign.

Barton, William E. THE LIFE OF ABRAHAM LINCOLN. 2 vols. Indianapolis: Bobbs-Merrill, 1925.

Volume 1 deals with Lincoln's life from birth to his election as
president. Volume 2 deals with the presidential years until his
assassination. The appendix includes such materials as the
Lincoln-Douglas debates, various versions of the Gettysburg
address and portions of the diary of John Wilkes Booth.

Bassett, John Spencer. LIFE OF ANDREW JACKSON. 2 vols. in one.
Garden City, N.Y.: Doubleday, Page, 1911. Reprint. Hamden, Conn.:
Archon Books, 1967.

Volume 1 of this biography begins with Jackson's early life and
career, covers his career in Tennessee and in the military and
ends with the first presidential campaign and the election of John
Quincy Adams by the House of Representatives. Volume 2 begins
with the second presidential campaign, covers his election, his
fights against nullification and the United States Bank, and ends
with the eight retirement years until his death on 8 June 1845.

Beveridge, Albert J. ABRAHAM LINCOLN: 1809-1858. 2 vols. Boston:
Houghton Mifflin Co., 1928.

Volume 1 covers the period from Lincoln's birth, through the
early phases of his political career in the state legislature and
Congress to his return to the practice of law. Volume 2 examines
the growing conflict between North and South, the Missouri Compromise, western development and slavery, Lincoln's return to
politics, the Dred Scott decision, the Lincoln-Douglas debates,
and Lincoln's presidential nomination.

Bishop, Arthur. RUTHERFORD BIRCHARD HAYES, 1822-1893: CHRONO-
LOGY-DOCUMENTS-BIBLIOGRAPHIC AIDS. Presidential Chronology Series.
Dobbs Ferry, N.Y.: Oceana, 1969.

The first section is a chronology of events in the life of Hayes:
his school years (1836-45), his years as a lawyer (1845-61), as
a soldier (1861-65) and as an Ohio politician (1865-76) as well
as his Washington years including his presidential years (1827-81)
and concluding with his years in retirement (1881-93). The
documents section includes his inaugural address and messages
to Congress, his executive order barring political acts by federal employees in 1877 and a number of his vetoes including
his veto of the Bland-Allison Act and of the Chinese Immigration
Bill in 1879. The bibliographic section includes citations of
biographies and of general works dealing with the disputed Hayes-
Tilden election and with the Reconstruction era.

_____. THOMAS JEFFERSON, 1743-1826: CHRONOLOGY-DOCUMENTS-
BIBLIOGRAPHIC AIDS. Presidential Chronology Series. Dobbs Ferry,
N.Y.: Oceana, 1971.

The first section is a chronology of events in Jefferson's early life (1743-60), his life as a student (1760-67), as a young lawyer (1767-73), as a radical leader (1773-84) and in his public career as a minister abroad, as secretary of state, as vice president and president and his postpresidential years. The second section includes such documents as his SUMMARY VIEWS OF THE RIGHTS OF BRITISH AMERICA, the Declaration of Independence, his NOTES ON VIRGINIA, his opinion on the constitutionality of the Bank of the United States, his inaugural addresses and addresses and messages to Congress, his proclamation on Burr's plot, and his letter to the Burr prosecutor explaining his reasons for refusing to appear personally at the trial. The bibliographic section contains citations to biographies and to Jefferson's papers as well as to general works on the "revolution of 1800" and on the presidency.

_____. THEODORE ROOSEVELT, 1858-1919: CHRONOLOGY-DOCUMENTS-BIBLIOGRAPHIC AIDS. Presidential Chronology Series. Dobbs Ferry, N.Y.: Oceana, 1969.

The first section is a chronology of major events in Roosevelt's early life (1858-1901), his first and second terms as president (1901-9) and his retirement (1909-19). The documentary section includes such materials as his inaugural addresses and messages to Congress. The bibliographic section notes the location of the Roosevelt papers, cites biographies and works on Roosevelt and on the progressive era.

_____. WILLIAM HOWARD TAFT, 1857-1930: CHRONOLOGY-DOCUMENTS-BIBLIOGRAPHIC AIDS. Presidential Chronology Series. Dobbs Ferry, N.Y.: Oceana, 1970.

The first section is a chronology of major events in Taft's early life (1857-80) and his prepresidential career (1880-1909), his presidential years (1909-13), the interim period between leaving the presidency, his assumption of the Chief Justiceship and his years on the Court until his death in 1930. The documentary section includes such materials as his messages to Congress. The last section includes citations to biographies and other works on Taft and to general works on the Progressive era and on the presidency.

Brady, Cyrus Townsend. THE TRUE ANDREW JACKSON. Philadelphia: J.B. Lippincott Co.,1906.

This biography examines Jackson's family and early years, his prepresidential and presidential careers and his place in history. The appendix includes South Carolina's Ordinance of Nullification, Jackson's Nullification Proclamation of 10 December 1832, his Farewell Address of 4 March 1837 and his will.

Brant, Irving N. THE FOURTH PRESIDENT: A LIFE OF JAMES MADISON. Indianapolis: Bobbs-Merrill, 1970.

This is a one-volume condensation of Brant's six-volume THE LIFE OF JAMES MADISON (see next entry).

_____. THE LIFE OF JAMES MADISON. 6 vols. Indianapolis: Bobbs-Merrill, 1941-61.

Despite Madison's acknowledged contributions to the framing of the Constitution, his presidency is not generally viewed as one of his more successful endeavors and there are few biographies of his life or examinations of his presidential years. This six-volume work is considered to be the definitive Madison biography. Volume 1 examines his role as revolutionist. Volume 2, entitled THE NATIONALIST, covers the years 1780 to 1787. Volume 3, entitled FATHER OF THE CONSTITUTION, covers 1787 to 1800 and examines his role in the formation of the Constitution. Volume 4 covers the years from 1800 to 1809 and concentrates on his role as secretary of state. Volume 5 covers the presidential years and volume 6 concentrates on his role as commander in chief.

Bremer, Howard F., ed. FRANKLIN DELANO ROOSEVELT, 1882-1945: CHRONOLOGY-DOCUMENTS-BIBLIOGRAPHIC AIDS. Presidential Chronology Series. Dobbs Ferry, N.Y.: Oceana, 1971.

The first section is a chronology of the major events in the life of Roosevelt from his youth through his early career, his years as governor of New York and his four terms as President. The documents section includes such materials as his inaugural addresses, messages to Congresses, numerous "fireside chats" and the undelivered Jefferson Day Address scheduled for 13 April 1945. The bibliographic section includes citations to biographies of Roosevelt and general works dealing with the New Deal and with foreign policy during the Roosevelt era.

_____. GEORGE WASHINGTON, 1732-1799. CHRONOLOGY-DOCUMENTS-BIBLIOGRAPHIC AIDS. Presidential Chronology Series. Dobbs Ferry, N.Y.: Oceana, 1971.

The first section is a chronology of Washington's life from his birth through his role in the French and Indian War and in the Revolutionary War, his presidential years and his retirement and death. The second section includes copies of such documents as Washington's first and second inaugural addresses, Hamilton's First Report on Public Credit, the Jefferson and Hamilton opinions on the constitutionality of the first national bank, the Proclamations of Neutrality and of the Whiskey Rebellion and his Farewell Address. The section on bibliographic aids includes a list of biographies of Washington and of works dealing with the Federalist era and with the presidency.

_____. JOHN ADAMS, 1735-1826: CHRONOLOGY-DOCUMENTS-BIBLIO-GRAPHIC AIDS. Presidential Chronology Series. Dobbs Ferry, N.Y.: Oceana, 1967.

This reference work includes a chronology of the life of Adams from 1737 to 1797, his term of office from 1797 to 1801 and his post presidential years from 1801-26. It includes documents such as his inaugural address and his messages and addresses to Congress. It also includes citations to publication of the Adams papers which were opened to the public in 1966, to biog-

raphies of Adams as well as to general works dealing with the
Federalist era and with the presidency.

Brooks, Noah. ABRAHAM LINCOLN AND THE DOWNFALL OF AMERICAN
SLAVERY. New York: G.P. Putnam's Sons, 1888.

> Written by a Lincoln contemporary and friend, this one-volume
> biography covers the prepolitical years but is devoted primarily
> to Lincoln's political life and presidential years.

Buchanan, James. THE WORKS OF JAMES BUCHANAN. Edited by John
Bassett Moore. 12 vols. New York: Noble Offset Printers, 1908-11. Reprint. New York: Antiquarian Press, 1960.

> This is a collection of Buchanan's writings from 1813 to 1868.
> Volume 12 contains biographical and autobiographical sketches.

Buell, Augustus C. HISTORY OF ANDREW JACKSON: PIONEER, PATRIOT,
SOLDIER, POLITICIAN, PRESIDENT. 2 vols. London: Bickers and Son,
1904.

> Volume 1 covers Jackson's ancestry, his early military career,
> his years in the House and in the Senate, his relationships with
> Burr and with Jefferson, the war with England, and his prep-
> arations for the Battle of New Orleans. Volume 2 opens with
> the Battle of New Orleans, and examines Jackson's performance
> as governor of Florida, his election to the presidency, his fight
> against nullification and for preservation of the Union, his war
> with the United States Bank, his foreign policy, and his function-
> ing as party leader after his retirement and ends with an assess-
> ment of his character and personality.

Charnwood, Godfrey Rathbone. ABRAHAM LINCOLN. New York: Henry
Holts Co., 1917.

> Although Lord Charnwood's biography deals with Lincoln's early
> life and political career in the state legislature and in Congress,
> it is principally concerned with such matters as the growth of
> American nationalism, secession, and Lincoln's role in the civil
> war.

COLLECTION OF MANUSCRIPTS AND ARCHIVES IN THE FRANKLIN DELANO
ROOSEVELT LIBRARY. Hyde Park, N.Y.: General Services Administration,
FDR Library, 1970.

> Most of the twenty million or so Roosevelt documents and papers
> are housed in the Hyde Park Library with microfilms of many
> available at the National Archives in Washington, D.C. This is
> a list of the materials at Hyde Park.

Colyar, Arthur St. Clair. LIFE AND TIMES OF ANDREW JACKSON:
SOLDIER, STATESMAN, PRESIDENT. 2 vols. Nashville, Tenn.: Marshall
and Bruce, 1904.

> This is a laudatory popular biography of "a great American
> citizen."

Convell, Russell H. THE LIFE, SPEECHES AND PUBLIC SERVICES OF JAMES A. GARFIELD, TWENTIETH PRESIDENT OF THE UNITED STATES, INCLUDING AN ACCOUNT OF HIS ASSASSINATION, LINGERING PAIN, DEATH AND BURIAL. Portland, Maine: George Stinson Co., 1881.

> Beginning with Garfield's genealogy and birth, this work examines his military career, his early speeches, his work in Congress, his inauguration as president and his assassination.

Curtis, James C. ANDREW JACKSON AND THE SEARCH FOR VINDICATION. Boston: Little, Brown, 1976.

> This slim volume, a psychohistorical study of Jackson, suggests that it was the insecurity of his early childhood that led him to channel his aggressive tendencies into hostile actions against real or imagined foes whether they be the Bank of the United States or secessionists.

Dickinson, John N., ed. ANDREW JOHNSON, 1808–1875: CHRONOLOGY-DOCUMENTS-BIBLIOGRAPHIC AIDS. Presidential Chronology Aids. Dobbs Ferry, N.Y.: Oceana, 1970.

> The chronological section covers Johnson's youth, his years as military governor (1862–65), his vice-presidential and presidential years (1865–69), his retirement from the presidency and his attempted return to politics (1869–75). The documentary section includes such materials as his first statement as president on 15 April 1865, his proclamations of mourning and of amnesty and pardon, his message to Congress, and the Articles of Impeachment. The bibliographic section includes citations to biographies, none of which is considered good by the editor, and to works on the Johnson impeachment and on Lincoln as well as on the Reconstruction era.

Durfee, David A., ed. WILLIAM HENRY HARRISON, 1773–1841. JOHN TYLER, 1790–1862. CHRONOLOGY-BIBLIOGRAPHIC AIDS. Presidential Chronology Series. Dobbs Ferry, N.Y.: Oceana, 1970.

> The first part of this slim volume covers major events in Harrison's life and his brief presidency from 4 March to 4 April 1941 and includes his inaugural address and his report on the battle of Tippecanoe. The second part deals with Tyler: major events in his life, his inaugural address, messages to Congress, the text of treaties with Texas and Mexico and a bibliographic guide to biographies and other materials related to his presidency.

Dyer, Brainer. ZACHARY TAYLOR. Baton Rouge: Louisiana University Press, 1946.

> This biography covers Taylor's early life, military career, and presidential years.

Eisenhower, Dwight D. THE WHITE HOUSE YEARS: MANDATE FOR CHANGE, 1953–1956. Garden City, N.Y.: Doubleday, 1963.

This volume of Eisenhower's memoirs covers his first term as president. He deals with such matters as the ending of the Korean War, the relationship between the executive and the congressional branches, the problems of Indochina, and his heart attack.

_____. THE WHITE HOUSE YEARS: WAGING PEACE, 1956-1961. Garden City, N.Y.: Doubleday, 1965.

This second volume of Eisenhower's memoirs covers his second presidential term. It deals with such matters as his second campaign, the Suez crisis, summit meetings, civil rights, the Middle East, and other foreign and domestic policy issues of his second term.

Elliot, Ian, ed. ABRAHAM LINCOLN, 1809-1865: CHRONOLOGY-DOCUMENTS-BIBLIOGRAPHIC AIDS. Presidential Chronology Series. Dobbs Ferry, N.Y.: Oceana Publications, 1970.

The first section is a chronology of Lincoln's early life (1809-35), his political career (1836-61), his terms of office (1861-65) and of events following his death. Documents included consist of his early political speeches, the first Lincoln-Douglas debate, his farewell to Springfield in February of 1861, his inaugural addresses, his arguments against the Emancipation Proclamation, and the Gettysburg address as well as letters. There are also citations to biographies of Lincoln, analyses of his presidency and works on his family members as well as to general works on the presidency.

_____. JAMES MADISON: 1751-1836: CHRONOLOGY-DOCUMENTS-BIBLIO-GRAPHICAL AIDS. Presidential Chronology Series. Dobbs Ferry, N.Y.: Oceana, 1969.

The first section contains a chronology of events in Madison's life divided into three major parts: his early life and governmental service (1751-1809), his term in office (1809-17) and his later life and retirement (1817-49). The "Documents" section contains such materials as "Federalist No. 10" and his inaugural addresses and messages to Congress. The last section contains citations to such materials as Irving Brant's biography of Madison and to general works dealing with the framing of the Constitution and the early days of the Republic, a period in which Madison played a major role as theoretician of government. There is also a short list of general works on the presidency.

Farrell, John J., ed. ZACHARY TAYLOR, 1784-1850. MILLARD FILLMORE, 1800-1874. CHRONOLOGY-DOCUMENTS-BIBLIOGRAPHIC AIDS. Presidential Chronology Series. Dobbs Ferry, N.Y.: Oceana, 1971.

The first half of this guide consists of a chronology of events in the life of Taylor and of such documents as his inaugural address and messages to Congress and the announcement of his death on 9 July 1850. The second half includes a chronology of events in Fillmore's life as a congressman, as vice-president, as president and as a Know-Nothing candidate, a compilation of documents such as the Compromise of 1850 and his messages to

Congress, and a list of biographies, monographs, and other
source materials.

Flexner, James T. GEORGE WASHINGTON. 3 vols. London: Little,
Brown, 1967-70.

Volume 1, entitled THE FORGE OF EXPERIENCE, covers the
period from Washington's birth in 1732 to the eve of the Revolution in 1775. Volume 2, entitled THE AMERICAN REVOLUTION,
is a day-by-day account of the years between 1775 and 1783.
Volume 3, entitled AND THE NEW NATION, covers 1783-93.

Freeman, Douglas Southall. GEORGE WASHINGTON: A BIOGRAPHY. 7
vols. New York: Charles Scribner's Sons, 1948-57.

The first five volumes cover the prepresidential years. Volumes
1 and 2 deal with YOUNG WASHINGTON. Volume 3 is entitled
PLANTER AND PATRIOT. Volume 4, LEADER OF THE REVOLU-
TION, and volume 5, VICTORY WITH THE HELP OF THE
FRENCH, focus on the revolutionary years. Volume 6, PATRIOT
AND PRESIDENT, deals with Washington's first administration.
At the time of his death, Freeman had completed his work to
Washington's sixty-first birthday on the eve of his second adminis-
tration. His work was concluded by John Alexander Carroll and
Mary Wells Ashworth who wrote volume 7, FIRST IN PEACE,
dealing with the second Washington administration, and his post-
presidential years. Volume 7 also contains a bibliography of
Washington's manuscripts, letters, diaries, and memoirs as well
as secondary works.

Freidel, Frank. FRANKLIN DELANO ROOSEVELT. 4 vols. to date.
Boston: Little, Brown, 1952-73.

Volume 1 of this biography of Roosevelt, subtitled THE APPREN-
TICESHIP, deals with the period through the First World War.
Volume 2, subtitled THE ORDEAL and published in 1954, covers
Roosevelt's campaign for vice-president, his struggle with polio,
and his first election as governor of New York by a narrow mar-
gin. Volume 3, subtitled THE TRIUMPH and published in 1956,
deals with the period from his governorship to the first presidential victory. Volume 4, subtitled LAUNCHING THE NEW DEAL,
deals with the first year of the New Deal.

Furer, Howard B., ed. HARRY S. TRUMAN, 1884--; CHRONOLOGY-
DOCUMENTS-BIBLIOGRAPHIC AIDS. Presidential Chronology Series.
Dobbs Ferry, N.Y.: Oceana, 1970.

The first section is a chronology of Truman's life from his birth
to his retirement. The second section includes such documents
as his addresses to Congress, his inaugural address, the Point
Four Program, his recall of MacArthur and his farewell address.
The last section includes not only citations to biographies of
Truman but reference to general works on the atomic bomb
decision, on the post-World War II era, on the Fair Deal, the
Cold War, and the Korean War.

_____. JAMES A. GARFIELD, 1831–1881. CHESTER A. ARTHUR, 1830–1886. CHRONOLOGY-DOCUMENTS-BIBLIOGRAPHIC AIDS. Presidential Chronology Series. Dobbs Ferry, N.Y.: Oceana, 1970.

> The first half of this guide contains a chronology of important events in Garfield's early life and his career in Congress and during his brief administration as well as a copy of his inaugural address. The second half consists of a chronology of events in Arthur's life, of documents such as his inaugural address, various messages to Congress, his vetoes of such legislation as the Chinese Exclusion Act of 1882 and a bibliography of such materials as biographies, letters, and diaries.

_____. LYNDON BAINES JOHNSON, 1908--; CHRONOLOGY-DOCUMENTS-BIBLIOGRAPHIC AIDS. Presidential Chronology Series. Dobbs Ferry, N.Y.: Oceana, 1971.

> The chronology section is divided into five parts: youth and early career (1908-37), congressional and senatorial years (1937-61), vice-presidential years (1961-63), first term as president (1963-65) and second presidential term (1965-69). The documentary section includes such materials as Johnson's address before a joint session of Congress on 27 November 1963, his state of the union messages, his inaugural address, the appointment of the Warren Commission and such messages as those on the war on poverty, civil rights, the war in Vietnam, Medicare, and the Economic Opportunity Act of 1964. The bibliographic section cites biographies and works on specialized aspects of his career, on politics and government during the Kennedy and Johnson years and general works on civil rights, the war on poverty, the Vietnam war, and the urban crisis.

Garfield, James A. THE DIARY OF JAMES A. GARFIELD. Edited by Harry J. Brown and Frederick D. Williams. 3 vols. East Lansing: Michigan State University Press, 1967.

> With an introduction by the editors, volume 1 covers the period from 1848-71, volume 2 covers the years from 1872-74 and volume 3 covers 1885-87.

_____. JAMES ABRAM GARFIELD, LIFE AND PAPERS. Edited by Theodore Clarke Smith. 2 vols. New Haven, Conn.: Yale University Press, 1925.

> Volume 1 covers the period from 1831 to 1877 and volume 2 covers the years from 1877 to 1882.

_____. WORKS OF JAMES ABRAM GARFIELD. Edited by B.A. Hinsdale. 2 vols. Boston: James R. Osgood Co., 1882.

> Volume 1 includes Garfield's speeches in the House on a variety of matters such as the confiscation of the property of southern rebels, the Fourteenth Amendment and the civil rights legislation of the 1860s and 1870s. Arranged chronologically, it covers the period from 1864 to 1872. Volume 2 includes House speeches beginning in 1872, speeches outside the House and such materials as his arguments before the Supreme Court. It concludes with his inaugural address on 4 March 1881.

Goldman, Eric F. THE TRAGEDY OF LYNDON JOHNSON. New York: Knopf, 1969.

This "memoir" by a Princeton historian who served as a special consultant to the president from 1963 to 1966 is a historical analysis of the Johnson presidency.

Grant, Ulysses. PAPERS OF ULYSSES S. GRANT. Edited by John T. Simon. 6 vols. Carbondale: Southern Illinois University Press, 1967-77.

The six volumes to date cover the years from 1837 to 1862. Volume 1 covers the years from 1837 to 1861. Volume 2 includes the papers from April through September of 1861. Volume 3 covers from 1 October 1861 to 7 January 1862. Volume 4 covers the period from 8 January to 31 March 1862. Volume 5 covers the period from 1 April to August 1862. Volume 6 published in 1977, covers the period from 1 September to 8 December 1862.

Hamilton, Holman. ZACHARY TAYLOR: SOLDIER IN THE WHITE HOUSE. Indianapolis: Bobbs-Merrill, 1951.

This scholarly biography begins with Taylor's return to the United States in 1847 after the Mexican War and focuses upon his political life and his presidential years. It concludes with Taylor's death and with an assessment of his place in history.

_____. ZACHARY TAYLOR: SOLDIER OF THE REPUBLIC. Indianapolis: Bobbs-Merrill, 1941.

This biography deals with Taylor's military career before he turned to politics.

Harwell, Richard. WASHINGTON. New York: Charles Scribner's Sons, 1968.

This is a one-volume abridgment of the seven-volume GEORGE WASHINGTON: A BIOGRAPHY by Douglas Southall Freeman published by Scribner, 1948-57.

Hayes, Rutherford Birchard. DIARY AND LETTERS OF RUTHERFORD BIRCHARD HAYES, NINETEENTH PRESIDENT OF THE UNITED STATES. Edited by Charles R. Williams. 5 vols. Columbus: Ohio State Archeological and Historical Society, 1922-26.

Volume 1 contains the diary and papers from 1834 to 1860. Volume 2 covers the period from 1860 to 1864. Volume 3 covers 1865 to 1881. Volume 4 covers 1881 to 1891. Volume 5 covers the period from 1891 until his death in January of 1893.

_____. THE DIARY OF A PRESIDENT, 1875-1881, COVERING THE DISPUTED ELECTION, THE END OF RECONSTRUCTION, AND THE BEGINNING OF CIVIL SERVICE. Edited by T. Harry Williams. New York: David McKay, 1964.

This reproduction of the diaries of Hayes from 1875 to 1881 includes explanatory notes by the editor who attempts to correct what he refers to as the scholarly shortcomings of the diary and letters edited by Charles R. Williams and published in five volumes from 1922 to 1926 (above).

Hecht, Marie V. JOHN QUINCY ADAMS: A PERSONAL HISTORY OF AN INDEPENDENT MAN. New York: Macmillan, 1972.

This one-volume biography, based on Columbia University's microfilmed copies of the Adams papers, deals with Adams's education, his years as a cabinet member, as president and as a member of the House of Representatives.

Hunt, Gaillard. THE LIFE OF JAMES MADISON. New York: Doubleday, Page, 1902. Reprint. Ann Arbor, Mich.: University Microfilms, 1965. Micro-xerography.

This one-volume biography by the editor of THE WRITINGS OF JAMES MADISON (p. 161) begins with Madison's family background, ends with his death and deals with important phases of his life such as his early contributions to liberty in Virginia, his role in the framing of the Constitution before and during the Philadelphia convention, and his leadership in the Congress which proposed the Bill of Rights as well as his presidential years.

Israel, Fred, ed. STATE OF THE UNION MESSAGES OF THE PRESIDENTS, 1790-1966. Introduction by Arthur Schlesinger. 3 vols. New York: Chelsea House, 1966.

With an index, this contains the texts of state of the union addresses from Washington to Lyndon B. Johnson.

Jackson, Andrew. CORRESPONDENCE OF ANDREW JACKSON. Edited by John Spencer Bassett. 7 vols. Vol. 7 prepared by D.M. Matteson. Washington, D.C.: Carnegie Institution of Washington, 1926-35.

With a preface by the editor and derived from the Jackson manuscripts in the Library of Congress, from the papers of Van Buren, Polk, and others in the Library of Congress and the Jackson papers in the New York Public Library, the Tennessee Historical Society, the Historical Society of Pennsylvania and other sources, this is a collection of letters to and from mostly from Jackson. Volume 1 includes letters written to April 1814. Volume 2 covers 1 May 1814 to 31 December 1819. Volume 3 covers 1820 to 1828. Volume 4 covers 1829 to 1832. Volume 5 covers 1833 to 1838. Volume 6 covers 1839 to 1845. Volume 7, prepared by D.M. Matteson, is a general index to letters contained in the first six-volumes.

Jefferson, Thomas. CALENDAR OF THE CORRESPONDENCE OF THOMAS JEFFERSON. 3 vols. Washington, D.C.: Bureau of Rolls and Library of Department of State, 1894-1903. Reprint. New York: Burt Franklin, 1970.

A guide to the published and unpublished correspondence of Jefferson held by the Library of Congress.

_____. JEFFERSON LETTERS: SELECTIONS FROM THE PRIVATE AND POLITICAL CORRESPONDENCE OF THOMAS JEFFERSON, TELLING THE STORY OF AMERICAN INDEPENDENCE, AND THE FOUNDING OF THE AMERICAN GOVERNMENT. Edited by William Whitman. Eau Claire, Wis.: E.M. Hale, n.d.

This is a brief selection of letters written by Jefferson between 1762 and June of 1826, the last an acknowledgment of an invitation to join a celebration in Washington of the fiftieth anniversary of the signing of the Declaration of Independence.

_____. THE PAPERS OF THOMAS JEFFERSON. Edited by Julian Boyd. 19 vols. Princeton, N.J.: Princeton University Press, 1950-- .

The writings contained in the 19 volumes published to date cover the prepresidential years, with volume 1 covering the years from 1760 to 1776 and volume 19, published in 1974, covering from January to March of 1791.

_____. THE WORKS OF THOMAS JEFFERSON. Edited by Paul L. Ford. 12 vols. New York: G.P. Putnam's Sons, 1904-05.

This collection of Jefferson's writings includes such materials as his letters, legal arguments, resolutions and political works. Volume 1 contains his autobiography and an introduction by the editor and, as the other volumes, contains an itinerary and a chronology of events covered by the volume.

_____. THE WRITINGS OF THOMAS JEFFERSON, BEING HIS AUTOBIOGRAPHY, CORRESPONDENCE, REPORTS, MESSAGES, ADDRESSES AND OTHER WRITINGS, OFFICIAL AND PRIVATE. Edited by H.A. Washington. 9 vols. Philadelphia: J.B. Lippincott Co., 1864.

Published by order of the Joint Committee of Congress on the Library, this collection is the published version of the original manuscripts deposited in the Department of State. Volume 1 begins with Jefferson's autobiography and volume 9 ends with a copy of his will.

_____. THE WRITINGS OF THOMAS JEFFERSON, CONTAINING HIS AUTOBIOGRAPHY, NOTES ON VIRGINIA, PARLIAMENTARY MANUAL, OFFICIAL PAPERS, MESSAGES AND ADDRESSES, AND OTHER WRITINGS, OFFICIAL AND PRIVATE, NOW COLLECTED AND PUBLISHED IN THEIR ENTIRETY FOR THE FIRST TIME, INCLUDING ALL OF THE ORIGINAL MANUSCRIPTS DEPOSITED IN THE DEPARTMENT OF STATE AND PUBLISHED IN 1853 BY THE ORDER OF THE JOINT COMMITTEE OF CONGRESS, WITH NUMEROUS ILLUSTRATIONS AND A COMPREHENSIVE INDEX. 20 vols. Washington, D.C.: Thomas Jefferson Memorial Association, 1903-5.

This collection contains the materials enumerated in the title. Volume 20 is an analytical index.

Jefferson, Thomas and DuPont de Nemours, Pierre Samuel. THE CORRES-PONDENCE OF JEFFERSON AND DuPONT de NEMOURS. Edited by Gilbert Chimard. Johns Hopkins Studies in International Thought. Baltimore: Johns Hopkins Press, 1931. Reprint. New York: Burt Franklin, 1971.

With an introduction on Jefferson and the physiocrats by the editor, this collection of correspondence covers the period between 1781 and Jefferson's death in 1826.

_____. CORRESPONDENCE BETWEEN THOMAS JEFFERSON AND PIERRE SAMUEL DU PONT de NEMOURS, 1798–1817. Edited by Dumas Malone. 1930. Reprint. New York: Da Capo Press, 1970.

This is a collection of the early correspondence between Jefferson and de Nemours. Latter correspondence is included in Gilbert Chinard's THE CORRESPONDENCE OF JEFFERSON AND DUPONT de NEMOURS (see p. 157).

Johnson, Andrew. THE PAPERS OF ANDREW JOHNSON. Edited by Leroy Graf and Ralph Haskins. 4 vols. Knoxville: University of Tennessee Press, 1967–76.

With an introduction by the editors, these four volumes of the papers of Johnson, who died in July of 1875, cover the period from 1822 to 1861. Volume 1 covers 1822 to 1851. Volume 2 covers the period from 1852 to 1857. Volume 3 covers the years from 1858 to 1860. Volume 4 covers 1860 to 1861.

Johnson, Lyndon Baines. THE VANTAGE POINT: PERSPECTIVES OF THE PRESIDENCY, 1963–1969. New York: Holt, Rinehart and Winston, 1971.

This is Johnson's memoirs of his presidency and an explanation of his foreign and domestic policies.

Jones, Kenneth V., ed. JOHN QUINCY ADAMS, 1767–1848: CHRONOLOGY-DOCUMENTS-BIBLIOGRAPHIC AIDS. Presidential Chronology Series. Dobbs Ferry, N.Y.: Oceana, 1970.

The first section is a chronology of major events in the life of Adams: his early life (1767–94), his early diplomatic career (1794–1803), his senate years (1803–8), his later diplomatic years (1809–16), his tenure as secretary of state (1816–25), his presidency (1825–28) and his years in Congress after he left the presidency (1829–52). The documentary section includes his diary comments on Henry Clay's visit on 9 January 1825, his inaugural address and messages to Congress and his diary entry after the gag rule was revoked in December 1844. The bibliographic section includes citations to biographies of Adams and to works dealing with his presidency and his congressional years, his role in specific areas such as foreign policy, his political philosophy and to general works dealing with the era of good feeling.

Kearns, Doris. LYNDON JOHNSON AND THE AMERICAN DREAM. New York: Harper and Row, 1976.

This is basically an analysis of the Johnson character by a Harvard professor who served as a White House Fellow in 1976 and became something of a Johnson confidante.

Klein, Philip S. PRESIDENT JAMES BUCHANAN: A BIBLIOGRAPHY. University Park: Pennsylvania State University Press, 1962.

This biography covers Buchanan's pioneering years in Pennsylvania, his entrance into politics and development as a Democratic party "kingmaker" and organizer along with Jackson and his presidential and retirement years. The bibliography contains citations to primary and secondary sources dealing with Buchanan's party and presidential role and to various official documents and contemporary writings of the Jacksonian era.

Lincoln, Abraham. ABRAHAM LINCOLN: COMPLETE WORKS. Edited by John G. Nicolay and John Hay. 12 vols. New York: Century, 1894. Reprint. New York: F.D. Tandy, 1905.

This collection of Lincoln's speeches, letters and state papers by his private secretaries was generally considered to be the most complete collection until the publication from 1953 to 1974 by the Abraham Lincoln Association of Springfield, Illinois of THE COLLECTED WORKS OF ABRAHAM LINCOLN under the editorship of Roy P. Basler (see p. 159). Most of volume 11 of the Nicolay collection is a bibliography of works on Lincoln. Volume 12 is an index to the first ten volumes.

_____. ABRAHAM LINCOLN: HIS SPEECHES AND WRITINGS. Edited by Roy P. Basler. Cleveland: World Publishing Co., 1946. Reprint. New York: Kraus, 1969.

With critical and analytical notes by the editor and a preface by Carl Sandburg, this is a one-volume selection of some of what the editor views as the "best" Lincoln letters and speeches, best in terms of historical importance, literary significance or human interest. Most of the selections are from the original manuscripts or from photostats of the original with a few from the Nicolay and Hay collection.

_____. ABRAHAM LINCOLN: SELECTED SPEECHES, MESSAGES AND LETTERS. Edited by T. Harry Williams. New York: Holt, Rinehart and Winston, 1957.

With an introduction and notes by the editor, a noted Civil War scholar and author of LINCOLN AND THE RADICALS AND LINCOLN AND HIS GENERALS, this is a paperback selection of materials from THE COLLECTED WORKS OF ABRAHAM LINCOLN edited by Roy P. Basler (below). The papers selected cover Lincoln's early years, the period of the controversy over slavery, his election as president, and the Civil War period.

_____. THE COLLECTED WORKS OF ABRAHAM LINCOLN. Edited by Roy P. Basler, assisted by Marion Dolores Pratt and Lloyd A. Dunlap. 8 vols. New Brunswick, N.J.: Rutgers University Press, 1953-74.

Published under the auspices of the Abraham Lincoln Association of Springfield, Illinois, this is the most recent and up-to-date collection of Lincoln's work superseding the twelve-volume ABRAHAM LINCOLN: COMPLETE WORKS edited by Lincoln's private secretaries, John G. Nicolay and John Hay and published originally in 1894, (above). Volume 1 covers 1824 to 1848. Volume 2 covers 1848 to 1858. Volume 3 covers 1858 to 1860. Volume 4

covers 1860 to 1861. Volume 5 covers 1861 to 1862. Volume
6 covers 1862 to 1863. Volume 7 covers 1863 to 1864. Volume
8 covers 1864 to 1865. An additional volume is an index to the
names, places and subjects of the documents and notes in the 8
volumes. The index also contains a list of the institutions where
the papers are located as well as such materials as a list of
forgeries of Lincoln papers. There is also a supplementary
volume containing additional papers for the years 1832 and 1865.

_____. THE LINCOLN READER. Edited by Paul M. Angle. New Bruns-
wick, N.J.: Rutgers University Press, 1947.

With an introduction by the editor, this biographical narrative
consists of selections from the writings of a variety of Lincoln
scholars such as Carl Sandburg, Ida Tarbell, Lord Charnwood,
John G. Nicolay, and James Randall. The selections examine
Lincoln's life from his childhood in Kentucky to his death.

Lincoln, Abraham. NEW LETTERS AND PAPERS OF LINCOLN. Edited by
Paul M. Angle. Boston: Houghton Mifflin Co., 1930.

This collection is primarily a supplement to ABRAHAM LINCOLN:
COMPLETE WORKS, edited by John G. Nicolay and John Hay
and published in 1894 (see p. 159), UNCOLLECTED LETTERS OF
ABRAHAM LINCOLN, edited by Gilbert A. Tracy and published
in 1917, and LINCOLN LETTERS AT BROWN, published by Brown
University in 1927. Although it includes some papers in other
collections, it excludes materials published in these three collections.

_____. UNCOLLECTED WORKS OF ABRAHAM LINCOLN: HIS LETTERS,
ADDRESSES AND OTHER PAPERS. Edited by Rufus Rockwell Wilson.
Introduction by George Fort Milton. 2 vols. Elmira, N.Y.: The Primanera
Press, 1947-48.

This is a supplement to and revision of the ABRAHAM LINCOLN:
COMPLETE WORKS by Nicolay and Hay (see p. 159). Volume 1
covers the period from 1824 to 1840. Volume 2 covers the period
from 1841 to 1845.

Link, Arthur S. WOODROW WILSON. 5 vols. Princeton, N.J.: Princeton
University Press, 1947-65.

Volume 1 of this biography is entitled WILSON: THE ROAD TO
THE WHITE HOUSE. Volume 2, entitled WILSON: THE NEW
FREEDOM, deals with domestic policy. Volume 3, entitled
STRUGGLE FOR NEUTRALITY, covers foreign policy from 1914
to 1915. Volume 4, entitled CONFUSIONS AND CRISES, covers
1915 to 1916. Volume 5, published in 1965 and entitled CAM-
PAIGNS FOR PROGRESSIVISM AND PEACE, covers 1916 to
1917.

_____. WOODROW WILSON: A BRIEF BIOGRAPHY. New York: New
Viewpoints, 1963.

This is a short biography by the renowned Wilson scholar.

McDonald, Forrest. THE PRESIDENCY OF THOMAS JEFFERSON. Lawrence: University Press of Kansas, 1976.

This study of Jefferson as president is critical of both the personal characteristics and attitudes he brought to the office and of his foreign and domestic policies.

Madison, James. THE PAPERS OF JAMES MADISON. Edited by William T. Hutchinson, William M.E. Rachal, Robert Rutland, Charles F. Hobson and Frederika Teute. 10 vols. Chicago: University of Chicago Press, 1962-- .

The first eight volumes of the ten volumes published to date include the correspondence and letters of Madison to 1786. Volumes 9 and 10, edited by Robert A. Rutland, Charles F. Hobson, William M.E. Rachal, and Frederika Teute contain his papers to 1788.

_____. THE WRITINGS OF JAMES MADISON: COVERING HIS PUBLIC PAPERS AND PRIVATE CORRESPONDENCE INCLUDING NUMEROUS LETTERS AND DOCUMENTS NOW FOR THE FIRST TIME PRINTED. 9 vols. Edited by Gaillard Hunt. New York: G.P. Putnam's Sons, 1900-1910. Ann Arbor, Mich.: University Microfilms, 1967. Microfilm-xerography.

Volumes 1 (1769-83) and 2 (1783-87) consist of letters written by Madison. Volumes 3 and 4 contain his JOURNAL OF THE CONSTITUTIONAL CONVENTION. Volume 5, covering 1787 to 1790, contains his letters and speeches in Virginia's ratifying convention. Volume 6, covering 1790 to 1802, contains letters to political associates and to newspapers as well as his congressional speeches and essays. Volume 7, covering 1802 to 1808, contains letters. Volume 8, covering 1808 to 1819, contains his letters, inaugural address and congressional messages. Volume 9, covering 1819 to 1836, contains letters and an alphabetical list of letters and papers printed in the other volumes with the exception of volumes 3 and 4 which contain the JOURNAL.

Malone, Dumas, JEFFERSON AND HIS TIMES. 5 vols. Boston: Little, Brown, 1948-75.

Volume 1 is entitled JEFFERSON THE VIRGINIAN. Volume 2 is entitled JEFFERSON AND THE RIGHTS OF MAN. Volume 3 is entitled JEFFERSON AND THE ORDEAL OF LIBERTY. Volumes 4 and 5 deal with the presidential years. Volume 4, JEFFERSON THE PRESIDENT, covers his first term from 1801 to 1805. Volume 5, JEFFERSON THE PRESIDENT, covers the second term from 1805 to 1809.

Marshall, John. THE LIFE OF GEORGE WASHINGTON. 5 vols. Philadelphia: C.R. Wayne, 1805. Reprint. Fredericksburg, Va.: Citizens Guild, 1926.

Volume 1 of Marshall's biography of Washington deals with colonial history. Volume 2 begins with the birth of Washington and the remaining volumes cover the period until his death.

Mearns, David C. THE LINCOLN PAPERS: THE STORY OF THE COLLEC-
TION WITH SELECTIONS TO JULY 4, 1861. 2 vols. Garden City, N.Y.:
Doubleday, 1948. Reprint. New York: Kraus.

> Many of Lincoln's papers were not publicly available until 26 July
> 1947. Held by Lincoln's son, who restricted access to them
> during his life and who prohibited access until twenty-one years
> after his death, the papers were made available only to a limited
> number of persons prior to 1947. The first portion of this work
> tells the story of the papers and the second portion includes some
> of the newly available Lincoln papers.

Moran, Philip R., ed. CALVIN COOLIDGE, 1872-1933: CHRONOLOGY-
DOCUMENTS-BIBLIOGRAPHIC AIDS. Presidential Chronology Series.
Dobbs Ferry, N.Y.: Oceana, 1970.

> The first section is a chronology of major events in the life of
> Coolidge from his birth through his vice-presidency and presidency
> to his retirement and death. The documents section includes his
> first and second inaugural addresses, the Kellogg-Briand Pact
> as well as the Supreme Court's decision in McGrain v. Daughtery.
> The last section includes citations to biographies of Coolidge as
> well as to general works dealing with policies during the Coolidge
> years.

_____. ULYSSES S. GRANT, 1822-1865: CHRONOLOGY-DOCUMENTS-
BIBLIOGRAPHIC AIDS. Presidential Chronology Series. Dobbs Ferry,
N.Y.: Oceana, 1968.

> The first section is a chronology of major events in Grant's youth
> and early army career (1822-60), his Civil War career (1861-65),
> his presidency (1869-77) and his retirement (1877-85). The docu-
> ments section includes such materials as his inaugural address
> and messages to Congress, various proclamations such as those
> on the Ku Klux Klan in 1871 and on the suspension of habeas
> corpus in 1871 and statements on Klan violence and on the 1875
> Louisiana elections. The bibliographic section contains citations
> to the papers of and biographies about Grant and to military
> studies and to general works on Reconstruction.

_____. WARREN G. HARDING, 1865-1923: CHRONOLOGY-DOCUMENTS-
BIBLIOGRAPHIC AIDS. Presidential Chronology Series. Dobbs Ferry,
N.Y.: Oceana, 1970.

> The first section is a chronology of major events in the early
> life and career of Harding and of his presidency. Major docu-
> ments, such as his inaugural address and addresses and messages
> to Congress, the Budget and Accounting Act of 1921 and the 1922
> treaty with Columbia are included in the second section. There
> is a bibliography of biographies and of general works dealing with
> Harding's foreign policy and on "normalcy."

Mugridge, Donald H., comp. THE PRESIDENTS OF THE UNITED STATES,
1789-1962: A SELECTED LIST OF REFERENCES. Washington, D.C.:
Government Printing Office, 1963.

This publication of the General Reference and Bibliography Division of the Library of Congress is a bibliography of general works on the presidency and the vice-presidency and on presidential elections as well as of works dealing with individual presidents from Washington through Kennedy.

Parton, James. LIFE OF ANDREW JACKSON. 3 vols. 1864. Reprint. New York: Mason Brothers, 1906. Reprint. New York: Johnson Reprint Corp., 1967.

The first two volumes deal with Jackson's life prior to his national political career. Volume 3 covers his years in the Senate and in the White House. Parton concludes that Jackson's "elevation to President was a mistake" because he was essentially just a "fighting man" and because his legacy was primarily corruption and inefficiency in government.

Polk, James K. CORRESPONDENCE OF JAMES K. POLK. Edited by Herbert Weaver and Paul H. Bergeron. 2 vols. to date. Nashville, Tenn.: Vanderbilt University Press, 1969-- .

These letters to and from Polk are arranged in chronological order. Volume 1 covers 1817 to 1832. Volume 2 covers 1833 to 1834.

_____. THE DIARY OF JAMES K. POLK, DURING HIS PRESIDENCY, 1845 TO 1849. Edited by Milo K. Quaefe. Introduction by Andrew C. McLaughlin. 4 vols. Chicago: A.C. McClurg, 1910.

With annotations by the editor, this diary was printed from the original manuscripts in the collection of the Chicago Historical Society. Volume 1 covers 1845, volume 2 covers 1846, volume 3 covers 1847, and volume 4 covers 1848 and 1849. There is a one-volume selection of materials from this diary edited by Allan Nevins and published in 1929.

_____. POLK: THE DIARY OF A PRESIDENT, 1845-1847, COVERING THE MEXICAN WAR, THE ACQUISITION OF OREGON AND THE CONQUEST OF CALIFORNIA AND THE SOUTHWEST. New York: Longmans, Green and Co., 1929. New York: Capricorn Books, 1952. Paper.

This one-volume collection consists of selections from the four-volume DIARY OF JAMES K. POLK, DURING HIS PRESIDENCY, 1845 to 1849 edited and annotated by Milo K. Quaefe (see above) and published in limited numbers in 1910.

Randall, James G., and Current, Richard N. LINCOLN THE PRESIDENT. 4 vols. New York: Dodd, Mead and Co., 1945-55.

The first two volumes of this work by Randall, a scholar of the Lincoln presidency, entitled LINCOLN THE PRESIDENT: FROM SPRINGFIELD TO GETTYSBURG, deal with the first half of the Lincoln administration. Volume 3, entitled LINCOLN THE PRESIDENT: MIDSTREAM, deals with the middle years of the presidency. These three volumes were written by Randall who died with about half of the fourth volume completed. Volume 4, entitled LINCOLN THE PRESIDENT: LAST FULL MEASURE, was completed by Current. Randall is also the author of LINCOLN

THE LIBERAL STATESMAN (Dodd, Mead, 1947) and CONSTITU-
TIONAL PROBLEMS UNDER LINCOLN (University of Illinois
Press, 1951).

Reid, John, and Eaton, John H. THE LIFE OF ANDREW JACKSON, MAJOR
GENERAL IN THE SERVICE OF THE UNITED STATES. Philadelphia: M.
Carey, 1817. Reprint. Introduction by Frank Lawrence Owsley. Univer-
sity of Alabama Press, 1974.

This biography focuses upon the military career of Jackson through
the War of 1812 and the Battle of New Orleans.

Rice, Arnold S., ed. HERBERT HOOVER, 1874–1963: CHRONOLOGY-
DOCUMENTS-BIBLIOGRAPHIC AIDS. Presidential Chronology Series.
Dobbs Ferry, N.Y.: Oceana, 1971.

The first section is a chronology of major events in Hoover's
youth and professional career (1874–1914), his early government
service (1914–21), his term as secretary of commerce and as
president and in his retirement from 1933 to his death in 1964.
Among the documents included are his inaugural address, messages
to Congress, his 1930 statement on the Hawley–Smoot Tariff Bill,
the Stimson doctrine of 1932 and his address on a balanced budget delivered in 1932. The bibliographic section cites biographies
of and works by Hoover and offers information on Hoover's unpublished papers, access to which is still restricted.

Rives, William C. HISTORY OF THE LIFE AND TIMES OF JAMES MADISON.
3 vols. Boston: Little, Brown, 1859–68.

This work deals with Madison's prepresidential years. Volume 1
covers the period through the Revolutionary War. Volume 2 covers
the period from the end of the war to the adoption of the Constitution. Volume 3 deals with his congressional years. The author
died before completing an intended fourth volume which was to
cover the period through Washington's second administration.

Rice, Arnold S., ed. HERBERT HOOVER, 1874–1963: CHRONOLOGY-
DOCUMENTS-BIBLIOGRAPHIC AIDS. Presidential Chronology Series. Dobbs
Ferry, N.Y.: Oceana, 1971.

The first section is a chronology of major events in Hoover's
youth and professional career (1874–14), his early government
service (1914–21), his term as secretary of commerce and as
president and in his retirement from 1933 to his death in 1964.
Among the documents included are his inaugural address, messages
to Congress, his 1930 statement on the Hawley–Smoot Tariff Bill,
the Stimson doctrine of 1932 and his address on a balanced budget delivered in 1932. The bibliographic section cites biographies
of and works by Hoover and offers information on Hoover's unpublished papers, access to which is still restricted.

Roosevelt, Franklin. THE COMPLETE PRESIDENTIAL PRESS CONFERENCE
OF FRANKLIN DELANO ROOSEVELT, 1933–1945. Introduction by Jonathan
Daniels. 12 vols. Franklin D. Roosevelt and the Era of the New Deal
Series. New York: Da Capo Press, 1973.

This twelve-volume work, prepared from the transcripts at the
Roosevelt Library at Hyde Park, is the first published record
of the Roosevelt press conferences held in a period when in-
formality rather than television cameras dominated.

_____. F.D.R.: HIS PERSONAL LETTERS. Edited by Elliott Roosevelt.
4 vols. Introduction by Eleanor Roosevelt. New York: Duell, Sloan and
Pearce, 1947-50.

This is a collection of letters to family and friends. Volume 1
covers the early years and consists primarily of Roosevelt's
letters to his mother and father. Volume 2 contains letters of
the 1905-28 period. The last two volumes contain letters written
as governor of New York and as president.

Roosevelt, Franklin Delano. THE PUBLIC PAPERS AND ADDRESSES OF
FRANKLIN DELANO ROOSEVELT. Edited by Samuel J. Rosenman. 13
vols. New York: Random House, Macmillan and Harper, 1938-50.
Reprint. New York: Russell and Russell, 1970.

Volumes 1 through 5 were published by Random House, volume 6
through 9 by Macmillan and volumes 10 through 13 by Harper.
Volume 1 includes Roosevelt's public papers and addresses for
the prepresidential years 1928-1932. Volumes 2 and 3, THE
YEARS OF CRISIS, cover 1933-1934. Volume 4, THE COURT
DISAPPROVES, covers 1935. Volume 5, THE PEOPLE APPROVE,
covers 1936. Volume 6, THE CONSTITUTION PREVAILS,
covers 1937. Volume 8 includes the papers of the last prewar
year of 1938. Volumes 9, 10, and 11 include the papers and
addresses of the years when Roosevelt's attention was riveted
on the war in Europe--1939, 1940, and 1941. The remaining
volumes cover the World War II years until the death of Roosevelt in 1945.

_____. THE WORKS OF THEODORE ROOSEVELT. Edited by Herman
Hagedorn. 20 vols. New York: Charles Scribner's Sons, prepared under
the auspices of the Theodore Roosevelt Memorial Association, 1913, 1925.

Each volume of this collection of the writings of Roosevelt has
a different title and deals with a different subject. Thus, volume
1 deals with hunting trips and ranching, volume 14 deals with
campaigns and political controversies, volume 15 contains Roosevelt's state papers while he was governor of New York and president, and volume 20 is his autobiography. Each of the first nine-
teen volumes has a brief study of Roosevelt during the period
covered, written by various scholars.

Sandburg, Carl. ABRAHAM LINCOLN: THE PRAIRIE YEARS. 2 vols.
New York: Harcourt, Brace and World, 1926.

This two-volume biography begins with Lincoln's ancestry and
early years and concludes with his last week in Springfield before
leaving for Washington and assumption of his presidential duties.

_____. ABRAHAM LINCOLN: THE WAR YEARS. 4 vols. New York: Har-
court, Brace and World, 1936-39.

Volume 1 begins with Lincoln's election as president and ends
with the resignations of Seward and Chase and the revocations
of their resignations. Volume 2 covers the period from the
Emancipation Proclamation to the problems surrounding Chase's
presidential ambitions. Volume 3 covers the period from the
spring of 1864 to the end of that year. Volume 4 covers the
adoption of the Thirteenth Amendment, the second inaugural and
ends with Lincoln's assassination, funeral, and burial in Springfield.

Sellers, Charles G. JAMES K. POLK. 2 vols to date. Princeton, N.J.:
Princeton University Press, 1957-- .

Volume 1, subtitled JACKSONIAN, 1795 to 1843, deals with
Polk's early life and his state political career. Volume 2, subtitled CONTINENTALIST, 1843 to 1846 and published in 1966,
begins with Polk's successful return to politics after his second
defeat for the governorship of Tennessee and covers his national
career to the presidency. The soon to be published third volume
will presumably deal with the last two and one half years of his
presidency. Volume 2 contains a bibliography of primary and
secondary sources.

Shaw, Ronald E., ed. ANDREW JACKSON, 1767-1845: CHRONOLOGY-
DOCUMENTS-BIBLIOGRAPHIC AIDS. Presidential Chronology Series.
Dobbs Ferry, N.Y.: Oceana, 1969.

The first section is a chronology of major events in the life of
Jackson from his youth in the Carolinas (1767-87), to his years
as a Tennessee lawyer and planter (1788-1810), his military
career during the Indian Wars and the War of 1812, his political
career in Tennessee and in Washington, including his two presidential terms, and his retirement years until his death in 1845.
The documents section includes his inaugural addresses and
messages to Congress, his veto of the bank bill in July of 1832,
his proclamation to the people of South Carolina in December of
1832, and his protest of the Senate censure resolution in April
of 1834. The bibliographic section cites source materials such
as Jackson's letters, biographies and general works on Jacksonian democracy and the presidency.

Sloan, Irving J., ed. FRANKLIN PIERCE, 1804-1869. CHRONOLOGY-
DOCUMENTS-BIBLIOGRAPHIC AIDS. Presidential Chronology Series.
Dobbs Ferry, N.Y.: Oceana, 1968.

The first section, listing the major events in the life of Pierce,
is divided into three major sections: early life (1804-54), his
years in office (1853-56) and the retirement years (1857-69). The
second section includes such materials as his inaugural address
and messages to Congress. The third section lists biographies
of Pierce and other source materials.

_____. JAMES BUCHANAN, 1791-1868. CHRONOLOGY-DOCUMENTS-
BIBLIOGRAPHIC AIDS. Presidential Chronology Series. Dobbs Ferry,
N.Y.: Oceana, 1968.

The first section is a chronology of events in the life of Pierce; it covers his early life and career (1791-1857), his presidential years (1857-61) and his retirement (1861-68). The documents include such materials as Pierce's inaugural address and messages to Congress, including his special message on South Carolina's secession on 8 January 1861. There is also a list of biographies and monographs on Pierce.

_____. MARTIN VAN BUREN, 1782-1862: CHRONOLOGY-DOCUMENTS-BIBLIOGRAPHIC AIDS. Presidential Chronology Series. Dobbs Ferry, N.Y.: Oceana, 1969.

The first eighteen pages are a chronology of important dates in Van Buren's career as senator, secretary of state, vice-president and president as well as his early career and his postpresidential years. Documents such as his inaugural address on 4 March 1837 and other messages to Congress are included. There is also a list of biographies and essays on Van Buren as well as guides to materials on the presidency in general.

Smith, Page. JOHN ADAMS. 2 vols. Garden City, N.Y.: Doubleday, 1962.

Volume 1 of this biography covers the years from 1735 to 1784. Volume 2 covers 1784 until the death of Adams on 4 July 1826.

Steinberg, Alfred. THE FIRST TEN: THE FOUNDING PRESIDENTS AND THEIR ADMINISTRATIONS. Garden City, N.Y.: Doubleday, 1967.

Intended for the general audience, this consists of brief biographical sketches of the presidential years of each of the first ten presidents. Each president--Washington, John Adams, Jefferson, Madison, Monroe, John Quincy Adams, Jackson, Van Buren, Harrison, and Tyler--is treated in a separate chapter and the contributions of each to the formation and evolution of the office is discussed. There is also a selected bibliography of general and specific histories, analyses, and biographies of works relevant to the role of each in shaping the office and country.

_____. SAM JOHNSON'S BOY: A CLOSE-UP OF THE PRESIDENT FROM TEXAS. New York: Macmillan, 1968.

This biography of Lyndon B. Johnson covers his boyhood years in Texas, his years under the tutelage of Franklin D. Roosevelt and Sam Rayburn and his years as vice-president and as president until mid-1968. Steinberg concludes that as of that period Johnson had failed to furnish the leadership necessary in the office he occupied, that Johnson indeed rivaled Hoover's inability to establish a warm relationship with the American people. This inability the author attributes to Johnson's failure to grow beyond being "Sam Johnson's boy" and the pursuit of personal power and wealth.

Stephenson, Nathaniel W., and Dunn, Waldo. GEORGE WASHINGTON. 2 vols. New York: Oxford University Press, 1940.

Volume 1 covers the period from 1732 to 1777. Volume 2 deals with the years from 1778 to 1799.

Stewart, William J., comp. THE ERA OF FRANKLIN DELANO ROOSEVELT: A SELECTED BIBLIOGRAPHY OF PERIODICAL AND DISSERTATION LITERATURE, 1945-1966. Hyde Park, N.Y.: General Services Administration, FDR Library, 1967.

With annotations by the editor, this is a bibliography of over one thousand articles and dissertations dealing with Roosevelt and the Roosevelt era.

Stone, Ralph A., ed. JOHN FITZGERALD KENNEDY, 1917-1963: CHRONO-LOGY-DOCUMENTS-BIBLIOGRAPHIC AIDS. Presidential Chronology Series. Dobbs Ferry, N.Y.: Oceana, 1971.

The first section is a chronology of events in the early life of Kennedy and his years in the Navy, in the House of Representatives, in the Senate and in the White House. The documents section includes such materials as his inaugural address and messages to Congress, a letter to Ngo Dinh Diem in December of 1961, a civil rights speech in June of 1961, a speech on Nuclear Test Ban in July of 1963 and two statements on the war in Vietnam in September of 1963. The bibliographic section cites works by and about Kennedy as well as works on his assassination and on the presidency in general.

Tarbell, Ida. THE LIFE OF LINCOLN, DRAWN FROM THE ORIGINAL SOURCES AND CONTAINING MANY SPEECHES, LETTERS AND TELEGRAMS HITHERTO UNPUBLISHED. 4 vols. New York: Lincoln History Society, 1895. New York: Doubleday, 1900.

Volume 1 deals with Lincoln's family background and his life to his election to Congress. Volume 2 covers the congressional years, his defeat and return to politics, the Lincoln-Douglas debates and his nomination in 1860. Volume 3 covers the years from his first inaugural to his reelection in 1864. Volume 4 covers 1864 to 1865.

U.S. Library of Congress. PRESIDENTS' PAPERS INDEX SERIES. Washington, D.C.: Government Printing Office, 1958-- .

This series of indexes to presidential papers includes the following:

CHESTER A. ARTHUR, 1959.
GROVER CLEVELAND, 1958.
CALVIN COOLIDGE, 1959.
UYLSSES S. GRANT, 1965.
BENJAMIN HARRISON, 1960.
WILLIAM H. HARRISON, 1958.
ANDREW JACKSON, 1967.
ANDREW JOHNSON, 1960.
ABRAHAM LINCOLN, 1960.
WILLIAM MCKINLEY, 1961.
JAMES MADISON, 1969.
JAMES MONROE, 1960.
FRANKLIN PIERCE, 1959.

JAMES POLK, 1964.
THEODORE ROOSEVELT, 1967.
WILLIAM HOWARD TAFT, 1969.
ZACHARY TAYLOR, 1958.
JOHN TYLER, 1958.
MARTIN VAN BUREN, 1960.
GEORGE WASHINGTON, 1964.

U.S. Presidents. COMPILATION OF THE MESSAGES AND PAPERS OF THE PRESIDENTS. 20 vols. Washington, D.C.: Government Printing Office, 1896-- .

> The first ten volumes, under the editorship of James D. Richardson, covers the period from 1789 to 1897. The second ten volumes, commercially published, bring the record to 1929. Beginning with the papers of the Truman administration, the PUBLIC PAPERS OF THE PRESIDENTS OF THE UNITED STATES have been compiled annually by the Office of the Federal Register, National Archives and Records Service, General Services Administration, Washington, D.C.: Government Printing Office, 1958-- . In addition, since 1965, a WEEKLY COMPILATION OF PRESIDENTIAL DOCUMENTS, which is an official publication of presidential speeches, statements, news conferences, messages to Congress, and other materials has been published with an index published annually.

Van Buren, Martin. THE AUTOBIOGRAPHY OF MARTIN VAN BUREN. Edited by John C. Fitzpatrick. 2 vols. Washington, D.C.: Government Printing Office, 1920. Reprint. New York: Augustus M. Kelley, 1969.

> Edited by the assistant chief of the Manuscript Division of the Library of Congress, Van Buren's autobiography is useful not only as a chronicle of the author's political career but for its observations about the roles of some of the political giants of the Jacksonian era.

Vexler, Robert I., ed. DWIGHT DAVID EISENHOWER, 1890-1969: CHRONOLOGY-DOCUMENTS-BIBLIOGRAPHIC AIDS. Presidential Chronology Series. Dobbs Ferry, N.Y.: Oceana, 1970.

> The first seventy-two pages of this 148-page guide consist of a chronology of important dates in the private and public life of Eisenhower from birth to death. A second section contains selected documents such as his first inaugural address, his news conferences, message to Congress and radio and television addresses. The bibliographic section contains a list of biographies of Eisenhower, works by Eisenhower himself, books on various aspects of his career such as Stephen Ambrose's EISENHOWER AND BERLIN, 1945: THE DECISION TO HALT AT THE ELBE and a list of works on the presidency in general.

Washington, George. THE FOUNDING FATHERS: GEORGE WASHINGTON: A BIOGRAPHY IN HIS OWN WORDS. Edited by Ralph K. Andrist. Founding Fathers Series. Introduction by Donald Jackson. New York: Newsweek, distributed by Harper and Row, n.d.

Published sometime in the mid–1970s, this is a one–volume selection of materials from the letters and diaries of Washington. Without footnotes, but with a selected bibliography, it is intended primarily for the general audience.

_____. THE WRITINGS OF GEORGE WASHINGTON FROM THE ORIGINAL MANUSCRIPT SOURCES, 1745–1799. Edited by John C. Fitzpatrick. 39 vols. Washington, D.C.: Government Printing Office, 1931–44.

Prepared under the direction of the United States George Washington Bicentennial Commission, this is a collection of Washington's papers. Volume 38 is a general index (A–N) as is volume 39 (O–Z).

Wilson, Woodrow. THE PUBLIC PAPERS OF WOODROW WILSON. Edited by Ray Stannard Baker and William Dodd. 3 vols. New York: Harper and Brothers, 1925–27.

Volume 1, entitled COLLEGE AND STATE: EDUCATION, LITERACY AND POLITICAL PAPERS, covers the period from 1875 to 1913. Volume 2, entitled THE NEW DEMOCRACY: PRESIDENTIAL MESSAGES, ADDRESSES AND OTHER PAPERS, covers the presidential years from 1913 to 1917. Volume 3, entitled WAR AND PEACE: PRESIDENTIAL MESSAGES, ADDRESSES AND PUBLIC PAPERS, covers the period from 1917 to 1924.

_____. WOODROW WILSON: LIFE AND LETTERS. Edited by Ray Stannard Baker. Garden City, N.Y.: Doubleday, 1927–39.

Volume 1, subtitled YOUTH, covers 1856 to 1890. Volume 2, subtitled PRINCETON, covers 1890 to 1910. Volume 3, subtitled GOVERNOR, covers 1910 to 1913. Volume 4, subtitled PRESIDENT, covers 1913 to 1914. Volume 5, subtitled NEUTRALITY, covers 1914 to 1915. Volume 6, subtitled FACING WAR, covers 1915 to 1917. Volume 8, subtitled ARMISTICE, covers March 1 to November 11.

_____. WOODROW WILSON PAPERS. Edited by Arthur S. Link. 24 vols. to date. Princeton, N.J.: Princeton University Press, 1966-- .

Volume 1 of this collection of Wilson papers covers the years from 1856 to 1880. Volume 24, published in 1977, covers to 1912.

Chapter 8
ARTICLE III: THE JUDICIARY
General Works, Primary Sources, Judicial Papers and Biographies

GENERAL WORKS

Abraham, Henry J. JUSTICES AND PRESIDENTS: A POLITICAL HIS-
TORY OF APPOINTMENTS TO THE SUPREME COURT. New York: Oxford University Press, 1974.

> This is an analysis of the process by which each president since
> Washington chose his Supreme Court nominees and an evaluation
> of the quality of each choice. There is also a paperback edition
> published by Penquin in 1975.

Acheson, Patricia. THE SUPREME COURT: AMERICA'S JUDICIAL HERI-
TAGE. New York: Dodd, Mead and Co., 1962.

> Intended for the general audience, this study of the role of the
> Supreme Court in American society looks at the political and
> economic origins of some of the Court's important decisions, such
> as Marbury v. Madison, McCulloch v. Maryland, Dred Scott and
> Brown, and some of the effects of these decisions.

Alsop, Joseph W., and Catledge, Turner. THE 168 DAYS. Garden City,
N.Y.: Doubleday, Doran and Co., 1938. Reprint. New York: Da Capo
Press, 1973.

> This is an account of the struggle over Roosevelt's court-packing
> proposal from its origin in the early New Deal to the presentation
> of the bill to and defeat by Congress in 1937.

Baker, Leonard. BACK TO BACK: THE DUEL BETWEEN FDR AND THE
SUPREME COURT. New York: Macmillan, 1967.

> This is a popular account of the 1937 attempt by Roosevelt to
> enlarge the Court and the final rejection of that effort by Congress
> on 22 July 1937 when the Senate voted to recommit the bill to
> committee.

Barth, Alan. PROPHETS WITH HONOR: GREAT DISSENTS AND GREAT
DISSENTERS IN THE SUPREME COURT. New York: Vintage Books, Knopf,
1974.

This is a study of six dissenting opinions which influenced the future course of constitutional change. The dissenters are the first Harlan, Brandeis, Black, Stone, and Douglas. The dissenting opinions are those in <u>Plessy</u>, <u>Olmstead</u>, <u>Betts</u>, <u>Colegrove</u>, <u>Gobitis</u>, and <u>Dennis</u>.

Bates, Ernest S. THE STORY OF THE SUPREME COURT. Indianapolis: Bobbs-Merrill, 1938.

With an introductory chapter on the organization of the Supreme Court and a prefatory conclusion dealing with Franklin D. Roosevelt's court-packing plan and the Court's "strategic retreat" in 1937, this history devotes one chapter to the Court under each Chief Justice from Jay to Hughes.

Beirne, Francis F. SHOUT TREASON: THE TRIAL OF AARON BURR. New York: Hastings House, 1959.

Written for the general reader, and without footnotes or bibliography, this is an account of Burr's treason trial in Richmond in 1807. It draws heavily on the account of the trial by Albert J. Beveridge in his work on Chief Justice John Marshall.

Benson, Paul R., Jr. THE SUPREME COURT AND THE COMMERCE CLAUSE: 1937-1970. New York: Dunellen Publishing Co., 1970.

This is a study of judicial interpretation of the commerce clause from its broad construction in <u>Gibbons</u> v. <u>Ogden</u> through the tumultuous years of its narrow interpretation as a basis for invalidation of New Deal legislation, with major emphasis upon the period from the "Constitutional Revolution of 1937" to the present. The author examines the commerce clause as a source of national power and as a limitation upon the powers of the state.

Berle, Adolph A. THREE FACES OF POWER. New York: Harcourt, Brace and World, 1967.

These three essays, originally presented as the Carpentier Lectures at Columbia University in 1967, examine the Supreme Court's acquisition and exercise of legislative power particularly in the areas of education and local government and its control over corporations under the antitrust laws. They also present some suggestions for redistribution and sharing of power by such means as increased congressional assumption of its legislative responsibilities and creation of a council of constitutional advisers in the White House.

Bickel, Alexander M. THE CASELOAD OF THE SUPREME COURT AND WHAT, IF ANYTHING, TO DO ABOUT IT. Washington, D.C.: American Enterprise Institute for Public Policy Research, 1973.

In 1972, Chief Justice Burger established a study group on the caseload of the Supreme Court. This brief work is an analysis of the proposals considered, rejected and recommended by the group with special attention paid to the recommendation that a new National Court of Appeals be created to screen all cases in which Supreme Court review is sought.

_____. THE LEAST DANGEROUS BRANCH: THE SUPREME COURT AT THE BAR OF POLITICS. Indianapolis: Bobbs-Merrill, 1962.

This is an analysis of the process of judicial review, the various concepts of the proper standards of review, the refusal to exercise power by denying jurisdiction or standing, and the relationship between the process of review and the theory and practice of democracy.

_____. THE MORALITY OF CONSENT. New Haven, Conn.: Yale University Press, 1974.

This short work consists of five essays in which the author looks at judicial policy making within a framework of the alternate models of the "contractarian" or liberal tradition and the Whig, Burkean or conservative tradition. The former tradition is more rigid, legalistic and "ultimately authoritarian" because it "rests on a vision of individual rights that have a clearly defined, independent existence predating society" whereas the latter is more pragmatic and flexible because it "begins not with theoretical rights but with a real society."

Bizzell, William B. JUDICIAL INTERPRETATION OF POLITICAL THEORY: A STUDY IN THE RELATION OF THE COURTS TO THE AMERICAN PARTY SYSTEM. 1919. Reprint. New York: Burt Franklin, 1971.

Originally prepared in 1910 as lectures at the Illinois College of Law, this is a criticism of the tendency of activist courts to substitute their own political theories for those of elected officials. Written in a period when judicial activism operated to benefit conservative theories of government, this study examines judicial implantation into the Constitution of its political philosophy concerning such matters as the basic nature of federalism, protective tariffs, the income tax, and internal improvements.

Boudin, Louis B. GOVERNMENT BY JUDICIARY. 2 vols. New York: William Godwin, 1932.

This work is an attack upon the doctrine of judicial review and its exercise by the courts. The author argues both that Marshall's opinion in Marbury v. Madison was unwarranted by the Constitution and that the subsequent expansion of that power was unwarranted by the initial opinion and represents an encroachment by the Court upon the legitimate power of the legislative and executive branches and of the people and makes judges superior even to the Constitution. Volume 1 covers the pre-Marbury theories about and role of the judiciary to the pre-Civil War period. Volume 2 covers the period from the Dred Scott opinion through the 1930 period of "government by a few conservatives."

Bruce, Andrew Alexander. THE AMERICAN JUDGE. New York: Macmillan, 1924.

Written in the 1920s during a high point of conservative constitutional interpretation and of criticism of the judiciary, this study of the role of Supreme Court justices and secondarily of state and local judges maintains that in order for law to reign lawyers must reject the role of hired hands and assert their role as

officers of the Court and that the demands of the public, particularly the rich, that lawyers serve as gladiators be rejected.

Butler, Charles H. A CENTURY AT THE BAR OF THE SUPREME COURT
OF THE UNITED STATES. New York: G.P. Putnam's Sons, 1942.

> Written for the 1940 sesquicentennial of the founding of the
> Supreme Court by a former reporter on the decisions of the
> Court who took office in 1902 and published posthumously, this
> book reminisces about such matters as important cases decided
> by the Court in the early part of the century, the arguments
> before the Court, and the rules, customs, and etiquette of the
> Court.

Cahill, Fred V., Jr. JUDICIAL LEGISLATION: A STUDY IN AMERICAN
LEGAL THEORY. New York: Ronald, 1952.

> Although prevailing legal philosophy at the time of the framing
> of the Constitution envisaged courts as applying rather than
> making law, by the twentieth century both opponents and pro-
> ponents of judicial legislation agreed that courts make law.
> Written before the Supreme Court's decision in Brown and the
> subsequent explosion of judicial policy making to protect indi-
> vidual rights, this is a study of legal theory, of the judicial
> function, and of the position of courts in the total governmental
> structure. Cahill examines the contemporary theories of those
> who view judicial law making as a legitimate means of social
> change.

Cahn, Edmond, ed. SUPREME COURT AND SUPREME LAW. Bloomington:
Indiana University Press, 1954.

> These 11 essays, including an introduction by the editor, are the
> result of meetings held in 1953 at New York University School
> of Law in observation of the 150th anniversary of Marbury v.
> Madison. They deal with various facets of judicial review such
> as the scope of judicial review, the principles of constitutional
> construction, and the effects of judicial review on such sub-
> stantive areas as federalism, individudal rights, majority rule,
> and separation of powers. The authors are Ralph F. Bischoff,
> John P. Frank, Paul A. Freund, Willard Hurst, and Charles
> P. Curtis.

Cardozo, Benjamin N. THE GROWTH OF THE LAW. 1924. Reissue. Foreword by Arthur L. Corbin. New Haven, Conn.: Yale University Press, 1963.

> These lectures, delivered at Yale in 1923 were, in Cardozo's
> view, a supplement to his 1921 lectures published as THE NATURE
> OF THE JUDICIAL PROCESS (below). He here expands upon
> some of the 1921 themes and deals with such matters as the need
> for a scientific restatement of the law to produce certainty and
> order in the legal system, the need for a philosophy of law to
> provide for growth in the law, the growth of law and methods
> of judging, and the functions and goals of law.

_____. THE NATURE OF THE JUDICIAL PROCESS. New Haven, Conn.:
Yale University Press, 1921.

This is Justice Cardozo's classic statement of the process by which judges interpret and apply law to concrete cases.

_____. THE PARADOXES OF LEGAL SCIENCE. New York: Columbia University Press, 1928. Reprint. New York: Greenwood Press, 1970.

In these 1928 James S. Carpenter Lectures, Justice Cardozo dealt with the legal paradoxes arising out of rest and motion in the law, the simultaneous need for stability and progress in the law, the needs of the individual and the society, and the compatibility and conflicts between individual liberty and governmental powers.

Carpenter, William S. JUDICIAL TENURE IN THE UNITED STATES WITH ESPECIAL REFERENCE TO THE TENURE OF FEDERAL JUDGES. New Haven, Conn.: Yale University Press, 1918.

Prior to the pronouncement in Marbury v. Madison, state courts exercised with--in Carpenter's view--popular approval the power to invalidate legislation, an exercise which led to legislative attacks upon the independence of the judiciary primarily by attacking the tenure of judges. This work is an analysis of the relationship between judicial review, judicial tenure and judicial independence in both national and state courts with emphasis upon the former.

Carson, Hampton L. THE HISTORY OF THE SUPREME COURT OF THE UNITED STATES WITH BIOGRAPHIES OF ALL THE CHIEF AND ASSOCIATE JUSTICES. 2 vols. 1902. Reprint. New York: Burt Franklin, 1971.

This history of the Supreme Court to the end of the nineteenth century begins with an analysis of the judicial system in the colonial period, the attempts by the Continental Congress to centralize judicial authority by establishing a court to hear appeals from the states and the establishment of a judicial system under the Articles of Confederation. Its primary focus, however, is upon the Supreme Court as established by the Constitution and organized by the Judiciary Act of 1789 and its activities from 1790 to 1900. Included are portraits and brief biographies of each of the fifty-eight justices who served on the court from 1790 to the turn of the century.

_____, ed. THE SUPREME COURT OF THE UNITED STATES. Philadelphia: John Y. Yuber, 1891.

This is an analysis of the role and power of the Supreme Court as envisaged by the framers of the Constitution.

Casper, Gerhard, and Posner, Richard A. THE WORKLOAD OF THE SUPREME COURT. Chicago: American Bar Association, 1976.

This is an analysis of the Court's workload, an evaluation of earlier research on its caseload, and a suggestion that the workload could be reduced through administrative reforms rather than by such drastic changes as creation of a National Court of Appeals proposed by the Commission on Revision of the Federal Court Appellate System.

Casper, Jonathan D. LAWYERS BEFORE THE WARREN COURT: CIVIL
LIBERTIES AND CIVIL RIGHTS, 1957-66. Urbana: University of
Illinois Press, 1972.

> In this analysis of judicial policy making, Casper argues that
> to understand the process by which the Court participates in
> national politics, it is necessary to go beyond the justices them-
> selves and to look at lawyers in private practice who argue
> before the Court. In this study of lawyers who argued civil
> liberties and civil rights cases before the Supreme Court between
> 1957 and 1966, he deals with such questions as how they became
> involved in litigation, what goals and interests they were pursuing
> and why they took cases to the Court which provided it with the
> opportunity to make national policy.

Chapin, Bradley. THE AMERICAN LAW OF TREASON: REVOLUTIONARY
AND EARLY AMERICAN ORIGINS. Seattle: University of Washington Press,
1964.

> This work traces the constitutional definition and application of
> the law of treason from its roots in medieval England to Chief
> Justice Marshall's interpretation in the Burr treason trial.

Chase, Harold W. FEDERAL JUDGES AND THE APPOINTING PROCESS.
Minneapolis: University of Minnesota Press, 1972.

> This is a study of the process of creating judgeships and of
> appointing judges at the district and court of appeals levels and
> the roles of the president, the White House staff, the Justice
> Department, the Senate, and the American Bar Association in
> that process. The focus of the analysis is the administrations
> of Eisenhower, Kennedy, and Johnson. The author suggests
> two alternative methods: selection of lower court judges by the
> Supreme Court or getting senators out of the process and leaving
> selection to the president and his subordinates.

Claude, Richard P. THE SUPREME COURT AND THE ELECTORAL PROCESS.
Baltimore: Johns Hopkins Press, 1970.

> This is an analysis of the role of the Court in nationalizing,
> democratizing and changing the process of elections. Claude
> examines the right to vote in congressional elections, the use
> of the Civil War Amendments and statutes in protecting the right
> to vote, the reapportionment controversy, questions related to
> presidential selection and the part played by the Voting Rights
> Act of 1965 in expanding the right to vote.

Clayton, James E. THE MAKING OF JUSTICE: THE SUPREME COURT
IN ACTION. New York: E.P. Dutton and Co., 1964.

> Written for the general audience by a journalist who covered the
> Court for the Washington Post in the 1960s, this book follows the
> Court in the 1962 term from its opening session in October to
> its last decisions in May. It is an account of the ceremonies
> (such as Chief Justice Warren's announcement of the retirement
> of Justice Frankfurter and the appointment of Justice Goldberg),

the arguments before the Court, the work over the midwinter
recess, and the major and minor opinions handed down during
the term.

Congressional Quarterly. THE SUPREME COURT, JUSTICE AND THE LAW.
2d ed. Washington, D.C.: 1977.

This brief examination of the development of the Court since
1789 focuses on the relationship between the Court and the
political branches during the Nixon and Ford administrations.
It examines the impact of the Nixon and Ford appointees to the
Court, surveys the major decisions from 1969 to 1977 and includes biographies of each justice. The appendix includes a list
of every law invalidated by the Court and excerpts from some
major opinions since 1969.

Cortner, Richard C. THE SUPREME COURT AND CIVIL LIBERTIES POLICY.
Palo Alto, Calif.: Mayfield Publishers, 1975.

Intended primarily for undergraduates, this paperback contains
case studies of litigation in the area of individual rights: nationalization of the Bill of Rights, searches and seizures, free
speech, religion, and sexual equality. In addition to excerpts
from the Supreme Court decision, there is an account of the
general legal framework within which each case fits and of the
background of each controversy.

Corwin, Edward S. THE TWILIGHT OF THE SUPREME COURT: A HISTORY
OF OUR CONSTITUTIONAL THEORY. New Haven, Conn.: Yale University
Press, 1934.

In this series of Storrshect Lectures at Yale, Corwin criticized
the Court's narrow construction of congressional power in the
1920s and early 1930s and urged a construction broad enough to
enable the national government to meet national economic needs.

Cox, Archibald. THE WARREN COURT: CONSTITUTIONAL DECISIONS AS
AN INSTRUMENT OF REFORM. Cambridge, Mass.: Harvard University
Press, 1975.

This is an analysis of the Warren Court's landmark opinions and
their implications for change.

Curtis, Charles P. LIONS UNDER THE THRONE: A STUDY OF THE
SUPREME COURT OF THE UNITED STATES ADDRESSED PARTICULARLY
TO THOSE LAYMEN WHO KNOW MORE CONSTITUTIONAL LAW THAN THEY
THINK THEY DO AND TO THOSE LAWYERS WHO KNOW LESS. Boston:
Houghton Mifflin Co., 1947.

This account of the Court's traditions, decisions, and doctrines,
addressed to a general audience but useful to the specialist, is
designed to remove the mystique attached to the Supreme Court
by documenting its long-standing role in the political process.

Dahl, Richard C., and Bolden, C.E. THE AMERICAN JUDGE: A BIBLIOG-
RAPHY. Vienna, Va.: Coiner Publications, 1968.

This is a bibliography of works dealing with trial and appellate judges in general at the state and local levels—their characters, qualifications, selections, tenure, removal and such matters as custom, decorum and dress.

Daly, John J. THE USES OF HISTORY IN THE DECISIONS OF THE SUPREME COURT, 1900-1930. Washington, D.C.: Catholic University of America Press, 1954.

This is an examination of selected decisions of the Fuller, White, and Taft courts with a view to determining if historical data is used by judges and if judges tend to be knowledgeable in this area of scholarship. The author concludes that judges use and have a comprehensive knowledge of the constitutional history of both the United States and England.

D'Amato, Anthony, and O'Neil, Robert M. THE JUDICIARY AND VIETNAM. New York: St. Martin's Press, 1972.

This analysis of judicial reaction to various attempts by individuals as well as by the state of Massachusetts to challenge the constitutionality of presidential prosecution of the war in Vietnam is made within the broad context of the role of the court in constitutional litigation and the concepts of judicial review and justiciability.

Davenport, William H., ed. VOICES IN COURT: A TREASURY OF THE BENCH, THE BAR AND THE COURTROOM. New York: Macmillan, 1958.

This anthology, organized on the basis of judges, courtroom activities, lawyers and the law, consists of essays, biographies, letters, judicial decisions, trials, and cross-examinations.

Early, Stephen T., Jr. CONSTITUTIONAL COURTS OF THE UNITED STATES: THE FORMAL AND INFORMAL RELATIONSHIPS BETWEEN THE DISTRICT COURTS, THE COURTS OF APPEALS, AND THE SUPREME COURT OF THE UNITED STATES. Totowa, N.J.: Littlefield, Adams and Co., 1977.

This basic text in intercourt relationships focuses primarily on lower federal courts and the various informal factors (such as localism, judicial socialization, spatial, and administrative distance) which influence the relationships.

Elliott, Ward E.Y. THE RISE OF GUARDIAN DEMOCRACY: THE SUPREME COURT'S ROLE IN VOTING RIGHTS DISPUTES, 1845-1969. Cambridge, Mass.: Harvard University Press, 1974.

This examination of Supreme Court opinions in voting cases from the pre-Civil War period to the late 1960s is critical of the interventionist policy of the judiciary, particularly the reapportionment role of the Warren Court.

Ernst, Morris L. THE GREAT REVERSALS: TALES OF THE SUPREME COURT. New York: Weybright and Talley, 1973.

Noting that the Supreme Court has reversed itself more than
one hundred times since its first about-face in 1810 and that
even Marshall reversed himself and his Court four times, Ernst
examines each reversal and the reasons, techniques and circumstances of each reversal. After an introductory chapter focusing
on the pace of change from 1800 to 1810 and from 1882 to 1967,
the work is organized chronologically and topically.

Ettrude, Dormin J., comp. POWER OF CONGRESS TO NULLIFY SUPREME
COURT DECISIONS. New York: H.W. Wilson, 1924.

Prepared primarily for debaters in the 1920s this slim volume
sets forth in outline form the major arguments in support of and
in opposition to the proposition that Congress should have the
power to overrule Supreme Court decisions. It also includes
a bibliography of relevant books and articles and pertinent
excerpts from such materials as Montesquieu on the separation
of powers doctrine, Marbury v. Madison and a summary of congressional laws invalidated by the Supreme Court.

Fairman, Charles. HISTORY OF THE SUPREME COURT OF THE UNITED
STATES: RECONSTRUCTION AND REUNION, 1864-1888. New York:
Macmillan, 1971.

This massive work is the first of two volumes on the Chase and
Waite courts by Fairman and the sixth volume of the OLIVER
WENDELL HOLMES DEVISE HISTORY OF THE SUPREME COURT
OF THE UNITED STATES. It is an analysis of the role the
Supreme Court played in the controversies of the Reconstruction
era, particularly through its interpretation of the Thirteenth and
Fourteenth Amendments, and the relationships between and the
views of individual justices. In addition to an examination of
Supreme Court opinions, this work includes the briefs and oral
arguments before the Court, the records of lower courts and the
reactions to the high Court's opinions.

Fish, Peter G. THE POLITICS OF FEDERAL JUDICIAL ADMINISTRATION.
Princeton, N.J.: Princeton University Press, 1973.

This study, designed to pick up where Felix Frankfurter and
James M. Landis in their 1928 THE BUSINESS OF THE SU-
PREME COURT (see p. 180) left off, examines judicial adminis-
tration since the reforms under Chief Justices Taft and Hughes.
It is a study of the administrative role and functioning of the
Judicial Conference and the Administrative Office of the United
States Courts. It also examines the part played by the Justice
Department in judicial administration, the relationship between
the Judicial Conference and the Congress, and the problems
surrounding both decentralized and centralized administration
of the federal court system.

Fleming, Macklin. THE PRICE OF PERFECT JUSTICE: THE ADVERSE
CONSEQUENCES OF CURRENT LEGAL DOCTRINE ON THE AMERICAN
COURTROOM. New York: Basic Books, 1974.

Written by a justice of the Court of Appeals of California, this
is an analysis of such "currently fashionable theories" as "per-
fectability, retroactivity, parallel review, multiple review, due

process of law and equal protection" which in the author's view contributes to the malfunctioning of the legal system. He argues that the boldness of courts in displacing legislators as chief law makers, coupled with judicial inability to achieve a final judgment in a concrete case have created a legal paralysis. He suggests that the effects of the elitism of appellate judges and of the absolute power of Supreme Court justices in particular could be minimized by limiting the term of office on the high court to sixteen years.

Forte, David E., ed. THE SUPREME COURT IN AMERICAN POLITICS: JUDICIAL ACTIVISM AND JUDICIAL RESTRAINT. Lexington, Mass.: D.C. Heath, 1972.

With an introduction by the editor, this collection of brief excerpts, drawn from the previously published works of a number of different scholars, focuses upon various facets of the conflict between judicial passivity and activism. It sets forth the basic arguments for and against each approach. There are excerpts from the works of such constitutional scholars as John P. Roche, Glendon Schubert, Learned Hand, Wallace Mendelson, Alpheus T. Mason, Martin Shapiro, Herbert Wechsler, Arthur Miller, Ronald F. Howell, Alexander Bickel, Charles L. Black, and Loren Beth.

Foster, G.W., Jr. THE STATUS OF CLASS ACTION LITIGATION. Chicago: American Bar Association, 1974.

This paper, delivered to the Chicago Bar Association, traces the development of the class action suit and assesses the effect of the 1966 revision.

Frank, Jerome. COURTS ON TRIAL: MYTH AND REALITY IN AMERICAN JUSTICE. Princeton, N.J.: Princeton University Press, 1949.

Emulating Blackstone's purpose in preparing his COMMENTARIES-- teaching the rulers of the country, in this instance, the American people, what the law is--Frank examines what courts actually do, what they are supposed to do, whether they do what they are supposed to do and whether they should do what they are supposed to do.

Frank, John P. MARBLE PALACE: THE SUPREME COURT IN AMERICAN LIFE. New York: Knopf, 1958.

Written at the height of the controversy swirling around the Court as a result primarily of its Public School Segregation Case in 1954, this is an analysis of the organization of the Court and the methods and procedures it employs in performing its basic functions of protecting liberty and controlling government.

Frankfurter, Felix, and Landis, James M. THE BUSINESS OF THE SUPREME COURT: A STUDY IN THE JUDICIAL SYSTEM. New York: Macmillan, 1928. Reprint. New York: Johnson Reprint Corp., 1972.

Article III gives to Congress the authority to create "inferior" courts and to regulate the federal judicial system. This work is an analysis of congressional use of that power from the Judiciary Act of 1789 to the Judiciary Act of 1925, legislation

which created, organized and regulated the power, procedures
and jurisdiction of the federal court system. It focuses upon
the Supreme Court with the major emphasis upon the 1925 legislation which, in the authors' view, gave the Supreme Court what
it wanted: a strictly confined and discretionary jurisdiction.

Freund, Paul A. ON UNDERSTANDING THE SUPREME COURT. Boston:
Little, Brown, 1950.

Originally delivered as the Rosenthal Foundation lectures at
Northwestern University Law School, this work examines the
ways by which a democratic federal government conditions and
controls the Supreme Court's activities, the traits of a liberal
judge (using Justice Brandeis as the focal point), and the impact
of the strategy and tactics employed by attorneys upon constitutional decisions.

_____. THE SUPREME COURT OF THE UNITED STATES: ITS BUSINESS,
PURPOSES AND PERFORMANCE. Cleveland: Meridan Books, 1961.

In this collection of seven previously published essays, Freund
deals with a broad range of matters relating to the Supreme Court.
Three essays from his ON UNDERSTANDING THE SUPREME
COURT (above) deal with Justice Brandeis as an example of a
liberal judge, with the role of lower courts and of counsel in
contributing to law making by the Supreme Court, and with the
question of whether judges make law. In other essays he examines the Court in terms of its jurisdictional and administrative
roles, its role as arbiter and as symbol, analyzes judicial
standards in the area of individual rights and in serving as um-
pire between national and state forces and discusses the potential
risk of lawlessness and cynicism that stems from criticism of
the Court and its decisions.

_____, ed. THE OLIVER WENDELL HOLMES DEVISE HISTORY OF THE
UNITED STATES. 3 vols. to date. New York: Macmillan, 1971-- . In
progress.

Justice Holmes willed his estate to the U.S. government and in
1955 Congress established the Oliver Wendell Holmes Devise
Fund to write a history of the Supreme Court. Eleven volumes
are to be published, of which three have thus far been published.
The eleven volumes are: volume 1: Julius Goebel, Jr., AN-
TECEDENTS AND BEGINNINGS TO 1801; volume 2: George
L. Haskins, FOUNDATIONS OF POWER--JOHN MARSHALL,
1801-1815; volume 3: Gerald Gunther, STRUGGLE FOR NATIONA-
LISM: THE MARSHALL COURT, 1815-1825; volume 4: Gerald
Gunther, THE CHALLENGE OF JACKSONIAN DEMOCRACY:
THE MARSHALL COURT, 1826-1835; volume 5: Carl B. Swisher,
THE TANEY PERIOD, 1835-1864; volumes 6 and 7: Charles
Fairman, RECONSTRUCTION AND REUNION, 1864-1888; volume
8: Philip C. Neal and Owen M. Fiss, NATIONAL EXPANSION
AND ECONOMIC GROWTH, 1888-1910; volumes 9 and 10:
Alexander Bickel, THE JUDICIAL AND RESPONSIBLE GOVERN-
MENT, 1910-1921 and 1921-1930, and volume 11: Paul A. Freund,
DEPRESSION, NEW DEAL AND THE COURT IN CRISIS, 1930-
1941. The three volumes that have thus far been published are

volume 1 by Goebel, volume 5 by Swisher, and volume 6 (part 1) by Fairman.

Friedman, Leon, ed. UNITED STATES v. NIXON: THE PRESIDENT BE-FORE THE SUPREME COURT. Introduction by Alan Westin. New York: Chelsea House in association with R.R. Bowker, 1974.

> With a preface by Friedman, this volume contains the documents relating to the special prosecutor's attempt to obtain the Nixon tapes--the lower courts' opinions, the petitions to the Supreme Court, the briefs submitted to the Court, the oral arguments and the Supreme Court opinion.

Frisbourg, Marjorie G. THE SUPREME COURT IN AMERICAN HISTORY: TEN GREAT DECISIONS: THE PEOPLE, THE TIMES, THE ISSUES. Philadelphia: Macrae Smith, 1965.

> This is a study of the background, litigants and constitutional issues in ten major Supreme Court decisions from Marbury v. Madison to Baker v. Carr.

Funston, Richard Y. CONSTITUTIONAL COUNTERREVOLUTION: THE WARREN COURT AND THE BURGER COURT: JUDICIAL POLICY MAKING IN MODERN AMERICA. New York: Halsted Press, 1977.

> This is an examination of the relationship between the Burger Court policies and the Warren Court policies in the areas of race relations, reapportionment, criminal procedures, church-state relations, and obscenity.

Goebel, Julius, Jr. HISTORY OF THE SUPREME COURT OF THE UNITED STATES: ANTECEDENTS AND BEGINNINGS TO 1801. New York: Macmillan, 1971.

> This is volume 1 of the OLIVER WENDELL HOLMES DEVISE HISTORY OF THE SUPREME COURT OF THE UNITED STATES, edited by Paul A. Freund (see p. 181). It deals with the pre-Marshall period of the Court.

Goldberg, Louis O., and Levenson, Eleanore. LAWLESS JUDGES. 1935. Reprint. New York: Da Capo Press, 1970.

> Originally published when judicial power was used to the ad-vantage of business and to the disadvantage of organized labor and when courts supported governmental regulation of speech, this is a criticism of what the authors view as judicial abuse of its discretionary power. To abolish the "dictatorship" of judges, the authors propose several remedies: recall of judges and of judicial opinions, the impeachment of judges who "deliber-ately misinterpret a statute," a constitutional amendment taking away from the courts the power to declare legislation uncon-stitutional and the establishment of legislative committees to hear complaints against judges in order to facilitate the impeachment process.

Gordon, Rosalie M. NINE MEN AGAINST AMERICA: THE SUPREME COURT AND ITS ATTACK ON AMERICAN LIBERTIES. 4th ed. Boston: Western Islands, 1965. Paperbound.

Written in the late 1950s for the general audience, this short
book is an attack upon the liberalism and activism of the Warren
Court and its "usurpation of the legislative functions of Congress."

Grey, David L. THE SUPREME COURT AND THE NEWS MEDIA. Evanston,
Ill.: Northwestern University Press, 1968.

This is an analysis of the problems, responsibilities, failures
and successes of press coverage of the Supreme Court. Grey
is particularly concerned with the difficulties encountered by
the press in attempting to understand the Court, and to communicate judicial actions to the public and the repercussions of press
failure to understand and to communicate. The work contains
case studies of news coverage of some important decisions. For
example, he suggests that the public was shocked by the 1962
Engel school prayer decision because the press had not adequately
covered the case prior to or at the time of the opinion, whereas
the 1963 Schempp decision was more quickly understood and
accepted because of better press coverage.

Haar, Charles M., ed. THE GOLDEN AGE OF LAW. New York: George
Braziller, 1965.

In this study of law and judicial developments from 1820 to
1860 from the vantage point of lawyers and laymen, Haar examines the division and system of political power, the reforms
in the practice and substance of law, the interrelationship of
law and economic change and the degree to which law in the
United States is unique.

Haines, Charles G. THE ROLE OF THE SUPREME COURT IN AMERICAN
GOVERNMENT AND POLITICS, 1789-1835. Berkeley: University of
California Press, 1944. Reprint. New York: Da Capo Press, 1973.

This study of the Court begins with an analysis of the political
divisions during the Revolutionary War and the influence of those
divisions on the framing of the Constitution and extends to the
end of the Marshall Court. It examines the political views and
constitutional theories of the major political figures of the first
forty-five years under the Constitution and the role of the Court
in the major political controversies during these formative years.
The disputes between nationalists and state sovereignists are
highlighted.

_____. THE ROLE OF THE SUPREME COURT IN AMERICAN GOVERNMENT
AND POLITICS, 1835-1864. New York: Da Capo Press, 1973.

This second volume (see above) covers the period from the appointment of Roger Taney as chief justice to the period of the Civil War.

Harris, Robert J. THE JUDICIAL POWER OF THE UNITED STATES.
Baton Rouge: Louisiana State University Press, 1940.

This analysis of the "judicial power" to hear "cases and controversies" conferred upon national courts by Article III focuses
upon judicial interpretation of the scope of and limitations upon
that power, the authority of Congress to control the jurisdiction
of constitutional courts and its authority to create legislative
courts.

Henderson, Dwight F. COURTS FOR A NEW NATION. Foreword by Justice Tom C. Clark. Washington, D.C.: Public Affairs Press, 1971.

> This is an account of the origins, organization, jurisdiction, procedures and functioning of lower federal courts from 1787 to 1801. After a brief discussion of the debates at Philadelphia over Article III and of congressional debates on the Judiciary Act of 1789, the work is principally concerned with the way in which lower courts operated during the administrations of Washington and Adams.

Honnold, John, ed. THE LIFE OF THE LAW: READINGS ON THE GROWTH OF LEGAL INSTITUTIONS. New York: Free Press of Glencoe, 1964.

> This is a collection of excerpts from the works of American and English scholars and commentators such as Blackstone, Holmès, Cardozo, Roscoe Pound and Morris L. Ernst. The excerpts deal with such matters as law making by judges, legislators and administrators, legal developments in the United States during its early formative years under the Constitution, codification of American law in the last century, and landmarks in the development of ideas and institutions in English legal history which contributed to American law.

Horowitz, Donald L. THE COURTS AND SOCIAL POLICY. Washington, D.C.: Brookings Institution, 1977.

> An analysis of the ability of courts to make and implement social policy and an examination of four substantive areas in which litigation has been the instrument of policy making: urban affairs, educational resources, juvenile courts, and delinquency and police conduct. Horowitz argues that courts as presently constituted cannot respond to the multiplicity of demands made on them.

Hughes, Charles Evans. THE SUPREME COURT OF THE UNITED STATES: ITS FOUNDATION, METHODS AND ACHIEVEMENTS: AN INTERPRETATION. 1928. Reprint. New York: Columbia University Press, 1966.

> Originally delivered as part of the Columbia University Lectures under the George Blumenthal Foundation, this is a far-ranging analysis of the establishment of the Court at Philadelphia, its organization by the judiciary acts of Congress, its achievements in "cementing the Union" by regulating the relations between nation and state, in protecting liberty and property and in providing for social justice.

Hughes, Graham. THE CONSCIENCE OF THE COURTS: LAWS AND MORALS IN AMERICAN LIFE. Garden City, N.Y.: Doubleday, 1975.

> Designed for the general audience, this is a study of decisions by the lower courts and the Supreme Court dealing with such moral issues as abortion, busing, obscenity, and drugs.

Hurst, James W. THE LAW OF TREASON IN THE UNITED STATES: COLLECTED ESSAYS. 1945. Reprint. Westport, Conn.: Greenwood Press, 1971.

This collection of previously published essays written at the request of Solicitor General Charles Faby and attached to the government's brief in the Cramer treason case in the 1940s deals with various legal and historical facets of the law of treason. The five essays in the original 1945 edition examine the historical background of the treason clause in the Constitution, the English sources of the treason law, the pre–Constitutional law of treason in the United States, the drafting of the treason provision at the Philadelphia convention and the interpretation and application of the provision from the adoption of the Constitution to the mid-1940s. A sixth essay, added in 1971, deals with treason cases and doctrines from 1945 to 1970.

Hyneman, Charles S. THE SUPREME COURT ON TRIAL. New York: Atherton Press, 1963.

This expansion of the Benjamin F. Shambaugh Lectures in Political Science at the State University of Iowa in 1961 is an examination of the role of the Supreme Court in the American political system beginning with the Brown decisions in 1954 and 1955. It is an account of the attacks upon the Court as a result of those decisions, such as Southern Manifesto and the Interposition resolutions, and of earlier attacks resulting from judicial interpretation of the commerce and due process clauses. The author seeks to offer "some explanations of why the nation has not lived comfortably under dramatic demonstrations of judicial power."

Jackson, Percival E. DISSENT IN THE SUPREME COURT: A CHRONO-LOGY. Norman: University of Oklahoma Press, 1969.

Organized chronologically and topically, this is a study of dissents from William Johnson's dissents on the Marshall Court to those of the final terms of the Warren Court. Divided into two major parts, the earlier years and the last decade, the study examines major judicial conflicts during the era of slavery, the Civil War, Reconstruction, the New Deal and the cold war in the first section and the conflicts over specific issues (the Fourth Amendment, race relations, crime, reapportionment, the First Amendment and labor) in the second.

Jackson, Robert H. THE SUPREME COURT IN THE AMERICAN SYSTEM OF GOVERNMENT. Cambridge, Mass.: Harvard University Press, 1955.

These essays were prepared for delivery as the 1954-55 Godkin lectures at Harvard. Justice Jackson completed the first two on "The Supreme Court as a Unit of Government" and "The Supreme Court as a Law Court" and partially completed the third on "The Supreme Court as a Political Institution" before his death. All three are here included.

Jaffee, Louis L. "The Citizen as Litigant in Public Actions: The Non-Hohfeldian or Ideological Plaintiff." UNIVERSITY OF PENNSYLVANIA LAW REVIEW 116 (April 1968): 1033-47.

This is an argument against the traditionally restrictive "case and controversy" interpretation which denies standing to a pro-

spective litigant whose personal rights are not dependent on the
outcome of a lawsuit. Jaffee argues that standing should be
accorded to an "ideological" plaintiff who wants to test the
constitutionality of governmental action to protect the public
interest rather than a personal right.

_____. "Standing Again." HARVARD LAW REVIEW 84 (January 1971):
633-38.

This brief comment is designed to clarify one point in Jaffee's
earlier published general argument in favor of liberalization
of the standing requirement. He emphasizes that while he believes that a plaintiff who does not have a personal stake in
the outcome of the litigation should be accorded standing to
protect the general interest, he does not believe that such
a plaintiff has right to standing. Rather, he believes that
a court, in its discretion, may accord standing if it believes that
the question raised by such a plaintiff is in the public interest.

_____. "Standing to Secure Judicial Review: Public Actions." HARVARD
LAW REVIEW 74 (May 1961): 1265-1314.

In this first installment of a two-part in-depth study of the law
of standing, Jaffee examines the law governing the standing of
a person attacking an administrative action whose asserted relation to the action is that of taxpayer, citizen, or consumer.
He looks at the background of public action and the use of the
writ of mandamus, injunction and declaratory judgment, the role
of the public action, the limitations on that action and judicial
treatment of the constitutional issues in the public action cases.
The second installment, entitled "Standing to Sue: Private
Action," appears in volume 75 of the HARVARD LAW REVIEW
(below).

_____. "Standing to Sue: Private Action." HARVARD LAW REVIEW 75
(December 1961): 255-305.

In this second installment of an analysis of the law of standing,
Jaffee focuses on private, rather than public, action and examines
the standing of a person who asserts a distinctive impact which
entitled him to challenge in an allegedly illegal administrative
action. He examines the development of the law of standing in
this area, the Administrative Procedures Act and state law.
The first installment, entitled "Standing to Secure Judicial Review: Public Actions" appears in volume 74 of the HARVARD
LAW REVIEW (above).

Klein, Fannie J. THE ADMINISTRATION OF JUSTICE IN THE COURTS:
A SELECTED AND ANNOTATED BIBLIOGRAPHY. Dobbs Ferry, N.Y.:
Oceana, 1976.

An update and expansion of Klein's 1963 JUDICIAL ADMINIS-
TRATION AND THE LEGAL PROFESSION, this is an extensive
bibliography, with a subject and personal name index, of materials
on such subjects as judges, trial procedures, appellate procedures,
criminal trials, and sentencing procedures. Book 1 deals with
the courts and book 2 deals with the administration of criminal
justice in the courts.

Kohlmeier, Louis M., Jr. "GOD SAVE THIS HONORABLE COURT." New York: Charles Scribner's Sons, 1972.

This is an analysis of the manner in which Johnson and Nixon used their appointive power to influence the Supreme Court and thus constitutional interpretation. Beginning with Adlai Stevenson's death, his replacement as United Nations ambassador by Justice Goldberg, and Johnson's appointment of Abe Fortas to fill the vacancy created by Goldberg's resignation, the work focuses on what the author views as Nixon's politicizing of the Court and ends with the Courts decisions in the Emporia, Virginia educational desegregation case, a case Kohlmeier says demonstrates that Nixon led "the Court, the Bill of Rights and the Fourteenth Amendment into retreat."

Kurland, Philip B. POLITICS, THE CONSTITUTION AND THE WARREN COURT. Chicago: University of Chicago Press, 1970.

Originally delivered as the 1969 Cooley Lectures at the University of Michigan Law School, this is an analysis of Warren Court policies in three areas: federalism, egalitarianism, and the relationships between the three branches of government.

_____, ed. THE SUPREME COURT AND THE CONSTITUTION: ESSAYS IN CONSTITUTIONAL LAW FROM THE SUPREME COURT REVIEW. Chicago: University of Chicago Press, 1965.

This is a selection of seven essays from the first few issues of the SUPREME COURT REVIEW. Included are Harry Kalven, "Metaphysics of the Law of Obscenity"; Edward L. Barrett, Jr., "Personal Rights, Property Rights and the Fourteenth Amendment"; Francis A. Allen, "Federalism and the Fourth Amendment: A Requiem for Wolf"; Walter E. Murphy, "In His Own Image: Mr. Chief Justice Taft and Supreme Court Appointments"; Robert G. McCloskey, "Economic Due Process and the Supreme Court: An Exhumantion and Reburial"; Phil C. Neal, "Baker v. Carr: Politics in Search of Law"; and Jerome H. Israel, "Gideon v. Wainwright: The Art of Overruling."

Kutler, Stanley. JUDICIAL POWER AND RECONSTRUCTION POLITICS. Chicago: University of Chicago Press, 1968.

This series of essays by Kutler on the Court during Reconstruction stresses two themes: congressional Republicans were not hostile to judicial power and indeed contributed to its growth, and despite the Dred Scott decision, the Court enlarged its power during Reconstruction.

Lawrence, David. NINE HONEST MEN. New York: Appleton-Century, 1936.

Written during the period when the Supreme Court invalidated both state and national legislation designed to regulate in the socioeconomic area, this is a defense of the pre-1937 Court's economic conservatism.

Leibman, Charles. DIRECTORY OF AMERICAN JUDGES WITH A TABLE OF FEDERAL AND STATE COURTS. Chicago: American Directories, 1955.

Outdated but useful for the period of the 1950s, this lists the
judges of each federal district court, federal Court of Appeals
and state and local courts, alphabetized by state and with an
alphabetized biographical sketch of sitting judges.

Levy, Beryl H. OUR CONSTITUTION: TOOL OR TESTAMENT? New
York: Knopf, 1941.

Designed for the general reader, this study employs a biographical technique to examine the role of the Court. Focusing primarily upon the question of activism v. restraint, the author examines
the attitudes of Marshall, Taney, Holmes and Brandeis and argues
for judicial self-restraint.

Levy, Leonard W. AGAINST THE LAW: THE NIXON COURT AND CRIMINAL
JUSTICE. New York: Harper and Row, 1974.

During the tenure of Chief Justice Warren, the procedural rights
of persons accused of crime were steadily expanded. This is a
comparison of the Warren and Burger courts and a criticism of
the "strict construction" and steady contraction of defendants'
rights by the Supreme Court under Chief Justice Burger.

Lytle, Clifford M. THE WARREN COURT AND ITS CRITICS. Foreword
by John P. Frank. Tucson: University of Arizona Press, 1968.

This is a systematic classification and examination of some of the
major criticisms directed against the liberalism of the Supreme
Court from 1954 to 1961. Organized in part on the basis of the
source of the criticism--Congress, pressure groups, state officials,
law enforcement officials and "professional critics" such as academicians and lawyers--it examines the opinions which produced
opposition and the basic arguments of the opponents.

McCloskey, Robert G. THE AMERICAN SUPREME COURT. Chicago: University of Chicago Press, 1960.

In this study of the role of the Court and the uses to which it has
put its power of judicial review, McCloskey examines the Court
under Marshall and Taney, constitutional evolution in the Gilded
Age, the Court's relationship to the welfare state and the modern
Court's handling of race and free speech questions.

_____. THE MODERN SUPREME COURT. Foreword by Martin Shapiro.
Cambridge, Mass.: Harvard University Press, 1972.

This is a study of the Court between 1941 and 1962. Divided
into four historical periods, the work deals with the Stone Court
in the World War II period, the Vinson Court during the cold war,
the early Warren Court from 1953 to 1960 and its handling of
desegregation, and the later Warren Court from the 1961 term
to Warren's resignation at the end of 1965.

McCune, Wesley. THE NINE YOUNG MEN. New York: Greenwood Press,
1947.

Written a decade after the Constitutional Revolution of 1937 and
in a spirit in contrast to the "nine old men" epithet hurled at
the conservative court of the early 1930s, this is an informal

study of the Court as reconstituted by Roosevelt and Truman.
It discusses some of the major constitutional issues before the
court, some of the conflicts within it, and contains sketches of
the individual justices on the Court in the late 1940s.

McGowan, Carl. THE ORGANIZATION OF JUDICIAL POWER IN THE
UNITED STATES. Evanston, Ill.: Northwestern University Press, 1969.

Originally delivered as the 1967 Rosenthal Lectures at Northwestern University School of Law, this is an analysis of the
relationship between the Supreme Court and lower federal courts
and between federal and state courts, of the strains imposed by
this dual judicial system and of the quest for accommodation.

Manwaring, David R.; Reich, Donald R.; and Wasby, Stephen L. THE
SUPREME COURT AS POLICY MAKER: THREE STUDIES ON THE IMPACT
OF JUDICIAL DECISIONS. Carbondale: Public Affairs Research Bureau,
Southern Illinois University, 1968.

Originally delivered at political science conventions, these three
papers examine the impact of Supreme Court decisions in three
areas: the impact of Mapp v. Ohio on search and seizures
practices, the impact of the school prayer cases and the impact
of obscenity decisions in Oregon.

Mason, Alpheus T. THE SUPREME COURT: PALLADIUM OF FREEDOM.
Ann Arbor: University of Michigan Press, 1962.

This expansion of the 1962 William W. Cook Lectures at the
University of Michigan is an exposition of the role of the court
as a forum for espousing the ideas of the American Revolution,
enforcing the guarantees of the Bill of Rights, developing and
using the power of judicial review and an examination of the
relationship between Jefferson and Marshall and between Roosevelt
and Hughes.

_____. THE SUPREME COURT FROM TAFT TO WARREN. Rev. ed.
Baton Rouge: Louisiana State University Press, 1968.

Originally published in 1958, this is an account of major constitutional developments and of the policy-making role of the Court
in the four decades from the activist Taft Court, through the retreat from socioeconomic policy making by the Hughes Court to
the Stone Court's attempt to carve out a new role for the Court,
and the adoption by the Court, culminating in the Warren years,
of the role of protector of egalitarian and libertarian principles.

Max Planck Institute. JUDICIAL PROTECTION AGAINST THE EXECUTIVE.
3 vols. Dobbs Ferry, N.Y.: Oceana, 1970-71.

This comparative study of the judiciary examines the authority
and effectiveness of courts in thirty-one countries, including
the United States, in checking and protecting against executive
use or abuse of power.

Mayers, Lewis. THE AMERICAN LEGAL SYSTEM: THE ADMINISTRATION
OF JUSTICE IN THE UNITED STATES BY JUDICIAL, ADMINISTRATIVE,
MILITARY AND ARBITRAL TRIBUNALS. New York: Harper and Brothers,
1955.

This is a study of the structure, power and the civil and criminal proceedings of varied legal institutions: federal and state courts, administrative tribunals, military tribunals, and voluntary arbitration tribunals.

Mendelson, Wallace. JUSTICES BLACK AND FRANKFURTER: CONFLICT IN THE COURT. 2d ed. Chicago: University of Chicago Press, 1966.

First published in 1961, this exploration of the nature of the role of the judiciary in constitutional interpretation focuses upon Black and Frankfurter as representatives of the two traditions of judicial activism and judicial self-restraint. Mendelson examines their views as expressed in a variety of cases dealing with substantive issues ranging from separation of powers through federalism to civil liberties to illustrate their different concepts of the proper role of a judge. In an epilogue written in 1966, Mendelson takes notes of Black's opinion in Bell v. Maryland and suggests that it is perhaps indicative of a major shift in Black's activist stance.

Miller, Arthur S. THE SUPREME COURT AND AMERICAN CAPITALISM. New York: Free Press, 1968.

This is an examination of Supreme Court decisions which had some influence in establishing the constitutional and legal framework within which business operates. Miller looks at the history of Supreme Court decisions and the role of that tribunal between 1787 and 1930, the implications of the constitutional revolution of the 1930s for business and the emergence of the "positive state" and the declining influence of the Supreme Court in economic policy matters. Noting that the Court no longer makes basic economic decisions and that this power now rests with Congress and the president, Miller argues for development of a new theory concerning the constitutional position of the corporation.

Miller, Charles A. THE SUPREME COURT AND THE USES OF HISTORY. Cambridge, Mass.: Belknap Press of Harvard University Press, 1969.

This is an examination of the two general types of history--intent of the framers and ongoing history since the framers--used in such areas of constitutional adjudication as presidential removal power, political expression, the sit-in-cases, reapportionment and the Minnesota mortgage moratorium case.

"The Mootness Doctrine in the Supreme Court." HARVARD LAW REVIEW 88 (December 1974): 373-95.

This is a brief overview of the basis of the mootness doctrine (originally grounded in the common law doctrine that courts lack the power to decide abstract questions where no dispute exists and then on the "cases and controversy" requirement of Article III) and the manner in which the Court has attempted to reconcile its role as policy maker and its purely legal role of settling legal disputes between parties. It examines such techniques as the "capable of repetition, yet evading review" approach and the "future recurrence of past injury" holding.

Muller, William H. EARLY HISTORY OF THE FEDERAL SUPREME COURT. Boston: Chipman Law Publishing Co., 1922.

This is a history of the Court prior to the ascension of Chief Justice Marshall to the bench, a period which has received little attention. It examines the debate on the judiciary at the Philadelphia convention, the organization of the early court under Chief Justice Jay in New York, the events surrounding Hayburn's case, the first major confrontation with a state over the question of state sovereignty in <u>Chisholm</u> v. <u>Georgia</u>, <u>Ware</u> v. <u>Jones</u> in which John Marshall appeared as counsel to argue that the judiciary had no authority to question the validity of legislation unless the Constitution expressly confers such authority, and the early growth of judicial power as exemplified by such cases as <u>Calder</u> v. <u>Bull</u>.

Murphy, Walter F.; Tanenhaus, Joseph; and Kastner, Daniel. PUBLIC EVALUATIONS OF CONSTITUTIONAL COURTS: ALTERNATIVE EXPLANATIONS. Sage Professional Papers in Comparative Politics. Beverly Hills, Calif.: Sage Publications, 1973.

This monograph summarizes the results of interviews with voting-age Americans designed to elicit patterns of support for the courts, uses these data to seek explanations for patterns of support and discusses some of the implications for the roles of courts suggested by these patterns for support.

Myers, Gustavus. HISTORY OF THE SUPREME COURT OF THE UNITED STATES. Chicago: Charles H. Kerr and Co., 1918.

This history begins not with the establishment of the Supreme Court by the Constitution but with an analysis of the creation of classes in the colonial period; the author argues that the landed aristocracy was created by royal grants, official favoritism and fraud while punitive law created a dependent, servile class. Although the working class sided with the upper class in rejecting English rule, it viewed the Constitution, and especially the judiciary it created, as a product of upper class privilege. It is against this background of upper class support for and working class fear of the Court that the author traces the development of the Court as an instrument of privilege from its origin to the chief justiceship of White.

North, Arthur H. THE SUPREME COURT: JUDICIAL PROCESS AND JUDICIAL POLITICS. New York: Appleton-Century-Crofts, Meredith Publishing Co., 1966.

In this study of judicial procedures, operations and doctrinal developments, North examines the movement from procedural to substantive due process, the nationalization of the Bill of Rights, selective incorporation of the Bill of Rights and the Preferred Position Doctrine.

Pfeffer, Leo. THIS HONORABLE COURT: A HISTORY OF THE UNITED STATES SUPREME COURT. Boston: Beacon Press, 1965.

This is a history of the Court from its "humble birth" and relative unimportance in the eyes of the framers of the Constitution, President Washington and the early Congress and its evolution into a major policy-making institution. It traces the major doctrinal shifts as embodied in the views of the Chief Justices and other leading members of the Court from Jay to Warren.

Post, Charles Gordon. THE SUPREME COURT AND POLITICAL QUES-
TIONS. Baltimore: Johns Hopkins University, 1936.

This is an analysis and classification of some Supreme Court
cases involving political questions. The author examines such
cases as Luther v. Borden, Texas v. White, the Prize Cases,
and some involving treaties and the status of Indian tribes with
a view to answering two questions: why the Court designates
certain problems as nonjusticiable and what the consequences of
such a designation are.

Pound, Roscoe. ORGANIZATION OF COURTS. Boston: Little, Brown,
1940.

With three background chapters on the court system in England
at the time of colonization and in the eighteenth century and on
the colonial courts in the seventeenth and eighteenth centuries,
this study of the organization and reorganizations of courts
examines national and state court systems from the formative
years under the Constitution, through the post-Civil War period
to the turn of the century and to the changes in the first three
decades of the twentieth century.

Pritchett, C. Hermann. CIVIL LIBERTIES AND THE VINSON COURT.
Chicago: University of Chicago Press, 1954.

Successor to Pritchett's classic work on THE ROOSEVELT COURT,
this is an analysis of the Court from 1946 to 1953, years during
which Fred Vinson served as Chief Justice. Focusing on individual rights, Pritchett examines the Vinson Court's handling of
speech, loyalty and segregation cases and examines the emergence
of liberal activism as exemplified by Black and liberal restraint
as exemplified by Frankfurter.

_____. THE POLITICAL OFFENDER AND THE WARREN COURT. Boston:
Boston University Press, 1958.

Delivered as the Gaspar G. Bacon Lectures on the Constitution
of the United States, this work examines the Court's reaction
to criminal punishment for political speech (in such cases as
Dennis, Yates, and Jencks), punishment by legislative investigating committees (in such cases as Watkins and Sweeney) as
well as to "quasipunishment" imposed by such governmental actions
as the loyalty security program and the denial of passports.

_____. THE ROOSEVELT COURT: A STUDY IN JUDICIAL POLITICS
AND VALUES, 1937-47. New York: Macmillan, 1948. Reprint. Chicago:
Quadrangle Books, 1969.

An examination of the politics and values of the Supreme Court
as reconstituted and redirected by the appointees of Franklin
D. Roosevelt and an analysis of the voting record of each of the
justices. There is a list of decisions overruled between 1937
and 1946, the case which overruled each and the vote in each
in the appendix.

Pusey, Merlo J. THE SUPREME COURT CRISIS. New York: Macmillan,
1937.

This short work is a contemporary attack on the "court-packing" proposal of Franklin Roosevelt which the author views as an attack upon the independence of the judiciary by a president "who has forgotten that there are three coordinate branches of government and he heads only one." To Pusey, the basic issue raised by the plan to enlarge the Court was whether modifications in government policy were to be made by the people or by a Court controlled by the president. His recommendation for settling disputes over constitutional provisions was the amending process which allowed the people to decide.

Ransom, William. MAJORITY RULE AND THE JUDICIARY: AN EXAMINATION OF CURRENT PROPOSALS FOR CONSTITUTIONAL CHANGE AFFECTING THE RELATION OF COURT TO LEGISLATION. New York: Charles Scribner, 1912. Introduction by Theodore Roosevelt. Reprint. New York: Da Capo Press, 1971.

This work was originally published at a time when a conservative Court was invalidating popular protective labor legislation and was, in general, reading conservative economic theory into the Constitution. This work examines various proposed methods by which a popular majority could have its programs legitimized and supports Roosevelt's proposal for the recall of judicial decisions on constitutional issues.

REPORTS OF CASES DECIDED BY CHIEF JUSTICE CHASE IN THE CIRCUIT COURT OF THE UNITED STATES, 4th CIRCUIT, 1865-1869. 1876. Reprint. New York: Da Capo Press, 1972.

As chief justice from 1864-73, Chief Justice Salmon P. Chase rode circuit in Maryland, Virginia, North Carolina and South Carolina. This is a collection of his opinions at the trial court level which in some ways may be more revealing of his political philosophy than are his collegiate opinions for the Supreme Court. This reprint has a new introduction in which an attempt is made to place Chase and his views in historical perspective. It challenges the traditional view that the Court under Chase hit a new low in power and prestige.

REPORTS OF THE TRIALS OF COLONEL AARON BURR FOR TREASON AND FOR A MISDEMEANOR IN PREPARING THE MEANS OF A MILITARY EXPEDITION AGAINST MEXICO IN THE CIRCUIT COURT OF THE UNITED STATES, SUMMER TERM, 1807. 2 vols. Philadelphia: Hopkins and Earle, 1808. Reprint, New York: Da Capo Press, 1969.

This contains the complete record of the Burr treason trial, including Marshall's examination of Burr, the evidence introduced, the motions made, the arguments before the court and the testimony.

Roberts, Owen J. THE COURT AND THE CONSTITUTION. Cambridge, Mass.: Harvard University Press, 1951. Reprint. Port Washington, N.Y.: Kennikat Press, 1969.

In these 1951 Holmes Lectures at Harvard, Justice Roberts discusses taxation, the states' police power and the Fourteenth Amendment.

Article III

Roche, John P. COURTS AND RIGHTS: THE AMERICAN JUDICIARY IN ACTION. New York: Random House, 1966.

> This is a brief overview of the judicial process and the role of the federal courts in protecting individual rights.

Rodell, Fred. NINE MEN: A POLITICAL HISTORY OF THE SUPREME COURT FROM 1790 TO 1955. New York: Random House, 1955.

> Without footnotes or bibliography and intended for the general reader, this work by Yale University Professor Rodell examines the Court as a political institution which uses the power of judicial review to influence and direct the course of public policy.

Rohde, David W., and Spaeth, Harold J. SUPREME COURT DECISION-MAKING. San Francisco: W.H. Freeman and Co., 1976.

> Focusing upon the Supreme Court justices of the present and recent past, this is an analysis of the decision-making process in terms of such factors as access, voting and coalition building.

Rosen, Paul L. THE SUPREME COURT AND SOCIAL SCIENCE. Urbana: University of Illinois Press, 1972.

> In this analysis of the role of social science research in judicial policy making, Rosen examines social Darwinism and the rise of sociological jurisprudence, the Court's defense of property rights in the period of economic substantive due process, the introduction of the Brandeis-type period in the early part of this century, racial discrimination and equal protection in the pre-Brown period and modern social science and the Brown opinion.

Rostow, Eugene V. THE SOVEREIGN PREROGATIVE: THE SUPREME COURT AND THE QUEST FOR LAW. New Haven, Conn.: Yale University Press, 1962.

> This look at what Holmes called the "sovereign prerogative of choice" exercised by courts in settling "conflicts between two social desires" is largely a collection of Rostow's articles and speeches in which he supports the legitimacy of "judge made law" and the doctrine of judicial review.

Sayler, Richard H.; Boyer, Barry B.; Gooding, Robert E., Jr., eds. THE WARREN COURT: A CRITICAL ANALYSIS. New York: Chelsea House Publishers, 1969.

> This is a collection of eleven essays by different scholars dealing with nine major substantive constitutional areas dealt with by the Warren Court: reapportionment, desegregation, criminal procedure, religion, speech, press, the political process, labor and antitrust law. One essay, by Anthony Lewis, is a biographical sketch of Warren and one, by Philip B. Kurland, is an analysis of "The Warren Court and the 'Warren Myth.'"

Scheingold, Stuart A. THE POLITICS OF RIGHTS: LAWYERS, PUBLIC POLICY AND POLITICAL CHANGE. New Haven, Conn.: Yale University Press, 1974.

This is an examination of the role of law and litigation in bringing about social and political change.

Schubert, Glendon [A.]. THE JUDICIAL MIND: ATTITUDES AND IDEO-
LOGIES OF SUPREME COURT JUSTICES, 1946-1963. Evanston, Ill.:
Northwestern University Press, 1965.

Using the sophisticated methodology associated with Schubert's
analyses of the judiciary, this work examines the voting records
in nonunanimous opinions of the eighteen justices who served from
1946 to 1963 to determine the factors which control the way judges
vote. He concludes that judicial attitudes are a product of the
social, economic, and political values of judges.

_____. JUDICIAL POLICY-MAKING: THE POLITICAL ROLE OF THE
COURTS. Chicago: Scott, Foresman, 1965.

This is an employment of the systems approach as a means of
examining the policy-making role of the judiciary.

Schwartz, Bernard. THE SUPREME COURT: CONSTITUTIONAL REVOLU-
TION IN RETROSPECT. New York: Ronald Press, 1957.

This is an analysis of the 1937 "constitutional revolution" in which
the Court turned to passive self-restraint and allowed the political
majority to determine socioeconomic policy.

Scott, Alfred M. THE SUPREME COURT V. THE CONSTITUTION: AN
ESSAY ON HOW JUDGES BECOME DICTATORS. New York: Exposition
Press, 1962.

This monograph is an attack upon the Supreme Court for violating
the principle of stare decisis and for making law in the guise of
interpreting the Constitution.

Shogan, Robert. A QUESTION OF JUDGMENT: THE FORTAS CASE AND
THE STRUGGLE FOR THE SUPREME COURT. Indianapolis: Bobbs-Merrill,
1972.

This is an analysis of the defeat of the nomination of Justice Abe
Fortas to be Chief Justice and his resignation from the Court in
May of 1969 set against a background of his career as a law professor, a practicing Washington lawyer and close advisor to
President Lyndon Johnson. In assessing the factors which led to
the first major defeat of a presidential nominee since the rejection
of Hoover's nomination of John J. Parker in the 1930s, the author
concludes that the most important factors were the clumsiness of
Johnson and Fortas, antipathy toward the Warren Court and the
low prestige of the president in the late 1960s. The ambivalence
of Chief Justice Warren's announcement that he would retire when
a successor was chosen made acceptance of his successor less
urgent.

Simon, James F. IN HIS OWN IMAGE: THE SUPREME COURT IN RICHARD
NIXON'S AMERICA. New York: David McKay, 1973.

Written by a TIME magazine legal reporter for the general audience, this is an account of changes in personnel on the Supreme
Court during the Nixon administation and a criticism of Nixon
and his "new conservative majority" on the Court which, in the
author's view, "cut back on the rights of criminal suspects,
largely ignored the constitutional demands of the poor and held
firmly but narrowly to the desegregation line that the Warren
Court drew in 1954." Simon .contends that as a result of Nixon's
appointees, the Court abandoned its "role of keeper of the nation's
conscience."

Sprague, John D. VOTING PATTERNS OF THE UNITED STATES SUPREME
COURT: CASES IN FEDERALISM, 1889-1959. Indianapolis: Bobbs-Merrill,
1968.

Building upon the methodology of C. Herman Pritchett's THE
ROOSEVELT COURT: A STUDY IN JUDICIAL POLITICS AND
VALUES (see p. 192) and Glendon A. Schubert's QUANTITATIVE
ANALYSIS OF JUDICIAL BEHAVIOR, this is a bloc analysis
of 831 cases over a seventy-year span involving federal-state
relations in which the Court was divided. The first three
chapters are devoted to an examination of the general method-
ological problems encountered in studying judicial behavior as
well as some specific problems arising out of the data analyzed
in the remainder of the book.

"Standing to Assert Constitutional Jus Tertii." HARVARD LAW REVIEW
88 (December 1974): 423-43.

This note criticizes the failure of the Supreme Court to distinguish between claims of statutory overbreath and jus tertti. It
argues that this failure to distinguish between the two claims,
combined with the Court's application of the same rule forbidding
assertion of rights of third parties to both, has further confused
the issue of what constitutes standing. It argues that different
considerations govern the appropriateness of adjudicating the
two types of claims and that the Court should adopt a more liberal rule according standing to third parties. It argues that
jus tertti claims are more compelling than overbreath claims.

Steamer, Robert J. THE SUPREME COURT IN CRISIS: A HISTORY OF
CONFLICT. Amherst: University of Massachusetts Press, 1971.

This is a history of the Supreme Court from Marshall to Warren
which focuses upon the recurring conflicts between the Court and
the other two branches and the constitutional crises which such
conflicts produce. Professor Steamer argues that such conflicts
are both inevitable and desirable. They are inevitable because
one branch is appointive and oligarchic, while the other two are
popularly elected and because the power of judicial review is not
explicitly conferred by the Constitution thus complicating the
power struggle between competing policy makers. They are
beneficial because pure majority rule sometimes results in bad
policy and because they furnish an occasion for public debate
on fundamental issues.

Strumm, Philippa. THE SUPREME COURT AND "POLITICAL QUESTIONS":
A STUDY IN JUDICIAL EVASION. University: University of Alabama
Press, 1974.

> The ambiguities inherent in the Court's attempts to explain the
> characteristics of a "political question" have led some Court
> observers to conclude that the major ingredient is judicial re-
> luctance to enter an area. This work examines the case law
> in the areas of elections, executive authority, republican form
> of government and reapportionment and concludes that the doc-
> trine is invoked by the Court to avoid rendering decisions which
> may be ignored or defied.

Swisher, Carl B. HISTORY OF THE SUPREME COURT OF THE UNITED
STATES: THE TANEY PERIOD, 1835-1864. New York: Macmillan, 1974.

> This is volume 5 of the projected eleven volume OLIVER WENDELL
> HOLMES DEVISE HISTORY OF THE SUPREME COURT OF THE
> UNITED STATES (see p. 181), three of which have been published.
> Written by the biographer of Chief Justice Taney, it covers the
> period from the Jackson era through most of the Civil War era.
> Like the other volumes in this ambitious HISTORY OF THE
> SUPREME COURT, this massive work of scholarship places the
> Supreme Court and its work within the context of the social,
> economic and political developments of the period covered as
> well as detailing the major and minor conflicts and relationships
> between members of the Court and their roles and relationships
> with the political figures and controversies of their day. It
> thus examines in detail not only such major issues and problems
> as sectionalism; nullification; slavery and the Civil War which
> dominated the later Taney years; territorial expansionism; and
> a variety of economic and business issues such as commerce
> contracts, land claims, patents and admiralty law which were
> important in the earlier years, but delves into such relatively
> minor skirmishes as judicial infighting over Court reporters.

Tompkins, Dorothy Campbell. COURT ORGANIZATION AND ADMINISTRA-
TION: A BIBLICGRAPHY. Berkeley: Institute of Governmental Studies,
University of California, 1973.

> This bibliography of materials on the organization of court and
> judicial administration published since 1957 is organized on the
> basis of the type of court: state and federal courts of general
> and limited jurisdiction and appellate courts. There is a section
> devoted to court administration and to periodicals.

_____. THE SUPREME COURT OF THE UNITED STATES: A BIBLIOG-
RAPHY. Berkeley: Bureau of Public Administration, University of California, 1959.

> Compiled in response to the attacks on the Supreme Court since
> its desegregation decision in 1954, this bibliography serves as a
> guide to bibliographies on the Supreme Court. It cites works
> dealing with the organization of the court, its jurisdiction,
> judicial review and the relationship of the court to the other
> branches of government. One section cites works dealing with
> controversies over the court.

Umbreit, Kenneth B. OUR ELEVEN CHIEF JUSTICES: A HISTORY OF THE SUPREME COURT IN TERMS OF THEIR PERSONALITIES. New York: Harper and Row, 1938. Reprint. Port Washington, N.Y.: Kennikat Press, 1969.

> This history examines the development and role of the Court as reflected and influenced by the personalities of its Chief Justices from John Jay to Charles Evans Hughes.

U.S. Congress. Senate. CREATION OF THE FEDERAL JUDICIARY: A REVIEW OF THE DEBATES IN THE FEDERAL AND STATE CONSTITU-TIONAL CONVENTIONS AND OTHER STATE PAPERS. Prepared by G.J. Schulz. 75th Cong., 1st sess. Document No. 91. Washington, D.C.: Government Printing Office, 1938.

> The various materials in this report include procedures at the constitutional and ratifying conventions, excerpts from the FEDER-ALIST PAPERS relative to the judiciary, the Judiciary Act of 1789, Marbury v. Madison, lists of the provisions of federal laws held unconstitutional, the decisions involving the constitution since 1933 to the time of the hearings, the five-to-four decisions by the Court, the cases decided by a majority of one, restrictions upon the appellate jurisdiction of the Supreme Court, changes in the number of Supreme Court justices, and the acts of Congress relating to the federal judiciary.

U.S. Congress. Senate. "Trial of Samuel Chase, An Associate Justice of the Supreme Court Impeached by the House of Representatives for High Crimes and Misdemeanors, Before the Senate of the United States." 14 ANNALS OF CONGRESS. 2 vols. 8th Cong., 2d sess. Washington, D.C.: Government Printing Office, 1805. Reprint. New York: Da Capo Press, 1970.

> In 1804, the House impeached a justice of the Supreme Court for the first and only time. This is the official record of the trial in the Senate which failed to convict Justice Chase on any of the eight charges brought by the House. Because Chase, a Federalist at a time when Republicans dominated the political branches, was highly partisan and used the bench for political pronouncements, one of the chief themes of the impeachment trial was the extent to which the political views and behavior of judges are appropriate bases for removal from office. Since the acquittal of Justice Chase, the conventional answer has been that such bases are illegitimate.

U.S. Congress. Senate. Committee on the Judiciary. LIMITATIONS OF APPELLATE JURISDICTION OF THE UNITED STATES SUPREME COURT. HEARINGS BEFORE THE SUBCOMMITTEE TO INVESTIGATE THE ADMINIS-TRATION OF THE INTERNAL SECURITY ACT AND OTHER INTERNAL SECURITY LAWS. 85th Cong., 1st sess. 7 August 1957. Washington, D.C.: Government Printing Office, 1957.

> These are the hearings on Senator Jenner's bill to remove certain matters from review by the Supreme Court, a bill prompted primarily by the Court's decisions calling into question the legiti-macy of some of the techniques of the House Un-American Activi-ties Committee.

U.S. Library of Congress. Legislative Reference Service. PROVISIONS OF THE FEDERAL LAW HELD UNCONSTITUTIONAL BY THE SUPREME COURT OF THE UNITED STATES. Washington, D.C.: Government Printing Office, 1936. Reprint. Westport, Conn.: Greenwood Press, 1976.

> This is a brief analysis of each Supreme Court opinion in which a provision of a federal law was held unconstitutional from the invalidation of Section 13 of the Judiciary Act of 1789 in Marbury v. Madison to the Guffey Coal Act invalidated in Carter v. Carter Coal in 1935. The analysis is organized chronologically on the basis of the date of the legislative provision, rather than the date of the Supreme Court decision. In addition to the analysis of cases, there are brief notes on such matters relative to judicial power as what constitutes a "case or controversy," procedures for seeking Supreme Court review, and the separability of constitutional from unconstitutional provisions of a statute. The list of the laws invalidated by the Supreme Court and the cases in which they were invalidated is kept up to date in the CONSTITUTION ANNOTATED and supplements. A list of invalidated laws to 1965 may also be found in Albert B. Saye, CONSTITUTIONAL LAW (Mundelein, Ill.: Callaghan, 1965), pp. 25-27. Such a list may also be found in the appendix of Volume IV of Leon Friedman and Fred L. Israel, THE JUSTICES OF THE UNITED STATES SUPREME COURT, 1789-1969: THEIR LIVES AND MAJOR OPINIONS (New York: Chelsea House Publishers in Association with R.R. Bowker, 1969).

Wasby, Stephen L. CONTINUITY AND CHANGE: FROM THE WARREN COURT TO THE BURGER COURT. Pacific Palisades, Calif.: Goodyear Publishing Co., 1976.

> This is an examination of the Supreme Court's transition from the late 1960s, when the Burger Court was completed with the seating of the four Nixon appointees, to the end of the 1973 terms in July of 1974. Examining the Warren Court briefly and the Burger Court in depth in terms of liberalism and conservatism, activism and self-restraint, Wasby suggests that the Burger Court is more liberal than its predecessor in some areas, less liberal in others and in conformity in others.

_____. THE IMPACT OF THE UNITED STATES SUPREME COURT: SOME PERSPECTIVES. Homewood, Ill.: Dorsey, 1970.

> The first section of this work deals with the broad problem of impact studies and the last section sets forth a set of hypotheses about the impact of judicial opinions. The major portion of the work is a substantive analysis of the impact of Supreme Court decisions in the areas of economic regulation, reapportionment, church-state relationships, obscenity, criminal procedure, school desegregation, and the political arena.

Wechsler, Herbert. THE COURTS AND THE CONSTITUTION. Athens: University of Georgia School of Law, 1965.

> Originally delivered as the 1965 John A. Sibley Lectures in Law, this slim volume addresses two major problems: the practical, political limits within which the Supreme Court exercises its power of judicial review and the moral limits.

_____. PRINCIPLES, POLITICS AND FUNDAMENTAL LAW: SELECTED ESSAYS. Cambridge, Mass.: Harvard University Press, 1961.

> In addition to the much lauded and much criticized essay entitled "Toward Neutral Principles of Constitutional Law," originally delivered at the 1959 Oliver Wendell Holmes Lectures, this work includes three other essays dealing with the Supreme Court and constitutional issues: "The Political Safeguards of Federalism," "Mr. Justice Stone and the Constitution," and "The Issues of the Nuremberg Trials."

Wechsler, Herbert, and Hart, Henry M., eds. THE FEDERAL COURTS AND THE FEDERAL SYSTEM. Brooklyn: Foundation Press, 1953.

> Because the Constitution confers upon Congress the authority to determine the appellate jurisdiction of the Supreme Court, Congress determines the jurisdiction of all federal courts. Until the last quarter of the nineteenth century, lower court exercised no general jurisdiction in constitutional cases.

Westin, Alan F. THE SUPREME COURT: VIEWS FROM THE INSIDE. New York: W.W. Norton, 1961.

> A collection of fourteen off-the-bench commentaries made by Supreme Court justices while on the Court or after leaving the Court on such topics as the role of oral arguments and of dissenting opinions and generally on the role and the work of the court and of the judicial process. It includes Justice Black's classic 1960 address on "The Bill of Rights."

White, G. Edward. THE AMERICAN JUDICIAL TRADITION: PROFILES OF LEADING AMERICAN JUDGES. New York: Oxford University Press, 1976.

> The author argues that there are certain traditions associated with the character of the American process of appellate judging. These traditions he identifies as: tension between independence and accountability, a delicate and unique relation to politics, and a recurrent trade-off between acknowledged constraints on the judiciary. He uses the profiles of individual judges (such as Marshall, Kent, Story, Taney, Harlan, Holmes, Hughes, and Frankfurter) to examine the developments of these elements.

Zeisel, Hans; Kalven, Harry, Jr.; and Buchholz, Bernard. DELAY IN THE COURTS. Boston: Little, Brown, 1959.

> This case study of congestion and delay in and the flow of cases through the Supreme Court of New York County (Manhattan) is designed to illuminate the problem in other local and state courts as well as in the national courts.

PRIMARY SOURCES

FEDERAL REPORTER: CASES DECIDED IN UNITED STATES COURTS OF APPEAL, COURT OF CLAIMS AND UNITED STATES COURT OF CUSTOMS AND PATENT APPEALS. St. Paul, Minn.: West Publishing Co., 1880-- .

Cited as F., the first series of the FEDERAL REPORTER (March 1880 - November 1924) consists of volumes 1 through 164 of the opinions of the federal court of claims and other appellate courts. The second series, cited as F. 2nd, picks up in 1924 and is published annually.

FEDERAL SUPPLEMENT: CASES ARGUED AND DETERMINED IN THE DISTRICT COURTS OF THE UNITED STATES AND THE COURT OF CLAIMS. St. Paul, Minn.: West Publishing Co., 1932-- .

Cited as F. SUPP., this series contains the opinions of the federal district courts and of the federal court of claims.

Kurland, Philip B., and Casper, Gerhard, eds. LANDMARK BRIEFS AND ARGUMENTS OF THE SUPREME COURT OF THE UNITED STATES: CON-STITUTIONAL LAW. 80 vols. Washington, D.C.: University Publications of America, 1975. 1974 TERM SUPPLEMENT, 2 vols., 1977. 1975 TERM SUPPLEMENT, 8 vols., 1977.

These ninety volumes consist of the briefs of opposing counsel and friends of the court and transcripts of oral arguments in basic constitutional law cases heard by the Supreme Court since Marbury v. Madison in 1803.

PREVIEW OF UNITED STATES SUPREME COURT CASES. Philadelphia: Association of American Law Schools and American Law Institute--American Bar Association--Committee on Continuing Professional Education, 6/month, September-May.

PREVIEW contains memoranda describing the background, signi-ficance, question of law and arguments of opposing counsel in each case pending before the Supreme Court.

UNITED STATES LAW WEEK: A NATIONAL SURVEY OF CURRENT LAW. Washington, D.C.: Bureau of National Affairs, 1932-- .

This weekly journal of the proceedings of the Supreme Court contains such materials as summaries of the orders of the Court, list of the cases docketed, summaries of cases recently filed, a calendar of hearings scheduled, summaries of oral arguments and of the major arguments in important cases, periodic reports on the cases argued as well as special articles on the Court's work.

UNITED STATES REPORTS: CASES ADJUDICATED IN THE SUPREME COURT. Washington, D.C.: Government Printing Office, 1789-- .

In addition to this official report of Supreme Court opinions, cited as U.S., there are two commercial editions, cited as S. Ct. and L. Ed. The latter, the Lawyers edition, contains not only the opinions of the Court but headnotes and summaries. In addition to these volumes published at the end of the court session, the Court issues slip opinions on the day the decision is rendered and these are available from the Government Printing Office.

UNITED STATES SUPREME COURT RECORDS AND BRIEFS IN UNITED STATES CASES DECIDED BY THE SUPREME COURT OF THE UNITED STATES. Washington, D.C.: Government Printing Office, 1897-- .

RECORDS AND BRIEFS contains all of the briefs presented
to the court by participating counsel and friends of the court as
well as all related documentation such as lower court opinions
and petitions. It is printed primarily for use by the Supreme
Court and is held by a limited number of law libraries. They
are now on microcards published by Microcard Editions, Washington, D.C. In addition, University Publications of America,
Washington, D.C., has published an eighty-volume LANDMARK
BRIEFS AND ARGUMENTS OF THE SUPREME COURT OF THE
UNITED STATES, 1975 (see p. 201) which contains the briefs
of opposing counsel and transcripts of oral arguments in 235
of the most important constitutional cases from 1803 and Marbury
v. Madison to the 1973 terms. Edited by Philip B. Kurland and
Gerhard Casper, the eighty-volume edition is kept up to date
through supplements. There is an index to RECORDS AND
BRIEFS (Englewood, Colo.: Information Handling Service, 1978--.
Quarterly. Cumulative hardbound published annually) which indexes
those briefs and records that have been microfiched by the Information Handling Service on the basis of 1) the docket number of
each case, 2) the assignment number designated by the Information
Handling Service, 3) the U.S. Reports number, and 4) the case
name.

JUDICIAL BIOGRAPHIES AND PAPERS

Baker, Leonard. JOHN MARSHALL: A LIFE IN LAW. New York: Macmillan, 1974.

This biography of Marshall focuses on his thirty-five years as
chief justice and on those judicial opinions which expanded the
power of the national government and of the Court.

Baker, Liva. FELIX FRANKFURTER. New York: Coward-McCann, 1969.

The first two-thirds of this biography examines Frankfurter's life
as a student and as a professor at Harvard and his political role
during the New Deal. The last one-third looks at his role on the
Supreme Court.

Ball, Howard. THE VISION AND DREAM OF JUSTICE HUGO L. BLACK:
AN EXAMINATION OF A JUDICIAL PHILOSOPHY. University: University
of Alabama Press, 1975.

This study of the constitutional theories of Justice Black focuses
upon his insistence that the due process clause of the Fourteenth
Amendment incorporates the guarantees of the Bill of Rights, no
more and no less, and upon his absolutist reading of the First
Amendment.

Bander, Edward J., comp. JUSTICE HOLMES EX CATHEDRA. Charlottesville, Va.: Michie Co., 1966.

Selected "to please those who seek the sheer joy of Holmes's
magic with the English language" rather than to reveal a coherent
legal philosophy, these one-sentence or one-paragraph extracts
from Holmes's judicial opinions and other writings are organized

on the basis of general propositions, legal definitions, "nuggets of [his] superb literary style" and anecdotes.

Beveridge, Albert J. THE LIFE OF JOHN MARSHALL. 4 vols. Boston: Houghton Mifflin Co., 1916-19.

This study of Marshall's life is probably still considered to be the most complete biography. Volume 1, subtitled FRONTIERS-MAN, SOLDIER AND LAWMAKER, covers the years from 1755 to 1788. Volume 2, subtitled POLITICIAN, DIPLOMATIST, STATEMAN, covers 1781 to 1801. Volumes 3 and 4 cover his Supreme Court years. Volume 3, subtitled CONFLICT AND CONSTRUCTION, covers 1800 to 1815. Volume 4, subtitled BUILDING A NATION, covers 1815 to 1835.

Black, Hugo. ONE MAN'S STAND FOR FREEDOM. Edited by Irving Dillard. New York: Knopf, 1963.

With an introductory biographical chapter, this is a selection of Black's major civil liberties opinions.

Bland, Randall W. PRIVATE PRESSURE ON PUBLIC LAW: THE LEGAL CAREER OF JUSTICE THURGOOD MARSHALL. Port Washington, N.Y.: Kennikat Press, 1973.

This analysis of the public life of Justice Marshall examines his role in expanding the constitutional protection afforded blacks as an attorney for the NAACP and his role as a Supreme Court justice who joined the liberal wing of the Warren and Burger Courts in an attempt to expand individual rights.

Brandeis, Louis D. LETTERS OF LOUIS D. BRANDEIS. Edited by Melvin I. Urofsky and David W. Levy. 4 vols. to date. Albany: State University of New York Press, 1971-- .

Volume 1, subtitled URBAN REFORMER, covers the period from 1870 to 1907. Volume 2, subtitled PEOPLE'S ATTORNEY, covers 1907 to 1912. Volume 3, subtitled PROGRESSIVE AND ZIONIST, covers 1913 to 1915. Volume 4, subtitled MR. JUSTICE BRAN-DEIS, covers 1916 to 1921.

_____. THE SOCIAL AND ECONOMIC VIEWS OF MR. JUSTICE BRANDEIS. Edited by Alfred Lief. Foreword by Charles A. Beard. New York: Vanguard Press, 1930.

With introductory notes by the editor, this is a collection of materials--largely judicial opinions--in which Brandeis expressed his views on various social and economic issues. Organized on the basis of various substantive issues important during his legal and judicial career, the work includes his attitudes toward such matters as labor, the regulation of business and taxation as well as about freedom and federalism.

_____. THE UNPUBLISHED OPINIONS OF MR. JUSTICE BRANDEIS: THE SUPREME COURT AT WORK. Edited by Alexander M. Bickel. Introduction by Paul A. Freund. Court and the Constitution Series. Chicago: University of Chicago Press, Phoenix Books, 1967.

This is a selection of materials from Brandeis's private papers
made available to Bickel by Frankfurter, to whom Brandeis had
entrusted the papers and which were then transferred to Harvard
Law School. It consists of such materials as memoranda and
drafts submitted to Brandeis by his law clerks, Brandeis's
successive drafts and revisions of his opinions, and the comments
made by other justices on his opinions.

Brennan, William J. WILLIAM J. BRENNAN, JR.: AN AFFAIR WITH
FREEDOM: A COLLECTION OF HIS OPINIONS AND SPEECHES DRAWN
FROM HIS FIRST DECADE AS A UNITED STATES SUPREME COURT
JUSTICE. Edited by Stephen J. Friedman. Foreword by Arthur J. Gold-
berg. New York: Atheneum, 1967.

> With an introduction by the editor, this selection of Brennan's
> opinions and speeches was published as a tribute on the tenth
> anniversary of his appointment to the Court. The selections
> include Brennan's James Madison Lecture on the Bill of Rights
> and the states, his Edward Douglass White Lectures on the role
> of the Court and some of his opinions in such areas as obscenity,
> speech and assembly, church and state, self-incrimination, searches
> and seizures and reapportionment. The appendix includes a list
> of his opinions from 1956 to 1965.

Brown, William Garrott. THE LIFE OF OLIVER ELLSWORTH. New York:
Macmillan, 1905. Reprint. New York: Da Capo Press, 1970.

> This biography of Ellsworth is largely devoted to his life as a
> lawyer, member of the Continental Congress, delegate to the
> Philadelphia convention, and senator. It also examines his three
> and one-half years as chief justice and the role of the Supreme
> Court during those years.

Brownfeld, Allan C. DOSSIER ON DOUGLAS. Washington, D.C.: New
Majority Book Club, 1970.

> In April of 1970, partly in response to charges by Rep. Gerald
> Ford, the House Judiciary Committee set up a select committee
> to study impeachment charges against Justice Douglas. This
> monograph looks at some of the charges, such as the Douglas
> connection with the Parvin Foundation and his role in the Ginz-
> burg case.

Chase, Harold, et al. BIOGRAPHICAL DICTIONARY OF THE FEDERAL
JUDICIARY. Detroit: Gale Research Co., 1976.

> This contains brief biographical sketches of every federal judge
> from 1789 to 1974.

Clark, F.B. THE CONSTITUTIONAL DOCTRINES OF JUSTICE HARLAN.
Baltimore: Johns Hopkins Press, 1915. Reprint. New York: Da Capo,
1969.

> This is a study of the constitutional doctrines of the first Justice
> Harlan as revealed in his dissenting opinions. The areas examined
> include the suing of states, the obligation of contracts, due process,

international and foreign commerce, equal protection and the jurisdiction of the Court.

Connon, Henry G. JOHN ARCHIBALD CAMPBELL, ASSOCIATE JUSTICE OF THE UNITED STATES SUPREME COURT. 1855-1861. Boston: Houghton Mifflin Co., 1920. Reprint. New York: Da Capo Press, 1971.

With a brief background chapter on Campbell's ancestry and early career, this biography focuses on his role as Supreme Court justice, during his relatively brief tenure from his appointment by President Pierce in 1853 to his retirement in 1861, in coping with such major national issues as slavery.

Corwin, Edward S. JOHN MARSHALL AND THE CONSTITUTION: A CHRONICLE OF THE CONSTITUTION. Chronicles of America Series. New Haven, Conn.: Yale University Press, 1919.

This brief volume is primarily a study of Marshall's work as chief justice. After a brief account of the establishment of the national judiciary and of Marshall's early life, Corwin looks at Jefferson's attack on the judiciary, the trial of Aaron Burr and Marshall's nationalist views and his protection of contracts.

Countryman, Vern. THE JUDICIAL RECORD OF JUSTICE WILLIAM O. DOUGLAS. Cambridge, Mass.: Harvard University Press, 1974.

This is a survey of major issues dealt with by the Court since Douglas went on the bench in 1939 and the attitude of Douglas toward each of these issues.

Danelski, David J. A SUPREME COURT JUSTICE IS APPOINTED. New York: Random House, 1964.

This is an examination of the process of the nomination and confirmation of the appointment of Pierce Butler to the Supreme Court.

Desmond, Charles S., et al. MR. JUSTICE JACKSON: FOUR LECTURES IN HIS HONOR. New York: Columbia University Press, 1969.

This contains four lectures, delivered under the auspices of the William Nelson Cromwell Foundation by Charles S. Desmond, Paul A. Freund, Potter Stewart, and Lord Shawcross, dealing with various facets of Jackson's career: his contributions during the Nuremberg trials, his influence on federal-state relations, his concept of individual rights, and his influence on the organized bar and the development of law.

Douglas, William O. DOUGLAS OF THE SUPREME COURT: A SELECTION OF HIS OPINIONS. Edited by Vern Countryman. Westport, Conn.: Greenwood Press, 1959; Garden City, N.Y.: Doubleday, 1959.

With a biographical sketch by the editor, this is a selection of Douglas's judicial opinions dealing with such topics as the powers of government, the economy, fair governmental procedures and liberty.

Dunham, Allison, and Kurland, Philip B., eds. MR. JUSTICE. Chicago: University of Chicago Press, 1964.

> This contains biographical essays on twelve justices, each by a different scholar. There are essays on Marshall, Taney, Bradley, Harlan, Holmes, Hughes, Brandeis, Sutherland, Stone, Cardozo, Murphy, and Rutledge by William Crosskey, Carl B. Swisher, Charles Fairman, Alan F. Westin, Francis Biddle, M.J. Pusey, Paul A. Freund, J.F. Pascal, Allison Dunham, A.L. Kaufman, John P. Roche, and John Paul Stevens.

Dunne, Gerlad T. HUGO BLACK AND THE JUDICIAL REVOLUTION. New York: Simon and Schuster, 1977.

> This is a study of Black's senatorial and judicial career and his role in moving the Court from its conservative position on individual rights when he assumed his place on the bench as Roosevelt's first appointee to the liberal position of the Warren Court.

_____. JUSTICE STORY AND THE RISE OF THE SUPREME COURT. New York: Simon and Schuster, 1970.

> In this biography of Story, the author examines the role of the Supreme Court in the emergence of the American nation state and the rise of a distinctive American law.

Fairman, Charles. MR. JUSTICE MILLER AND THE SUPREME COURT, 1862-1890. Cambridge, Mass.: Harvard University Press, 1939.

> This work examines the new constitutional issues facing the post-Civil War Court and Miller's role in confronting the forces unleashed by the war and its aftermath.

Faulkner, Robert K. THE JURISPRUDENCE OF JOHN MARSHALL. Princeton, N.J.: Princeton University Press, 1968.

> Organized topically, this examination of Marshall's legal and political principles seeks to portray his "blend of knowledge verging on the theoretical, with judgment eminently practical." Faulkner analyzes Marshall's "constitutional understanding" of such concepts as sovereignty, the nature of a republic, and the role of the Court and the Constitution in a republic.

Fine, Sidney. FRANK MURPHY: THE DETROIT YEARS. 1 vol. to date. Ann Arbor: University of Michigan Press, 1975--.

> This first volume deals primarily with Murphy's service on Detroit's recorder court and as Detroit's mayor during the Depression. A projected second volume is to encompass his New Deal years as governor-general and high commissioner of the Philippines and as governor of Michigan. A concluding third volume is to deal with his Washington career as attorney general and as justice of the Supreme Court.

Flanders, Henry. LIVES AND TIMES OF CHIEF JUSTICES OF THE SUPREME COURT OF THE UNITED STATES. 2 vols. Philadelphia: Lippincott, Grambo, 1855-58. New York: James Cockcroft, 1875.

Volume 1 contains biographies of John Jay and of John Rutledge.
Volume 2 contains biographies of William Cushing, Oliver Ellsworth, and John Marshall.

Frank, John P. JUSTICE DANIEL DISSENTING: A BIOGRAPHY OF
PETER V. DANIEL, 1784-1860. Cambridge, Mass.: Harvard University
Press, 1964.

> This biography of "the last Jeffersonian to hold public office
> in the United States," "the last exponent of the Virginia and
> Kentucky Resolutions," and "possibly the first exponent of
> secession" examines Daniel's role as the most extreme antibusi-
> ness and prostates' rights man to sit on the Court.

_____. MR. JUSTICE BLACK: THE MAN AND HIS OPINIONS. Intro-
duction by Charles A. Beard. New York: Knopf, 1949.

> This is a biographical sketch of Black and a collection of his
> opinions during his first ten years on the Court. Written by one
> of Black's former law clerks and designed for the general audi-
> ence, the first half of the book deals with Black before his
> appointment to the Court.

_____. THE WARREN COURT. New York: Macmillan, 1964.

> This contains portraits and brief biographical sketches of each
> justice in 1964: Warren, Black, Douglas, Clark, Brennan,
> Stewart, White, and Goldberg.

Frankfurter, Felix. THE CONSTITUTIONAL WORLD OF MR. JUSTICE
FRANKFURTER: SOME REPRESENTATIVE OPINIONS. Edited by Samuel
J. Konefsky. New York: Macmillan, 1949.

> This is a selection of Frankfurter's opinions dealing with such
> matters as judicial restraint, the relationship between government
> and economic interests, federalism, freedom and democracy and
> criminal justice.

_____. FELIX FRANKFURTER ON THE SUPREME COURT: EXTRA-
JUDICIAL ESSAYS ON THE COURT AND THE CONSTITUTION. Edited
by Philip B. Kurland. Cambridge, Mass.: Harvard University Press, 1970.

> Selected with Frankfurter's aid and published shortly after his
> death on 22 February 1965, the essays here included were ori-
> ginally published primarily in such popular periodicals as the
> NEW REPUBLIC. The essays deal with a variety of topics,
> such as the nomination of Brandeis, Taft and the Supreme Court,
> John Marshall and the judicial function, and the judicial process
> and the Supreme Court.

_____. FROM THE DIARIES OF FELIX FRANKFURTER. Edited by Joseph
O. Lash. New York: W.W. Norton, 1975.

> With a biographical essay and notes by the editor, this consists
> of irregular entries from Frankfurter's diaries from 1911 to
> 1948. The 1911 entries deal with his stay in Washington. There
> are entries from 1928 and from 1933 dealing with his Harvard

years. His judicial role is the subject of entries in 1943, in
1945, 1946, and 1948.

_____. OF LAW AND LIFE AND OTHER THINGS THAT MATTER: PAPERS
AND ADDRESSES OF FELIX FRANKFURTER, 1956-1963. Edited by Philip
B. Kurland. Cambridge, Mass.: Harvard University Press, 1965.

Published in the period between Frankfurter's retirement from
the Court and his death, this small volume consists of his brief
addresses. It contains such materials as his Memorial day
address at Hyde Park in 1956, a tribute to Brandeis on the centennial of his birth, remarks made on the occasion of Learned
Hand's fiftieth anniversary as a federal judge in 1959 and an
address on federalism.

_____. OF LAW AND MEN: PAPERS AND ADDRESSES OF FELIX FRANK-
FURTER, 1939 TO 1956. Edited by Philip Elman. New York: Harcourt,
Brace and World, 1956. Reprint. Hamden, Conn.: Archon Books, 1965.

This is a collection of Frankfurter's brief addresses, informal
talks, book reviews, memorials, and biographical sketches.

_____. LAW AND POLITICS: OCCASIONAL PAPERS OF FELIX FRANK-
FURTER, 1913-1938. Edited by Archibald MacLeish and E.F. Prichard.
New York: Harcourt, Brace, 1939. Reprint. Gloucester, Mass.: Peter
Smith, 1971.

With a foreword by MacLeish, this contains some of Frankfurter's
pre-judicial papers such as addresses, letters to the editors, book
reviews, essays in popular magazines and scholarly journals.
They are organized on the basis of such broad categories as
liberty, labor and courts, and government and administration.

_____. MR. JUSTICE HOLMES AND THE SUPREME COURT. Cambridge,
Mass.: Harvard University Press, 1961.

In 1938, Frankfurter delivered three lectures at Harvard. In
1944, he wrote a biographical note on Holmes which appeared in
the DICTIONARY OF AMERICAN BIOGRAPHY. Harvard University asked for and received permission to combine the three lectures and the biographical sketch and this book is the result.

_____, ed. MR. JUSTICE BRANDEIS. Introduction by Oliver Wendell
Holmes. New Haven, Conn.: Yale University Press, 1932.

With a brief tribute by Charles Evans Hughes, these five previously published essays were published in honor of Brandeis'
seventy-fifth birthday. Focusing on various facets of his work
as a jurist, the essays were written by Max Lerner, Donald R.
Richberg, Henry Wolf Bikle, Walton H. Hamilton, and Frankfurter. There is a list of the opinions of Brandeis in the index.

Friedman, Leon, and Israel, Fred L., eds. THE JUSTICES OF THE UNITED
STATES SUPREME COURT: 1789-1969: THEIR LIVES AND MAJOR OPIN-
IONS. Introduction by Louis H. Pollak. 4 vols. New York: Chelsea House
Publishers in association with R.R. Bowker, 1969.

This contains a short biographical sketch, each by a different scholar, of each of the ninety-seven justices through the appointment of Chief Justice Burger. The work is arranged chronologically with one or two opinions of each justice reprinted and with a selected bibliography at the end of each essay. Volume 4 contains an appendix which includes a variety of information about the Court and its actions, such as lists of acts invalidated by the Court and decisions which were overruled.

Gerhardt, Eugene. AMERICA'S ADVOCATE: ROBERT JACKSON. Indianapolis: Bobbs-Merrill, 1958.

Begun before Jackson's death, this work deals with his public life as lawyer, solicitor general, attorney general, and especially his role as "America's advocate" at the Nuremberg trials.

Goldberg, Arthur J. THE DEFENSES OF FREEDOM: THE PUBLIC PAPERS OF ARTHUR J. GOLDBERG. Edited by Patrick Daniel Moynihan. New York: Harper and Row, 1964, 1966.

With an introduction by the editor, this collection is divided into two major sections: public papers and judicial opinions. It includes twenty-four of Goldberg's Supreme Court opinions and various addresses and speeches.

Hamilton, Virginia Van Der Veer. HUGO BLACK: THE ALABAMA YEARS. Baton Rouge: Louisiana State University Press, 1972.

This political biography of Black is primarily concerned with reconciling the apparent conflict between his early membership in the Ku Klux Klan and his libertarian philosophy as a member of the Court. It examines his pre-judicial years and his career in Alabama politics prior to his appointment to the bench. It includes brief, one-paragraph excerpts from his Supreme Court opinions between 1940 and 1964.

Harlan, John M. THE EVOLUTION OF A JUDICIAL PHILOSOPHY: SELECTED OPINIONS AND PAPERS OF JUSTICE JOHN M. HARLAN. Edited by David L. Shapiro. Foreword by Paul A. Freund. Cambridge, Mass.: Harvard University Press, 1969.

With a biographical sketch by the editor, these selections from Harlan's opinions from 1954 to 1967 and from other writings are organized on the basis of such topics as the concept of ordered liberty in a federal system, the First Amendment and the Fourteenth Amendment, the individual and the administration of federal justice, and the art of judging.

Hendel, Samuel. CHARLES EVANS HUGHES AND THE SUPREME COURT. New York: Columbia University Press, 1951.

This work deals with Hughes first as an associate justice and then with his role as chief justice upon his return to the Court. It examines the attitudes of Associate Justice Hughes toward such issues as the relationship between liberty and authority, the due process clause, the equal protection clause and the police power and national and state power under the commerce

clause. It examines the Hughes Court's interpretation of due
process and governmental power, the contract clause and equality.

Holmes, Oliver Wendell. COLLECTED LEGAL PAPERS. Selected by Harold
Laski. New York: Peter Smith, 1952.

With a preface by Holmes, this is a one-volume collection of the
pre-Supreme Court articles, essays and lectures by Holmes
on a diversity of legal topics.

_____. JUSTICE HOLMES TO DOCTOR WU: AN INTIMATE CORRESPON-
DENCE, 1921-1932. New York: Central Book, n.d.

This small volume is a collection of brief notes and letters
written by Holmes over a twelve-year period to a young Chinese
law student. They were originally published in the October 1935
issue of I'IEN HSIA MONTHLY.

_____. JUSTICE OLIVER WENDELL HOLMES: HIS BOOK NOTICES AND
UNCOLLECTED LETTERS AND PAPERS. Edited by Harry C. Shriver.
New York: Central Book Co., 1936. Reprint. Introduction by Justice
Harlan Fiske Stone. New York: Da Capo Press, 1973.

With annotations by the editor, this is a collection of letters and
of signed and unsigned articles and book reviews which originally
appeared in the AMERICAN LAW REVIEW from 1870 to 1880.
Holmes edited the REVIEW from 1870 to 1873.

_____. THE MIND AND FAITH OF MR. JUSTICE HOLMES: HIS SPEECHES,
ESSAYS, LETTERS AND JUDICIAL OPINIONS. Edited by Max Lerner.
New York: Modern Library, 1943. Reprint. Garden City, N.Y.: Halcyon
House, 1948.

With a foreword by the editor, this selection of the writings of
Holmes includes such pre-Supreme Court materials as excerpts
from the COMMON LAW and from his opinions while on the Massachusetts courts and his opinions while on the Supreme Court as
well as various essays on such topics as law and courts and on
such legal thinkers as Montesquieu and Marshall.

_____. REPRESENTATIVE OPINIONS OF MR. JUSTICE HOLMES. Edited
by Alfred Lief. Foreword by Harold J. Laski. New York: Vanguard Press,
1931.

With introductory notes by the editor, this selection of Holmes's
Supreme Court opinions is arranged topically: federalism, trade
combinations and boycotts, statutory interpretation, constitutional
guarantees, regulation of public utilities and state taxation.
There is also a selection of his opinions while on the Massachusetts court.

Holmes, Oliver Wendell, and Einstein, Lewis. THE HOLMES-EINSTEIN
LETTERS: CORRESPONDENCE OF MR. JUSTICE HOLMES AND LEWIS
EINSTEIN, 1903-1935. Edited by James Bishop Peabody. New York: St.
Martin's Press, 1964.

At twenty–six, Lewis Einstein met Holmes in 1903 when Einstein was about to be appointed as third secretary in the American Embassy in Paris and Holmes was sixty–one and on the Supreme Court. The two corresponded until Holmes died on 6 March 1935. This is a collection of 207 letters from Holmes to Einstein and of fifty–six letters from Einstein to Holmes.

Holmes, Oliver Wendell, and Laski, Harold. HOLMES–LASKI LETTERS: THE CORRESPONDENCE OF MR. JUSTICE HOLMES AND HAROLD J. LASKI, 1916–1935. Edited by Mark De Wolfe Howe. Foreword by Felix Frankfurter. 2 vols. Cambridge, Mass.: Harvard University Press, 1953.

This is a collection of the extensive correspondence between Holmes and Laski from the time of their first meeting in the summer of 1916 when Holmes was nearing seventy–five and Laski was a young instructor at Harvard, a correspondence that continued for twenty years until the death of Holmes. Volume 1 covers the years from 1916 to 1925. Volume 2 contains the letters written between 1926 and 1935.

Holmes, Oliver Wendell, and Pollock, Frederick. HOLMES–POLLOCK LETTERS: THE CORRESPONDENCE OF MR. JUSTICE HOLMES AND SIR FREDERICK POLLOCK, 1874–1932. Edited by Mark De Wolfe Howe. Introduction by John Gorham Palfrey. 2 vols. Cambridge, Mass.: Harvard University Press, 1941.

On a visit to England in the early 1870s, Holmes met Pollock and began a firm friendship that survived few actual meetings but which deepened through correspondence. This is a collection of that correspondence. Volume 1 covers 1874 to 1918. Volume 2 covers 1919 to 1932.

Holmes, Oliver Wendell, and Sheehan, Patrick. HOLMES–SHEEHAN CORRESPONDENCE: THE LETTERS OF JUSTICE OLIVER WENDELL HOLMES AND CANON PATRICK AUGUSTINE SHEEHAN. Edited by David H. Burton. Port Washington, N.Y.: Kennikat Press, 1976.

This is a collection of letters exchanged between Justice Holmes and an Irish priest on a wide range of subjects including philosophy and law.

Howe, Mark De Wolfe. OLIVER WENDELL HOLMES: THE SHAPING YEARS, 1841–1870. Cambridge, Mass.: Harvard University Press, 1957.

This biography deals with Holmes's pre–Supreme Court years: his childhood, his undergraduate years at Harvard, his military service during the Civil War, his Harvard law school years, and his European travels and studies after leaving school.

Hughes, Charles Evans. THE AUTOBIOGRAPHICAL NOTES OF CHARLES EVANS HUGHES. Edited by David J. Danelski and Joseph S. Tulchin. Cambridge, Mass.: Harvard University Press, 1973.

This is a collection of notes dictated by Hughes between November of 1941 and the end of 1945 with an introduction and clarifying notes by the editors.

Hurst, James W. JUSTICE HOLMES ON LEGAL HISTORY. New York: Macmillan, 1964.

> This collection of essays focuses upon Holmes as a legal historian rather than as a jurist. Hurst examines some of Holmes's theories such as the logic of experience and the logic of law.

Iredell, James. THE PAPERS OF JAMES IREDELL. Edited by Don Higginbottom. 2 vols. to date. Raleigh: Division of Archives and History, Department of Cultural Resources, North Carolina Historical Commission, 1976--. In progress.

> The first two volumes of a projected four-volume collection contain letters to and from Iredell, his diary and his political essays. Volume 1 covers the years 1767 to 1777. Volume 2 covers the years from 1778 to 1783. A projected fourth volume, to be edited by John E. Semonche, is to be devoted exclusively to his legal papers.

Jay, John. THE CORRESPONDENCE AND PUBLIC PAPERS OF JOHN JAY, FIRST CHIEF JUSTICE OF THE UNITED STATES, MEMBER AND PRESIDENT OF THE CONTINENTAL CONGRESS, MINISTER TO SPAIN, MEMBER OF COMMISSION TO NEGOTIATE TREATY OF INDEPENDENCE, ENVOY TO GREAT BRITAIN, GOVERNOR OF NEW YORK, ETC., 1763-1826. Edited by Henry P. Johnston. 4 vols. New York: G.P. Putnam's Sons, 1890-93. Reprint. New York: Burt Franklin, 1968.

> These volumes consist primarily of Jay's letters. Volume 1 covers the period from 1763 to 1781. Volume 2 covers the years from 1781 to 1782. Volume 3 included 1782 to 1793. Volume 4 contains his correspondence from 1794 to 1826. Because his role as one of the three authors of the FEDERALIST PAPERS and as the first chief justice (1789-95), Jay's papers serve as a major primary source on the making of the Constitution and its development in its formative years.

Jones, W. Melville, ed. CHIEF JUSTICE JOHN MARSHALL: A REAPPRAISAL. Ithaca, N.Y.: Cornell University Press, 1956. Reprint. Foreword by Chief Justice Warren. New York: Da Capo Press, 1971.

> This is a collection of ten essays which were originally presented at the College of William and Mary in 1955 as part of the Marshall Bicentennial Program which had as its general theme "John Marshall: 200 Years Later." Divided into three parts, "Marshall and His Times," "Judicial Review" and "Special Contributions of Marshall to the Law," it contains papers by such scholars as Carl B. Swisher, Irving Brant, Charles Fairman, Julius Goebel, Jr., and Donald G. Margan.

Katcher, Leo. EARL WARREN: A POLITICAL BIOGRAPHY. New York: McGraw-Hill, 1967.

> Designed for the general audience, this biography is about equally divided between Warren's political career and his judicial career.

King, Willard L. MELVILLE WESTON FULLER: CHIEF JUSTICE OF THE UNITED STATES, 1888-1910. New York: Macmillan, 1950.

With a brief look at Fuller's early life in Maine and as a student
at Bowdoin and Harvard, this biography is concerned primarily
with his judicial career: his appointment and confirmation, his
early cases, his relations with Gray and Bradley, his growing
influence by 1890, Leisy v. Hardin, and his long relationship
with Holmes.

Konefsky, Samuel J. CHIEF JUSTICE STONE AND THE SUPREME COURT.
New York: Macmillan, 1946. Reprint. Ann Arbor, Mich.: University
Microfilms, 1970. Microfilm-xerography.

Written while Stone was still on the bench, this is an analysis
of the major issues before the Court at that time, Stone's concept of the Court's role in confronting those issues and his
effort to develop a methodology for the exercise of judicial
power. Konefsky examines such issues as intergovernmental
tax immunity, the commerce clause and state power, the scope
of federal power, censorship, and civil liberties.

_____. THE LEGACY OF HOLMES AND BRANDEIS: A STUDY IN THE
INFLUENCE OF IDEAS. New York: Macmillan, 1956.

This is an examination of the constitutional ideas of Justice
Holmes and Brandeis and the effect of these ideas on the course
of the development of American constitutional law.

Kurland, Philip B. MR. JUSTICE FRANKFURTER AND THE CONSTITUTION.
Chicago: University of Chicago Press, 1971.

This examination of Frankfurter's philosophy on a wide variety
of constitutional issues (such as separation of powers, the
"political thicket," speech and association, religion, due process,
equal protection, judicial restraint, stare decisis and commerce)
includes numerous but brief excerpts from his opinions.

Leonard, Charles A. A SEARCH FOR A JUDICICAL PHILOSOPHY: MR.
JUSTICE ROBERTS AND THE CONSTITUTIONAL REVOLUTION OF 1937.
Port Washington, N.Y.: Kennikat Press, 1971.

This is an examination of the role of Justice Owen Roberts who
furnished the swing vote on New Deal legislation and whose ultimate alliance with the liberal wing legitimized New Deal legislation. It looks at the Court in the three years before the election of Roosevelt, its invalidation of New Deal legislation, its
switch in 1937 and its consolidation of the new view between 1937
and 1941.

Levy, Beryl H. CARDOZO AND FRONTIERS OF LEGAL THINKING: WITH
SELECTED OPINIONS. New York: Oxford University Press, 1938. Reprint. Port Washington, N.Y.: Kennikat Press, 1972.

This is an analysis of the process by which judges interpret and
apply law, a subject which Cardozo explored in his classic NATURE
OF THE JUDICIAL PROCESS.

McDevitt, Matthew. JOSEPH MCKENNA, ASSOCIATE JUSTICE OF THE
UNITED STATES. Washington, D.C.: Catholic University Press, 1946.

Although this biography deals with McKenna's years as congressman, circuit court judge and attorney general, it is principally
an examination of his opinions while on the Supreme Court.   It
discusses his opinions on due process, labor, federal power
over commerce and civil rights, and the states' police power.

Magrath, C. Peter. MORRISON D. WAITE: THE TRIUMPH OF CHARACTER.
New York: Macmillan, 1963.

This biography of the seventh chief justice, appointed by Grant
in 1874, is primarily a study of the consolidation and concilia-
tion role of the essentially conservative Waite Court. Magrath
examines the major issues--such as race relations, the civil
war amendments, and the relationship between government and
economic interests--facing the Court in the aftermath of the
Reconstruction changes.

Marshall, John. JOHN MARSHALL: COMPLETE CONSTITUTIONAL DECI-
SIONS. Edited by John M. Dillon. Chicago: Callaghan, 1903.

With commentaries and annotations by the editor, this is a collection of Marshall's opinions in twenty-nine cases, including his
opinion in the Burr case.

_____. JOHN MARSHALL: MAJOR OPINIONS AND OTHER WRITINGS.
Edited by John P. Roche. American Heritage Series. Indianapolis: Bobbs-
Merrill, 1967.

With an introduction and commentaries by the editor, this selection includes such pre-judicial statements as his remarks at the
Virginia ratifying convention in 1788 and a campaign tract of
1798 when he sought a congressional seat as well as judicial
opinions dealing with such topics as the jurisdiction of the Supreme Court, contracts and state authority, the protection of
federal finance, commerce, treaties and civil rights.

_____. THE PAPERS OF JOHN MARSHALL. Edited by Herbert A. John-
son. 2 vols. to date. Chapel Hill: University of North Carolina Press,
1974-- .

This collection of Marshall's letters and other papers is being
published in association with the Institute of Early American
History and Culture. Volume 1 includes his correspondence and
papers from 10 November 1775 to 23 June 1788, and his account
book from September 1783 to June of 1788. Volume 2, published
in 1977, contains his correspondence, papers and account book
from July 1788 to December 1795.

_____. THE POLITICAL AND ECONOMIC DOCTRINES OF JOHN MAR-
SHALL. . .AND ALSO HIS LETTERS, SPEECHES, AND HITHERTO UN-
PUBLISHED AND UNCOLLECTED WRITINGS. Edited by John Edward Oster.
New York: Burt Franklin, 1914.

This is an extensive collection of the papers of John Marshall in
which he expounded the same Federalist political and economic
theories as a political leader in Virginia and in the cabinet as
he was to read into the Constitution as chief justice.

Mason, Alpheus T. BRANDEIS: A FREE MAN'S LIFE. New York: Viking Press, 1946.

> This biography, by the author of BRANDEIS: LAWYER AND JUDGE IN THE MODERN STATE (1933) and THE BRANDEIS WAY (1938), examines the life of Brandeis from his family background to his retirement and death, and focuses upon his career as a reform lawyer and as Supreme Court justice.

_____. HARLAN FISKE STONE: PILLAR OF THE LAW. New York: Viking Press, 1956.

> This biography is generally considered to be the most important scholarly study of Stone's public career. It is primarily concerned with his role on the Supreme Court.

Morgan, Donald G. JUSTICE WILLIAM JOHNSON: THE FIRST DISSENTER: THE CAREER AND CONSTITUTIONAL PHILOSOPHY OF A JEFFERSONIAN JUDGE. Columbia: University of South Carolina Press, 1954.

> This biography of Jefferson's first Supreme Court appointee, who remained on the Court for thirty years, examines the areas in which this Jeffersonian agreed with Marshall (economic conservatism, implied powers and a strong Union), his relations with Jefferson while on the Court, and his emergence in his third year on the Court as the first dissenter of the Marshall Court.

Morris, Richard B. JOHN JAY, THE NATION AND THE COURT. Boston: Boston University Press, 1967.

> This slim volume contains three essays on Jay originally delivered as the Gaspar G. Bacon Lectures on the Constitution. The lectures examine the wellsprings of Jay's nationalism, the Jay Court's subordination of the states to the nation and its insistence upon the supremacy of treaties.

Paschal, Joel Francis. MR. JUSTICE SUTHERLAND: A MAN AGAINST THE STATE. Princeton, N.J.: Princeton University Press, 1951.

> Noting that no other justice spoke for the majority in so many great cases as did Sutherland, the author examines the development of the political philosophy of this major spokesman of a conservative Court's insistence upon a limited government. He looks at the decisive influence which the theories of Herbert Spencer exerted on the views that Sutherland read into the Constitution and Sutherland's role on the Court from the time of his appointment in 1922 to the overthrow of his conservative constitutional theories in 1937.

Perkins, Dexter. CHARLES EVANS HUGHES AND AMERICAN DEMOCRATIC STATESMANSHIP. The Library of American Biography Series. Boston: Little, Brown, 1956.

> This study of Hughes's public career in New York politics, as associate justice and as chief justice focuses on his years as secretary of state.

Pollard, Joseph P. MR. JUSTICE CARDOZO: A LIBERAL MIND IN
ACTION. Foreword by Roscoe Pound. New York: Yorktown Press, 1935.

> This is a study of Cardozo's constitutional and judicial philosophy
> as revealed by his opinions while on the United States Supreme
> Court. It examines Cardozo's views on a wide range of issues
> such as family strife, crime, civil rights, social welfare, work-
> men's compensation, business and government and morals and the
> New Deal.

Pusey, Merlo J. CHARLES EVANS HUGHES. 2 vols. New York: Macmillan, 1951.

> Volume 1 of this biography examines Hughes's background and
> childhood and his career as lawyer, governor and as associate
> justice. Volume 2 examines his return to politics, his role as
> secretary of state and his return to the Court as chief justice.

Schubert, Glendon, ed. DISPASSIONATE JUSTICE: A SYNTHESIS OF
THE JUDICIAL OPINIONS OF ROBERT H. JACKSON. Indianapolis: Bobbs-
Merrill, 1969.

> In his introductory and concluding chapters, Schubert examines
> Jackson's personality, his legal ideology, literary style and po-
> litical career. The excerpts from Jackson's opinions are orga-
> nized on the basis of such topics as liberty demogoguery, property,
> bureaucracy, policy, comity, and advocacy. Preceding each
> group of excerpts is a brief sketch of Jackson's position on the
> major constitutional question addressed in the opinions.

Schwartz, Mortimer, and Hogan, John C., eds. JOSEPH STORY: A
COLLECTION OF WRITINGS BY AND ABOUT AN EMINENT AMERICAN
JURIST. New York: Oceana, 1959.

> This slim volume contains brief excerpts from various primary
> and secondary sources on the role of Story in the development
> of American legal and political history. Dealing both with his
> personal and professional life, the excerpts include such materials
> as his letters and essays by and about him during his years as
> state legislator, lawyer, judge, and Harvard law professor.

Severn, William M. MR. CHIEF JUSTICE: EARL WARREN. New York:
David McKay, 1968.

> Designed for the popular audience, this short book is primarily
> concerned with Warren's personal and political life before his
> appointment to the Supreme Court and only briefly with his judi-
> cial career.

Smith, Charles W. ROGER B. TANEY: JACKSONIAN JURIST. Chapel
Hill: University of North Carolina Press, 1936. Reprint. New York: Da
Capo Press, 1973.

> In this study of Taney's political theory and his contributions to
> constitutional law, the author examines the chief justice's views
> on such matters as sovereignty, the nature of the Union, the
> states' police power, slavery, individual rights, and the problem
> of reconciling liberty with the sovereignty of the state.

Steiner, Bernard. LIFE OF ROGER BROOKE TANEY: CHIEF JUSTICE
OF THE UNITED STATES SUPREME COURT. Baltimore: Williams and
Wilkins, 1922.

> This study of Taney as a "border state Federalist" who the
> author credits with being one of the four men responsible for
> keeping Maryland in the Union, examines his years as a student
> at Dickinson and at Annapolis, as a lawyer, as attorney general,
> as Secretary of the Treasury and as chief justice. The author
> looks at Taney's friendship with Jackson, his Dred Scott opinion,
> his Supreme Court opinions during the Civil War and his circuit
> court opinions.

Story, Joseph. LIFE AND LETTERS OF JOSEPH STORY, ASSOCIATE
JUSTICE OF THE SUPREME COURT AND DANE PROFESSOR AT HARVARD
UNIVERSITY. Edited by William W. Story. 2 vols. Boston: Charles C.
Little and James Brown, 1851.

> Edited and with introductory comments by Story's son, this is a
> collection of his papers, primarily letters. Volume 1 covers his
> childhood and college years but deals primarily with his political
> life from 1805 to 1810 and his judicial life from 1811 to 1829.
> Volume 2 consists primarily of letters from 1829 to 1845 dealing
> with his professorial and judicial life.

Strickland, Stephen Parks, ed. HUGO BLACK AND THE SUPREME COURT.
Introduction by Charles A. Beard. Indianapolis: Bobbs-Merrill, 1967.

> This work contains nine essays on Black's constitutional views,
> each by a different scholar. There are essays on such topics
> as the reconstituted Court and the New Deal, race relations, the
> Bill of Rights, federal taxation and antitrust laws by such scholars
> as Carl B. Swisher, John P. Frank, Daniel Berman, Irving
> Dillard, and W. Wallace Kirkpatrick.

Swisher, Carl B. ROGER B. TANEY. Washington, D.C.: Brookings
Institution, 1935. Reprint. New York: Macmillan, 1936. Reprint. Hamden,
Conn.: Archon Books, 1961.

> Focusing primarily on Taney's political and judicial life, this
> biography is still generally considered to be the most perceptive
> analysis of his public career.

_____. STEPHEN J. FIELD: CRAFTSMAN OF THE LAW. Washington, D.C.:
Brookings Institution, 1930. Reprint. Hamden, Conn.: Archon Books, 1963.

> This biography of the "first judicial representative of the new
> empire on the Pacific Coast," deals briefly with Field's youth,
> his early years in California, his public service in California
> and focuses upon his long tenure on the United States Supreme
> Court. Appointed to the Taney Court by Lincoln in 1863, Field
> retired in 1897, having written 620 Supreme Court opinions and
> fifty-seven circuit court opinions and having participated in basic
> constitutional changes during the Civil War, Reconstruction, and
> the rise of big business.

Article III

Thomas, Helen Shirley. FELIX FRANKFURTER: SCHOLAR ON THE BENCH. Baltimore: Johns Hopkins University Press, 1960.

> This study of Frankfurter as successor to the Holmes and Cardozo "scholar seat" examines the influence of Harvard on his thinking, his emergence on the national scene during the New Deal, his appointment to the Court and his judicial performance and philosophy.

Trimble, Bruce R. CHIEF JUSTICE WAITE: DEFENDER OF THE PUBLIC INTEREST. Princeton, N.J.: Princeton University Press, 1938. Reprint. Ann Arbor, Mich.: University Microfilm, 1965. Microfilm-xerography.

> This biography examines Waite's early life and his career in Ohio politics but focuses upon his relatively brief tenure as Chief Justice from 1874 to 1888 and the role of the Waite Court in "demolishing Reconstruction" with its reaffirmation of Slaughter-house in Minor v. Happersett and its decisions, such as in Munn, upholding the state's regulatory powers.

Warren, Charles. THE STORY-MARSHALL CORRESPONDENCE (1819-1831). Anglo-American Legal History Series. New York: New York University School of Law, 1942.

> In 1926, the Massachusetts Historical Society published twenty-six letters from Marshall to Story in which Marshall acknowledged receipt of eighteen letters from Story, none of which had been published. In this brief monograph, Warren discusses this exchange of correspondence and includes excerpts.

Warren, Earl. THE PUBLIC PAPERS OF CHIEF JUSTICE EARL WARREN. Edited by Henry M. Christmas. Rev. ed. New York: G.P. Putnam's Sons, Capricorn, 1966. Paperbound.

> Divided into three major sections ("California and the Nation," "Liberty and the Law," and the "Scales of Justice"), this book contains some of Governor Warren's addresses (on such topics as education, equal rights, penal reform and the Republican Party), some of Chief Justice Warren's addresses (on such topics as Cardozo and LaFollette) and Supreme Court opinions (in such cases as Brown and Reynolds).

Westin, Alan F., ed. AN AUTOBIOGRAPHY OF THE SUPREME COURT: OFF-THE-BENCH COMMENTARY BY THE JUSTICES. New York: Macmillan, 1963.

> With an introduction by the editor, this is a selection of materials from speeches and other nonjudicial writings of Supreme Court justices from Chief Justice Jay and other justices on the first Court under the Constitution to justices on the Warren Court in the 1960s. It is organized chronologically and topically. There is a selected bibliography of speeches and extralegal writings by Supreme Court justices from 1790 to 1962.

Williams, Charlotte. HUGO L. BLACK: A STUDY IN THE JUDICIAL PROCESS. Baltimore: Johns Hopkins University Press, 1950.

This study of the career of Franklin D. Roosevelt's first appointee to the Court looks at Black's years as a senator, his Klan affliation, his first thirteen years on the Court and the significant changes in constitutional interpretation during those years.

Chapter 9

ARTICLES IV, V, VI, AND VII

Interstate Relations, Ratifying and Amending the Constitution, Constitutional and National Supremacy

American Bar Association. AMENDMENT OF THE CONSTITUTION BY THE CONVENTION METHOD UNDER ARTICLE V. Chicago: American Bar Association, 1974.

> This special American Bar Association report suggests rules, regulations, procedures which it recommends that Congress adopt to govern the convention device for proposing constitutional amendments.

Ames, Herman V. THE PROPOSED AMENDMENTS TO THE CONSTITUTION OF THE UNITED STATES DURING THE FIRST CENTURY OF ITS HISTORY. 1896. Reprint. New York: Burt Franklin, 1970.

> This is a compilation and discussion by the American Historical Association of the 1,736 proposals to amend the Constitution between 1787 and the late nineteenth century.

Averill, Lawrence H., Jr. "Choice-of-Law Problems Raised By Sister-State Judgments and the Full Faith and Credit Mandate." NORTHWESTERN UNIVERSITY LAW REVIEW 64 (November-December 1969): 686-703.

> Suggesting that many of the problems concerning the full faith and credit clause could be solved by analyzing them from a choice-of-law point of view, this article defines and examines first line choice-of-law issues and second line choice-of-law issues.

Baldwin, Leland Dewitth. REFRAMING THE CONSTITUTION: AN IMPERATIVE FOR MODERN AMERICA. Santa Barbara, Calif.: American Bibliographic Center, Clio Press, 1972.

> This is a discussion of what the author views as the defects of the present Constitution and a proposal for a new constitution which would remedy these defects. The proposed constitution, a copy of which is included, is designed to be more flexible, increase the power of the electorate and provide for a "guardian" to assure that government is responsive to the popular will.

Birkby, Robert H. "Politics of Accommodation: The Origin of the Supremacy Clause." WESTERN POLITICAL QUARTERLY 19 (March 1966): 123-35.

This analysis of the debates at the Philadelphia convention suggests that the national supremacy clause, which has become the basis for centralization and for nationalization of certain rights, was a compromise between those who wanted a veto by the national legislature over state statutes and those who wanted state courts to construe the Constitution. As with many other provisions of the Constitution, thus, a clause designed to meet one specific and immediate problem became the basis for dealing with a different problem in a different way.

Black, Charles L. "Amending the Constitution: A Letter to a Congressman." YALE LAW JOURNAL 82 (December 1972): 189–215.

In this letter to the chairman of the House Judiciary Committee, Black criticizes the defects in a proposed constitutional amendment to change Article V. The proposal to change the procedure for handling state requests for a national convention to amend the Constitution had, in Black's view, a multiplicity of defects any one of which would have justified rejection.

_____. "The Proposed Amendment of Article V: A Threatened Disaster." YALE LAW JOURNAL 72 (April 1963): 957–68.

Partly as a result of Baker v. Carr and other decisions limiting the power of the states, a number of constitutional amendments were advocated in the early 1960s designed to curb the power of the Supreme Court in particular and of the federal government in general. One suggestion was that Article V be amended so that two-thirds of the states could, in effect, initiate constitutional amendments. Under this proposal, Congress would be required to submit to the states for ratification any amendment when two-thirds of the states called upon it to do so. It would in effect confer upon the states both the power to propose and to ratify and would take away from Congress its authority to determine whether the ratification process would be by the legislature or by state convention. This is a criticism of the proposal to so change Article V.

Brickfield, Cyril F. PROBLEMS RELATING TO A FEDERAL CONSTITUTIONAL CONVENTION. Washington, D.C.: Government Printing Office, 1957.

Article V provides for two methods of proposing constitutional amendments. The usual method of proposal has been by Congress; the other method of proposal by a constitutional convention is the subject of this work. It examines both the legal and practical problems raised by the device and presents drafts of legislation designed to cope with these problems. It was drafted for the Committee on the Judiciary of the House of Representatives of the 85th Congress.

Brown, Everett S. "The Ratification of the Twenty-First Amendment." AMERICAN POLITICAL SCIENCE REVIEW 29 (December 1935): 1005–17.

When submitting the Twenty-First Amendment to the states, Congress required conventions to be called to vote on ratification. This brief article examines some of the questions raised by convention ratification--the power of Congress to prescribe the rules

governing such conventions, whether state laws should provide
for all future conventions or just the one at hand, how delegates
should be chosen—and analyzes the state statutes governing the
conventions called.

_____, comp. RATIFICATION OF THE TWENTY-FIRST AMENDMENT
TO THE CONSTITUTION OF THE UNITED STATES: STATE CONVENTION
RECORDS AND LAWS. 1938. Reprint. New York: Da Capo Press, 1970.

This is a state by state record of the laws pertaining to constitutional conventions and a state by state record of the conventions called to ratify the Twenty-First Amendment. It was
originally published as volume 7 of the UNIVERSITY OF MICHI-
GAN PUBLICATIONS IN LAW.

Burton, Weldon V. INTERSTATE COMPACTS IN THE POLITICAL PRO-
CESS. Chapel Hill: University of North Carolina Press, 1967.

This study of the proper role of the interstate compact in the
American federal system examines two major questions: by whom
and for what purposes was the compact established and what
individuals and groups seem to have benefitted from the compact.

CERTIFICATES OF RATIFICATION OF THE CONSTITUTION AND THE
BILL OF RIGHTS, INCLUDING RELATED CORRESPONDENCE AND REJEC-
TION OF PROPOSED AMENDMENTS, 1787-1792. Washington, D.C.: Na-
tional Archives. Microfilm. M338, 1 roll.

This includes the states' certificates of ratification and various
other materials relating to the states' ratification of the Constitution and the Bill of Rights.

Chase, Harold. "The Lawyers Need Help with the 'Lawyers Clause.'" In
ESSAYS ON THE AMERICAN CONSTITUTION, edited by Gottfried Dietz,
pp. 101-24. Englewood Cliffs, N.J.: Prentice-Hall, 1964.

In this call for political scientists to bring their skills to those
problems which the full faith and credit clause has been used to
solve and those inherent in the clause itself, Chase argues that
these are essentially problems of intergovernmental relations
rather than purely legal ones.

Corwin, Edward S. "The 'Full Faith and Credit' Clause," UNIVERSITY
OF PENNSYLVANIA LAW REVIEW 81 (February 1933): 371-89.

In this brief analysis of the intention of the framers of the Constitution and of judicial interpretation of the full faith and credit
clause, Corwin suggests that judicial interpretation of the clause
has probably not met the expectations of the framers and that the
Constitution reserves to Congress rather than to the courts the
initiative in applying Article IV, Section 1.

Dunker, William L. "Constitutional Amendments: The Justiciability of
Ratification and Retraction." TENNESSEE LAW REVIEW 41 (Fall 1973):
93-111.

This note examines the question of the authority of the state to reverse its decision to ratify or not to ratify a proposed constitutional amendment. It suggests three major theories: that rejection or ratification is reversible, that a state may ratify after rejection but not reject after ratifying and that the state has the freedom to choose until the matter is foreclosed by adoption. The author suggests that if the Court were to find the issue justiciable, it would settle the question on the basis of one of these theories, probably the second.

Elliott, William Yandell. NEED FOR CONSTITUTIONAL REFORM: A PROGRAM FOR NATIONAL SECURITY. New York: Whittlesey House, McGraw-Hill, 1935.

Written during the height of the constitutional and political controversy over the New Deal, this is an analysis of proposals for constitutional changes and an argument that the reforms needed for security at home and abroad should be thought through and not imposed in a moment of national hysteria as was the NRA.

Engdahl, David E. "Characterization of Interstate Arrangements: When Is A Compact Not A Compact?" MICHIGAN LAW REVIEW 64 (November 1965): 63-104.

Noting that one of the most significant developments in federalism in the last forty years has been interstate arrangements commonly referred to as "compacts," the author deals with the question of the applicability to these agreements of the limitations imposed by Article I, Section 10. He concluded that not all "compacts" in the loose sense of that term fall within the compact clause and that the courts, not the states, should interpret the compact clause.

Hazlitt, Henry. A NEW CONSTITUTION NOW. New York and London: Whittlesey House, McGraw-Hill, 1942.

Written in the early period of World War II and published shortly after Franklin D. Roosevelt's 1942 Labor Day message in which he proclaimed that "if Congress fails to act and act adequately, I shall accept the responsibility and I will act," this book urges adoption of a new constitution. The author suggests that the Constitution is too inflexible and that it should be changed to allow government to respond to emergencies without disregarding the Constitution. At the least, he urges abandonment of Article V and adoption of an easier method of amendment.

Herbstreith, Lloyd G., and King, George Van B. THE LIBERTY AMENDMENT. Los Angeles: Operation America, 1963.

This is a polemic in support of the "liberty amendment" introduced in Congress in the early 1950s to repeal the Sixteenth Amendment, to prohibit governmental levying of taxes on income, estates, or gifts and to require governmental sale of all business-type operations.

Jackson, Robert H. FULL FAITH AND CREDIT: THE LAWYER'S CLAUSE OF THE CONSTITUTION. New York: Columbia University Press, 1945.

> This address by Justice Jackson was delivered as the fourth annual Benjamin N. Cardozo Lecture to the New York Bar Association and was originally printed in volume 45 of the COLUMBIA LAW REVIEW. Reviewing the written law of the full faith and credit clause and judicial review as to judgments under that clause, Jackson suggests that Congress is in a better position to assure compulsory reciprocal recognition of process and execution of judgments than are courts.

Kauper, Paul G., ed. THE ARTICLE V CONVENTION PROCESS: A SYMPOSIUM. New York: Da Capo Press, 1971.

> The papers reprinted here originally appeared in the MICHIGAN LAW REVIEW 66 (March 1968). The essays include: Sen. Everett Dirksen on "The Supreme Court and the People," Sen. Sam Ervin on "Proposed Legislation to Implement the Convention Method of Amending the Constitution," Paul G. Kauper on "The Alternative Amending Process: Some Observations," Ralph M. Carson on "Disadvantages of a Federal Constitutional Convention," Robert G. Dixon, Jr. on "Article V: The Comatose Article Of Our Living Constitution?" Arthur Earl Bonfield on "The Dirksen Amendment and the Article V Convention Process," and Clifton McCleskey on "Along the Midway: Some Thoughts on Democratic Constitutional Amending."

Lacy, Donald P., and Martin, Philip L. "Amending the Constitution: The Bottleneck in the Judiciary Committees." HARVARD JOURNAL OF LEGISLATION 9 (May 1972): 666-93.

> In this examination of the historical and contemporary process by which each house of Congress considers proposed constitutional amendments, the authors conclude that the use of existing procedures has allowed Congress to avoid hasty changes, has protected against undue influence by pressure groups, and has maintained the Constitution as it was conceived by the framers.

Levine, Henry D. "Limited Federal Constitutional Convention: Implications of the State Experience." HARVARD JOURNAL ON LEGISLATION 11 (December 1973): 127-29.

> When thirty-two states, of the required thirty-four, petitioned Congress for a constitutional convention in the late 1960s, questions were raised about the possibility of such a convention proposing far-reaching, multiple changes. Examining the experience at the state level in limiting constitutional conventions to specified purposes, this note concludes that Article V could be interpreted to permit a limited constitutional convention at the national level; the limits imposed would be those specified in the state petitions calling upon Congress to convene the convention.

Martin, Philip L. "The Application Clause of Article V." POLITICAL SCIENCE QUARTERLY 85 (December 1970): 616-28.

Noting that between 1789 and 1961 there have been 226 applications from states for a constitutional convention, the author examines the reasons why the convention mode has not been successfully initiated. Looking at the precedent of legislation proposal, the applications of the first one-hundred years, and twentieth-century applications, he concludes that the application clause will probably remain unused because of fears that such a convention could not be limited to specific resolutions and that it might precipitate a constitutional crisis.

_____. "Convention Ratification of Federal Constitutional Amendments."
POLITICAL SCIENCE QUARTERLY 82 (March 1967): 61-71.

With the exception of the Twenty-First Amendment, state ratification of proposed amendments has been by the legislature. This article briefly discusses those other instances, usually during times of political and social crisis such as in the pre-Civil War period, when Congress discussed, though rejected, requiring the convention alternative for ratification. The author suggests that the convention is the more democratic of the two methods of ratification.

Musmanno, Michael A. PROPOSED AMENDMENTS TO THE CONSTITUTION:
A MONOGRAPH ON THE RESOLUTIONS INTRODUCED IN CONGRESS PRO-
POSING AMENDMENTS TO THE CONSTITUTION OF THE UNITED STATES
OF AMERICA. House Document Number 551, 70th Cong., 2d sess. Washington, D.C.: Government Printing Office, 1929.

This is a follow-up to the Ames list of proposed constitutional amendments introduced between 1789 and 1889. In addition to a brief summary of those proposals in Congress prior to 1889, this brings the list of accepted and rejected proposals up to 1929. The proposals are organized on the basis of subject matter: those affecting the form of government with subdivisions of proposals affecting the legislative, executive, and judicial branches: those affecting the powers of government by limiting or expanding congressional power and those proposing changes in the procedures for amending the Constitution. There is a separate section on the Fourteenth through the Nineteenth Amendments.

Myers, Denys P. THE PROCESS OF CONSTITUTIONAL AMENDMENT.
Washington, D.C.: Government Printing Office, 1941.

Written by a member of the World Peace Foundation and printed as Senate Document Number 314, 76th Congress, this is a brief summary of the constitutionally prescribed methods of amending the Constitution, including a discussion of Supreme Court cases involving questions arising out of the ratification role and authority of the states.

Nadelmann, Kurt H. "Full Faith and Credit to Judgments and Public Acts:
A Historical-Analytical Reappraisal." MICHIGAN LAW REVIEW 56 (November 1957): 33-88.

This is an examination of the judicial assumption that the full faith and credit clause is self-executing as it applies to both public acts and judgments.

Ober, Frank. "The Treaty-making and Amending Powers: Do They Protect Our Fundamental Rights?" AMERICAN BAR ASSOCIATION JOURNAL 36 (March 1950): 715-19, 793-96.

> Prompted primarily by opposition to American participation in international human rights agreements in 1950, this is an argument for a constitutional amendment to limit the treaty-making power of the president and the Senate and for an amendment to the Article V amending process on the grounds that neither provision provides adequate safeguards against fundamental changes being made without the consent of the people. To assure greater popular participation in the amending process, Ober suggests ratification by state convention rather than by state legislatures.

Orfield, Lester B. THE AMENDING OF THE FEDERAL CONSTITUTION. Ann Arbor: University of Michigan Press, 1942. Reprint. New York: Da Capo Press, 1971.

> This analysis of Article V covers such areas as the origins of the provisions, judicial review of the validity of amendments and the question of justiciability as well as standing and procedural questions, the scope of the amending power and proposals for reform of Article 5.

"Proposed Legislation on the Convention Method of Amending the Constitution." HARVARD LAW REVIEW 85 (1972): 1612-48.

> This note is an analysis of legislation proposed by Senator Sam Ervin in 1967 to govern the call and conduct of a constitutional convention to amend the Constitution.

Reynolds, Harry W., Jr., ed. "Intergovernmental Relations in the United States." ANNALS OF AMERICAN ACADEMY OF POLITICAL AND SOCIAL SCIENCES 359 (May 1965): Entire issue.

> This issue of the ANNALS contains fifteen essays, each by a different scholar, dealing with different facets of federalism. It is divided into three major parts: the substantive dimensions of intergovernmental relations, its procedural dimensions, and its social and political implications.

Rice, William G. A TALE OF TWO COURTS: JUDICIAL SETTLEMENT BETWEEN THE STATES OF THE SWISS AND AMERICAN FEDERATIONS. Madison: University of Wisconsin Press, 1967.

> This is a comparative study of the respective roles of the judiciary in the United States and in Switzerland in settling controversies between states in a federal system.

Ridgeway, Marion E. INTERSTATE COMPACTS: A QUESTION OF FEDERALISM. Carbondale: Southern Illinois University Press, 1971.

> This is a study of the interstate compacts, through June of 1969, to which Illinois is a party: the number, kind, nature and potentialities of this device for dealing with problems that cross state lines.

Scott, James B., ed. JUDICIAL SETTLEMENT OF CONTROVERSIES
BETWEEN STATES OF THE AMERICAN UNION. 2 vols. Clarendon, Calif.:
Carnegie Endowment for International Peace, 1918.

> Although the role of the Supreme Court in maintaining the federal
> system by defending the supremacy of national law against state
> challenge is one of its most controversial roles, an equally im-
> portant role in protecting federalism involves dealing with dis-
> putes between states, a task that occupied much judicial time
> in the first century under the Constitution. These two volumes
> contain excerpts and reprints of Supreme Court cases dealing
> with such threats to domestic tranquility.

Steinbaum, Robert S. "Federal Question Jurisdiction to Interpret Interstate
Compacts." GEORGETOWN LAW JOURNAL 64 (October 1975): 87-111.

> In this examination of federal judicial authority to hear cases
> involving interstate compacts, the author argues that even though
> such compacts are neither federal nor state law but a legislative
> centaur--half state and half federal law--federal courts should
> resolve disputes over these agreements even if they refuse to
> accept them as federal law.

Thursby, Vincent. INTERSTATE COOPERATION: A STUDY OF THE INTER-
STATE COMPACT. Introduction by Carl B. Swisher. Washington, D.C.:
Public Affairs Press, 1953.

> This work focuses on the increasing use of the interstate compact
> to deal with problems that do not respect the territorial boundaries
> of the states.

Tugwell, Rexford G. THE EMERGING CONSTITUTION. New York: Harper's
Magazine Press, 1974.

> This extensive volume recommending a new model constitution con-
> sists of revisions of discussion papers presented at the Center
> for the Study of Democratic Institutions. In the first part, the
> basic criteria and reasoning of the group on such matters as
> federalism and the separation of powers is set forth. The second
> part deals with the structure of the executive, legislative and
> judicial branches. There is a copy of the proposed constitution
> in the appendix.

Turner, Lonnie. THE RIGHTS OF NATIONAL CITIZENSHIP: THE
ABOLITIONISTS' CAUSE IN THE COURTS. Occasional Papers on Politics
Series. Northridge: California State University at Northridge, 1974.

> This monograph is an analysis of the little noticed privileges and
> immunities clause of Article IV. It examines the usual inter-
> pretation, that the provision applies to "sojourners" or citizens
> of other states, and the abolitionists' unsuccessful attempts to
> have the Court construe it to protect the rights of national citizen-
> ship.

U.S. Congress. Senate. Committee on the Judiciary. Subcommittee on
Separations of Powers. HEARINGS. FEDERAL CONSTITUTIONAL CON-
VENTION PROCEDURES. Washington, D.C.: Government Printing Office,
1973.

These hearings were held to examine the problems and procedures
of the convention as opposed to the congressional method of proposing constitutional amendments.

U.S. Library of Congress. Legislative Reference Service. PROPOSED
AMENDMENTS TO THE CONSTITUTION OF THE UNITED STATES INTRO-
DUCED IN CONGRESS FROM DECEMBER 4, 1889 TO JULY 2, 1926.
Washington, D.C.: Government Printing Office, 1926. Reprint. Westport,
Conn.: Greenwood Press, 1976.

This chronological list of proposed constitutional amendments from
1889 to 1926 gives the resolution or bill number, the sponsor,
and the subject of the proposal.

Wiecek, William M. THE GUARANTEE CLAUSE OF THE UNITED STATES
CONSTITUTION. Ithaca, N.Y.: Cornell University Press, 1972.

This is an examination of the guarantee clause in terms of its
drafting, its restrictive interpretation in Luther v. Borden, its
use by both slavery and abolitionist forces, its use by the Radical
Republicans in the Reconstruction era to legitimize their control
of southern states, and its demise as both a judicial and political
tool by the twentieth century.

Chapter 10

THE BILL OF RIGHTS AND THE
PRE-CIVIL WAR AMENDMENTS

Abernathy, Glenn. THE RIGHT OF ASSEMBLY AND ASSOCIATION.
Columbia: University of South Carolina Press, 1961.

This is a study of the First Amendment guarantee of the right
to peaceably assemble and of the judicially created right of
association. Noting that the right of association has received
less attention than other First Amendment rights, Abernathy
argues that it is clearly a right cognate to the right of assembly
even though it is not specifically mentioned in the Constitution
and examines such aspects as the intention of the framers and
assemblies in streets and parks.

Abraham, Henry J. FREEDOM AND THE COURT: CIVIL RIGHTS AND
LIBERTIES IN THE UNITED STATES. 3d ed. New York: Oxford University Press, 1977.

In this study of the historic role of the Court in drawing lines
between the rights of the individual and the rights of society,
Abraham examines such problems as the applicability of the Bill
of Rights to the states, the expansion of due process to include
new substantive rights, the expanding concept of free expression,
the relationship between the two religious clauses, and race
relations.

Ackerman, Bruce A. PRIVATE PROPERTY AND THE CONSTITUTION.
New Haven, Conn.: Yale University Press, 1977.

The Fifth Amendment prohibits the taking of private property for
public use without just compensation. This is an analysis of the
clash between the constitutional protection of private property
and environmental law, a conflict intensified by the increasing
numbers of environmental statutes and the growing tendency of
private property owners to demand greater compensation.

Adams, John Quincy. SPEECH OF JOHN QUINCY ADAMS UPON THE
RIGHT OF THE PEOPLE, MEN AND WOMEN, TO PETITION: ON THE
FREEDOM OF SPEECH AND OF DEBATE IN THE HOUSE OF REPRESEN-
TATIVES OF THE UNITED STATES: ON THE RESOLUTIONS OF SEVEN
STATE LEGISLATURES AND THE PETITIONS OF MORE THAN ONE
HUNDRED THOUSAND PETITIONERS RELATING TO THE ANNEXATION
OF TEXAS TO THIS UNION. DELIVERED IN THE HOUSE OF REPRESEN-
TATIVES OF THE UNITED STATES IN FRAGMENTS OF THE MORNING
HOURS FROM THE 16TH OF JUNE TO THE 7TH OF JULY, 1838, INCLUSIVE.
1838. Reprint. New York: Arno Press, 1969.

This is a reprint of one of the many attacks by Adams upon the constitutionality of the "gag rule" imposed by the House in an attempt to prevent his continued presentation to the House of antislavery petitions.

THE AMERICAN CIVIL LIBERTIES UNION RECORDS AND PUBLICATIONS, 1917-1975. Glen Rock, N.J.: Microfilming Corp. of America, 1976.

The records and publication include: Series I, "Minutes of the Board of Directors, 1926-1973"; Series II, "Mailings to the Board of Directors, 1942-1973"; Series III, "Biennial Conference Papers, 1954-1974"; Series IV, "ACLU Policy Guides, 1938-1971"; Series V, "National Legal Docket, 1972-1975"; Series VI, "Organization Manuals, 1968-1975"; Series VII, "Constitutions and By-Laws, 1957-1975"; Series VIII, "Legal Briefs"; Series IX, "ACLU Publications, 1917-1975." There is a guide to the series: THE AMERICAN CIVIL LIBERTIES UNION RECORDS AND PUBLICATIONS, 1917-1975: A GUIDE TO THE MICROFILM COLLECTION. Glen Rock, N.J.: Microfilming Corp. of America, 1976.

Anastaplo, George. THE CONSTITUTIONALIST: NOTES ON THE FIRST AMENDMENT. Dallas: Southern Methodist University Press, 1971.

Focusing upon the First Amendment guarantees of speech and press, this work is an analysis of the nature of liberty and of constitutional government. It is the author's argument that the First Amendment, originally proposed as a limitation upon states as well as the national government, an idea that was rejected, was designed to absolutely prohibit congressional interference but left the states free to deal with abuses of these freedoms.

Annual Chief Justice Earl Warren Conference on Advocacy in the United States. FINAL REPORT: PRIVACY IN A FREE SOCIETY. Cambridge, Mass.: Roscoe Pound-American Trial Lawyers Foundation, 1974.

This 1974 report contains background papers and final recommendations on electronic surveillance, political informing, and data banks and dossiers.

Antieau, Chester J., et al. FREEDOM FROM FEDERAL ESTABLISHMENT: FORMATION AND EARLY HISTORY OF THE FIRST AMENDMENT RELIGION CLAUSES. St. Paul, Minn.: Bruce Publishing Co., 1964.

This work argues that the intention of the religious protection afforded by the First Amendment was to prohibit preferential treatment of one religion, compulsion, and exclusiveness and that the Supreme Court has deviated from this original intention in its construction and application.

Asch, Sidney H. CIVIL RIGHTS AND RESPONSIBILITIES UNDER THE CONSTITUTION. Foreword by Robert M. Morganthau. New York: Arco, 1968.

This work by a judge of the Civil Court of New York City is designed to acquaint a general audience with the operation of the federal judicial system and with judicial interpretation of the guarantees of the Bill of Rights. Without footnotes or bibliog-

raphy, it discusses the leading cases on the first eight amendments as well as on the Thirteenth, Fourteenth, Fifteenth, and
Nineteenth Amendments.

Ashmore, Harry S. FEAR IN THE AIR: BROADCASTING AND THE
FIRST AMENDMENT: THE ANATOMY OF A CONSTITUTIONAL CRISIS.
New York: W.W. Norton, 1973.

> This study of governmental power to control the electronic media
> focuses upon the Nixon administration's attacks on the broadcasting
> media and the response of the communications industry to that
> threat to free speech.

Barbour, Alton B. FREE SPEECH YEARBOOK, 1975. Falls Church, Va.:
Speech Communications Association, 1976.

> This publication of the Commission on Freedom of Speech of the
> Speech Communications Association contains essays by different
> scholars reviewing various aspects of free speech during 1975
> and a bibliography of books and articles on free speech published
> in the same year.

Barron, Jerome A. FREEDOM OF THE PRESS FOR WHOM: THE RIGHT
OF ACCESS TO MASS MEDIA. Bloomington: Indiana University Press,
1973.

> This study argues that the First Amendment guarantee of free
> speech imposes upon the mass media of communications an affirma-
> tive obligation to afford their readers, listeners or viewers access
> to their facilities. Absent such access, the First Amendment pro-
> tects not the rights of individuals nor the interests of the public
> but serves only the interests of a few.

Becker, Carl L., ed. SAFEGUARDING CIVIL LIBERTY TODAY. Ithaca,
N.Y.: Cornell University Press, 1945.

> Originally delivered as the Edward L. Bernays Lectures of 1944
> at Cornell, this contains six essays by different scholars on
> various facets of civil liberties at issue during the World War II
> era: political freedom, public opinion, free speech and press,
> and federal protection of civil rights.

Bedau, Hugo A. THE COURTS, THE CONSTITUTION AND CAPITAL
PUNISHMENT. Lexington, Mass.: D.C. Heath, 1977.

> This is a collection of essays by Bedau dealing with constitutional
> challenges to capital punishment and the Supreme Court's responses
> to these challenges.

Bedau, Hugo A., and Pierce, Chester M., eds. CAPITAL PUNISHMENT
IN THE UNITED STATES. New York: AMS Press, 1976.

> This contains twenty-five essays by political scientists, economists,
> historians, and psychologists covering a wide spectrum of research
> done on various facets of the controversy over capital punishment
> since the Supreme Court's 1972 decision in Furman v. Georgia.

It covers such areas as the legislative response to <u>Furman</u>,
public attitudes toward capital punishment, the deterent effect
of this penalty and the manner in which the criminal justice system deals with the two major crimes, murder and rape, for which
the penalty is imposed.

Belknap, Michal R. COLD WAR POLITICAL JUSTICE: THE SMITH ACT,
THE COMMUNIST PARTY, AND AMERICAN CIVIL LIBERTIES. Contributions in American History Series. Westport, Conn.: Greenwood Press, 1977.

This study of the Smith Act prosecutions leads the author to conclude that they were an example of American "political justice,"
that is, the use of the machinery of justice for partisan ideological purposes. He suggests that just as government may abuse
the judicial process in this fashion so may radical minorities
exploit it to facilitate their attack on the established order.

Berkson, Larry Charles. THE CONCEPT OF CRUEL AND UNUSUAL PUNISH-
MENT. Lexington, Mass.: D.C. Heath, 1975.

This is an analysis of the Eighth Amendment concept of cruel and
unusual punishment from its English origins to Supreme Court interpretation in the 1970s. After a brief overview of judicial
interpretation between 1798 to 1910 and 1910 to 1974, Berkson
divides punishments into corporeal and uncorporeal categories
and examines judicial responses to the challenges to each.

Berns, Walter F. THE FIRST AMENDMENT AND THE FUTURE OF AMERI-
CAN DEMOCRACY. New York: Basic Books, 1976.

This examination of the foundations of the constitutional protections
of religion and speech and of Supreme Court interpretations of
these guarantees criticizes judicial distortion of these principles
to defeat their compatibility with freedom, public morality, and
republican government.

_____. FREEDOM, VIRTUE AND THE FIRST AMENDMENT. Baton Rouge:
Louisiana State University Press, 1957. Reprint. Chicago: Henry Regnery,
Gateway, 1965.

This is an exploration of the nature of the problem of free speech
and religion and a criticism of the liberal conception of law and
politics underlying Supreme Court decisions and commentaries
on these rights.

Black, Hugo L. "The Bill of Rights." NEW YORK UNIVERSITY LAW
REVIEW 35 (April 1960): 865-81.

Delivered as the first James Madison Lecture at New York University, this is a classic statement of Justice Black's views that the
constitutionally guaranteed rights of individuals (those in the first
ten amendments and those in the original Constitution) are absolute.
This lecture is reprinted in Edmond Cahn's THE GREAT RIGHTS
(see p. 236), along with a series of other James Madison Lectures.

Blackburn, Sara, ed. WHITE JUSTICE: BLACK EXPERIENCE TODAY IN
AMERICA'S COURTROOM. New York: Harper and Row, 1971.

Designed for the general reader, this indictment of the legal
system's denial of constitutional rights to blacks accused of crime
examines the trials of such defendants as Huey Newton and Bobby
Seale among others.

Blakely, William A., ed. AMERICAN STATE PAPERS AND RELATED
DOCUMENTS ON FREEDOM IN RELIGION. 4th rev. ed. Washington, D.C.:
Review and Herald Press, 1949.

Published for the Religious Liberty Association, this contains
documents on religious freedom in America from the colonial
period to the 1940s.

Boles, Donald E. THE TWO SWORDS: COMMENTARIES AND CASES IN
RELIGION AND EDUCATION. Ames: Iowa State University Press, 1965.

This is a comprehensive analysis of the major constitutional issues
in the area of the relationship between the state and religion in
the fields of education, transportation, released time, prayer
and bible reading, state distribution of textbooks, flag saluting,
school buildings, religious garb in public schools, curriculum,
compulsory education, and special public benefits such as tax
exemptions for parochial education.

Bosmajian, Haig A. OBSCENITY AND FREEDOM OF EXPRESSION. New
York: Burt Franklin, 1976.

This is a study of judicial opinions dealing with obscenity from
the nineteenth century through the recent Supreme Court deter-
mination that local communities are to determine the "community
standards." An introductory chapter details the various standards used since the nineteenth century. The appendix includes
a list of the five hundred cases cited and materials indicating
the manner in which foreign countries deal with the legal problem.

Brant, Irving N. THE BILL OF RIGHTS: ITS ORIGIN AND MEANING
Indianapolis: Bobbs-Merrill, 1965. Reprint. New York: New American
Library, 1967.

This study of individual rights by the author of the six-volume
biography of JAMES MADISON (see p. 149) traces the development of the more than sixty guarantees in the Constitution from
Magna Carta through the constitutional convention and the First
Congress which proposed the first ten amendments. It also deals
with the erosion of rights during times of crisis from the Alien
and Sedition Acts of 1789 to the House Un-American Activities
Committee in the 1950s.

Breckenridge, Adam C. THE RIGHT TO PRIVACY. Lincoln: University
of Nebraska Press, 1970.

This is an examination of the rise of a constitutional right of
privacy beginning with the Brandeis-Warren article in 1890, its
acceptance in state courts beginning at the turn of the century
and its more gradual acceptance by federal courts. The concept
as used here traces its lineage to the "right to be let alone"
usage of Brandeis and not to its use in Roe to embrace the

right to abort a fetus. Written before Roe, though after Griswold, the work traces the concept in its more traditional sense. A copy of the Brandeis-Warren article is included in the appendix.

Buranelli, Vincent, ed. THE TRIAL OF PETER ZENGER. New York: New York University Press, 1957.

This is a brief account of the Zenger seditious libel case, a hallmark in the development of freedom of the press. The second half of the book contains the arguments of Andrew Hamilton and James Alexander, attorney for the defendant, and other materials from the trial transcript.

Cahn, Edmond, ed. THE GREAT RIGHTS. New York: Macmillan, 1963.

With an introductory essay by Cahn, this is a collection of four James Madison Lectures on individual rights delivered by Supreme Court justices at New York University School of Law and an essay by Irving Brant, a Madison scholar and biographer. The lectures were delivered by Justices Black, Brennan, Douglas, and Chief Justice Warren.

Capaldi, Nicholas, ed. CLEAR AND PRESENT DANGER: THE FREE SPEECH CONTROVERSY. New York: Pegasus, 1969.

This anthology includes arguments for and against limitations on free speech by such commentators as John Stuart Mill, Justice Holmes, and William Buckley.

Carmen, Ira H. MOVIES, CENSORSHIP AND THE LAW. Ann Arbor: University of Michigan Press, 1966.

This is an examination of the process by which motion pictures are censored within the context of constitutional standards established by the Supreme Court in the "early period" between 1915 and 1952 and in the "modern period" between 1953 and 1965. Included in the appendix are the questionnaires submitted to the censors in a number of states and cities and the interviews conducted by the author.

Carosell, Philip A. QUEST FOR ORDERED LIBERTY. New York: Carlton Press, 1969.

Partially inspired by Cardozo's concept of a scheme of ordered liberty as used in the Palko sense, this slim volume is a broad review of doctrines (such as federalism, separation of powers, due process, privileges and immunities, and the rule of law) which affect the quest for ordered liberty.

Carter, Dan T. SCOTTSBORO: A TRAGEDY OF THE AMERICAN SOUTH. Baton Rouge: Louisiana State University Press, 1969.

This is a scholarly examination of the trial and subsequent fates of nine black youths convicted of rape in Scottsboro, Alabama, in the 1930s. Their case became a cause celebre of the era and resulted in two important Supreme Court opinions, the Powell and Norris cases, further clarifying the constitutional guarantees of counsel and trial by jury.

Casper, Jonathan D. THE POLITICS OF CIVIL LIBERTIES. New York: Harper and Row, 1972.

This is an examination of doctrinal developments in a number of substantive areas of civil liberties within the context of the attitudes and behavior that shaped their development and affected their implementation. The areas covered include freedom of expression and the problem of loyalty and security; the civil rights movement and free expression; racial, economic, and voting equality; and criminal justice.

Chaffee, Zechariah, Jr. FREE SPEECH IN THE UNITED STATES. Cambridge, Mass.: Harvard University Press, 1954.

Copyrighted in 1941, this is still the most thorough analysis of judicial interpretation of the First Amendment guarantee of free speech from the 1920s to the eve of American entrance into the Second World War. With a brief summary of the World War I cases, the book examines the sedition and criminal syndicalism cases of the postwar peace decade of 1920 to 1930, the speech cases in the Hughes Court from 1930 to 1940, and the various methods by which government controls speech in times of peace. A concluding chapter examines the status of free speech in 1941.

_____. GOVERNMENT AND MASS COMMUNICATIONS. 2 vols. in 1. Hamden, Conn.: Archon Books, 1965.

This report of the Commission on Freedom of the Press is an extensive survey of the relationship between government and mass communications. Volume 1 deals with the use of government power to limit expression. Volume 2 deals with affirmative government activities for encouraging the communication of news and ideas. The appendix includes the recommendations of the commission.

_____. THE INQUIRING MIND. New York: Harcourt, Brace and Co., 1928.

This is a collection of Chafee's previously published articles dealing with such civil liberties issues in the 1920s as state and federal sedition laws, judicial interpretation of such laws and governmental attacks on labor groups such as the IWW.

_____. THREE HUMAN RIGHTS IN THE CONSTITUTION OF 1787. Lawrence: University of Kansas Press, 1956.

Originally delivered as the Nelson Timothy Stephens Lectures at the University of Kansas School of Law, this is an examination of three basic rights protected by the Constitution prior to the adoption of the Bill of Rights: freedom of debate in Congress, freedom of movement and the prohibition against bills of attainder.

_____, ed. DOCUMENTS ON FUNDAMENTAL HUMAN RIGHTS. 3 vols. Cambridge, Mass.: Harvard University Press, 1951-52.

This is an extensive collection of European and American documents concerned with individual liberties.

Clark, Leroy D. THE GRAND JURY: THE USE AND ABUSE OF POLITI-
CAL POWER. Foreword by Sen. Philip A. Hart. New York: Quadrangle/
New York Times Book Co., 1975.

> This is a brief study of the grand jury system, an evaluation of
> its uses and abuses (mostly abuses) from its birth as a forum for
> political struggles in England to the early 1970s when, the author
> charges, the Nixon administration used it to harass opponents.
> Arguing that the grand jury is now controlled by prosecutors,
> the author urges reforms that would strengthen its independence.

Clor, Harry M., ed. CENSORSHIP AND FREEDOM OF EXPRESSION:
ESSAYS ON OBSCENITY AND THE LAW. Chicago: Rand McNally, 1971.

> In addition to reprinting a concurring opinion in Roth at the
> lower court level and the Supreme Court opinion, this is a
> collection of essays presenting differing views toward the ques-
> tion of the need for and constitutionality of laws censoring obscene
> materials written from the perspectives of law, religion and psy-
> chiatry. The authors include Charles Rembar, Walter Berns,
> Richard F. Hettlinger, Harry M. Clor, Richard H. Kuh, and
> William Gaylin.

Cohen, William; Schwartz, Murray; and Sobel, De Anne. THE BILL OF
RIGHTS: A SOURCE BOOK. New York: Benziger Brothers, 1968.

> This presents a general overview of judicial application of the
> guarantees of the equal protection clause to voting, housing,
> education, and employment, its interpretation of the due process
> clause in criminal cases and its construction of the First Amend-
> ment guarantees of speech and press.

THE COLLEGES AND THE COURTS: JUDICIAL DECISIONS REGARDING
INSTITUTIONS OF HIGHER LEARNING. 7 vols. Vols. 1-3, edited by
M.M. Chambers. New York: Carnegie Foundation for the Advancement of
Teaching, Columbia University Press, 1946-67. Vols. 4-7, edited by
Edward C. Elliott. Danville, Ill.: Interstate Printers and Publishers,
1946-72.

> The first three volumes cover the period from the nineteenth
> century through 1935. The remaining volumes keep the material
> up to date. Volume 7, subtitled THE DEVELOPING LAW OF
> THE STUDENT AND THE COLLEGE, deals only with federal
> and state judicial decisions governing the relationship between
> students and colleges with the focus on the post-1965 period.

Conference on American Freedom. PAPERS FROM THE CONFERENCE ON
AMERICAN FREEDOM: PRESS, PRIVACY, RELIGION, SPEECH. Washington, D.C.: Conference on American Freedom, 1973.

> Held during the Nixon administration when journalists and civil
> libertarians were troubled by what they perceived to be govern-
> mental assaults upon individual freedom, this conference was
> called to discuss these concerns. This publication includes
> five papers written for the conference by constitutional scholars
> and journalists on the freedoms of press, speech and religion
> and the right to privacy.

CONSTITUTIONAL PROBLEMS IN CHURCH-STATE RELATIONS. A SYM-POSIUM. New York: Da Capo Press, 1971.

This collection of four articles, originally published in the NORTHWESTERN UNIVERSITY LAW REVIEW 61 (November-December 1966) deals with various facets of judicial interpretation of the First Amendment religion clauses. One article reviews the history of the establishment clause in terms of the debates in the First Congress and the evolution of Supreme Court construction. Others examine the limitations imposed on financial aid to religion, the problems in defining a "wall of separation" and potential conflicts between the free exercise and establishment clauses.

Cooper, Thomas. A TREATISE ON THE LAW OF LIBEL AND THE LAW OF THE PRESS; SHOWING THE ORIGIN, USE, AND ABUSE OF THE LAW OF LIBEL: WITH COPIUS NOTES AND REFERENCES TO AUTHORI-TIES IN GREAT BRITAIN AND THE UNITED STATES AS APPLICABLE TO INDIVIDUALS AND TO POLITICAL AND ECCLESIASTICAL BODIES AND PRINCIPLES. 1830. Reprint. New York: Da Capo Press, 1970.

This argument in support of free expression of opinion takes the view that truth will emerge from unrestrained speech.

Corwin, Edward S. LIBERTY AGAINST GOVERNMENT: THE RISE, FLOWERING AND DECLINE OF A FAMOUS JURIDICAL CONCEPT. Baton Rouge: Louisiana State University Press, 1941.

This is an analysis of the "liberty of contract" concept read into the due process clause of the Fourteenth Amendment and the rejection of that doctrine by the Court in the "constitutional revolution" of 1937.

Cowles, Willard B. TREATIES AND CONSTITUTIONAL LAW: PROPERTY INTERFERENCES AND DUE PROCESS OF LAW. Washington, D.C.: American Council on Public Affairs, 1941.

This is an examination of the question of whether or not the due process and just compensation clauses of the Fifth Amendment are applicable to, and constitute limitations upon, the operation of treaties in the domestic realm.

Cross, Harold L. THE PEOPLE'S RIGHT TO KNOW: LEGAL ACCESS TO PUBLIC RECORDS AND PROCEEDINGS. New York: Columbia University Press, 1953.

Written two decades before passage of the Freedom of Information Act and intended primarily for news editors and reporters, this is a survey of national and state laws governing the right of inspection of public records.

Dash, Samuel; Knowlton, Robert E.; and Schwartz, Richard F. THE EAVESDROPPERS. New Brunswick, N.J.: Rutgers University Press, 1959. Reprint. New York: Da Capo Press, 1971.

This is a study of the techniques, use and legality of wiretapping and electronic surveillance.

Destro, Robert A. "Abortion and the Constitution: The Need for a Life-Protective Amendment." CALIFORNIA LAW REVIEW 63 (September 1975): 1250-1351.

> This is an analysis of the reasoning and effect of Roe v. Wade
> and of Doe v. Bolton and of the background, rationale and con-
> tent of proposed constitutional amendments designed to change
> the Court's abortion decisions. Of the two major proposed amend-
> ments, the "states' rights" amendment and the "life protective"
> amendment, Destro prefers the latter which recognizes the rights
> of the unborn.

Devol, Kenneth S., ed. MASS MEDIA AND THE SUPREME COURT: THE LEGACY OF THE WARREN YEARS. 2d ed. New York: Hastings House, 1976.

> Basically a case book dealing primarily with free speech issues
> such as judicial standards for applying the First Amendment,
> prior restraint, obscenity and privacy, this also includes journal
> articles on each topic covered and a separate section entitled
> "The Legacy of the Warren Court and the 1973-74 Term of the
> Burger Court."

Dienes, C. Thomas. LAW, POLITICS, AND BIRTH CONTROL. Urbana: University of Illinois Press, 1972.

> Written after Griswold but before Roe, this is a study of the
> process by which courts and legislatures have responded to the
> demands of a changing society. It examines the emergence of
> birth control as a legislative issue in the early nineteenth cen-
> tury and the contemporary responses at the national level and
> in the states of New York, Connecticut, and Massachusetts to
> changed attitudes.

Dixon, Robert G., et al. "Symposium on the Griswold Case and the Right of Privacy." MICHIGAN LAW REVIEW 64 (December 1965): 197-288.

> This contains five papers, each by a different scholar, dealing
> with Griswold: Robert G. Dixon, "The Griswold Penumbra:
> Constitutional Charter For An Expanded Law of Privacy"; Thomas
> I. Emerson, "Nine Justices in Search of a Doctrine"; Paul
> Kauper, "Penumbras, Peripheries, Emanations, Things Fundamen-
> tal and Things Forgotten"; Robert McKay, "The Right of Privacy";
> and Arthur E. Sutherland, "Privacy in Connecticut."

Dolbeare, Kenneth M., and Hammond, Phillip E. THE SCHOOL PRAYER DECISIONS: FROM COURT POLICY TO LOCAL PRACTICE. Chicago: University of Chicago Press, 1971.

> This is an analysis of judicial interpretation of the establishment
> clause prohibiting prayer in public schools and of the extent to
> which school policy is responsive to the Court's opinions.

Donner, Frank. "Electronic Surveillance: The National Security Game." CIVIL LIBERTIES REVIEW 2 (Summer 1975): 15-45.

Noting that wiretapping was not held to fall within the searches and seizures provision until 1967, this article traces governmental use of electronic surveillance from 1928 and the Olmstead case through the Nixon administration when national security became a favorite ploy to justify this intrusion at a time when the Court tightened restrictions on its employment.

Dorsen, Norman. FRONTIERS OF CIVIL LIBERTIES. Introduction by Louis H. Pollak. Preface by Robert F. Kennedy. New York: Pantheon Books, 1968.

This is an examination of the role of the Supreme Court in protecting civil liberties in general and its policies in specific First Amendment areas (such as military censorship, blacklisting, and academic freedom), in procedural due process (counsel, juvenile courts, trial by TV, and capital punishment) and in discrimination (voting, de facto segregation, segregation in private schools, and illegitimate children).

Douglas, William O. A LIVING BILL OF RIGHTS. Garden City, N.Y.: Doubleday, 1961.

This slim volume by Justice Douglas is a brief explanation of the kinds of values which he believes are embodied in the Bill of Rights along with a declaration of his faith in the viability of human freedom.

Downs, Robert B., ed. THE FIRST FREEDOM: LIBERTY AND JUSTICE IN THE WORLD OF BOOKS AND READINGS. Chicago: American Library Association, 1960.

This is a collection of writings and commentaries on Supreme Court speech and press cases, of statements by groups concerned with preventing censorship and of popular and scholarly discussions of what constitutes obscenity.

Drinker, Henry S. SOME OBSERVATIONS ON THE FOUR FREEDOMS OF THE FIRST AMENDMENT: FREEDOM OF SPEECH; FREEDOM OF THE PRESS; FREEDOM OF ASSEMBLY AND PETITION; FREEDOM OF RELIGION. Boston: Boston University Press, 1957.

Originally delivered as the 1957 Gaspar G. Bacon Lectures, this examines the evils in England and the American colonies which the First Amendment was designed to correct and discusses such issues as the right of labor to picket, of Jehovah's Witnesses to preach on the streets, and the released time controversy.

Drouin, Edmond G. THE SCHOOL QUESTION: A BIBLIOGRAPHY ON CHURCH–STATE RELATIONSHIPS IN AMERICAN EDUCATION, 1940–1960. Washington, D.C.: Catholic University Press, 1963.

Useful for the period covered, this bibliography is of somewhat limited value because the Supreme Court decisions which most affect church–state relationships, and thus the scholarly analyses of those relationships, postdate this work.

Bill of Rights & Pre-Civil War Amendments

Ducker, Sam. THE PUBLIC SCHOOL AND RELIGION: THE RELIGIOUS CONTEXT. New York: Harper and Row, 1966.

> This is an account of Supreme Court First Amendment and due process decisions affecting public schools from the 1923 <u>Meyer</u> case to the 1963 <u>Schempp</u> decision.

Dumbald, Edward. THE BILL OF RIGHTS AND WHAT IT MEANS TODAY. Norman: University of Oklahoma Press, 1957.

> This is a study of the events leading to the adoption of the Bill of Rights: the constitutional convention's rejection of a bill of rights, the states' ratifying conventions' demands for such protection, Madison's proposals in the First Congress, the changes in the Senate and in conference and its adoption; and a legal analysis of the scope of the amendments as interpreted by the judiciary.

Emerson, Thomas I. THE SYSTEM OF FREEDOM OF EXPRESSION. New York: Random House, 1970.

> Suggesting that the Supreme Court has failed to develop a comprehensive theory of the meaning of the free speech guarantee and that the absence of such a theory has had a detrimental effect upon the work of public officials and upon public understanding, Emerson argues for judicial structuring of a system that would assure that speech be given full protection and that other values be required to yield. Maintaining the distinction between expression and action, Emerson would confer full protection only on the former.

_____. TOWARD A GENERAL THEORY OF THE FIRST AMENDMENT: THE UNIQUE EXAMINATION OF THE NATURE OF FREEDOM OF EXPRESSION AND ITS ROLE IN A DEMOCRATIC SOCIETY. New York: Random House, 1966.

> This is an analysis of judicial interpretation of the First Amendment guarantee of free expression and of the preeminent role of such a guarantee in a free society.

Ernst, Morris L., and Lindey, Alexander. THE CENSOR MARCHES ON: RECENT MILESTONES IN THE ADMINISTRATION OF OBSCENITY LAW IN THE UNITED STATES. New York: Doubleday, Doran, and Co., 1940. Reprint. New York: Da Capo Press, 1971.

> This is a review of the status of obscenity laws in 1940.

Ernst, Morris L., and Schwartz, Alan U. PRIVACY: THE RIGHT TO BE LET ALONE. New York: Macmillan, 1962.

> Viewing the right of privacy as an American invention rather than as a right rooted in the common law of England, this work is a general overview of the development and status of that right. It includes a copy of and commentary upon the classic 1880 HARVARD LAW REVIEW article by Louis Brandeis and Samuel Warren on the right of privacy.

Fellman, David. THE CONSTITUTIONAL RIGHT OF ASSOCIATION. Chicago: University of Chicago Press, 1963.

> This is a brief explanation of the right of association as judicially derived from the first amendment guarantees of speech and assembly.

_____. THE DEFENDANT'S RIGHTS TODAY. Madison: University of Wisconsin Press, 1977.

> This is an analysis of the constitutional rights of persons accused of crime as those rights have been expanded and modified through the 1970s.

_____. THE LIMITS OF FREEDOM. New Brunswick, N.J.: Rutgers University Press, 1959.

> This is a brief study of the development of the concept of liberty from government and the restraints upon that liberty imposed by such acts as the Alien and Sedition Acts. Written before the explosion of Supreme Court decisions expanding individual rights in the 1960s, the work explores the clear and present danger doctrine and the judicial search for a new formula.

_____. RELIGION IN AMERICAN PUBLIC LAW. Boston: Boston University Press, 1965.

> This is a short analysis of judicial interpretation of the religion clauses of the First Amendment.

Fischer, Louis, and Schimmel, David. THE CIVIL RIGHTS OF TEACHERS. Critical Issues in Education Series. New York: Harper and Row, 1973.

> Designed for elementary and high school teachers, this work deals with such issues as freedom of speech inside and outside the classroom, the personal appearance and private lives of teachers, loyalty oaths and political associations and activities.

Fleming, Walter L. DOCUMENTARY HISTORY OF RECONSTRUCTION: POLITICAL, MILITARY, SOCIAL, RELIGIOUS, EDUCATIONAL AND INDUSTRIAL FROM 1865 TO THE PRESENT TIME. 2 vols. Cleveland, Ohio: Arthur H. Clark Co., 1906. Reprint. New York: McGraw-Hill, 1966.

> This work contains materials relating to various facets of the Reconstruction era from the end of the Civil War to the late 1890s. Volume I covers the period from the beginning of Reconstruction to the readmission of the seceding states to the Union. Volume II covers the rest of the Reconstruction era and continues through the 1890s. In addition to brief excerpts from newspaper articles and editorials, speeches of public figures and provisions in state constitutions concerning race relations, these volumes contain more lengthy excerpts from or reprints in full of such materials as testimony before congressional committees dealing with constitutional amendments and civil rights legislation and the text of Reconstruction legislation.

Freedom of Information Center. MIAMI HERALD V. TORNILLO: THE TRIAL OF THE FIRST AMENDMENT. Columbia, Mo.: Freedom of Information Center, 1975.

This monograph includes the opinions of the Florida Supreme Court and of the United States Supreme Court in the Tornillo right to reply case, along with an account of the trial by Roy M. Fisher and an analysis of the legal framework of the case by Paul A. Freund.

Freund, Paul A., and Ulrich, Robert. RELIGION AND THE PUBLIC SCHOOLS. Cambridge, Mass.: Harvard University Press, 1966.

This contains two brief essays originally delivered as the Burton Lecture and the Inglish Lecture at Harvard in 1965. The Freund essay deals with "The Legal Issue" and the Ulich essay deals with "The Educational Issue."

Friendly, Fred W. THE GOOD GUYS, THE BAD GUYS AND THE FIRST AMENDMENT. New York: Random House, 1976.

This is an examination of the tension between the First Amendment guarantee of a free press and the fairness doctrine in which Friendly considers the rights of broadcasters, the rights of individuals and the desirability of debate between opposing viewpoints.

Galloway, John, ed. THE SUPREME COURT AND THE RIGHTS OF THE ACCUSED. New York: Facts on File, 1973.

This is a review of Supreme Court decisions of the 1960s and early 1970s dealing with the rights of persons accused of crime: counsel, cross-examination of witnesses, obtaining witnesses, speedy trial, double jeopardy, confessions, searches and seizures, self-incrimination, capital punishment, plea bargaining, eyewitness identification, nonunanimous verdicts in state courts and the rights of juveniles. It includes extensive excerpts from Supreme Court opinions.

Gaylin, Willard. PARTIAL JUSTICE: A STUDY OF BIAS IN SENTENCING. New York: Random House, 1974. New York: Vintage Books, 1975. Paper.

This is a study of the disparity in sentencing practices of different judges.

Gellhorn, Walter. INDIVIDUAL FREEDOM AND GOVERNMENT RESTRAINTS. Baton Rouge: Louisiana State University Press, 1956.

Originally delivered as the 1956 Edward Douglass White Lectures, this deals with administrative restraints on freedom. Gellhorn examines changing attitudes toward the administrative process and administrative restraints on book reading and the right to make a living.

_____. SECURITY, LOYALTY AND SCIENCE. Ithaca, N.Y.: Cornell University Press, 1950.

This is a study of the detrimental effects of the national loyalty programs upon the scientific community.

Gerald, James E. THE PRESS AND THE CONSTITUTION, 1931-1947. Minneapolis: University of Minnesota Press, 1948.

This is an analysis of judicial decisions dealing with censorship, unions, contempt of court, post office powers, and taxes in which the central issue was freedom of the press.

Gillmor, Donald M. FREE PRESS AND FAIR TRIAL. Washington, D.C.: Public Affairs Press, 1966.

This is a review of some of the major aspects of the confrontation between the constitutional guarantees of a free press and a fair trial. It examines the conflicts at issue in Sheppard and subsequent such cases and other problems such as those presented by cameras in the courtroom.

Ginger, Ann Fagan, ed. CIVIL LIBERTIES DOCKET. Berkeley, Calif.: National Lawyers Guild, 1955-- . 5/year.

This publication published by the Guild's National Committee on Constitutional Rights and Liberties, lists the cases on court dockets which raise issues involving individual rights. The lists are organized on the basis of the constitutional issue involved.

Gordon, William I. NINE MEN PLUS: SUPREME COURT OPINIONS ON FREE SPEECH AND FREE PRESS: AN ACADEMIC GAME-SIMULATION. Dubuque, Iowa: William C. Brown, 1971.

This work first sets forth the rules for game simulation and then presents Supreme Court cases for games in five major areas: academic freedom, censorship, defamation and libel, political dissent, and privacy.

Graebner, Norman A., ed. FREEDOM IN AMERICA: A 200-YEAR PERSPECTIVE. University Park: Pennsylvania State University Press, 1977.

With an introduction by the editor, this contains fifteen essays written as part of a bicentennial project. Divided into four parts, the essays deal with such concerns as the foundations of American freedom, constitutional protection of political freedom, the economy, and the environment.

Graham, Fred P. THE SELF-INFLICTED WOUND. New York: Macmillan, 1970.

This is an examination of the incorporation of the guarantees of the Bill of Rights into the due process clause of the Fourteenth Amendment and of the Court's opinions protecting the rights of persons accused of crime. It focuses upon Miranda which the author views as a "colossal blunder" and "a serious self-inflicted" wound. He both criticizes the Court's opinions in the area of criminal justice and defends its role in assuring a fair trial.

Griswold, Erwin. THE FIFTH AMENDMENT TODAY. Cambridge, Mass.: Harvard University Press, 1955.

> Written at the height of the equation of invocation of the Fifth Amendment guarantee against self-incrimination with admission of guilt of Communist affiliation, this work is a defense of the right to invoke that guarantee as a basis for refusal to answer questions.

Grodzins, Morton. AMERICANS BETRAYED: POLITICS AND THE JAPANESE EVACUATION. Chicago: University of Chicago Press, 1949.

> Although the focus of this political and social history of the evacuation of persons of Japanese ancestry from the West Coast during World War II is upon the decision-making process and is primarily concerned with the roles of regional pressure groups, of congressional delegations from the West, and of the Justice and War Departments, it also examines the role of the Court in the policy process and judicial interpretation of the constitutionality of the policy in the Hirabayashi and Korematsu cases.

Habenstreit, Barbara. ETERNAL VIGILANCE: THE AMERICAN CIVIL LIBERTIES UNION IN ACTION. New York: Julian Messner, 1971.

> This is an account of the activities of the American Civil Liberties Union in protecting individual rights from its role in such early naturalization cases as Schwimmer to its more recent participation in battles over sexual equality.

Hachten, William A. THE SUPREME COURT ON THE PRESS: DECISIONS AND DISSENTS. Ames: Iowa State University Press, 1968.

> This study of the ideas and principles underlying freedom of the press examines majority and minority opinions dealing with such aspects of the problem as censorship, licensing, contempt, pretrial publicity, broadcasting, and governmental regulation of business aspects of the press.

Hand, Learned. BILL OF RIGHTS. Cambridge, Mass.: Harvard University Press, 1958. Reprint. New York: Atheneum, 1964.

> This is the published version of the Oliver Wendell Holmes 1958 Lecture in which Judge Hand examines three major and related issues: the justification for judicial invalidation of legislation, the conditions under which the power of invalidation should be exercised when based on the Fifth and Fourteenth Amendment due process and equal protection clauses, and the reasons that the First Amendment guarantees are entitled to no greater protection than any other interest. Generally, Hand argues against judicial invalidation on the grounds of "unreasonableness."

Haney, Robert W. COMSTOCKERY IN AMERICA: PATTERNS OF CENSORSHIP AND CONTROL. Boston: Beacon Press, 1960. Reprint. New York: Da Capo Press, 1974.

> This is an examination of various kinds of legal and extralegal limitations imposed upon books, movies and television.

Harris, Richard. FREEDOM SPENT. Boston: Little, Brown, 1976.

> Designed for the general audience, most of the material included
> originally appeared in the NEW YORKER. Taking the position
> that the most fundamental parts of the Constitution, especially
> the Bill of Rights, are rarely enforced and that the rhetoric of
> freedom has tended to drown out the practices of tyranny, Harris
> narrates the experiences of six individuals who fought govern-
> mental violations of their rights guaranteed by the First, Fourth
> and Fifth Amendments.

Heller, Francis H. THE SIXTH AMENDMENT TO THE CONSTITUTION
OF THE UNITED STATES. Lawrence: University of Kansas Press, 1951.

> Written before Gideon started the judicial trend toward defining
> with greater specificity the ingredients of a fair trial and thus
> somewhat outdated, this is an in-depth study of judicial construc-
> tion of the right to counsel and a trial by jury and of the stan-
> dards for a fair trial.

Herman, Lawrence. THE RIGHT TO COUNSEL IN MISDEMEANOR COURT.
Columbus: Ohio State University Press, 1974.

> This slim volume contains an expanded version of lectures pre-
> sented at Ohio Law School in 1972. At that time, the case of
> Argersinger v. Hamlin was before the Court and the lectures
> dealt with the problems of that case. They were revised after
> the Court's decision and this book includes an added section
> dealing with Argersinger and its implications for the right to an
> appointed counsel in misdemeanor cases.

Hofstadter, Samuel H. THE FIFTH AMENDMENT AND THE IMMUNITY ACT
OF 1954: ASPECTS OF THE AMERICAN WAY. New York: Fund for the
Republic, 1956.

> This is a brief overview of Supreme Court application of the
> self-incrimination provision of the Fifth Amendment from the Boyd
> case in the nineteenth century to the 1950s and the 1954 congres-
> sional legislation which conferred immunity from prosecution upon
> those forced to testify after invoking the Fifth Amendment. The
> book examines the question of whether the statute protects a
> witness as fully as does the Fifth.

Hogan, John C. THE SCHOOLS, THE COURTS AND THE PUBLIC IN-
TEREST. Lexington, Mass.: Lexington Books, 1974.

> This is an extensive review of the changing role of courts in
> education--judicial attempts to bring about racial equality, to
> scrutinize expenditures in order to assure equal access by the
> poor and the increasing willingness to enlarge and protect the
> civil liberties of students not only in such basic areas as the
> right of expression involved in the Tinker case but freedoms
> surrounding such decisions as the length of hair.

Hook, Sidney. COMMON SENSE AND THE FIFTH AMENDMENT. New
York: Criterion Books, 1957.

This is a criticism of the increasing use by witnesses in the
1950s of the guarantee against self-incrimination to avoid answering questions.

Horton, David S., ed. FREEDOM AND EQUALITY: ADDRESSES BY
HARRY S. TRUMAN. Columbia: University of Missouri Press, 1960.

With an introductory chapter by the editor, this slim volume contains nine of Truman's addresses and messages to Congress on
civil rights and civil liberties, including his veto message returning the 1952 Immigration and Nationality Act, his request
for legislation to protect blacks and addresses dealing with the
threat of internal communism.

Howard, A.E. Dick. THE ROAD FROM RUNNEYMEDE: MAGNA CARTA
AND CONSTITUTIONALISM. Charlottesville: University of Virginia Press,
1968.

This is "a biography of a document and the ideas it set loose--
the document being Magna Carta and the most significant idea
being constitutionalism." It explores the development of the
concepts embodied in Magna Carta during the colonial, revolutionary and constitutional periods and analyzes due process as
it took shape and expanded in American law.

Hudson, Edward G. FREEDOM OF SPEECH AND PRESS IN AMERICA.
Introduction by Morris L. Ernst. Foreword by Justice Douglas. Washington, D.C.: Public Affairs Press, 1963.

This study of the historical development of free speech and press
from the early colonial period to the 1960s argues that from the
beginning the law governing speech and press has vacillated partly
because of the lack of a basic philosophy.

IN THE MATTER OF KAREN QUINLAN. THE COMPLETE LEGAL BRIEFS,
COURT PROCEEDINGS, AND DECISION IN THE SUPERIOR COURT OF
NEW JERSEY. THE COMPLETE BRIEFS, ORAL ARGUMENTS AND OPINION
IN THE NEW JERSEY SUPREME COURT. Washington, D.C.: University
Publications, 1977.

The Quinlan case raised new constitutional as well as medical and
ethical questions concerning the right to die, the rights of incom-
petent patients, and the responsibilities of physicians. Volume
1 contains the materials relevant to the lower court's opinion.
Volume 2 contains the materials relevant to the opinion of the
Supreme Court of New Jersey.

Invau, Fred E., ed. CONFERENCE ON PREJUDICIAL NEWS REPORTING
IN CRIMINAL CASES. Chicago: Northwestern University Press, 1962.

This discussion of the conflict between a free press and a fair
trial by scholars from the journalistic and legal communities
consists of papers delivered at a conference conducted by Northwestern University School of Law and the Medill School of Journalism at Northwestern in 1962.

Jacobs, Clyde. THE ELEVENTH AMENDMENT AND SOVEREIGN IMMUNITY. Westport, Conn.: Greenwood Press, 1972.

> This is an examination of the factors leading to the adoption of the Eleventh Amendment placing limitations on federal judicial power to hear suits against the state, an account of judicial application of that amendment to suits against the state and state officials and a criticism of the doctrine of sovereign immunity.

Kalven, Harry, Jr. THE NEGRO AND THE FIRST AMENDMENT. Columbus: Ohio State University Press, 1965. Chicago: University of Chicago Press, 1966.

> Originally delivered at the Ohio State Law Forum in 1964, these lectures examine the contributions of the civil rights movement to judicial expansion of individual and group rights such as the right of association.

Kaplan, Morton A. DISSENT AND THE STATE IN PEACE AND WAR: AN ESSAI ON THE GROUNDS OF PUBLIC MORALITY. New York: Dunellen Publishing Co., 1970.

> Prompted by the extremism of the protest movement against the Vietnam War and its ultimate attack upon the legitimacy of the government, this "essai" is a polemical exploration of the issues of legitimate dissent and political obligations in a free society.

Kauper, Paul G. CIVIL LIBERTIES AND THE CONSTITUTION. Ann Arbor: University of Michigan Press, 1962.

> This is an examination of the major civil libertarian controversies of the early 1960s: obscenity, freedom of association, the role of the national government in protecting individual rights and the applicability of constitutional prohibitions to private actions.

_____. RELIGION AND THE CONSTITUTION. Baton Rouge: Louisiana State University Press, 1964.

> Originally delivered as the 1964 Edward Douglass White Lecture, this work examines the free exercise and establishment clauses of the First Amendment. With reference to the former, Kauper poses the problem of whether it was designed to be an independent protection of religion or a part of the general protection of free expression. With reference to the latter, he analyzes three Supreme Court theories: no aid or strict separation, strict neutrality, and the accommodation theory.

Kelly, Alfred H., ed. FOUNDATIONS OF FREEDOM IN THE AMERICAN CONSTITUTION. New York: Harper and Brothers, 1958.

> Originally written in the early 1950s era of loyalty programs, of domestic anti-Communist fervor and of the cold war, some of the six essays in this volume reflect these concerns and were revised for the 1958 edition. Three of the essays, essentially historical in nature, deal with the broad issue of freedom: the nature of constitutionalism, the Bill of Rights and free speech and press. The other three deal with the loyalty program,

congressional investigations and anticommunism.

Kemper, Donald J. DECADE OF FEAR: SENATOR HENNINGS AND CIVIL LIBERTIES. Columbia: University of Missouri, 1965.

This is a study of the threat to civil liberties posed by the fear of internal communism in the 1950s and the Warren Court's response to governmental restrictions within the context of the career of Senator Thomas Carey Hennings of Missouri who came on the national political scene at the same time as did McCarthy.

Knight, Harold V. WITH LIBERTY AND JUSTICE FOR ALL: THE MEANING OF THE BILL OF RIGHTS TODAY. Rev. ed. Dobbs Ferry, N.Y.: Oceana, 1968.

With an introduction by Roger Baldwin and designed for a general audience, this is a study of the status of the First Amendment guarantees and some of the procedural guarantees in the mid-1960s.

Konvitz, Milton R. RELIGIOUS LIBERTY AND CONSCIENCE: A CONSTITUTIONAL INQUIRY. New York: Viking Press, 1968.

Originally delivered as the Paley Lectures in American Culture and Civilization at the Hebrew University in Israel in 1968, this work looks at changes within religious groups and within society in the 1960s and examines the question of what constitutes a religion for constitutional purposes, the relationship between religion and secularism, and the First Amendment's protection of conscience.

Konvitz, Milton R., and Rossiter, Clinton, eds. ASPECTS OF LIBERTY: ESSAYS PRESENTED TO ROBERT E. CUSHMAN. Ithaca, N.Y.: Cornell University Press, 1958.

This is a collection of seventeen essays written in honor of Professor Cushman upon his retirement. The essays deal with such subjects as the uses of social science in civil rights litigation, the Marshall Court and civil liberties, the Bill of Rights, the Fourteenth Amendment and the federal system, and procedural due process of the Fifth Amendment. There is also a bibliography of works by Cushman.

Krantz, Sheldon, et al. RIGHT TO COUNSEL IN CRIMINAL CASES: THE MANDATE OF ARGERSINGER V. HAMLIN. Cambridge, Mass.: Ballinger, 1976.

In June of 1972, the Supreme Court held in the Argersinger case that the Sixth Amendment prohibits the imprisonment of a person unless he or she has been represented by an attorney. Prepared by the Boston University School of Law Center for Criminal Justice, this is a mammoth report on the problems, implications and implementation of that decision. It finds that in most jurisdictions there has been little or no effort to comply with the spirit or principle of Argersinger.

Krislov, Samuel. THE SUPREME COURT AND POLITICAL FREEDOM. New York: Free Press, 1968.

Noting that the heart of the democratic process is defended by a legal process remote from majoritarian principles, Krislov examines the theoretical underpinnings of political freedom, the power of the Court to protect that freedom, and the relationship between the Court and the public.

Kurland, Philip B. RELIGION AND THE LAW OF CHURCH AND STATE AND THE SUPREME COURT. Chicago: Aldine Publishing Co., 1963.

This is a brief study of judicial interpretation of the First Amendment prohibition of governmental interference with the free exercise of religion and of governmental establishment of religion.

Lader, Lawrence. ABORTION II: MAKING THE REVOLUTION. Boston: Beacon Press, 1973.

Written before and published shortly after Roe, with a summation of the Court's opinion in that case, this is a proabortion tract by the one-time chairman of the National Association for the Repeal of Abortion Laws. It is an account of the abortion movement and its use of direct action tactics as well as litigation to overturn abortion laws.

Lapidus, Edith J. EAVESDROPPING ON TRIAL. Roselle Park, N.J.: Hayden Book Co., 1974.

This study of "four decades of indecision" about wiretapping characterized by "vacillating action" by the executive, legislative, and judicial branches from 1928 and Olmstead to 1967 and Berger v. New York and Katz v. U.S. focuses on Title III of the Omnibus Crime Control and Safe Streets Act of 1968 in which Congress for the first time authorized wiretapping and electronic surveillance.

Lasson, Nelson B. THE HISTORY AND DEVELOPMENT OF THE FOURTH AMENDMENT TO THE UNITED STATES CONSTITUTION. Baltimore: Johns Hopkins University Press, 1937. Reprint. New York: Da Capo Press, 1970.

This history of the origins of the guarantee against unreasonable searches and seizures examines early English and French practices, the use of writs of assistance in the colonies, the adoption of a guarantee against such searches and seizures in the 1776 Virginia Bill of Rights, the proposal of the Fourth Amendment by the First Congress and its interpretation and application to the national government by the Supreme Court through the 1920s.

Laubach, John H. SCHOOL PRAYERS: CONGRESS, THE COURTS AND THE PUBLIC. Washington, D.C.: Public Affairs Press, 1965.

Relying on extensive testimony given at congressional hearings on the unsuccessful Becker and Dirksen proposed amendments to reverse the Supreme Court's school prayer decisions, this work examines the intentions of the framers of the First Amendment on the question of the separation of church and state, the disputes over the school-religion problem in state and national jurisdictions, and the Engel, Abington v. Schempp and Murray opinions of the Supreme Court.

Levy, Leonard W. JEFFERSON AND CIVIL LIBERTIES: THE DARKER SIDE. Cambridge, Mass.: Belknap, Harvard University Press, 1963.

In this examination of the validity of Jefferson's historical reputation as the apostle of liberty, Levy concludes that by Jefferson's own articulated standards and the libertarian standards of
his day, he fell far short as a protector of liberty. He not only
used governmental power in violation of these standards but he
never risked his career or his reputation to champion any libertarian value and failed even to condemn publicly the Alien and
Sedition Acts about which he complained in private.

_____. LEGACY OF SUPPRESSION, FREEDOM OF SPEECH AND PRESS
IN EARLY AMERICAN HISTORY. Cambridge, Mass.: Harvard University
Press, 1960.

This analysis of attempts to curb the circulation of political ideas
from the Zenger case to the American Revolution leads the author
to conclude that "the generations which adopted the Constitution
and the Bill of Rights did not believe in a broad scope of freedom
of expression." Levy examines seditious libel laws in the colonial
period, early English theory of free speech from Milton to Cato,
American practice from the Revolution to the adoption of the
First Amendment and the emergence of American libertarian theory.
A paperback edition, with a new preface, was published by Harper
and Row in 1963 under the title FREEDOM OF SPEECH AND PRESS
IN EARLY AMERICAN HISTORY: LEGACY OF SUPPRESSION.

_____. ORIGINS OF THE FIFTH AMENDMENT: THE RIGHT AGAINST
SELF-INCRIMINATION. New York: Oxford University Press, 1968.

This is a history of the right against self-incrimination from its
origins in English law, its evolution in the colonies and the
establishment of the right after the Revolution to the ratification
of the Fifth in 1791. Because the work is concerned with the
origins of the right and because the right originated in England,
the bulk of this massive work of scholarship is devoted to English law.

_____, ed. FREEDOM OF THE PRESS FROM ZENGER TO JEFFERSON:
EARLY AMERICAN LIBERTARIAN THEORIES. Indianapolis: Bobbs-Merrill,
1966.

With a general introduction and a headnote to each excerpt by the
editor, this is an anthology of fifty-nine documents from Andrew
Hamilton's argument in the Zenger case to the Jeffersonian advocacy of free expression which illustrate the editor's view that
freedom of the press emerged with the late eighteenth century's
rejection of the notion of seditious libel, a crime supported by
such earlier libertarians as Locke and Milton.

Lewis, Anthony. GIDEON'S TRUMPET. New York: Random House, 1964.

This is a study of the Gideon case from the commission of the
crime in 1961 to the Supreme Court decision and ultimately Gideon's
release following that decision and his retrial and acquittal.

Bill of Rights & Pre-Civil War Amendments

Lewis, Felice Flanery. LITERATURE, OBSCENITY AND LAW. Carbondale: Southern Illinois University Press, 1976.

With excerpts from both censored works and judicial opinions upholding or rejecting governmental attempts to suppress these works, this is an examination of the changing moral values and sexual explicitness in literature since the 1890s and evolving constitutional standards for determining what constitutes unprotected obscenity.

Lofton, John. JUSTICE AND THE PRESS. Boston: Beacon Press, 1966.

Written by a journalist and lawyer, this is an examination of the historic and contemporary problems produced by the conflicts between the organized bar and bench on the one hand and the press on the other as one attempts to protect the defendant's due process rights and the other seeks to publish free from all restrictions.

McAuliffe, Mary Sperling. CRISIS ON THE LEFT: COLD WAR POLITICS AND AMERICAN LIBERALS, 1947-1954. Amherst: University of Massachusetts Press, 1978.

This is a study of the responses of the left, particularly of liberal politicians such as Senator Humphrey and organizations such as the American Civil Liberties Union, to the cold war and to the anti-Communist politics in the postwar and McCarthy era, a response that not infrequently paralyzed normally liberal impulses.

McCloskey, Robert G., ed. ESSAYS IN CONSTITUTIONAL LAW. New York: Random House, 1957.

This is a collection of essays, ten reprints and two original, which examine basic aspects of constitutional interpretation such as judicial review, presidential power, church-state relationships, race relations, criminal procedures and the role of the Court in the socioeconomic realm through its interpretation of the commerce and due process clauses.

Mackey, Philip E., ed. VOICES AGAINST DEATH: CLASSIC APPEALS AGAINST THE DEATH PENALTY IN AMERICA, 1787-1973. New York: Burt Franklin, 1976.

This is a collection of arguments advanced by members of such diverse groups as lawyers, legislators, social scientists, men on death row and journalists. Arranged chronologically, the earlier selections tend to rely more heavily upon moral and religious considerations whereas the more recent arguments rely more heavily upon the constitutional prohibition against cruel and unusual punishment.

Manwaring, David R. RENDER UNTO CAESAR: THE FLAG SALUTE CONTROVERSY. Chicago: University of Chicago Press, 1962.

This work uses the flag salute cases as a basis for analysis of the role of group pressures in constitutional change.

Marion, George. THE COMMUNIST TRIAL: AN AMERICAN CROSSROADS. New York: Fairplay Publications, 1949.

> Written before the Supreme Court's decision in the Dennis case, this is an account of and attack upon governmental prosecutors in that trial and upon Judge Medina's conduct of the trial.

Marnell, William H. THE FIRST AMENDMENT: THE HISTORY OF RELI-GIOUS FREEDOM IN AMERICA. Garden City, N.Y.: Doubleday, 1964.

> The First Amendment both prohibits governmental interference with the free exercise of religion and governmental establishment of religion. This work, rather than viewing the guarantees as compatible, points to the potential conflict if the Supreme Court interprets either rigidly.

Mayer, Milton, ed. THE TRADITION OF FREEDOM: SELECTIONS FROM THE WRITERS WHO SHAPED THE TRADITIONAL CONCEPTS FOR FREE-DOM AND JUSTICE IN AMERICA. New York: Oceana, 1957.

> Sponsored by the Fund for the Republic, this is a collection of such classic statements on free speech as those of Milton, Locke, and Mill as well as a selection of Supreme Court decisions.

Mayers, Lewis. SHALL WE AMEND THE FIFTH AMENDMENT? New York: Harpers, 1959.

> Written against the backdrop of a period when the self-incrimina-tion provision was widely viewed as a shield for the guilty in general and for Communists in particular, this is a study of the origins, use and meaning of the Fifth Amendment guarantee.

Medalie, Richard J. FROM ESCOBEDO TO MIRANDA: THE ANATOMY OF A SUPREME COURT DECISION. Foreword by Samuel Dash. Washington, D.C.: Lerner Law Books, 1966.

> This is a compilation of opinions, briefs and oral arguments in Miranda set against the background of the opinion in Escobedo.

Medina, Harold R., chairman. FINAL REPORT: FREEDOM OF THE PRESS AND FAIR TRIAL. New York: Columbia University Press, 1967.

> This is the final report of a Special Committee on Radio, TV and the Administration of Justice of the Association of the Bar of the City of New York. It analyzes and makes recommendations in four major areas in which the guarantees of a fair trial and of a free press clash: contempt of court, Canon 20 restricting comments by lawyers, police practices and comments and the court's role in minimizing pretrial publicity and utilizing its powers of continuance, change of venue and sequestration.

Meiklejohn, Alexander. POLITICAL FREEDOM: THE CONSTITUTIONAL POWERS OF THE PEOPLE. New York: Harpers, 1960.

> This is a declaration of the important roles of the guarantees of speech and voting in assuring political freedom.

Meltsner, Michael. CRUEL AND UNUSUAL: THE SUPREME COURT AND CAPITAL PUNISHMENT. New York: Random House, 1973.

This study of capital punishment focuses upon the lawyers involved in such cases, the strategies they employed in challenging the death penalty and their victories. It includes summaries of oral arguments before the Supreme Court.

Metzger, Walter P., ed. THE CONSTITUTIONAL STATUS OF ACADEMIC TENURE. The Academic Profession Series. New York: Arno Press, 1977.

This anthology contains reprints of five law review articles dealing with academic freedom and tenure plus seven judicial opinions from 1878 to 1974 which deal with the subject.

Miller, Leonard G. DOUBLE JEOPARDY AND THE FEDERAL SYSTEM. Chicago: University of Chicago Press, 1968.

Originally a Ph.D. thesis, this slender volume examines the "dual sovereignty" aspect of double jeopardy, i.e., successive state and federal prosecutions of an individual for a single act. The author argues that such prosecutions are an intrinsic and legitimate by-product of a federal system.

Morgan, Richard E. THE SUPREME COURT AND RELIGION. New York: Free Press, 1972.

This is an examination of the Supreme Court's interpretation of the free exercise and establishment clauses of the First Amendment in terms of a tension between doctrinal consistency and political acceptability. Morgan agrees with the Court's rejection of prayers in public schools but argues that the Court has gone too far in accomodating religious minorities at the expense of the majority and in prohibiting aid to parochial schools.

Mott, Rodney. DUE PROCESS OF LAW: A HISTORICAL AND ANALYTICAL TREATISE OF THE PRINCIPLES AND METHODS FOLLOWED BY THE COURTS IN THE APPLICATION OF THE CONCEPT OF "LAW OF THE LAND." Indianapolis: Bobbs-Merrill, 1926.

This is a comprehensive analysis of the development and functions of the concept of due process from Magna Carta to judicial interpretations in the early part of this century. It examines the varied phrasings of the guarantee in England, the growth of this protection in the colonies, states and nation, procedural requirements traditionally imposed by this guarantee, its relationship to equality and its use in limiting the state's police power.

Muir, William K. PRAYER IN THE PUBLIC SCHOOLS: LAW AND ATTITUDE CHANGE. Chicago: University of Chicago Press, 1967.

Muir approaches the broad question of the relationship between law and attitude by focusing on the narrow question of the effect of the Schempp decision on the attitudes of a group of educators toward prayer in public schools. In asking under what circumstances law does and does not change attitudes, he suggests four general patterns of effect: the nulist, the backlash, the conversion, and the liberating hypotheses.

Murphy, Paul L. THE MEANING OF FREEDOM OF SPEECH: FIRST AMEND-
MENT FREEDOMS FROM WILSON TO FDR. Contributions in American History Series. Westport, Conn.: Greenwood Press, 1972.

In this analysis of the meaning of freedom of speech in the years
from the World War I armistice to the inauguration of Roosevelt,
Murphy suggests that the idea of liberty was cast largely in terms
of freedom of expression and was one of the major instruments
for redefining social relationships. Winner of the American Bar
Association's 1972 Gavel Award, this work examines the attempts
of those who were shocked by governmental restrictions during
World War I to broaden the scope of constitutional protection
of free expression, their opponents, and their failures, frustrations, and successes.

Murphy, Walter P. WIRETAPPING ON TRIAL: A CASE STUDY IN THE
JUDICIAL PROCESS. New York: Random House, 1965.

Essentially an analysis of the interaction of administrative, legislative and judicial officials in the formulation of public policy,
this work focuses on the wiretapping problem from the prohibition
era and the Olmstead case to the early 1960s.

Nagata, Ernest A. "Federal Powers and the Eleventh Amendment: Attorneys'
Fees in Private Suits Against the State." CALIFORNIA LAW REVIEW 63
(September 1975): 1167-1225.

Although focusing upon the question of federal judicial authority
to award attorney's fees, this work examines that question within
the framework of the broader problem of the scope of the remedial
powers of federal courts in a private suit against a state or its
officials--or, more specifically, the extent to which federal courts
can compel states to take affirmative actions requiring expenditures
of state funds without violating the Eleventh Amendment. The
author suggests an Eleventh Amendment interpretation that would
give the national government greater flexibility by expanding congressional authority to require states to waive immunity.

Nelson, Harold L., ed. FREEDOM OF THE PRESS FROM HAMILTON TO
THE WARREN COURT. Indianapolis: Bobbs-Merrill, 1967.

This is a collection and analysis of documents relevant to the
evolution of the concept of a free press from Hamilton's 1804
argument that truth with good motive and justifiable ends should
be a defense in a criminal libel suit to Warren Court opinions
such as that in New York TIMES v. Sullivan. It includes cases
in such areas as criminal libel, contempt of court, and obscenity.

Oaks, Dallin H., ed. THE WALL BETWEEN CHURCH AND STATE. Chicago:
University of Chicago Press, 1963.

This contains nine essays, each by a different scholar, dealing
with various facets of the controversy over the proper relationship between state and religion. The overall problem is viewed
from a Protestant and a Catholic perspective. Other essays deal
with the constitutionality of aid to parochial schools, the constitutionality of tax exemptions for religious activities, the problem of utilizing a religious factor in adoption and placement of

children, and the school prayer cases of the 1961 terms.

Oboler, Eli M. THE FEAR OF THE WORD: CENSORSHIP AND SEX. Metuchen, N.J.: Scarecrow Press, 1974.

This work deals primarily with the origins and history of govern- mental censorship of words and only incidentally with the Supreme Court's response to such limitations. The author's position is that if government and society were to cease to concern them- selves with words, attention could then be turned to the "true obscenities of our time" such as hunger and poverty.

O'Brian, John Lord. NATIONAL SECURITY AND INDIVIDUAL FREEDOM. Cambridge, Mass.: Harvard University Press, 1955.

Originally delivered as the 1955 Godkin Lectures and concerned with the effects of McCarthyism upon individual rights, this work discusses the changes in constitutional theory, law and public attitudes precipitated by national anxieties about internal security.

O'Brien, F. William. JUSTICE REED AND THE FIRST AMENDMENT: THE RELIGION CLAUSES. Washington, D.C.: Georgetown University Press, 1958. Reprint. Westport, Conn.: Greenwood Press, 1976.

Shortly after Reed took his seat on the bench in 1938, the first of a long series of religion cases that the Court was to consider during his nineteen-year tenure came before the Court. This is a study of the position that Reed took in the free exercise and establishment cases.

O'Neil, Robert M. FREE SPEECH: RESPONSIBLE COMMUNICATION UN- DER LAW. Bobbs-Merrill Series in Speech Communications. Indianapolis: Bobbs-Merrill, 1966.

This slim volume is designed to inform public speakers when and to what extent they may be liable for abusing the constitutional rights of speech, assembly and petition. It deals with such matters as free speech on college campuses, hostile audiences, the regulation of the time, place and manner of speech, the legal liability of speakers and the application of copyright laws to the speaker's words.

_____. PRICE OF DEPENDENCY: CIVIL LIBERTIES IN THE WELFARE STATE. New York: E.P. Dutton and Co., 1970.

This is a criticism of the conditions attached to receipt of govern- ment benefits that undermine basic civil rights, rights constitution- ally guaranteed to all persons including those accused of crime but systematically denied to beneficiaries of government largess and an analysis of judicial participation in and/or rejection of the imposition of such conditions.

Patterson, Bennett B. THE FORGOTTEN NINTH AMENDMENT: A CALL FOR LEGISLATIVE AND JUDICIAL RECOGNITION OF RIGHTS UNDER SOCIAL CONDITIONS OF TODAY. Indianapolis: Bobbs-Merrill, 1955.

Written over a decade before the Court noticed the potentialities of the Ninth Amendment as a basis for enlarging the specific guarantees of the Constitution, this is a study of the origins, history, and state and national judicial interpretations of this Amendment. It analyzes the debates over the Bill of Rights and concludes that legislative and judicial expansion of individual rights is not only warranted by and consistent with the intention of the framers but that the Amendment imposes upon government an affirmative obligation to protect the natural and inalienable rights of the individual.

Paul, James C.N., and Schwartz, Murray L. FEDERAL CENSORSHIP: OBSCENITY IN THE MAIL. New York: Free Press, 1961.

This is a study of the evolution of national censorship of obscenity. Organized chronologically, it examines censorship laws to 1930, the developments from 1930 to 1945, postwar Supreme Court decisions from 1945 to 1956 and the changes in obscenity control between 1957 and 1960.

Pember, Don R. PRIVACY AND THE PRESS: THE LAW, THE MASS MEDIA AND THE FIRST AMENDMENT. Seattle: University of Washington Press, 1972.

This is a "defense oriented" treatment of the conflicts between the statutory and constitutional right of privacy and the constitutional guarantee of a free press. The appendix includes various cases in the development of the law of privacy, the texts of existing privacy law and a chart on the status of the law of privacy in each of the states and the District of Columbia.

Perry, Richard L., ed. SOURCES OF OUR LIBERTIES: DOCUMENTARY ORIGINS OF INDIVIDUAL LIBERTIES IN THE UNITED STATES CONSTITUTION AND BILL OF RIGHTS. Chicago: American Bar Association Foundation, 1959.

This is a collection of thirty-two documents from Magna Carta to the Bill of Rights which serve as the legal foundation for protecting individual rights, each with an introductory commentary by the editor.

Pfeffer, Leo. GOD, CAESAR AND THE CONSTITUTION: THE COURT AS REFEREE OF CHURCH-STATE CONFRONTATION. Boston: Beacon Press, 1975.

This is an examination of the contemporary status of the confrontations between the state and religion and how the Supreme Court has acted to resolve these conflicts in such arenas as the family, the military, public schools, parochial schools, and the community.

Pound, Roscoe. THE DEVELOPMENT OF CONSTITUTIONAL GUARANTEES OF LIBERTY. New Haven, Conn.: Yale University Press, 1957.

This examines four major periods in the history of legally enforceable protection of individual liberty: medieval England, the period from the Reformation to the Glorious Revolution of

1688, the American colonial period to the 1774 Declaration of
Rights by the Continental Congress, and the period of written
constitutions culminating in the adoption of the Bill of Rights.

Prettyman, Barrett, Jr. DEATH AND THE SUPREME COURT. New York:
Harcourt, Brace and World, 1961. Reprint. New York: Harvest Books,
1971.

   Written before Furman v. Georgia and designed for the general
   audience, this is a narrative of six capital punishment crimes,
   the defendants in each case, their trials and their appeals to
   the Supreme Court.

Randall, Richard S. CENSORSHIP OF THE MOVIES: THE SOCIAL AND
POLITICAL CONTROL OF A MASS MEDIA. Madison: University of Wisconsin Press, 1968.

   Written within the context of continuing judicial removal of restrictions on motion pictures, this is a study not only of the procedural and substantive aspects of the law of censorship but of
   censorship as seen by the censors and by film proprietors and
   their lawyers and of informal and nongovernmental control.

Rankin, Robert S. WHEN CIVIL LAW FAILS: MARTIAL LAW AND ITS
LEGAL BASIS IN THE UNITED STATES. Durham, N.C.: Duke University
Press, 1939.

   This is a review of state and national use of martial law. It
   discusses its imposition and exercise by Jackson following the
   Battle of New Orleans, by Rhode Island during the Dorr rebellion,
   by both state and national governments during the Civil War,
   presidential opposition to its use in World War I, its use by
   states during and after that war, and judicial interpretation of
   the constitutionality of such uses.

Reardon, Paul C., and Daniels, Clifton. FAIR TRIAL AND FREE PRESS.
Washington, D.C.: American Enterprise Institute, 1968.

   This contains lectures by Reardon and Daniels, a rebuttal by each
   and answers to questions directed to the debaters.

Regan, Richard J. PRIVATE CONSCIENCE AND PUBLIC LAW: THE
AMERICAN EXPERIENCE. New York: Fordham University Press, 1972.

   Prompted by protests against the Vietnam war and domestic in-
   justices and by the revival in the 1960s of "higher law" appeals
   of conscience as justification for immunity from public laws, this
   is a comparative study of conflicts between private conscience and
   public law in the American constitutional system. It examines
   such problems as the relationship between conscience on the one
   hand and, on the other, national security, public order, public
   welfare and family and education.

Reitman, Alan, ed. THE PULSE OF FREEDOM: AMERICAN LIBERTIES,
1920-1970. Foreword by Ramsey Clark. New York: W.W. Norton, 1975.

These six essays examine various facets of civil liberties in
the five decades from the 1920s through the 1960s, a period
chosen because it coincides with the fifty-year history of the
American Civil Liberties Union. Organized chronologically, they
deal with World War I internal repression of individual rights,
the postwar threat to civil liberties, the domestic crises posed
by World War II, postwar McCarthyism, and the turmoil of the
1960s.

Rice, Charles E. THE SUPREME COURT AND PUBLIC PRAYER: THE
NEED FOR RESTRAINT. New York: Fordham University Press, 1964.

This is a criticism of the 1962 and the 1963 Schempp school
prayer decisions. The author argues that the decisions, in
contrast to American constitutional tradition which favors religion,
introduced the novel and unsupportable concept of governmental
neutrality toward religion into constitutional law.

Rogge, Oetje John. THE FIRST AND THE FIFTH: WITH SOME EX-
CURSIONS INTO OTHERS. New York: Thomas Nelson and Sons, 1960.

This is a survey of the constitutional right to speak and the
right not to speak through the Supreme Court term ending June,
1959 and the first session of the 86th Congress. It examines
such aspects of the First Amendment as the intention of the
framers, the Sedition Act of 1789, the power of the states before
and after the adoption of the Fourteenth Amendment and the concept of "ordered liberty." It examines the Fifth Amendment in
terms of its origins and operations and various compulsory testimony acts.

_____. OUR VANISHING CIVIL LIBERTIES. Foreword by Thomas I.
Emerson. New York: Gaer Associates, 1949.

Written for a popular audience by a former head of the Criminal
Division of the Department of Justice, this is a polemic on what
the author saw as a civil liberties crisis in the 1940s resulting
in part from government secrecy and refusal to make public
reports on fascist activities and ties between German and American
industrialists.

Ruchelshaus, William, et al. FREEDOM OF THE PRESS. Washington, D.C.:
American Enterprise Institute for Public Policy Research, 1976.

This pamphlet contains the proceedings of an American Enterprise
Institute roundtable discussion by journalists of the First Amendment guarantee of a free press and of the regulation of the media.

Rutland, Robert A. THE BIRTH OF THE BILL OF RIGHTS, 1776-1791.
Chapel Hill: University of North Carolina Press, 1955.

This is an examination of the background and the process by
which Americans came to rely on legal guarantees to protect
personal liberty. Rutland argues that the Bill of Rights was the
culmination of the English common law, colonial charters, legislative enactments and represented the sum total of American experience and experimentation with civil liberty up until its adoption.

St. John-Stevas, Norman. OBSCENITY AND THE LAW. 1956. Reprint. New York: Da Capo Press, 1974.

This analysis of obscenity law is devoted primarily to the development of the English law from the period of ecclesiastical courts and Star Chamber to the 1955 Obscene Publications bill. There is, however, some material on American and Irish law.

Samuel, Howard D., ed. TOWARD A BETTER AMERICA. New York: Macmillan, 1968.

With an introduction by the editor, this contains essays, speeches, and newspaper articles and editorials dealing with various public policy issues, including civil rights and civil liberties, which were taken from programs sponsored by the Sidney Hillman Foundation: the foundation's prize awards, reprint series, and lectureship programs.

Schafer, William J. III. CONFESSIONS AND STATEMENTS. Springfield, Ill.: Charles C Thomas, 1968.

This monograph examines the standards of a "voluntary" confession that will meet the Supreme Court's criteria.

Schauer, Frederick F. THE LAW OF OBSCENITY. Washington, D.C.: Bureau of National Affairs, 1976.

This treatise on the law of obscenity, designed for legal scholars, judges, lawyers, prosecutors and legislators, examines the historical origins of American obscenity law, existing state and federal obscenity laws and constitutional standards from Roth to Miller. It deals with such problems as who sets the standards for defining the "average person," the meaning of "prurient interest," of "patently offensive," of "taken as a whole," and of "community standards." It also analyzes the free press, fair trial controversy.

Schimmel, David, and Fisher, Louis. THE CIVIL RIGHTS OF STUDENTS. Critical Issues in Education Series. New York: Harper and Row, 1975.

Designed primarily for high school and college students but touching rights of elementary school pupils, this deals with such issues as freedom of the press, speech, association, and religion, the personal appearance of students, racial and ethnic segregation, sexual discrimination and such due process rights as those enunciated in Gault. The appendix includes such materials as the relevant constitutional provisions and sample dress codes.

Schlesinger, Steven R. EXCLUSIONARY JUSTICE: THE PROBLEM OF ILLEGALLY OBTAINED EVIDENCE. New York: Marcel Dekker, 1977.

This slim volume examines the exclusionary rule as it pertains to searches and seizures and asks whether the rule constitutes good public policy. Schlesinger concludes that it runs counter to reason, has done little to deter official misconduct and offers no aid, compensation or remedy to innocent victims. He suggests that the states be left free to experiment so that out of the

diversity of experience, the information needed to fashion a new
rule to deter misconduct could be obtained.

Schmidt, Benno C., Jr. FREEDOM OF THE PRESS VERSUS PUBLIC
ACCESS. New York: Praeger Publishers, 1976.

This is an examination of the general question of whether there
is a constitutional right of access to the media of communications
and of the Supreme Court decision in Miami Herald v. Tornillo.
The author agrees with the Court's rejection of the right to
reply argument in that case and argues that newspapers in particular enjoy broad immunity under the First Amendment from demands for access. He suggests, however, that the press has
an obligation to act in a responsible fashion.

Schroder, Theodore A. FREE SPEECH FOR RADICALS. 1916. Reprint.
New York: Burt Franklin, 1970.

This is a collection of early twentieth-century essays critical
of governmental interference with the constitutional guarantee of
free speech and press, including one essay on the "Method of
Constitutional Construction" prevalent prior to the absorption
of the First Amendment into the Fourteenth.

_____. "OBSCENE" LITERATURE AND CONSTITUTIONAL LAW: A FO-
RENSIC DEFENSE OF FREEDOM OF THE PRESS. 1911. Reprint. New
York: Da Capo Press, 1972.

This work argues that the First Amendment prohibits any governmental interference with obscene materials.

Schwartz, Bernard. THE GREAT RIGHTS OF MANKIND: A HISTORY OF
THE AMERICAN BILL OF RIGHTS. New York: Oxford University Press,
1977.

This work treats in narrative form the materials contained in
Schwartz's two-volume BILL OF RIGHTS: A DOCUMENTARY
HISTORY (below). Organized chronologically, it begins with
a discussion of the charters of English liberty, continues with
the colonial and revolutionary antecedents of the Bill of Rights
and discusses the movement that culminated in the adoption of
those constitutional amendments.

_____, ed. THE BILL OF RIGHTS: A DOCUMENTARY HISTORY. 2
vols. New York: Chelsea House in association with McGraw-Hill, 1971.

This is an extensive collection of documents relevant to the
liberties guaranteed in the Bill of Rights from Magna Carta to
ratification, each preceded by an introductory comment by the
editor. Volume 1 contains English and American documents prior
to the adoption of the Bill of Rights. Volume 2 contains materials
relevant to the proposal and ratification of the first ten amendments.

Seibert, Fred S., et al. FREE PRESS AND FAIR TRIAL: SOME DIMEN-
SIONS OF THE PROBLEM. Athens: University of Georgia Press, 1970.

This contains five brief reports on the findings of several studies designed to determine the relationship between jury verdicts in felony cases and pretrial publicity.

Shapiro, Martin W. FREEDOM OF SPEECH: THE SUPREME COURT AND JUDICIAL REVIEW. Englewood Cliffs, N.J.: Prentice-Hall, 1966. Reprint. Ann Arbor, Mich.: University Microfilms, 1974. Microfilm-xerography.

In this analysis of the role of the Court in American politics and in determining the boundaries of free speech, Shapiro examines the clear and present danger doctrine and the balancing test. He suggests that the conflict between the two is in reality a debate between the advocates of judicial restraint and the activists with the former using the balancing test as a means of abandoning judicial defense of the First Amendment.

_____, ed. THE PENTAGON PAPERS AND THE COURTS. San Francisco: Chandler, 1972.

This is a collection of papers, documents, and opinions related to the Pentagon papers controversy.

Sherwood, Margaret. "The Newsman's Privilege: Government Investigations, Criminal Prosecutions and Private Litigation." CALIFORNIA LAW REVIEW 58 (October 1970): 1198-1250.

Suggesting that efforts by governments at all three levels to force newsmen to reveal both their sources of information and the information itself are intensifying, this article examines the possible constitutional bases for challenging governmental power and urges judicial resolution of the conflict.

Sigler, Jay A. DOUBLE JEOPARDY: THE DEVELOPMENT OF A LEGAL AND SOCIAL POLICY. Ithaca, N.Y.: Cornell University Press, 1969.

This traces the history and development of the legal and social policy of double jeopardy in each of the states and in the nation and compares American policy with the practices in other countries.

Simon, Rita James, ed. THE JURY SYSTEM IN AMERICA: A CRITICAL OVERVIEW. Sage Criminal Justice System Annual Series. Beverly Hills, Calif.: Sage Publications, 1975.

This work examines the jury system from the perspectives of historians, political scientists, lawyers, judges, journalists, literary critics and jurors. The eleven essays deal with the history of the jury system, describe the research of behavioral scientists and convey the impressions of those professionally involved in the system.

Simons, Howard, and Califano, Joseph A., Jr., eds. THE MEDIA AND THE LAW. New York: Praeger Publishers, 1976.

Based on the transcript of a conference of judges, journalists and government officials sponsored by the WASHINGTON POST and the Ford Foundation, this is a discussion of the various areas in which the rights of the press come into conflict with

other rights and with legitimate government concerns such as
the right of privacy, the secrecy of grand jury proceedings and
the claims of national security.

Slough, M.C. PRIVACY, FREEDOM AND RESPONSIBILITY. Springfield,
III.: Charles C Thomas, 1969.

> This is an examination of the origins of the right to privacy in
> the English law protecting personal correspondence and in
> American consciousness with the publication in 1880 of the right
> to privacy article by Louis Brandeis and Samuel Warren in the
> HARVARD LAW REVIEW, and its evolution in American constitu-
> tional law in First and Fourteenth Amendment cases. It deals
> with such problems as administrative inspections, wiretapping,
> police interrogations, and with the general question of "order in
> a disobedient society."

Smith, James M. FREEDOM'S FETTERS: THE ALIEN AND SEDITION
LAW AND AMERICAN CIVIL LIBERTIES. Ithaca, N.Y.: Cornell University Press, 1956.

> In this work, the Alien and Sedition Act is viewed as an unwar-
> ranted infringement of individual rights, an expected manifestation
> of the intolerance and authoritarianism of Federalist rule.

Sorauf, Frank J. THE WALL OF SEPARATION: THE CONSTITUTIONAL
POLITICS OF CHURCH AND STATE. Princeton, N.J.: Princeton University Press, 1976.

> In this examination of sixty-seven establishment cases between
> 1951 and 1971, Sorauf focuses upon the individuals and groups
> involved, the plaintiffs, attorneys, and groups bringing the suit,
> their strategies and goals and their successes and failures rather
> than upon doctrinal development. He also looks at the trial and
> appellate judges involved.

Spinrad, William. CIVIL LIBERTY. Chicago: Quadrangle Books, 1970.

> This is an exploration of the characteristics of a society or of
> a particular historical period which accounts for the relative
> presence or absence of civil liberties. It examines civil liber-
> ties in a broad historical and sociological context, the role of
> the courts in protecting individual rights, the problems of the
> McCarthy era and of the mid-1960s and such continuing concerns
> as censorship and academic freedom.

Stein, Meyer L. FREEDOM OF THE PRESS: A CONTINUING STRUGGLE.
New York: Julian Messner, 1966.

> Intended for the general audience, this is a review of various
> aspects of the constitutional protection of newspapers, books
> and movies and of such problems as press ethics and the public's
> right to know.

Stephens, Otis H., Jr. THE SUPREME COURT AND CONFESSIONS OF
GUILT. Knoxville: University of Tennessee Press, 1973.

This is a study of the evolving involvement of the Supreme Court in confession cases from the earlier "fair trial" rule to the interventionism of <u>Miranda</u> in 1966.

Stevens, George E., and Webster, John B. LAW AND THE STUDENT PRESS. Ames: Iowa State University Press, 1973.

This work deals with the demands in the late 1960s and early 1970s for free expression in student publications and judicial response to these demands. It examines judicial decisions affecting high school, college and underground publications on such questions as censorship, libel, obscenity and contempt of court.

Tarr, George Alan. JUDICIAL IMPACT AND STATE SUPREME COURTS. Lexington, Mass.: D.C. Heath, 1977.

This is a comparative study of judicial responses to the Supreme Court's religion decisions. In attempting to determine the factors which account for compliance or noncompliance by state supreme courts, Tarr examines three possible answers: judicial backgrounds, the Neustadtian theory, and the state impact hypothesis.

Taylor, Telford. TWO STUDIES IN CONSTITUTIONAL INTERPRETATION: SEARCH, SEIZURE AND SURVEILLANCE AND FAIR TRIAL AND FREE PRESS. Columbus: Ohio State University Press, 1969.

These two essays are an expanded version of 1967 lectures at the College of Law of Ohio State. There is also a postscript to each essay adding important Supreme Court decisions in search and seizure decided after the lectures and noting the changes made by the American Bar Association in its recommendations regarding the fair trial, free press conflict.

Thayer, Frank. LEGAL CONTROL OF THE PRESS. 4th ed. Brooklyn, N.Y.: Foundation Press, 1969.

This general journalism work is a description of the law which protects and regulates the press. It deals with a wide variety of issues involving the legal rights and responsibilities of the press including libel, privacy and contempt of court.

Tinder, Glenn E. TOLERANCE: TOWARD A NEW CIVILITY. Amherst: University of Massachusetts, 1976.

This study of "tolerance of expression" examines the weaknesses of traditional arguments in support of free speech and sets forth new bases for tolerance leading toward civility in public discourse.

Torpey, William George. JUDICIAL DOCTRINES OF RELIGIOUS RIGHTS IN AMERICA. Chapel Hill: University of North Carolina Press, 1948.

Although out of date insofar as the status of judicial doctrines is concerned, this is a useful analysis of early common, statutory, and constitutional law in the colonies, states and nation and the use of national delegated powers and of states' police power to govern and/or affect religious belief and action.

Tussman, Joseph. GOVERNMENT AND THE MIND. New York: Oxford University Press, 1977.

> Although the Supreme Court view that the First Amendment pro-
> hibits governmental invasion of the spheres of the intellect and
> of the spirit appears to be plausible and obvious on the surface,
> Tussman argues that it is neither. In this exploration of the
> range of legitimate governmental concern with the mind, he
> examines what he calls the "politics of cognition" or the problem
> of awareness, the inherent constitutional power of government
> in education and its role in providing and protecting the forum of
> communication.

Ungar, Sanford J. THE PAPERS AND THE PAPERS: AN ACCOUNT OF THE LEGAL AND POLITICAL BATTLES OVER THE PENTAGON PAPERS. New York: E.P. Dutton and Co., 1972.

> Written by a WASHINGTON POST reporter who covered the
> government's case against the POST in the federal district court
> of the District of Columbia, this is an account of the Pentagon
> Papers case from the events leading up to the institution of
> litigation by the government to resolution of the conflict by the
> Supreme Court.

U.S. Congress. House. Committee on the Judiciary. PROPOSED AMEND-MENT TO THE CONSTITUTION RELATING TO SCHOOL PRAYERS. 88th Cong., 2d sess. Washington, D.C.: Government Printing Office, 1964.

> This is a staff study of the various proposals to amend the Con-
> stitution to overrule Supreme Court decisions prohibiting prayers
> in public schools.

_____. SCHOOL PRAYERS. HEARINGS. 88th Cong., 2d sess. Wash-ington, D.C.: Government Printing Office, 1964.

> These hearings were held to consider proposals to amend the
> Constitution to permit prayers in public schools.

U.S. Congress. Senate. Committee on the Judiciary. PRAYERS IN PUB-LIC SCHOOLS AND OTHER MATTERS. HEARINGS. 87th Cong., 2d sess. Washington, D.C.: Government Printing Office, 1962.

> These hearings were held in July and August of 1962 to consider
> the means and desirability of reversing the Supreme Court school
> prayer decisions.

Vreeland, Hamilton, Jr. TWILIGHT OF INDIVIDUAL LIBERTY. 1944. Reprint. New York: Arno Press, 1972.

> This is an analysis and criticism of national governmental regula-
> tion of business, regulations which the author contends exceed
> the powers delegated to the national government by the Constitu-
> tion.

Warren, Earl. A REPUBLIC, IF YOU CAN KEEP IT. New York: Quad-rangle Books, 1972.

This consists of some reflections by the former chief justice on various facets of individual freedom in civil society in general and the status and problems encountered in maintaining individual liberty in America from the creation of the nation to the 1970s.

Whisker, James B. OUR VANISHING FREEDOM: THE RIGHT TO KEEP AND BEAR ARMS. McLean, Va.: Heritage House, 1972.

Originally a Ph.D. thesis, this work argues that restrictions on the right to bear arms are associated with tyranny while protection of this right is associated with freedom. He criticizes civil libertarians for attempts to contract this right, the only guarantee of the Bill of Rights which they seek to narrow rather than to expand.

Williamson, Chilton. AMERICAN SUFFRAGE: FROM PROPERTY TO DEMOCRACY, 1760-1860. Princeton, N.J.: Princeton University Press, 1960.

This is a study of the removal of the first major barrier to voting and the institution of universal white manhood suffrage, a less controversial extension of the vote than its expansion to blacks and women.

Zelermyer, William. INVASION OF PRIVACY. Syracuse, N.Y.: Syracuse University Press, 1959.

Although two chapters of this work deal with privacy as an issue in public law, it is primarily an analysis of state judicial decisions in which the right of privacy developed as a right in tort law. It deals with invasions of privacy by advertisers, creditors, magazines, newspapers, books, motion pictures and wiretapping. There are no footnotes or case citations.

Chapter 11

THE CIVIL WAR AMENDMENTS

Adams, John Quincy. ARGUMENTS OF JOHN QUINCY ADAMS. BEFORE THE SUPREME COURT OF THE UNITED STATES, IN THE CASE OF THE UNITED STATES V. CINQUE AND OTHERS, AFRICANS, CAPTURED IN THE SCHOONER AMISTAD, BY LT. GEDNEY, DELIVERED ON THE 24TH OF FEBRUARY AND THE IST OF MARCH, 1841; WITH A REVIEW OF THE CASE OF THE ANTELOPE, REPORTED IN THE 10TH, 11TH, AND 12TH VOLUMES OF WHEATON'S REPORTS, 1841. Reprint. New York: Arno Press, 1969.

> After his presidency and during his tenure in the House of Representatives, Adams represented before the Supreme Court a group of black slaves who killed the captain and crew of a Spanish slave ship which was transporting them. This is a reprint of Adams's argument before the Supreme Court, an argument that came to be viewed as a classic legal attack upon slavery in the pre-Civil War period. He argued that the slave trade was illegal under Spanish law and in conflict with the natural rights of man. The slaves were ordered released by the Supreme Court.

Anderson, John W. EISENHOWER, BROWNELL, AND THE CONGRESS: THE TANGLED ORIGINS OF THE CIVIL RIGHTS BILL OF 1956-1957. Interuniversity Case Program Series. University: University of Alabama Press, 1964.

> This is a study of the unsuccessful attempt to pass a civil rights bill in 1956.

Avins, Alfred, ed. THE RECONSTRUCTION AMENDMENTS DEBATE: THE LEGISLATIVE HISTORY AND CONTEMPORARY DEBATES IN CONGRESS ON THE 13TH, 14TH AND 15TH AMENDMENTS. Richmond: Virginia Commission on Constitutional Government, 1967.

> This includes excerpts from congressional debates from 1849 to 1875 relevant to the Civil War amendments and civil rights legislation adopted by the Reconstruction congresses along with materials culled from such sources as committee reports.

Baker, Gordon E. THE REAPPORTIONMENT REVOLUTION: REPRESENTATION, POLITICAL POWER AND THE SUPREME COURT. New York: Random House, 1966.

> Written after the Supreme Court decision in Baker v. Carr and its 1964 opinions requiring equality in state legislatures, this is a study of reactions to and effects of those decisions. It also

The Civil War Amendments

examines the development of the notion of equality in representation, legislative refusal to reapportion, the resulting urban-
rural conflicts and the reassertion of the theory and practice
by the Court in the 1960s. Although outdated in terms of its
examination of effects of reapportionment, it is a useful study
of the problem of malapportionment to which the Court addressed
itself in the 1960s.

Bardolph, Richard, ed. THE CIVIL RIGHTS RECORD: BLACK AMERICANS
AND THE LAW, 1849-1970. New York: Thomas Y. Crowell, 1970.

Organized chronologically, this is an extensive collection of legal
materials--state, local and national legislation, administrative
actions, and judicial decisions, concerning race relations and
public law in the United States.

Bedau, Hugo A., ed. JUSTICE AND EQUALITY. Englewood Cliffs, N.J:
Prentice-Hall, 1971.

This consists of ten excerpts from the works of such thinkers
as Aristotle, Hobbes, and John Rawls, as well as of the editor,
on the question of the relationship between justice and equality.

Belz, Herman. A NEW BIRTH OF FREEDOM: THE REPUBLICAN PARTY
AND FREEDMEN'S RIGHTS, 1861-1866. Westport, Conn.: Greenwood
Press, 1977.

This is an analysis of the development of the constitutional and
legislative guarantee of equality in the tumultuous Civil War and
immediate postwar period. Against the background of attempts
by the Republican party to prevent Confederate use of slaves to
fight the war, a national policy of equality emerged. This work
examines the emancipation legislation, presidential and congressional policies on Reconstruction, the Freedmen's Bureau legislation, the Thirteenth Amendment and the 1866 civil rights settlement.

Berger, Monroe. EQUALITY BY STATUTE. New York: Columbia University Press, 1952.

This short work focuses upon state laws prohibiting racial discrimination. A shortened version was published by UNESCO in
1954 under the title of RACIAL EQUALITY AND THE LAW.

Berger, Raoul. GOVERNMENT BY JUDICIARY: THE TRANSFORMATION
OF THE FOURTEENTH AMENDMENT. Cambridge, Mass.: Harvard University Press, 1978.

This massive study of the intentions of the 39th Congress which
proposed the Fourteenth Amendment and of judicial interpretation
of that Amendment concludes that the Warren Court's application
in such areas as voting and education, for example, was much
broader than and in conflict with the comparatively narrow aims
of its framers and was thus a usurpation of power.

Berman, Daniel M. IT IS SO ORDERED: THE SUPREME COURT RULES
ON SCHOOL SEGREGATION. New York: W.W. Norton, 1966.

This is a study of Brown: the strategy of litigation, the lower court cases, the oral arguments before the Supreme Court, the Court's 1954 and 1955 opinions and the problems of implementation.

Bernstein, Barton J., ed. POLITICS AND POLICIES OF THE TRUMAN ADMINISTRATION. New York: New Viewpoints, 1970.

This collection of original essays on the Truman era includes works on the loyalty program instituted by the Truman adminis- tration in response to the McCarthy attacks and on the civil rights efforts of that administration.

Berry, Mary Frances. BLACK RESISTANCE/WHITE LAW: A HISTORY OF CONSTITUTIONAL RACISM IN AMERICA. New York: Appleton- Century-Crofts, 1971.

This is an analysis of the use and abuse of constitutional theory and practice to actively repress and to refuse national protection to blacks. The author argues that the theory of federalism coupled with the use, the threat to use, and the failure to use national military power legally sanctioned racial oppression and that law has been an instrument for maintaining a racist status quo.

Black, Earl. SOUTHERN GOVERNORS AND CIVIL RIGHTS: RACIAL SEGREGATION AS A CAMPAIGN ISSUE IN THE SECOND RECONSTRUC- TION. Cambridge, Mass.: Harvard University Press, 1976.

This is a study of the role of racial segregation as an issue in gubernatorial campaigns in the primaries, first and run-offs, and general elections in the South from 1950 through 1973 with empha- sis upon the era which began on 17 May 1954 with the Brown decision.

Blackstone, William T., and Heslep, Robert D., eds. SOCIAL JUSTICE AND PREFERENTIAL TREATMENT: WOMEN AND RACIAL MINORITIES IN EDUCATION AND BUSINESS. Athens: University of Georgia Press, 1977.

This is a collection of ten papers, most of which were presented at a conference at the University of Georgia at which scholars met to discuss the moral and legal aspects of discrimination and of preferential treatment of women and minority racial and ethnic groups in the academic and professional worlds.

Blaustein, Albert P., and Ferguson, Clarence C. DESEGREGATION AND THE LAW. 2d rev. ed. New York: Vintage Books, 1962.

This work focuses upon the efforts of the southern states to defy, circumvent, and delay the Supreme Court's public school segre- gation decision of 1954.

Blaustein, Albert P., and Zangrando, Robert L., eds. CIVIL RIGHTS AND THE BLACK AMERICANS: A DOCUMENTARY HISTORY. New York: Simon and Schuster, 1970.

Originally published in 1968 under the title CIVIL RIGHTS AND THE AMERICAN NEGRO, this is a collection of excerpts from ninety-eight documents relating to race relations from 1618 attitudes toward slavery to the 1968 Kerner Commission report on urban riots.

Blumberg, Abraham S., ed. THE SCALES OF JUSTICE. 2d ed. New Brunswick, N.J.: Transaction Books, 1973.

This collection of thirteen essays, which originally appeared in TRANSACTION/SOCIETY magazine, examines a variety of legal issues such as pornography and lawyers for the poor.

Bolner, James. RACIAL IMBALANCE IN PUBLIC SCHOOLS: A BASIC ANNOTATED BIBLIOGRAPHY. Baton Rouge: Louisiana State University Institute of Governmental Research, 1968.

This annotated bibliography is organized alphabetically by author.

Bolner, James, and Shanley, Robert. BUSING: THE POLITICAL AND JUDICIAL PROCESS. New York: Praeger, 1975.

This is an examination of busing in terms of the constitutional context and the way in which courts have dealt with the issue (the Richmond, Detroit, and Denver cases are treated in some detail), the role of the controversy in the presidential campaigns of 1964, 1968, and 1972 and the presidential and congressional reactions to court-ordered busing. State and local politics and the community conflicts produced by busing are covered in less detail.

Bork, Robert H. CONSTITUTIONALITY OF THE PRESIDENT'S BUSING PROPOSALS. Washington, D.C.: American Enterprise Institute for Public Policy Research, 1972.

This brief paper examines the constitutionality of the Student Transportation Moratorium Act and the Equal Education Opportunity Act which President Nixon proposed to Congress in 1972. There is also a brief general discussion of the power of Congress to regulate busing. The appendix includes the texts of the two proposals examined.

Brauer, Carl M. JOHN F. KENNEDY AND THE SECOND RECONSTRUC-TION. New York: Columbia University Press, 1977.

Originally a Ph.D. thesis and based in large part on the archives and oral histories in the Kennedy library, this study of Kennedy's civil rights record suggests that while he started as a moderate indifferent to strong national action and did little to advance equality in the early phase of his presidency, he became an activist who spearheaded the "second Reconstruction."

Brisbane, Robert H. THE BLACK VANGUARD: ORIGINS OF THE NEGRO SOCIAL REVOLUTION. Valley Forge, Pa.: Judson Press, 1970.

This is a historical account of the development of black leadership from Dubois, the NAACP and other groups and individuals
viewed by the author as "the first militants" to the "new militants"
of the 1960s.

Burgess, John W. RECONSTRUCTION AND THE CONSTITUTION, 1866–
1876. 1902. Reprint. Port Washington, N.Y.: Kennikat, 1971.

This analysis of the Reconstruction era argues that the national
decision to give political power to blacks rather than to return
power to loyal whites and to afford national protection of individual liberty was an erroneous policy of punishment. The
author suggests that the Hayes policy of returning power to
whites in the South was both the correct policy and the only
policy that could have brought about reconciliation between the
former rebels and the unionists.

Burke, Joan Martin. CIVIL RIGHTS: A CURRENT GUIDE TO THE PEOPLE,
ORGANIZATIONS AND EVENTS. A CBS News Reference Book. New York:
R.R. Bowker, 1974.

This is an alphabetized list of the names, along with the addresses
and background material on leading civil rights figures and private
civil rights groups. The one hundred-page appendixes include
the voting records of individual congressmen on civil rights acts
from 1957 through 1970; the names and addresses of state and
federal governmental agencies with civil rights responsibilities
(organized alphabetically by state); a civil rights chronology
from 1954 to 1974; leading black public officials as of April,
1973; and civil rights informational sources (such as library
collections of papers and documents) organized by state.

Byrson, Conrey. DR. LAWRENCE A. NIXON AND THE WHITE PRIMARY.
El Paso, Tex.: Western Press, 1974.

This monograph is a study of the efforts of a black physician
to vote in the Texas Democratic Party primary, efforts which
led to the invalidation of the white primary in Nixon v. Herndon
and Nixon v. Condon. It also discusses Grovey v. Townsend in
which the Supreme Court upheld the party's exclusion of blacks
from its primaries.

Carmichael, Robert A. THE SOUTH AND SEGREGATION. Washington,
D.C.: Public Affairs Press, 1965.

This is an attack upon the Supreme Court's decision in Brown
which the author believes precipitated worsening relations between blacks and whites in the South and which he views as a
usurpation of power by the Court.

Carr, Robert K. FEDERAL PROTECTION OF CIVIL RIGHTS: QUEST
FOR A SWORD. 1947. Reprint. Ithaca, N.Y.: Cornell University Press,
1964.

This is a study of the Civil Rights Section of the Justice Department during the Truman administration and its resurrection of the
remnants of Reconstruction legislation enacted to afford national
protection of civil rights.

Catterall, Helen T. JUDICIAL CASES CONCERNING SLAVERY AND THE NEGRO. 5 vols. Washington, D.C.: Carnegie Institution of Washington, 1926-37. Reprint. New York: Octagon, 1968.

> This is an extensive collection of opinions dealing with the myriad of issues arising out of the existence of slavery and conflicting laws and attitudes toward the institution and the status of blacks and slaves.

CIVIL RIGHTS AND THE SOUTH: A SYMPOSIUM. New York: Da Capo Press, 1971.

> This is a collection of papers, originally published in the NORTH CAROLINA LAW REVIEW 42 (December 1963), delivered by various scholars and public officials, some of whom advocated further national protection of civil rights and some of whom argued that further national action was constitutionally and politically defective.

Claude, Richard P. "Nationalizing Electoral Process Standards: Is An Obituary for States' Rights Premature?" IDAHO LAW REVIEW 13 (Summer 1977): 373-402.

> By the author of THE SUPREME COURT AND THE ELECTORAL PROCESS, this article analyzes four instruments of nationalization of the electoral process (constitutional amendment, Supreme Court decisions, congressional legislation, and the Federal Election Commission) and explores the question of what electoral power is left for the states.

Cobb, Thomas R. AN INQUIRY INTO THE LAW OF NEGRO SLAVERY IN THE UNITED STATES OF AMERICA, TO WHICH IS PREFIXED AN HISTORICAL SKETCH OF SLAVERY. 1858. Reprint. New York: Negro Universities Press, 1968.

> This is a massive review of laws governing slavery in ancient governments and in the middle ages as well as in the United States. Its primary concern is slavery in the United States and the laws in the states defining the status, rights, and dis- abilities of slaves. It also examines the abolition of slavery in other countries and in some of the states of the United States before the Civil War.

Commager, Henry Steele, ed. A STRUGGLE FOR RACIAL EQUALITY: A DOCUMENTARY RECORD. Gloucester, Mass.: Peter Smith, 1972.

> This collection of excerpts from thirty-eight documents includes such materials as Gunnar Myrdal's AN AMERICAN DILEMMA, the Civil War amendments, speeches by Frederick Douglass, Booker T. Washington, and Stokely Carmichael, Truman's orders creating the Civil Rights Commission, the text of the Southern Manifesto, and Johnson's message urging passage of the Voting Rights Act of 1965.

THE COMPLETE SUPREME COURT BAKKE ARCHIVE. New York: Law Reprints, 1978. Microfiche.

This contains all of the documents, including all of the briefs and arguments, in the case of Regents of the University of California v. Bakke. These records are also contained in volumes 99 and 100 of LANDMARK BRIEFS AND RECORDS edited by Philip B. Kurland and Gerhard Casper (see p. 201).

CONFERENCE ON MILLIKEN V. BRADLEY: THE IMPLICATIONS FOR METROPOLITAN DESEGREGATION. Washington, D.C.: Commission on Civil Rights, 1975.

The lower court opinion in Milliken was one of the early attempts to use metropolitan consolidation as a remedy for school segregation. This conference was called to deal with the effects of such a remedy.

"Congressional Power Under the Civil War Amendments." DUKE LAW JOURNAL, October 1969, pp. 1247-84.

This comment examines judicial expansion of congressional power derived from the Thirteenth, Fourteenth, and Fifteenth Amendments in Jones v. Mayer, Katzenbach v. Morgan and South Carolina v. Katzenback against a background of the post-Civil War contraction of the amendments and the beginning of a more expansive interpretation in the 1950s.

Congressional Quarterly Service. CIVIL RIGHTS PROGRESS REPORT. Washington, D.C.: 1970.

This is a review of civil rights developments from 1968 to 1970, with a background chapter on the period from 1948 to 1968. It covers such issues as the Haynsworth-Carswell controversy and the Court's decisions on busing and racial balance.

_____. REVOLUTION IN CIVIL RIGHTS. Washington, D.C.: 1968.

This is a review of civil rights developments from post-World War II to 1968.

Cook, Lady Tennessee Celeste. CONSTITUTIONAL EQUALITY: A RIGHT OF WOMAN. 1871. Reprint. Westport, Conn.: Hyperion Press, 1976.

Written by a nineteenth-century feminist and sister of Victoria Woodhull, this work is an impassioned argument in support of the proposition that the Constitution and the newly adopted Fourteenth Amendment prohibit the state from withholding from women the basic rights guaranteed to men.

Cortner, Richard C. THE APPORTIONMENT CASES. Knoxville: University of Tennessee Press, 1970.

Baker v. Carr and Reynolds v. Sims are used to examine the questions of judicial enunciation and implementation of public policy, the weaknesses and strengths of this judicial role and the emergence of the constitutional guarantee of equality. The author also compares the apportionment and segregation cases and discusses group pressure through litigation, in this case "litigating coalitions," that is, ad hoc alliances of individuals and groups who join together for the performance of one specific task.

Cover, Robert M. JUSTICE ACCUSED: ANTISLAVERY AND THE JUDI-
CIAL PROCESS. New Haven, Conn.: Yale University Press, 1975.

> This is an attack upon judges, the American system of justice
> and courts for their complicity in antebellum slavery and an
> analysis of the legal traditions, language and principles in which
> pre-Civil War law was steeped and which allowed judges to avoid
> striking down an oppressive system.

Cox, Archibald; Howe, Mark De Wolfe; and Wiggins, J.R. CIVIL RIGHTS,
THE CONSTITUTION AND THE COURTS. Cambridge, Mass.: Harvard
University Press, 1967.

> This slim volume contains three papers delivered by the authors
> to the Massachusetts Historical Society. Cox discusses "Di-
> rect Action, Civil Disobedience and the Constitution." Howe
> deals with "Federalism and Civil Rights." Higgins examines
> "The Press and the Courts."

De Santis, Vincent P. REPUBLICANS FACE THE SOUTHERN QUESTION:
THE NEW DEPARTURE YEARS, 1877–1897. Baltimore: Johns Hopkins
Press, 1959. Reprint. Westport, Conn.: Greenwood Press, 1969.

> This study of Republican policy and strategies in the South in
> the twenty years from the formal end of Reconstruction to the
> election of 1896 suggests that in these years there was a dis-
> tinct break with the past that established the basis for the lily-
> white movement of the 1920s.

Dillon, Merton L. THE ABOLITIONISTS: THE GROWTH OF A DISSENT-
ING MINORITY. DeKalb: Northern Illinois University Press, 1974.

> This is a history of the ideas and activities of the abolitionists.

Dixon, Robert G., Jr. DEMOCRATIC REPRESENTATION: REAPPORTION-
MENT IN LAW AND POLITICS. New York: Oxford University Press, 1968.

> Taking the view that the "one man, one vote" principle is too
> simplistic as a theory of representation because it is interests
> common to groups of individuals rather than to individuals as
> such that are represented in legislative bodies, this extensive
> work examines representation theories and practices. It examines
> traditional representation theories of Hobbes, Locke and Burke,
> the American traditions as represented by Madison and Jackson,
> the practices in the states from statehood to Baker v. Carr, the
> apportionment cases of 1964, the apportionment efforts following
> the 1964 cases, the Dirksen amendment attempts to ameliorate
> the population egalitarianism of judicial decisions and the impact
> of the "one man, one vote" principle of representation.

Dulles, Foster Rhea. THE CIVIL RIGHTS COMMISSION, 1957–1965. East
Lansing: Michigan State University Press, 1968.

> This is a history of the organization and work of the Civil Rights
> Commission from its creation in 1957 to 1965. It examines the
> Commissions' investigations, its reports and recommendations for
> legislation. The emphasis is upon its first report in 1959 and
> its second report in 1961.

Eidenberg, Eugene, and Morey, Roy D. AN ACT OF CONGRESS: THE LEGISLATIVE PROCESS AND THE MAKING OF EDUCATIONAL POLICY. New York: W.W. Norton, 1969.

> Although primarily a case study of the passage of the Elementary and Secondary Education Act of 1965 from a legislative process, not a constitutional perspective, this examination of the enactment of the legislation and of the period to 1967 is relevant to the problem of implementation of the egalitarian promise of the Civil War amendments. When the administration joined the 1965 education act with the 1964 Civil Rights Act prohibition against federal funding of discriminatory programs, the desegregation which began with the 1954 public school segregation case accelerated.

Elliott, Ward E.Y. THE RISE OF GUARDIAN DEMOCRACY: THE SUPREME COURT'S ROLE IN VOTING RIGHTS DISPUTES, 1845-1968. Cambridge, Mass.: Harvard University Press, 1974.

> This is a criticism of the Warren Court's reapportionment role and of the Guardian Ethnic--the mystique of standardization, expertise, crisis and progress--which played a predominant role in intellectuals' reformist thought in the modern era. Elliott argues that the Court's entrance into voting rights disputes in the 1940s and in Smith v. Allwright in particular was a triumph of equality of practice over equality in form whereas its reapportionment opinions, such as in Reynolds, was a triumph of equality in form over equality in practice and that reapportionment has contributed little but disruption.

Fairman, Charles, and Morrison, Stanley. THE FOURTEENTH AMENDMENT AND THE BILL OF RIGHTS: THE INCORPORATION THEORY. Introduction by Leonard W. Levy. New York: Da Capo Press, 1970.

> This work includes the Court's opinion in Adamson v. California along with the Black dissent insisting that the due process clause incorporated the Bill of Rights; a reprint of Fairman's article entitled "Does the Fourteenth Amendment Incorporate the Bill of Rights? The Original Understanding"; Morrison's article entitled "Does the Fourteenth Amendment Incorporate the Bill of Rights? The Judicial Intrepretation"; and the Supreme Court's opinion in Duncan v. Louisiana. Both articles appeared originally in the STANFORD LAW REVIEW (December 1949).

Fisher, Sidney G. THE TRIAL OF THE CONSTITUTION. 1862. Reprint. New York: Negro Universities Press, 1969.

> Written shortly before and during the Civil War and thus touched by some of the burning issues of that day such as secession, slavery, and presidential power, this is an analysis of the nature of written constitutions in general and of the nature of the American Constitution in particular. Attached as an appendix and written at the time of Lincoln's Emancipation Proclamation is a brief analysis of presidential authority to free the slaves in the rebellious states.

Flack, Horace E. THE ADOPTION OF THE FOURTEENTH AMENDMENT. Baltimore: Johns Hopkins University Press, 1908.

This is a historical study of the intent of the framers of the
Fourteenth Amendment.

Franklin, John Hope. RACIAL EQUALITY IN AMERICA. Chicago: University of Chicago Press, 1976.

Originally delivered as the 1976 Jefferson Lecture for the
National Endowment for the Humanities, this work examines the
American tradition of inequality. In the first, Franklin deals
with the revolutionary era and the willingness of that generation
to ignore racial equality. In the second, he finds the devotion
of abolitionists to equality shallow. In the third, he suggests
that twentieth-century Americans still view equality as divisible
and argues that the task facing the present generation is to view
equality as indivisible.

Friedman, Leon, ed. ARGUMENT: THE ORAL ARGUMENTS BEFORE THE
SUPREME COURT IN BROWN V. BOARD OF EDUCATION OF TOPEKA,
1952–1955. New York: Chelsea House, 1969.

This is a complete record of the oral arguments in Brown from
its beginning in 1952 through its redocketing with attorneys for
both sides asked to argue the question of implementation which
resulted in the 1955 "deliberate speed" order.

Friendly, Henry J. THE DARTMOUTH COLLEGE CASE AND THE PUBLIC-
PRIVATE PENUMBRA. Austin: University of Texas at Austin, 1968.

Originally delivered in 1968 at Dartmouth's celebration of the
sesquicentennial of Webster's argument before the Supreme Court
in the Dartmouth College case and published as a supplement to
volume 12 of the TEXAS QUARTERLY, this lecture examines the
question of the extent to which the Fourteenth Amendment applies
to "private" institutions such as Dartmouth.

Gerteis, Louis S. FROM CONTRABAND TO FREEDMAN: FEDERAL POLICY
TOWARD SOUTHERN BLACKS, 1861–1865. Contributions in American
History. Westport, Conn.: Greenwood Press, 1973.

This study of national policy toward blacks beginning in 1861
when Union forces occupied portions of Virginia and South
Carolina argues that decisions made during the war shaped postwar policies and precluded effective social changes in the status
of blacks despite formal legal and constitutional protections.

Gillette, William. THE RIGHT TO VOTE: POLITICS AND THE PASSAGE
OF THE FIFTEENTH AMENDMENT. Baltimore: Johns Hopkins University
Press, 1965.

In contrast to the more general view that the Fifteenth Amendment,
like the Fourteenth, was aimed primarily at the South, this work
argues that the Fifteenth was designed by political moderates to
confer the right to vote on northern blacks.

Ginger, Ann Fagan, ed. DE FUNIS V. ODEGAARD: THE UNIVERSITY
ADMISSIONS CASE. 3 vols. Dobbs Ferry, N.Y.: Oceana, 1974.

Prepared for the Council on Legal Education Opportunity (CLEO), this contains the full record of the first case accepted by the Supreme Court dealing with the problem of "reverse discrimination." Volume 1 contains the records of the state courts, petitions for certiorari and motions for leave to file amicus curiae briefs. Volumes 2 and 3 contain the briefs filed with the Supreme Court and the majority, concurring and dissenting opinions.

Glazer, Nathan. AFFIRMATIVE DISCRIMINATION: ETHNIC INEQUALITY AND PUBLIC POLICY. New York: Basic Books, 1976.

This is an analysis of and attack upon the basic idea and methods of affirmative action requirements imposed by the judiciary and other governmental agencies in an attempt to rectify racial and ethnic discrimination that violated constitutional prohibitions and egalitarian principles.

Goldwin, Robert A., ed. REPRESENTATION AND MISREPRESENTATION: LEGISLATIVE REAPPORTIONMENT IN THEORY AND PRACTICE. Chicago: Rand McNally, 1968.

These eight essays, by political scientists who take differing views of the propriety of judicially ordered reapportionment, deal with such matters as reapportionment before Baker v. Carr, the distinction between political and judicial questions, the problems stemming from judicially constructed reapportionment standards, the techniques of reapportionment, congressional reaction to reapportionment cases and the fight over and defeat of the Dirksen amendment to overrule the Reynolds holding that both houses of a state legislature must be based on population.

Graglia, Lino A. DISASTER BY DECREE: SUPREME COURT DECISIONS ON RACE AND THE SCHOOLS. Ithaca, N.Y.: Cornell University Press, 1977.

This is an analysis of judicial decisions in the area of educational desegregation and a criticism of judicially devised remedies designed to implement substantive constitutional rights, particularly the controversial busing remedy.

Graham, Gene. ONE MAN, ONE VOTE: BAKER V. CARR AND THE AMERICAN LEVELLERS. Boston: Little, Brown, 1972.

In this popular account of the apportionment controversy in Tennessee, Baker v. Carr is examined in terms of the actors in that political drama: the plaintiffs, defendant, judges.

Graham, Howard Jay. "The 'Conspiracy Theory' of the Fourteenth Amendment." YALE LAW JOURNAL 47 (January 1938): 371-403.

This examination or reexamination of the socalled "conspiracy theory," the theory that the framers of the Fourteenth Amendment intended the due process and equal protection clauses to protect business interests, is an attempt to determine the basis for and the validity of that theory. The author examines Roscoe Conkling's arguments before the Supreme Court in 1883 in San Mateo v. Southern Pacific in which it was asserted that the committee which drafted the amendment intended to protect corporations, the con-

gressional debates in 1866 and three of Congressman Bingham's
speeches in 1856, in 1857 and in 1859 on due process. This
article is reprinted in several collections of essays on constitutional law including volume 1 of SELECTED ESSAYS ON CON-
STITUTIONAL LAW (see p. 79).

_____. EVERYMAN'S CONSTITUTION: HISTORICAL ESSAYS ON THE
FOURTEENTH AMENDMENT, THE "CONSPIRACY THEORY" AND AMERICAN
CONSTITUTIONALISM. Foreword by Leonard Levy. Madison: State His-
torical Society of Wisconsin, 1968.

This is a collection of fourteen of Graham's essays on the Fourteenth Amendment, including a reprint of his famous article on the
"conspiracy theory." Also included are such essays as "Justice
Field and the Fourteenth Amendment," "The Early Antislavery
Background of the Fourteenth Amendment," "Procedure to Substance: Extra-Judicial Rise of Due Process, 1830-1860," "Crosskey's Constitution: An Archeological Blue-Print," and "The
Waite Court and the Fourteenth Amendment."

Greenberg, Jack. RACE RELATIONS AND AMERICAN LAW. New York:
Columbia University Press, 1959.

Written after the 1954 Brown case and the Civil Rights Act of
1957 but before the outpouring of national civil rights legislation
in voting, housing, public accommodations and employment in the
1960s, this is a study of state and federal laws on race relations
as they existed in the late 1950s. It covers public accommodations,
interstate travel, elections, employment, education, property,
criminal law, domestic law and the military. Included in the
appendix are citations to state laws requiring and prohibiting
racial discrimination.

Gross, Barry R., ed. REVERSE DISCRIMINATION. Buffalo, N.Y.:
Prometheus Books, 1977.

This is a collection of excerpts from thirty-two sources--Supreme
Court decisions, briefs presented to the Court, and scholarly
books and articles--dealing with the facts, laws, and values of
preferential treatment as a means of redressing past discrimination.
Included are excerpts from such materials as Douglas's dissent
in DeFunis, Nathan Glazer's argument against affirmative discrimination from the periodical PUBLIC INTEREST, and Archibald Cox's amicus curiae brief in DeFunis.

Guthrie, William G. LECTURES ON THE FOURTEENTH ARTICLE OF AMEND-
MENT TO THE CONSTITUTION OF THE UNITED STATES. 1898. Reprint.
New York: Da Capo Press, 1970.

The first of these four lectures on the Fourteenth Amendment
examines the factors leading to its adoption, congressional intent
with regard to each of its provisions and late nineteenth-century
judicial interpretations in such cases as the Slaughterhouse Cases
and the Civil Rights Cases which narrowed the protection afforded.
The other lectures deal with judicial interpretation of the due
process and equal protection clauses and such questions as federal
judicial interpretation.

Hamilton, Charles V. THE BENCH AND THE BALLOT: SOUTHERN FEDERAL
JUDGES AND BLACK VOTERS. New York: Oxford University Press, 1973.

This is an account of the role of federal judges at the district
and court of appeals levels in advancing and retarding the effort
to lower racial barriers to voting in the six-year period before
Congress and the executive branch became extensively involved
in protecting the right to vote with the passage of the Voting
Rights Act of 1965, a period when civil rights forces relied
primarily on the judiciary to protect the rights of blacks.

Hamilton, Howard, ed. LEGISLATIVE APPORTIONMENT: KEY TO POWER.
New York: Harper and Row, 1964.

This is a collection of essays which deal with such facets of
apportionment as malapportionment and the power of rural areas
prior to judicially ordered reapportionment, reapportionment cases
in national and state courts from Colegrove to Baker, the impact
of Baker and reapportionment standards and procedures.

Harris, Robert J. THE QUEST FOR EQUALITY: THE CONSTITUTION,
CONGRESS AND THE SUPREME COURT. Baton Rouge: Louisiana State
University Press, 1960.

Originally delivered as the 1959 Edward Douglass White Lectures
at Louisiana State University, this study of the theory of equality
examines its roots in Greco-Roman thought, its developments in
Christian theology and natural law, and focuses upon its emergence
as a constitutionally and legislatively protected right in the Reconstruction era and judicial interpretation of the equal protection
clause in race relations cases.

Harvey, James C. CIVIL RIGHTS DURING THE KENNEDY ADMINISTRA-
TION. Hattiesburg: University and College Press of Mississippi, 1971.

This is an analysis of the civil rights record of the Kennedy
administration.

Higginbotham, A. Leon, Jr. IN THE MATTER OF COLOR: RACE AND
THE AMERICAN LEGAL PROCESS. THE COLONIAL PERIOD. New York:
Oxford University Press, 1978.

This first of a projected four-volume study of the law of slavery
by a United States circuit judge examines the legal underpinnings
of slavery in the colonies of Virginia, Massachusetts, New York,
South Carolina, Georgia, and Pennsylvania.

Hollander, Barnett. SLAVERY IN AMERICA. New York: Barnes and
Noble, 1964.

This is a collection of brief excerpts from official documents,
judicial decisions, statutes, newspaper editorials and census
figures dealing with the introduction, growth, regulation and
finally state and national constitutional abolition of slavery and
the post-Civil War national legislation protecting the rights of
blacks.

Howard, Benjamin C. REPORT OF THE DECISION OF THE SUPREME
COURT OF THE UNITED STATES AND THE OPINIONS OF THE JUDGES
THEREOF IN THE CASE OF DRED SCOTT VERSUS JOHN F.A. SAND-
FORD. DECEMBER TERM, 1856. Washington, D.C.: Cornelius Wendell, 1857.
Reprint. New York: Da Capo Press, 1970.

> This is a separately bound volume of the entire 239 pages of the
> majority, concurring and dissenting opinions in the Dred Scott
> case.

Hyman, Harold M. NEW FRONTIERS OF THE AMERICAN RECONSTRUC-
TION. Urbana: University of Illinois Press, 1966.

> Originally presented at a 1965 Reconstruction Conference called
> to provide a forum for scholarly reevaluation of the Reconstruction
> era, the five essays here reprinted, along with comments by
> panelists on the papers, deal with various constitutional and
> political facets of that period. Included are Harold M. Hyman's
> "Reconstruction and Political-Constitutional Institutions—the
> Popular Expressions," John Hope Franklin's "Reconstruction and
> the Negro," and C. Vann Woodward's "Seeds of Failure in Radical
> Race Policy."

Ianniello, Lynne, ed. MILESTONES ALONG THE MARCH: TWELVE HIS-
TORIC CIVIL RIGHTS DOCUMENTS FROM WORLD WAR II TO SELMA.
Introduction by John P. Roche. New York: Frederick A. Praeger, 1965.

> With an introductory note to each document by the editor, this con-
> tains such "milestones" as Franklin D. Roosevelt's 1941 executive
> order creating a Fair Employment Practices Committee, Harry S.
> Truman's executive orders establishing the Committee on Civil
> Rights and desegregating the armed services, Supreme Court de-
> cisions in Shelley and Brown, the Civil Rights Act of 1957 and
> 1964 and speeches by John F. Kennedy and Lyndon B. Johnson.

James, Joseph B. THE FRAMING OF THE FOURTEENTH AMENDMENT.
Urbana: University of Illinois Press, 1956.

> This is a historical analysis of the intentions of the framers
> of the Fourteenth Amendment.

Kendrick, Benjamin B. THE JOURNAL OF THE JOINT COMMITTEE OF
FIFTEEN ON RECONSTRUCTION, THIRTY-NINTH CONGRESS, 1865-1867.
New York: Columbia University Press, 1914.

> More than a reprint of the journal of the committee which was
> largely responsible for the Fourteenth Amendment, this work
> is a study of the history of the committee and its work. In
> addition to the journal, which is reprinted in part I, this work
> includes biographical sketches of the members of the committee,
> analyzes the reasons for and development of the Fourteenth Amend-
> ment from introduction to passage as well as the evolution of
> civil rights legislation, and documents the committee's battles
> with the president.

King, Donald B., and Quick, Charles W., eds. LEGAL ASPECTS OF THE
CIVIL RIGHTS MOVEMENT. Detroit: Wayne State University Press, 1965.

This volume contains fifteen essays, each by a different scholar, dealing with various substantive issues involved in the civil rights movement: education, transportation, voting, employment, public accommodations, housing, justice and association.

Klein, Herbert S. SLAVERY IN THE AMERICAS: A COMPARATIVE STUDY OF VIRGINIA AND CUBA. New York: New Viewpoints, 1967.

This is a comparative study of the system of slavery in Virginia and Cuba, including a comparative study of the different legal structures in the two jurisdictions.

Kluger, Richard. SIMPLE JUSTICE: THE STORY OF BROWN V. BOARD OF EDUCATION AND BLACK AMERICA'S STRUGGLE FOR EQUALITY. New York: Knopf, 1976.

This is a massive, in-depth analysis of the history of the Court's decision in the public school segregation case and of the struggle for racial equality in the United States.

Konvitz, Milton R., and Leskes, Theodore. A CENTURY OF CIVIL RIGHTS, WITH A STUDY OF STATE LAWS AGAINST DISCRIMINATION. New York: Columbia University Press, 1961.

This analysis of civil rights since the Civil War focuses upon national and state legislation designed to combat racial discrimination in education, housing, public accommodations and employment. Written prior to the enactment of the most significant national legislation in the 1960s, this work is valuable not only for its study of state law but for its analysis of Reconstruction legislation, legislation which continues to serve an important role in civil rights particularly since the Supreme Court's revitalization of this old legislation in the 1960s.

_____. EXPANDING LIBERTIES. New York: Viking Press, 1966-67.

Part 1 deals with the First Amendment freedoms. Part 2 focuses upon civil rights and the Supreme Court's role in enlarging and protecting racial equality.

Kutler, Stanley F., ed. THE DRED SCOTT DECISION: LAW OR POLITICS? Boston: Houghton Mifflin Co., 1967.

With an introduction by the editor, this is a selection of contemporary materials related to the Dred Scott case. In addition to excerpts from the opinions of Chief Justice Taney and of Justices Nelson and Curtis, excerpts from editorial reactions (Republican and Democratic) to the decision are included as are the views expressed by various political figures of the day (portions of the Lincoln-Douglas debates, for example), of judges and of congressmen. One chapter includes more recent scholarly assessments of the decision--Edward S. Corwin and Wallace Mendelson, for example.

Lawson, Steven F. BLACK BALLOTS: VOTING RIGHTS IN THE SOUTH, 1944-1969. New York: Columbia University Press, 1976.

This is a study of the responses of legal and political institutions in the post-World War II period to demands that the Fifteenth Amendment be implemented.

Levinsohn, Florence H., and Wright, Benjamin D., eds. SCHOOL DESEGRE-GATION: SHADOW OR SUBSTANCE? Chicago: University of Chicago Press, 1977.

These thirteen essays by scholars of and/or participants in desegregation, written for the May 1976 issue of SCHOOL REVIEW in response to the question "Is School Desegregation Still a Good Idea," examine the effects, techniques and process of desegregation and the roles of academic research and TV coverage. Each concluded that desegregation is a worthy goal and some suggest more effective and less agonizing means to that end.

Levy, Leonard W., and Jones, Douglas L., eds. JIM CROW IN BOSTON: THE ORIGIN OF THE SEPARATE BUT EQUAL DOCTRINE. New York: Da Capo Press, 1974.

With an introduction by the editors relating Roberts to Plessy, this is a collection of documents surrounding the case of Roberts v. City of Boston in which the Massachusetts judiciary upheld the validity of the separate but equal doctrine. It contains such documents as reports and petitions to abolish separate schools for blacks, the arguments of Charles Sumner against segregation in the Roberts case, the state court's opinion and the 1855 Massachusetts legislation forbidding segregation.

Lewinson, Paul. RACE, CLASS AND PARTY: A HISTORY OF NEGRO SUFFRAGE AND WHITE POLITICS IN THE SOUTH. New York: Oxford University Press, 1932. Reprint. New York: Russell and Russell, 1963.

This is a study of the interaction between the racial question and the white class and party struggle in the South. Part 1 examines the period of slavery, emancipation, and the disfranchisement movement of 1890 to 1908. Part 2 deals with the operation of the disfranchising constitutions to 1930.

McCord, John H., ed. WITH ALL DELIBERATE SPEED: CIVIL RIGHTS THEORY AND PRACTICE. Urbana: University of Illinois Press, 1969.

This collection of six papers presented at a symposium on the progress or lack of progress of the civil rights movement in the 1960s examines such matters as the Public Accommodations Act of 1964, equal educational opportunity for blacks, and the role of legal institutions in civil rights.

McKay, Robert B. REAPPORTIONMENT: THE LAW AND POLITICS OF EQUAL REPRESENTATION. New York: Simon and Schuster, 1966.

In these eight essays, McKay analyzes the 1964 Supreme Court apportionment standard of "one man, one vote" and subsequent attempts in each of the states to apportion its congressional districts.

McPherson, Edward. THE POLITICAL HISTORY OF THE UNITED STATES OF AMERICA DURING THE PERIOD OF RECONSTRUCTION, APRIL 15, 1865-1870; INCLUDING A CLASSIFIED SUMMARY OF THE LEGISLATION OF THE THIRTY-NINTH, FORTIETH, AND FORTY-FIRST CONGRESSES WITH THE VOTES THEREON: TOGETHER WITH THE ACTION, CONGRESSIONAL AND STATE, ON THE FOURTEENTH AND FIFTEENTH AMENDMENTS TO THE CONSTITUTION OF THE UNITED STATES AND OTHER IMPORTANT EXECUTIVE, LEGISLATIVE, POLITICO-MILITARY, AND JUDICIAL FACTS OF THAT PERIOD. 1871. Reprint. Introduction by Harold M. Hyman and Hans L. Trefousse. New York: Da Capo Press, 1972.

> The introduction details McPherson's role and influence as an elected and appointed public official, as journalist and as author of successive editions of the POLITICAL MANUAL, beginning in 1866 and culminating in the 1871 edition of this reprint. This POLITICAL HISTORY contains such basic source materials on the post-Civil War period as the reports of the various congressional committees on Reconstruction legislation, on the Civil War amendments, and on congressional debate on these subjects. It also includes copies of the civil rights acts between 1866 and 1870, as well as such legislation as the Tenure of Office Act which attempted to limit President Johnson's removal power; presidential veto messages and proclamations; proceedings in the impeachment and trial of Johnson; judicial opinions dealing with the Civil War amendments and Reconstruction legislation; a proposed women's suffrage constitutional amendment which was voted down; and correspondence between Grant and Johnson.

McPherson, James M. THE STRUGGLE FOR EQUALITY: ABOLITIONISTS AND THE NEGRO IN THE CIVIL WAR AND RECONSTRUCTION. Princeton, N.J.: Princeton University Press, 1964.

> This history of the abolitionist movement, a movement transformed by the war from a group of fanatics to a respected wing of the Republican party, traces the programs and contributions it made during and after the war in attempting to achieve equality for blacks, contributions culminating in the adoption of the Fifteenth Amendment.

Marshall, Burke. FEDERALISM AND CIVIL RIGHTS. Foreword by Robert F. Kennedy. New York: Columbia University Press, 1964.

> Originally delivered as the Gino Speranza Lectures for 1964 at Columbia, this work by the head of the Civil Rights Division during the Kennedy administration focuses on the limitations imposed by federalism upon the national government's authority to protect the rights of blacks. The first lecture deals with the national government's experiences in enforcing voting rights. The second deals with national efforts to control abuses in the administration of justice.

Martin, Charles H. THE ANGELO HERNDON CASE AND SOUTHERN JUSTICE. Baton Rouge: Louisiana State University Press, 1976.

> This study of the background of Herndon v. Lowry touches on the problems of protecting the free speech guarantees of radicals, in this instance Communists, in times of social and economic

upheaval and of assuring equal justice for black defendants in
the South during the 1930s.

Mathews, John Mabry. LEGISLATIVE AND JUDICIAL HISTORY OF THE
FIFTEENTH AMENDMENT. Baltimore: Johns Hopkins University Press,
1909. Reprint. New York: Da Capo Press, 1971.

This is a history of the Fifteenth Amendment from the time that
the Joint Committee on Reconstruction first considered extension
of the suffrage to blacks to early twentieth-century judicial interpretation. It examines the committee's work in drafting the amendment, the presentation of the proposal to Congress, its adoption
by the states, and the enactment of legislation to implement the
amendment.

Mendelson, Wallace. DISCRIMINATION: BASED ON THE REPORT OF THE
UNITED STATES COMMISSION ON CIVIL RIGHTS. Englewood Cliffs, N.J.:
Prentice-Hall, 1962.

This is a condensation of and commentaries upon the 1961 five-
volume report of the commission on racial discrimination in voting,
education, employment, housing, and police conduct, along with
the Commission's recommendations.

Meyer, Howard. THE AMENDMENT THAT REFUSED TO DIE. Radnor, Pa.:
Chilton Book Co., 1973.

This is a historical study of the Fourteenth Amendment.

Miller, Arthur S. RACIAL DISCRIMINATION AND PRIVATE EDUCATION.
Chapel Hill: University of North Carolina Press, 1957.

Written a decade before the resurrection of the Thirteenth Amendment in Jones and its use to support national prohibition of segregation in private schools in Runyon, and in a period when the
"state action" concept had not yet been expanded to its present
scope, this is a somewhat outdated but nonetheless useful analysis
of some of the constitutional problems involved in preventing racial
segregation in private schools.

Mills, Nicolaus, ed. THE GREAT SCHOOL BUS CONTROVERSY. New
York: Teachers College Press, 1973.

This collection of readings focusing on the busing controversy
examines the legal basis for such court orders as well as research on the problem of busing and the political strategy used
to secure this legal remedy for racial discrimination in education.

Moreland, Lois B. WHITE RACISM AND THE LAW. African Afro-American
Studies Series. Columbus, Ohio: Charles E. Merrill, 1970.

This analysis of the Supreme Court's interpretation of the Four-
teenth Amendment and the state action doctrine from the Civil
Rights Cases through the sit-in cases and Guest concludes that the
Court "was and still is a decisive force in maintaining racism."
Moreland argues that it is not the Constitution that prevents the
Court from declaring that "there is no legal right of white

Americans to discriminate against Black Americans." Rather, the Court itself has imposed limitations.

Morris, Thomas D. FREE MEN ALL: THE PERSONAL LIBERTY LAWS OF THE NORTH, 1780–1861. Baltimore: Johns Hopkins University Press, 1974.

This is an analysis of various laws known as "personal liberty" laws (anti-kidnapping, trial by jury, and writ of habeas corpus requirements) which were used in nonslave states to protect blacks from seizure without court proceedings and of the conflicts which such use produced between North and South. These safe-guards, in the author's view, translated into the presumption that all persons are free, a presumption which served as a back-drop to the Civil War amendments.

Murray, Pauli, ed. STATES' LAWS ON RACE AND COLOR AND APPEN-DICES CONTAINING INTERNATIONAL DOCUMENTS, FEDERAL LAWS AND REGULATIONS, LOCAL ORDINANCES AND CHARTS. N.p.: Women's Division of Christian Service of the Methodist Church, 1950.

This is an extensive collection of state, local, and national laws regarding race relations in effect in the late 1940s. In addition to a summary of state legislation which prohibited or required segregation, the work lists each state alphabetically and repro-duces its laws regulating race relations. The appendix includes various international documents as well as American documents such as court decisions, executive orders, briefs submitted to the Court and charts and tables of race relations laws.

Muse, Benjamin. TEN YEARS OF PRELUDE: THE STORY OF INTEGRA-TION SINCE THE SUPREME COURT'S 1954 DECISION. New York: Viking Press, 1964.

Designed primarily for the general audience, this project for the Southern Regional Council is a review of the impact of Brown in the first ten years following that decision. Written prior to the passage and implementation of congressional legislation prohibiting the use of federal funds in programs that discriminate, it examines the reaction of the border states to desegregation, the desegre-gation crisis at Little Rock and Ole Miss and the beginning of a move toward compliance.

_____. VIRGINIA'S MASSIVE RESISTANCE. Bloomington: Indiana University Press, 1961.

This is a study of the efforts by Virginia to defy the Supreme Court's decision in Brown.

National Lawyers Guild. Committee to Assist Southern Lawyers. CIVIL RIGHTS AND LIBERTIES HANDBOOK: PLEADINGS AND PRACTICE. Berkeley, Calif.: 1963-- . Irregular. Looseleaf.

Designed to aid lawyers in combatting governmental interference with individual rights, this handbook contains practical informa-tion such as the forms of motions and complaints as well as cita-tions to civil rights and civil liberties cases since the mid-1950s.

National Municipal League. APPORTIONMENT IN THE 1960'S: STATE
LEGISLATURES, CONGRESSIONAL DISTRICTS. New York, 1967-- .
Irregular. Looseleaf.

> First issued in 1962 at the time of <u>Baker</u> v. <u>Carr</u> but not pub-
> lished until 1967 and kept up to date by use of a loose-leaf for-
> mat, this work contains district by district population data and
> maps for all state legislative and congressional districts. The
> league calculates the percentage deviation from the average
> population for each district and the theoretical percentage of
> the state's population that could elect a majority of each house.
> Organized on the basis of states, the work contains a brief
> history and analysis of reapportionment for each state.

Nelson, Bernard H. THE FOURTEENTH AMENDMENT AND THE NEGRO
SINCE 1920. Washington, D.C.: Catholic University Press, 1946. Reprint.
New York: Russell and Russell, 1957.

> This is a study of judicial interpretation of the Fourteenth Amend-
> ment between 1920 and 1943 to protect blacks. It deals with such
> issues as residential segregation, white primaries, juries and fair
> trials as well as higher education.

Nerken, Ira. "A New Deal for the Protection of Fourteenth Amendment
Rights: Challenging the Doctrinal Bases of the Civil Rights Cases and the
State Action Theory." HARVARD CIVIL RIGHTS AND CIVIL LIBERTIES
LAW REVIEW 12 (Spring 1977): 297-366.

> In this examination of the state action doctrine, Nerken argues
> that much of the doctrinal power which sustained this concept was
> derived from the nineteenth-century concept of "liberty of contract."
> With the downfall of <u>Lochner</u> and with the post-New Deal legal,
> intellectual and social developments culminating in <u>Shelley</u> v.
> <u>Kraemer</u> which broke with the Lochnerian view of private property
> and individual rights, there is no longer any doctrinal support
> for the <u>Civil Rights Cases</u>.

Newby, Idus A. CHALLENGE TO THE COURT: SOCIAL SCIENTISTS AND
THE DEFENSE OF SEGREGATION, 1954-1966. Baton Rouge: Louisiana
State University Press, 1969.

> This is an examination of the ideas and writings of social scien-
> tists whose works were, in the author's view, a direct response
> to and repudiation of <u>Brown</u> and are largely responsible for a
> resurgence of "scientific racism." It also reviews the evidence
> presented in <u>Brown</u>. First published in 1967, the 1969 edition
> includes the responses and criticisms of those whose works were
> discussed in the earlier edition.

Nye, Russel Blaine. FETTERED FREEDOM: CIVIL LIBERTIES AND
THE SLAVERY CONTROVERSY, 1830-1860. Rev. ed. East Lansing: Michigan State University Press, 1963.

> In this examination of the relationship between civil liberties and
> the controversy over slavery, Nye argues that the question of the
> right of a minority--the abolitionists--to speak became as impor-
> tant in the abolition of slavery as the slavery question itself.
> As the two became intertwined, the abolitionist movement gained

strength because those who supported free expression but were indifferent or neutral toward slavery became increasingly anti-South and ultimately antislavery.

O'Neil, Robert M. DISCRIMINATING AGAINST DISCRIMINATION: PREF-ERENTIAL ADMISSIONS AND THE DE FUNIS CASE. Bloomington: Indiana University Press, 1975.

In this examination of preferential admissions policies in pro-fessional education and similar preferential programs for minori-ties in other areas, the author argues that such plans are good constitutional law and desirable social policy.

_____. "Preferential Admission: Equalizing the Access of Minority Groups to Higher Education." YALE LAW JOURNAL 80 (March 1971): 699-767.

Although concluding that the fate of preferential admission pro-grams will not be determined by courts and constitutional law but by legislators and financial supporters of educational institu-tions, this article discusses some of the constitutional issues that have been raised by such programs. Three possible judicial reactions to the question of constitutionality are examined: a holding that racially based classifications are unconstitutional per se, employment of the rational test or use of the compelling interest test.

Orfield, Gary. THE RECONSTRUCTION OF SOUTHERN EDUCATION. THE SCHOOLS AND THE 1964 CIVIL RIGHTS ACT. New York: John Wiley and Sons, 1969.

Ten years after the Supreme Court held that racial segregation in education was unconstitutional, Congress prohibited racial discrimination in any program supported by federal funds. This is an analysis of the development of guidelines by HEW and of the impact of legislative and administrative action in support of racial equality in education in North and South.

O'Rourke, Terry B. REAPPORTIONMENT: LAW, POLITICS, COMPUTERS. Washington, D.C.: American Enterprise Institute for Public Policy Research, 1972.

This study of the Supreme Court's 1964 reapportionment decisions and of the political reactions to and consequences of those decisions concludes that the Court's insistence upon absolute equality as the sole standard of constitutionality for legislative districting at the expense of other considerations will encourage gerrymandering and that computer technology will make gerrymandering more sophisticated.

Paludan, Phillip S. COVENANT WITH DEATH: THE CONSTITUTION, LAW AND EQUALITY IN THE CIVIL WAR ERA. Urbana: University of Illinois Press, 1975.

This is an analysis of the ideas of representative thinkers of the nineteenth century with a view to supporting the contention that from the Jacksonian era to the Civil War the threat of disunion was seen primarily as a threat to the status quo and not as an

opportunity to develop ideas that would support a constitutional
system based on the notion of racial equality. In reacting against
secession and thus change, opinion makers created an ideological
climate which made it impossible to develop a legal and constitutional order which would guarantee equality after the Civil War.

Panetta, Leon E., and Gall, Peter. BRING US TOGETHER: THE NIXON
TEAM AND THE CIVIL RIGHTS RETREAT. Philadelphia: J.B. Lippincott,
1971.

Designed for the popular audience, this is an assessment of
the educational desegregation policies of the Nixon administration
by the director of the Office of Civil Rights who was forced to
resign in 1970 and an associate. The authors conclude that
Nixon's treatment of civil rights "bodes ill for the nation."

Peltason, Jack W. FIFTY-EIGHT LONELY MEN: SOUTHERN FEDERAL
JUDGES AND SCHOOL DESEGREGATION. Introduction by Sen. Paul A.
Douglas. New York: Harcourt, Brace and World, 1961.

This is a study of the fifty-eight U.S. District Court and Court
of Appeals judges who were charged in the 1955 Brown implementing decision with overseeing educational desegregation in the
South.

Polsby, Nelson W., ed. REAPPORTIONMENT IN THE 1970S. Berkeley:
University of California Press for the Institute for Governmental Studies,
1971.

This collection of eight essays by such scholars as Robert G.
Dixon, Alexander Bickel, Douglas Rae, and Gordon Baker examines various facets of the theory and practice of reapportionment.

Porter, Kirk Harold. A HISTORY OF SUFFRAGE IN THE UNITED STATES.
Chicago: University of Chicago Press, 1918. Reprint. Ann Arbor, Mich.:
University Microfilms, 1967. Microfilm-xerography. Reprint. New York:
AMS Press, 1971.

Relying heavily upon debates in state constitutional conventions,
this is a study of the various fights since 1776 to expand the
suffrage to include large new groups. Written in 1918 before
the adoption of the Nineteenth Amendment but during the struggle
for woman suffrage, it discusses that fight briefly but is more
concerned with conflicts over property qualifications and black
voting.

"The Problem of Malapportionment: A Symposium on Baker v. Carr." YALE
LAW JOURNAL 72 (November 1962): Entire issue.

These eight articles on various aspects of apportionment include
E.E. Schattschneider, "Urbanization and Reapportionment";
Charles L. Black, Jr. "Inequities in Districting for Congress";
Allan P. Sindler, "Baker v. Carr: How to Sear the Conscience";
Alexander Bickel, "The Durability of Colegrove v. Green"; F.
William O'Brien, "Baker v. Carr Abroad"; Thomas I. Emerson,

"Malapportionment and Judicial Power"; Louis H. Pollak, "Judicial Power and the Politics of the People"; and Arthur L. Goldbert, "The Statistics of Malapportionment."

RACE RELATIONS IN THE USA, 1954-1968. Keesing's Research Report. New York: Charles Scribner's Sons, 1970.

Organized chronologically and topically, this is a report on major events in the civil rights movement from the decision in Brown to the assassination of Martin Luther King and the conviction of James Earl Ray. It covers educational desegregation, voting rights legislation and its implementation, and racial demonstrations from the sit-in movement to urban rioting.

REPORT OF THE JOINT COMMITTEE TO ENQUIRE INTO THE CONDITION OF AFFAIRS IN THE LATE INSURRECTIONARY STATES MADE TO THE TWO HOUSES OF CONGRESS ON FEBRUARY 19, 1872. 13 vols. Washington, D.C.: Government Printing Office, 1872.

This report of congressional investigations into the activities of the Ku Klux Klan in the South in the Reconstruction era led to the adoption of some still significant national legislation protecting the constitutional rights of blacks.

Ruchames, Louis, ed. THE ABOLITIONISTS: A COLLECTION OF THEIR WRITINGS. New York: G.P. Putnam's Sons, 1964.

With an introduction by the editor, this collection of abolitionist literature includes writings by such leaders as Garrison and Whittier.

Schechter, Alan H. CONTEMPORARY CONSTITUTIONAL ISSUES. New York: McGraw-Hill, 1972.

Designed primarily for undergraduate students, each of the six case studies focuses on a different constitutional issue related to civil rights and civil liberties. The author seeks to blend the traditionalist and the behavioral approaches by examining the political origins and conflicts in each area as well as the legal issues, arguments and judicial opinions.

Schurz, Carl. REPORT ON THE CONDITION OF THE SOUTH. 1865. Reprint. New York: Arno Press, 1970.

This is the report of the findings of a committee sent to the South by President Andrew Johnson to investigate post-Civil War conditions in that region. The report was used by Radical Republicans to support the necessity for greater national intervention to reconstruct the South.

Schwartz, Bernard. A COMMENTARY ON THE CONSTITUTION OF THE UNITED STATES. 2 vols. New York: Macmillan, 1968.

Volume 2, entitled EQUALITY, BELIEF AND DIGNITY, deals with judicial interpretation of the Civil War amendments.

_____, ed. THE FOURTEENTH AMENDMENT: CENTENNIAL VOLUME.
New York: New York University Press, 1970.

> This work includes sixteen papers delivered at a centennial
> conference at New York University in 1968. The three major
> themes of the conference papers were: the Fourteenth Amend-
> ment in historical perspective, the amendment and contemporary
> constitutional problems and constitutionalism in a changing world.
> The authors include Justice Brennan, Henry Steele Commager,
> Justice Abe Fortas, Erwin N. Griswold, and Chief Justice
> Warren.

_____. STATUTORY HISTORY OF THE UNITED STATES. CIVIL RIGHTS.
2 vols. New York: Chelsea House in association with McGraw-Hill, 1970.

> This work contains extensive materials on the origins, congres-
> sional debate and presidential actions on each Civil War amend-
> ment, each piece of civil rights legislation from 1866 to 1968,
> plus some relevant Supreme Court decisions.

Sobel, Lester A., ed. CIVIL RIGHTS, 1960-1966; 1967-1968. 2 vols.
New York: Facts on File, 1967-73.

> This is a chronology of important events in the civil rights move-
> ment in the 1960s. The first volume covers the first six years
> of the decade. Volume 2 covers 1967 and 1968.

Southern Education Reporting Service. RACE RELATIONS LAW REPORTER.
Nashville, Tenn.: School of Law, Vanderbilt University, 1957-67. Quarterly.

> This work was prompted by the Supreme Court's public school
> segregation case and the reaction to that decision. It includes
> all state and local legislative, executive and judicial documents
> dealing with race relations as well as national judicial opinions
> beginning with Brown and legislative and presidential actions
> in the area of race. It was superseded by RACE RELATIONS
> LAW SURVEY (below).

_____. RACE RELATIONS LAW SURVEY. Nashville, Tenn.: School of
Law, Vanderbilt University, 1969-- . Bimonthly.

> This newsletter supersedes the RACE RELATIONS LAW REPORTER.
> Rather than containing full copies of official documents, it is a
> survey of laws dealing with race.

Spooner, Lysander. THE UNCONSTITUTIONALITY OF SLAVERY. 2d ed.
1860. Reprint. New York: Burt Franklin, 1965.

> This is a pre-Civil War condemnation of slavery by a major nine-
> teenth-century anarchist who argued that the Constitution forbade
> slavery.

Strong, Donald S. NEGROES, BALLOTS, AND JUDGES: NATIONAL VOTING
RIGHTS LEGISLATION IN THE FEDERAL COURTS. University: University
of Alabama Press, Bureau of Public Administration, 1968.

This is a study of the effect of the Civil Rights Acts of 1957 and 1960 on black voting. In exploring the reasons for the relative ineffectiveness of this early legislation, Strong examines the problems of judicial enforcement and of the resistance of segregationist judges and of state legislatures. The epilogue examines the Voting Rights Act of 1965.

Strum, Philippa. THE SUPREME COURT AND POLITICAL QUESTIONS: A STUDY IN JUDICIAL EVASION. University: University of Alabama Press, 1974.

This is an examination of the judicially constructed political question doctrine in terms of its nature, its development in the guaranty clause cases, its role in the areas of reapportionment and elections, and its general utility.

Taper, Bernard. GOMILLION VERSUS LIGHTFOOT: THE TUSKEGEE GERRYMANDER CASE. New York: McGraw-Hill, 1962.

This slim volume is a study of the background of the successful effort to obtain judicial intervention to prohibit Alabama's re-drawing of the boundaries of Tuskegee in such a way as to leave blacks outside the boundaries of that predominantly black city.

tenBroek, Jacobus. EQUAL UNDER LAW. Rev. ed. New York: Collier-Macmillan, 1965.

Originally published in 1951 as THE ANTISLAVERY ORIGINS OF THE FOURTEENTH AMENDMENT by the University of California Press and with a new introduction to the revised edition which suggests that even with Brown the Court did not achieve the far-reaching goals of the framers of the Fourteenth Amendment, this classic analysis of the background of that amendment concentrates not on the Thirty-ninth Congress but on the theories of the abolitionist movement which were accepted by that Congress.

Thomson, David. EQUALITY. Cambridge: Cambridge University Press, 1959.

This is an examination of various aspects of the concept of equality, legal, political, and economic.

Tuckerman, Bayard. WILLIAM JAY AND THE CONSTITUTIONAL MOVEMENT FOR THE ABOLITION OF SLAVERY. 1893. Reprint. New York: Burt Franklin, 1970.

This is a study of the role of William Jay, a judge and abolitionist, in the movement for the abolition of slavery in the District of Columbia and an analysis of his argument that slavery was unconstitutional before the Civil War and the adoption of the Thirteenth Amendment.

U.S. Commission on Civil Rights. THE CIVIL RIGHTS DIGEST: A QUARTERLY OF THE UNITED STATES COMMISSION ON CIVIL RIGHTS. Washington, D.C.: United States Commission on Civil Rights, 1968-- .

This quarterly contains brief articles on current issues and controversies in the area of civil rights.

_____. CIVIL RIGHTS DIRECTORY. Rev. ed. Washington, D.C.: U.S. Commission on Civil Rights, 1970.

This is a directory of national officials who are involved in the administration of civil rights legislation and of private civil rights organizations, and state and local agencies which have some responsibility for administering civil rights programs.

_____. POLITICAL PARTICIPATION BY NEGROES IN THE ELECTORAL AND POLITICAL PROCESSES IN TEN SOUTHERN STATES SINCE PASSAGE OF THE VOTING RIGHTS ACT OF 1965. Washington, D.C.: U.S. Commission on Civil Rights, 1968.

This is a study of the effects of the Voting Rights Act of 1965 on black voting in the South in the first few years of its implementation by the Johnson administration.

_____. REPORTS. Washington, D.C.: U.S. Commission on Civil Rights, 1957-- .

Created first as a presidential committee to study the status of civil rights and then, in the Civil Rights Act of 1957, as an independent advisory commission, the Civil Rights Commission issues periodic reports, ranging from TO SECURE THESE RIGHTS, issued during the Truman administration, to DESEGREGATING THE BOSTON PUBLIC SCHOOLS: A CRISIS IN CIVIC RESPONSIBILITY, issued in the Ford administration, dealing with both the general question of the status of civil rights and with specific issues.

_____. VOTING: HEARINGS. Washington, D.C.: U.S. Commission on Civil Rights, 1959.

This contains the hearings held by the commission in Alabama in late 1958 and early 1959 after the enactment of the first civil rights legislation of the modern era. The commission staff heard testimony about continued state interference with the rights of blacks to register to vote. It was the findings of hearings such as these throughout the South that furnished much of the ammunition needed to strengthen the 1957 legislation and to increase national protection of the right to vote.

U.S. Congress. Senate. Committee on the Judiciary. LIST OF PUBLICATIONS OF THE SUBCOMMITTEE ON CONSTITUTIONAL RIGHTS, 1955-1972. Washington, D.C.: Government Printing Office, 1972.

This list of publications, prepared for the Ninety-third Congress, second session, along with the LIST OF PUBLICATIONS OF THE SENATE COMMITTEE ON THE JUDICIARY, 1964 and PUBLICATIONS RELATIVE TO THE WORK OF THE SUBCOMMITTEE ON CIVIL RIGHTS, 1959 are especially useful as sources to the continued congressional debate over the meaning of the Civil War amendments because all of the civil rights measures considered by Congress during the most active civil rights period since

Reconstruction were filtered through the judiciary committee.

U.S. Congress. Senate. Select Committee on Equal Education Opportunity. SELECTED COURT DECISIONS RELATIVE TO EQUAL EDUCATION OPPOR-TUNITY. Washington, D.C.: Government Printing Office, 1972.

This 663-page collection of judicial opinions was printed for use by the committee considering the need for national legislation dealing specifically with discrimination in education.

Warsoff, Louis A. EQUALITY AND THE LAW. New York: Liveright, 1938.

The most useful aspect of this study of the equal protection clause is its account of the congressional proposal of the Fourteenth Amendment, its ratification by the states and its subsequent congressional interpretation. It also discusses the concept of equality in England and the United States before 1868 and judicial application of the equal protection and due process clauses to the socioeconomic order in the first three decades of the twentieth century.

Wasby, Stephen L.; D'Amato, Anthony A.; and Metrailer, Rosemary. DE-SEGREGATION FROM BROWN TO ALEXANDER: AN EXPLORATION OF SUPREME COURT STRATEGIES. Carbondale: Southern Illinois University Press, 1977.

This examination of Supreme Court desegregation cases from Brown in 1954 to Alexander in 1909 and of the Court's evolving strategy suggests that as the Court became aware of the in-effectiveness of the sweeping approach of Brown, it adopted the more effective strategy of turning a large dispute into a series of smaller disputes.

Wechsler, Herbert. THE NATIONALIZATION OF CIVIL LIBERTIES AND CIVIL RIGHTS. Austin: University of Texas at Austin, 1968.

Originally delivered as the Oliver Wendell Holmes Devise Lecture for 1967 at the University of South Dakota, expanded to include the subsequently decided case of Jones v. Mayer, and published as a supplement to the TEXAS QUARTERLY (volume 12), this brief work examines the way in which congressional legislation and Supreme Court decisions transformed rights protected by the states into nationally protected rights. The appendix includes the civil rights laws enacted between 1866 and 1875, those that were repealed or changed and those that remain.

Weinbert, Meyer. RACE AND PLACE: A LEGAL HISTORY OF THE NEIGH-BORHOOD SCHOOL. Washington, D.C.: Government Printing Office, 1967.

This monograph is an account of the origins of neighborhood schools, the relationship between residence and constitutional rights, judicial alteration of attendance zones and the use of busing to remedy segregation, and a suggestion that the constitutional problems presented by adherence to neighborhood school zoning might be solved by judicial reliance on legislative appor-tionment cases as precedent in dealing with school segregation.

Westin, Alan F. FREEDOM NOW: THE CIVIL RIGHTS STRUGGLE IN
AMERICA. New York: Basic Books, 1964.

> This contains excerpts from the writings of a wide variety of
> contemporary observers, participants, writers and scholars
> which deal with the history of civil rights, the moral dimensions
> of the struggle and the areas of tension in race relations.

Weyl, Nathaniel, and Marina, William. AMERICAN STATESMEN ON SLAVERY
AND THE NEGRO. New Rochelle, N.Y.: Arlington House, 1971.

> This is a study of the views of American statesmen from the
> colonial period to President Kennedy's assassination toward both
> slavery in particular and blacks in general.

Wilhoit, Francis. THE POLITICS OF MASSIVE RESISTANCE. New York:
George Braziller, 1973.

> Following the Supreme Court's Brown opinion, southern officials
> responded with a call for resistance. This is a study of the
> rise of resistance in the late 1950s and early 1960s, congres-
> sional response to that movement with passage of the Civil Rights
> Act of 1964 and the Voting Rights Act of 1965, and the abatement
> of defiance.

Winter, Ralph K., et al. AFFIRMATIVE ACTION: THE ANSWER TO
DISCRIMINATION? Washington, D.C.: American Enterprise Institute for
Public Policy Research, 1975.

> This pamphlet consists of an American Enterprise Institute round-
> table discussion by journalists and law professors of the question
> of the desirability of affirmative action programs.

Wirt, Frederick M. POLITICS OF SOUTHERN EQUALITY: LAW AND
SOCIAL CHANGES IN A MISSISSIPPI COUNTY. Foreword by Gunnar
Myrdal. Chicago: Aldine, 1970.

> This is a study of the effects of national civil rights legislation
> in Panola County, Mississippi, in the areas of voting, education
> and economic opportunities.

Wolff, Miles. LUNCH AT THE FIVE AND TEN, THE GREENSBORO SIT-
IN: A CONTEMPORARY HISTORY. New York: Stein and Day, 1970.

> This is a popular account of the activities of black students in
> Greensboro, North Carolina who began a region-wide movement
> when they sat at a white-only lunch counter at Woolworth's and
> refused to move, thereby launching a movement which led to judi-
> cial expansion of the state action concept of the Fourteenth Amend-
> ment and to congressional enactment of the Public Accommodations
> Act of 1964.

Wolk, Allan. THE PRESIDENCY AND BLACK CIVIL RIGHTS: EISEN-
HOWER TO NIXON. Rutherford, N.J.: Fairleigh Dickinson University
Press, 1971.

This is a study of the implementation of civil rights legislation by the Civil Rights Division and the Community Relations Service in the Department of Justice and the Office of Education and the Office for Civil Rights in HEW. It focuses primarily upon the Kennedy and Johnson administrations.

Wood, Virginia. DUE PROCESS, 1923-1949: THE SUPREME COURT'S USE OF A CONSTITUTIONAL TOOL. Port Washington, N.Y.: Kennikat Press, 1951.

This is an analysis of the due process clause as a basis for judicial scrutiny of socioeconomic legislation, criminal procedures and governmental interference with substantive liberties.

Ziegler, Benjamin, ed. DESEGREGATION AND THE SUPREME COURT. Problems in American Civilization Series. Boston: D.C. Heath, 1958.

This small volume contains brief excerpts from a number of articles, books, resolutions, proclamations and judicial decisions relevant to the role of the Court in general and in the educational desegregation process in particular.

Chapter 12

TWENTIETH-CENTURY AMENDMENTS

16 (Income Tax), 17 (Direct Election of Senators), 18 (Prohibition),
19 (Women's Suffrage), 20 (Presidential Term), 21 (Prohibition
Repeal), 22 (Two-Term Limitation), 23 (Presidential Vote for D.C.),
24 (Poll Tax), 25 (Presidential Succession and Disability), 26 (18-Year-
Old Vote), and Proposed 27 (Equal Rights for Women)

Beman, Lamar T., comp. SELECTED ARTICLES ON PROHIBITION:
MODIFICATION OF THE VOLSTEAD LAW. The Handbook Series. New
York: H.W. Wilson, 1924. Supplement, 1927.

The first half of this work is a bibliography of and excerpts from
articles, pamphlets, debates, addresses and official documents
dealing with the Eighteenth Amendment, the Volstead Act and the
physiological, economic, political and social effects of alcohol.
The second half contains affirmative and negative sides of a debate
over the desirability of the amendment.

Blocker, Jack S., Jr. RETREAT FROM REFORM: THE PROHIBITION
MOVEMENT IN THE UNITED STATES, 1890-1913. Contributions in American History Series. Westport, Conn.: Greenwood Press, 1976.

In this analysis of the development of the prohibition movement,
Blocker focuses upon the 1890s as the period in which that movement underwent a fundamental change. He argues that the third
wave of the prohibition movement, which began in 1907 and culminated in the ratification of the Eighteenth Amendment in 1919,
was not the same movement which had enjoyed limited success in
the 1880s. The change between 1890 and 1913 accounted for its
success. The epilogue deals with the Eighteenth and the Twenty-
First Amendments.

Brown, Barbara, et al. "The Equal Rights Amendment: A Constitutional
Basis for Equal Rights for Women." YALE LAW JOURNAL 80 (April 1971):
871-985.

This extensive article is a discussion of the inadequacy of the
equal protection clause in protecting the rights of women, an
argument in support of the adoption of an equal rights amendment
and an in-depth analysis of the interpretation and application of
such an amendment to a variety of situations. It discusses such
matters as the development in Congress of the proposed amendment,

the constitutional framework, the problems of transition the
amendment would require, and the effect of the amendment in such
areas as protective labor laws, domestic relations law, criminal
law, and the military.

Bruere, Maratha B. DOES PROHIBITION WORK: A STUDY OF THE
OPERATION OF THE EIGHTEENTH AMENDMENT MADE BY THE NATIONAL
FEDERATION OF SETTLEMENTS, ASSISTED BY SOCIAL WORKERS IN
DIFFERENT PARTS OF THE UNITED STATES. New York: Harpers, 1927.

This is a report of a commission appointed by the Federation and
consisting of a "wet," a "dry," and a "doubter" to investigate the
effect of the Eighteenth Amendment on urban family life.

Bushnell, Horace. WOMAN'S SUFFRAGE: THE REFORM AGAINST NATURE.
New York: Scribner, 1869. Reprint. Ann Arbor, Mich.: University Microfilms, 1974. Microfilm-xerography.

This tract in opposition to women's suffrage argues that women
were not created to govern and that political participation by
women would create such undesirable behavioral changes as
aggressiveness and selfishness and such physical changes as
bigger hands and feet.

Catt, Carrie Chapman, and Shuler, Nettie Rogers. WOMAN SUFFRAGE
AND POLITICS: THE INNER STORY OF THE SUFFRAGE MOVEMENT.
New York: Charles Scribner's Sons, 1926. Reprint. Introduction by T.A.
Larson. Seattle: University of Washington Press, 1969.

This one-volume study of the women's suffrage movement by
Susan B. Anthony's successor as president of the National American Woman Suffrage Association covers the movement from the
1840s to the adoption of the Nineteenth Amendment.

Cherrington, Ernest H. THE EVOLUTION OF PROHIBITION IN THE UNITED
STATES OF AMERICA: A CHRONOLOGICAL HISTORY OF THE LIQUOR
PROBLEM AND THE TEMPERANCE REFORM IN THE UNITED STATES
FROM THE EARLIEST SETTLEMENTS TO THE CONSUMMATION OF
NATIONAL PROHIBITION. 1920. Reprint. Montclair, N.J.: Patterson
Smith, 1969.

Written by the general secretary of the World League Against
Alcoholism, this is an account of the attempts by colonial, state
and national governments to impose restrictions on the manufacture,
sale and consumption of alcoholic beverages. The author concludes
that the prohibition movement was an evolutionary rather than a
revolutionary movement and that each period examined revealed
a more advanced temperance sentiment.

Chodorov, Frank. THE INCOME TAX: ROOT OF ALL EVIL. New York:
Devin-Adair, 1954.

This is an attack upon the income tax and a call for repeal of
the Sixteenth Amendment. The author argues that adoption of
that amendment constituted a coup d'etat because it shifted political power from the people and their elected representatives to
the bureaucracy. Repeal of the amendment would similarly con-

stitute not a reform but a revolution because it would severely restrict governmental power by reducing its revenues.

Coolidge, Olivia E. WOMEN'S RIGHTS: THE SUFFRAGE MOVEMENT IN AMERICA, 1848-1920. New York: E.P. Dutton and Co., 1966.

This work traces the women's suffrage movement through its pioneers, its later leaders, its cessation of activities during the Civil War, its internal splits, failures and successes.

Delsman, Mary A. EVERYTHING YOU NEED TO KNOW ABOUT ERA (THE EQUAL RIGHTS AMENDMENT). Riverside, Calif.: Meranza Press, 1975.

Designed for the general audience, this is an argument in support of the equal rights amendment. Drawing upon scholarly studies, it discusses the effects of ERA upon law in general and in such areas as education, employment, sex crimes, marriage, and the family.

Dobyns, Fletcher. THE AMAZING STORY OF REPEAL: AN EXPOSE OF THE POWER OF PROPAGANDA. Chicago: Willett, Clark, 1940.

Relying heavily upon a congressional investigation of lobbying, this work is an attack upon financial, industrial, and social leaders who used the instruments of publicity to wage a pro-paganda war to repeal the Eighteenth Amendment and to induce the public "to follow actions inimical to its economic and spiritual interests."

Duarte, Joseph S. THE INCOME TAX IS OBSOLETE. New Rochelle, N.Y.: Arlington House, 1974.

Arguing that the problem of taxation cannot be divorced from politics and that tax laws may degenerate into an instrument of political despotism, this scholarly polemic examines alternatives to the income tax that would be fair, that would raise sufficient revenue, and that would remedy the defects of congressional use of the power derived from the Sixteenth Amendment. The author recommends taxation of consumption rather than income.

Equal Rights Amendment Project. THE EQUAL RIGHTS AMENDMENT: A BIBLIOGRAPHIC STUDY. Westport, Conn.: Greenwood Press, 1976.

This is a comprehensive bibliography of materials dealing with women's issues since the early twentieth century. It includes citations to newspapers, popular magazines, scholarly journals, government documents, dissertations, and books. There is a subject index to the microfilm collections of HERSTORY AND WOMEN AND THE LAW, a separate index to EQUAL RIGHTS, a publication of the National Woman's Party, and a list of the addresses of women's publications and organizations as well as a chronological list of the newspapers indexed. The Equal Rights Amendment Project was founded to undertake a study of the impact of the Equal Rights Amendment.

Equal Rights Amendment Project of the California Commission on the Status of Women. A COMMENTARY ON THE EFFECT OF THE EQUAL RIGHTS AMENDMENT ON STATE LAWS AND INSTITUTIONS. Sacramento, Calif.: Commission on the Status of Women, 1975.

> This lists typical state laws in such areas as education, labor, and property and indicates what changes would have to be made to bring them into conformity with the Equal Rights Amendment.

_____. IMPACT ERA: LIMITATIONS AND POSSIBILITIES. Millbrae, Calif.: Les Femmes Publishing, 1976.

> This is an analysis of the possible effects of the proposed Twenty-Seventh Amendment in such areas as employment, education and domestic relationships, the reasons for opposition to the amendment and the possible problems its implementation might produce.

Feerick, John D. FROM FAILING HANDS: THE STORY OF PRESIDEN-TIAL SUCCESSION. New York: Fordham University Press, 1965.

> Written after the assassination of President Kennedy but before adoption of the Twenty-Fifth Amendment, this is a study of the original constitutional provision relating to presidential succession and of congressional legislation dealing with this problem. In the first half of the book, Feerick examines the problems, crises, and near crises produced by the death or disability of presidents. The second part of the book is an analysis of ways to cope more effectively with the problems of succession and disability. The author, who participated in the American Bar Association work on this subject, urges adoption of a constitutional amendment.

_____. THE TWENTY-FIFTH AMENDMENT: ITS COMPLETE HISTORY AND EARLIEST APPLICATION. New York: Fordham University Press, 1976.

> This sequel to FROM FAILING HANDS (above) deals with the Twenty-Fifth Amendment in terms of its meaning, its legislative history, and its applications in 1973 and 1974 following the resignations of Vice-President Agnew and President Nixon.

Flexner, Eleanor. CENTURY OF STRUGGLE. 2d ed. Cambridge, Mass.: Harvard University Press, 1975.

> Written in the 1950s and first published in 1959, this is a history of feminist efforts to open the political arena to women. After a survey of the general position occupied by women during the colonial and revolutionary era, it traces the hesitant beginnings of the women's movement in the early nineteenth century in education, employment, and politics to the successful culmination of its suffrage efforts with the adoption of the Nineteenth Amendment.

Gillet, Ranson Hooker, and Haynes, John. REPEAL OF THE PROHIBITION AMENDMENT. New York: H.W. Wilson, 1923.

> This is a debate between the general counsel of the Association Against the Prohibition Amendment and a Protestant minister over the question of the desirability of repealing the Eighteenth Amendment.

Gordon, Ernest. THE WRECKING OF THE EIGHTEENTH AMENDMENT. Francestown, N.H.: Alcohol Information Press, 1943.

In this attack upon the various political, religious, economic and press forces which combined to adopt the Twenty-First Amendment, the author argues that the Eighteenth Amendment proved to be an ideal method of treating social alcoholism and that it accomplished precisely what it was designed to accomplish.

Gusfield, Joseph R. SYMBOLIC CRUSADE: STATUS POLITICS AND THE AMERICAN TEMPERANCE MOVEMENT. Urbana: University of Illinois Press, 1963.

In this study of the temperance movement as a reflection of the clashes and conflicts between rival social systems, cultures and status groups, Gusfield argues that the Eighteenth Amendment was the high point of the struggle to assert the dominance of old middle class values and represented a victory of Protestant over Catholic, rural over urban, tradition over modernity and the middle class over both the lower and upper strata of society. Adoption of the Twenty-First Amendment represented a decline of old middle-class values.

Kersfelt, David S. "The Effect of the Twenty-First Amendment on State Authority to Control Intoxicating Liquors." COLUMBIA LAW REVIEW 75 (December 1975): 1578-1610.

In this examination of judicial interpretation of the effect of the "ambiguously worded" Twenty-First Amendment on the state's authority, the author looks at early Supreme Court decisions which granted virtually absolute authority to the state to control alcoholic beverages but which later gradually limited such authority.

Kobler, John. ARDENT SPIRITS: THE RISE AND FALL OF PROHIBITION. New York: G.F. Putnam's Sons, 1973.

This popular account of the prohibition movement, the adoption of the Eighteenth Amendment, and its repeal by the Twenty-First relies heavily upon the reminiscences of participants in the struggle over national control of alcohol.

Kraditor, Aileen S. THE IDEAS OF THE WOMAN SUFFRAGE MOVEMENT. 1890-1920. New York: Columbia University Press, 1965. New York: Doubleday, 1971.

This study of the women's suffrage movement focuses on the ideas of its leaders, its varying justifications from justice to expediency to broaden the suffrage and its attitudes toward minority racial and ethnic groups who acquired the right to vote before women.

Krichmar, Albert. THE WOMEN'S RIGHTS MOVEMENT IN THE UNITED STATES, 1848-1970: A BIBLIOGRAPHY AND SOURCEBOOK. Metuchen, N.J.: Scarecrow Press, 1972.

This bibliography contains over five thousand citations, some of which are annotated, to books, doctoral theses, periodical literature, and government documents dealing with various aspects of the status of women. It also contains about four hundred citations to manuscript sources. In addition to the legal and political status of women, the suffrage movement, and the Equal Rights Amendment, topics such as women and employment, education, and religion are covered.

Lee, Henry Walsh. HOW DRY WE WERE: PROHIBITION REVISITED. Englewood Cliffs, N.J.: Prentice-Hall, 1963.

This is a popular, anecdotal account of the effect of the Eighteenth Amendment and its repeal by the Twenty-First.

Merz, Charles. THE DRY DECADE. Garden City, N.Y.: Doubleday, Doran and Co., 1930. Reprint. Seattle: University of Washington Press, 1969.

Written before the repeal of the Eighteenth Amendment when prohibition was still a controversial political issue and designed for the general audience, this is a study of the adoption of the Eighteenth Amendment, the operation of the Volstead Act, its enforcement, and the organization of opposition to prohibition. In an introduction written for the 1969 edition, the Twenty-First Amendment is discussed.

Morgan, David. SUFFRAGISTS AND DEMOCRATS: THE POLITICS OF WOMAN SUFFRAGE IN THE UNITED STATES. East Lansing: Michigan State University Press, 1972.

This is a study of the political struggle culminating in the Nineteenth Amendment. Arguing that the women's suffrage movement was not a serious issue in national politics until 1916 but that by late 1918 it had become thoroughly enmeshed in party politics, the author discusses the political, legal, and economic changes prior to 1915 and then focuses upon the national fight over the right of women to vote.

National American Woman Suffrage Association. VICTORY: HOW WOMEN WON IT: A CENTENNIAL SYMPOSIUM, 1840-1940. Foreword by Carrie Chapman Catt. New York: H.W. Wilson Co., 1940.

This contains nine essays by women on the history of the attempt by women to gain the right to vote in local, state, and national elections. The appendix contains a chronology of congressional actions on women's suffrage and of partial gains made at lower governmental levels prior to the adoption of the Nineteenth Amendment.

_____. WOMAN SUFFRAGE: ARGUMENTS AND RESULTS. 1910-1911. New York: National American Woman Suffrage Association, 1911. Reprint. New York: Kraus, 1971.

This is an extensive collection of pamphlets, monographs, leaflets and resolutions supporting woman suffrage by such activists as Carrie Chapman Catt, Alice Stone Blackwell and Jane Addams and by such organizations as the American Federation of Labor.

Paulson, Ross Evans. WOMEN'S SUFFRAGE AND PROHIBITION: A COMPARATIVE STUDY OF EQUALITY AND SOCIAL CONTROL. Glenview, Ill.: Scott, Foresman, 1973.

Using the methods of comparative history, this is a study of the interaction of the women's suffrage movement and the prohibition movement. Paulson argues that the "woman question" of the nineteenth and early twentieth centuries was an aspect of the debate over the meaning of equality and, like the temperance and prohibition movements, involved questions concerning the nature of democracy and the means of social control. He compares the American movements to those in other countries which experienced significant interactions between suffrage and prohibition, such as England and the Scandinavian countries.

Phelps, Edith M., comp. SELECTED ARTICLES ON WOMAN SUFFRAGE. Debaters Handbook Series. 3d ed. White Plains, N.Y.: N.W. Wilson, 1916.

This contains a bibliography and excerpts from articles dealing with women's suffrage organized on the basis of general, affirmative, and negative discussions.

Pickett, Elbert Deets. THEN AND NOW: THE TRUTH ABOUT PROHIBITION AND REPEAL. Columbus, Ohio: School and College Service, 1952.

This brief pamphlet by the managing editor of publications of the Methodist Board of Temperance contends that the Eighteenth Amendment embodied the will of the people and that its repeal, engineered by big cities and big money, led to an increase in crime and aggravated the abuse of alcohol.

PROCEEDINGS OF THE WOMAN'S RIGHTS CONVENTION HELD AT SENECA FALLS AND ROCHESTER, NEW YORK, JULY, AUGUST, 1848. New York: Robert J. Johnston, 1870. Reprint. New York: Arno Press, 1968.

This contains two brief reports on women's rights: the report of the two-day discussion of the session of the Woman's Rights Convention held at Rochester on August 2, 1848 to discuss the "social, civil and religious conditions of women," and the report of the Woman's Rights Convention held at Seneca Falls on July 19 and 20, 1848.

Seligman, Edwin Robert. THE INCOME TAX: A STUDY OF THE HISTORY, THEORY AND PRACTICE OF TAXATION AT HOME AND ABROAD. 2d ed., rev. and enl. 1914. Reprint. New York: A.M. Kelly, 1970.

This history of the income tax deals with taxation in England, Germany, and France as well as the United States. It examines the American colonial experience with the income tax, its imposition during times of emergency such as the Civil War and the invalidation of the 1894 tax in Pollock. First published in 1911 before the adoption of the Sixteenth Amendment, the second edition devotes a chapter to the proposed income tax amendment and the 1913 law.

Sinclair, Andrew. PROHIBITION: THE ERA OF EXCESS. Preface by Richard Hofstadter. Boston: Little, Brown, 1962.

This work argues that prohibition was an attempt by rural Pro-
testants to impose their standards upon a heterogeneous urban
society and that repeal of that amendment by the Twenty-First
was a manifestation of the old order of the country giving way to
the new order of the cities and a replacement of rural morality
by urban morality.

Stanton, Elizabeth Cady, et al., eds. THE HISTORY OF WOMAN SUF-
FRAGE. 6 vols. 1881-1922. Reprint. New York: Arno Press, 1969.

This massive work is the most complete study of the woman
suffrage movement from 1848 to 1920. The first three volumes
were edited by Stanton, Susan B. Anthony, and Matilda Gage and
published by Anthony. Volume 4 was edited by Anthony and Ida
Husted Harper and published by Anthony. Volumes 5 and 6 were
edited under the guidance of Harper and published by the National
American Woman Suffrage Association.

Timberlake, James H. PROHIBITION AND THE PROGRESSIVE MOVEMENT,
1900-1920. Cambridge, Mass.: Harvard University Press, 1963.

This examination of the prohibition movement culminating in the
adoption of the Eighteenth Amendment argues that this movement
was an integral part of the progressive movement and drew its
strength from the same middle-class, urban sources.

U.S. Congress. House. Committee on the Judiciary. ABOLITION OF THE
POLL TAX IN FEDERAL ELECTIONS. HEARINGS. Washington, D.C.:
Government Printing Office, 1962.

These hearings led to the recommendation to propose the Twenty-
Fourth Amendment.

_____. AMEND THE CONSTITUTION RELATIVE TO EQUAL RIGHTS FOR
MEN AND WOMEN. STATEMENTS. Washington, D.C.: Government Printing
Office, 1945.

The Equal Rights Amendment was first introduced in 1923. These
statements presented to the committee of the 79th Congress were
among the many on this proposal prior to its acceptance by Congress in 1972.

_____. APPLICATION OF THE 25TH AMENDMENT TO VACANCIES IN THE
OFFICE OF THE VICE-PRESIDENT: LEGISLATIVE HISTORY. Washington,
D.C.: Government Printing Office, 1973.

This committee print contains the 1965 hearings before the Judiciary Committee on Presidential Disability, the texts of various
proposals on this topic, and the testimony and statements to the
committee. It also contains the House debate and copies of the
Senate report and the conference committee report.

_____. CONSTITUTIONAL AMENDMENT TO REDUCE VOTING AGE TO 18.
HEARINGS. Washington, D.C.: Government Printing Office, 1943.

These hearings are among the many held on lowering the voting
age to eighteen both during and after World War II, proposals
which culminated in adoption of the Twenty-Sixth Amendment.

_____. A DIRECT VOTE ON PROHIBITION REPEAL. HEARINGS. Washington, D.C.: Government Printing Office, 1933.

> These hearings considered the desirability of a popular vote on prohibition.

_____. EQUAL RIGHTS FOR MEN AND WOMEN. HEARINGS. Washington, D.C.: Government Printing Office, 1971.

> This copy of the hearings held 24 March through 5 April 1971 includes bibliographic reference to literature dealing with the question of discrimination on the basis of sex.

_____. NOMINATION OF GERALD R. FORD TO BE VICE-PRESIDENT OF THE UNITED STATES. HEARINGS. Washington, D.C.: Government Printing Office, 1973.

> These are the hearings before the Judiciary Committee of the first session of the Ninety-third Congress on the first use of the Twenty-Fifth Amendment to nominate a vice-president. It includes the testimony before and correspondence with the committee and such additional materials as Ford's House speech on Justice Douglas and the congressional debate on the Twenty-Fifth Amendment reprinted from the CONGRESSIONAL RECORD.

_____. REPORT, 92-359. Washington, D.C.: Government Printing Office, 1971.

> This is the HOUSE REPORT of the Ninety-second Congress accompanying the resolution proposing the Twenty-Seventh Amendment.

U.S. Congress. Joint Committee on the Economic Report. CONSTITUTIONAL LIMITATION ON FEDERAL INCOME, ESTATE AND GIFT TAX RATES. Washington, D.C.: Government Printing Office, 1952.

> This is a study for the Eighty-second Congress of a proposed constitutional amendment to limit to 25 percent the rate of income, inheritance and gift taxes.

_____. CONGRESSIONAL RECORD, 188, NO. 42, S 4247-S4273, AND NO. 44, S 4531-4537. Washington, D.C.: Government Printing Office, 1972.

> This contains the senate debate on the proposed Twenty-Seventh Amendment.

U.S. Congress. Senate. WOMEN AND THE "EQUAL RIGHTS" AMENDMENT: SENATE SUBCOMMITTEE HEARINGS ON THE CONSTITUTIONAL AMENDMENT. Edited by Catharine Stimpson in conjunction with the Congressional Information Service. New York: R.R. Bowker, 1972.

> This is a reprint of the documents and testimony presented to the Senate committee hearings in the 91st Congress in 1970. Included in the appendix is the House and Senate floor debate.

U.S. Congress. Senate. Committee on the Judiciary. CONGRESSIONAL REPRESENTATION FOR THE DISTRICT OF COLUMBIA. HEARINGS. Washington, D.C.: Government Printing Office, 1968.

These hearings before the subcommittee on constitutional amendments in the Ninetieth Congress are among the many on-going hearings on the still unsuccessful effort to provide for congressional representation for the District of Columbia.

_____. LOWERING VOTING AGE TO 18. HEARINGS. Washington, D.C.: Government Printing Office, 1968.

These hearings before the subcommittee on constitutional amendments of the Ninetieth Congress culminated in the proposal and adoption of the Twenty-Sixth Amendment.

_____. THIRD TERM FOR PRESIDENT OF THE UNITED STATES. Washington, D.C.: Government Printing Office, 1940.

This contains letters and statements submitted to a subcommittee of the Senate Judiciary Committee of the third session of the Seventy-fifth Congress in support of and in opposition to proposals to limit the presidential term of office--one proposal to limit the president to one six-year term and the other to impose a limitation of two four-year terms.

Vose, Clement E. CONSTITUTIONAL CHANGE: AMERICAN POLITICS AND SUPREME COURT LITIGATION SINCE 1900. Lexington, Mass.: D.C. Heath, 1972.

This is an examination of the process by which the eleven twentieth-century amendments were adopted as well as those advocated but not adopted. This analysis is designed to demonstrate the social and political ingredients in the Constitution and how these ingredients have contributed to the changes brought about by the Court and by constitutional amendment. Emphasis is placed on those amendments (prohibition, repeal of prohibition, and women's suffrage) which represent fundamental changes in social attitudes.

WOMEN'S LEGAL HANDBOOK SERIES ON JOB AND SEX DISCRIMINATION. 7 vols. Butler, Ind.: Ford Associates, 1971.

These seven volumes deal with the following subjects: (1) the Civil Rights Act of 1964; (2) national implementation; (3) Title VII and its interpretation and application; (4) the Equal Pay Act of 1963; (5) the proposed Equal Rights Amendment; (6) state commissions on women, and (7) administrative agencies.

AUTHOR INDEX

In addition to authors, this index includes all editors, compilers, and other contributors to works cited in the text. Numbers refer to page numbers and alphabetization is letter by letter.

A

Abair, Douglass 99
Abernathy, Glenn 231
Abraham, Henry J. 171, 231
Acheson, Patricia 171
Ackerman, Bruce A. 231
Adair, Douglass 35
Adams, Abigail 145
Adams, Charles Francis 145
Adams, Henry 57
Adams, John 13, 144, 145–46
Adams, John Quincy 145, 146, 231, 269
Alfange, Dean 79
Allen, Francis A. 96
Alsop, Joseph W. 171
Ambrose, Stephen 169
American Assembly, Columbian University 87
American Bar Association 221
Ames, Herman V. 57, 221
Ames, John G.B. 1
Ammon, Harry 62
Anastaplo, George 232
Anderman, Nancy 1
Anderson, John W. 269
Anderson, Thornton 27
Andrews, William G. 67
Andriot, John L. 2
Andrist, Ralph K. 169
Angle, Paul M. 160
Annual Chief Justice Earl Warren Conference on Advocacy in the United States of America 115, 232
Antieau, Chester J. 232
Apple, R.W. 134
Arnold, Isaac W. 146
Asch, Sidney H. 232

Ashmore, Harry S. 55, 233
Ashworth, Mary Wells 153
Association of American Law Schools 1, 35, 57, 79
Auerback, Jerold S. 35
Averill, Lawrence H., Jr. 221
Avins, Alfred 269

B

Bailey, Stephen K. 87
Bailyn, Bernard 13
Baker, Gordon E. 106, 269
Baker, Leonard 171, 202
Baker, Liva 202
Baker, Ray Stannard 170
Baldwin, Leland Dewitth 221
Baldwin, Roger 250
Ball, Howard 202
Ballagh, James Curtis 46
Bancroft, George 13
Bander, Edward J. 202
Barber, Sotirios A. 68
Barbour, Alton B. 233
Bardolph, Richard 270
Barnett, William M., Jr. 87
Barre, W.L. 146
Barrett, Joseph H. 146
Barron, Jerome A. 233
Barth, Alan 88, 135, 171
Barton, William E. 147
Basler, Roy P. 9, 159
Bassett, John Spencer 147, 156
Bates, Ernest S. 172
Bauer, Elizabeth 35
Baxter, Maurice G. 36
Bayh, Birch 115, 127
Beard, Charles A. 36, 80, 203, 207, 217
Beck, Carl 88

Author Index

Author Index

Author Index

Author Index

Author Index

Author Index

TITLE INDEX

This index includes all titles of books, proceedings, and published reports cited in the text. References are to page numbers and alphabetization is letter by letter.

Title Index

Title Index

Title Index

Title Index

Title Index

Title Index

P

Title Index

Title Index

Title Index

Title Index

SUBJECT INDEX

Court cases involving state or federal governments are cited under the name
of the individual preceding the government unit, regardless of plaintiff.
References are to page numbers and underlined numbers refer to main entries within the subject. Alphabetization is letter by letter.

A

Subject Index

Calder v. Bull 191
Calhoun, John C.
  interpretation of federalism by 63
  investigation of his conduct as
      Secretary of War 108
  nullification and 118
Callender, James 44
Campaigns. See Political campaigns
Campbell, John Archibald 205
Canada
  constitutionalism in 54
  party and convention organization
      and candidate selection in
      130
Canals, federal government in the
    construction of 55
Capitalism
  legal foundations of 39
  Supreme Court and 83
Capital punishment 253
  Supreme Court and 233–34, 244,
      255, 259
Cardozo, Benjamin Nathan
  biographies of 206, 213, 216
  Warren on 218
Carmichael, Stokely 274
Carswell, G. Harrold 73, 275
Carter v. Carter Coal 199
Catholic schools. See Parochial
    schools
Catt, Carrie Chapman, on women's
    suffrage 304
Censorship 245, 245, 258, 264
  in the military 241
  of motion pictures 236, 259
  Stone on 213
  of the student press 265
  Supreme Court and 236, 238, 241,
      245, 246
  See also Freedom of speech; Ob-
    scenity
Center for the Study of Democratic
    Institutions, model consti-
    tution of 55, 228
Charles River Bridge case 103
Charters, colonial 10, 32, 45, 52
Chase, Salmon P.
  impeachment of 198
  opinions of 193
Checks and balances 134
  threats to 106
  See also Separation of powers
Chicago Bar Association, papers of
    180
Child labor, regulation of
  interstate commerce in 88, 106,
      114
  through taxation 103, 114

Children. See Juveniles
Chinese Exclusion Act (1882),
      Arthur's veto of 154
Chinese Immigration Bill (1879),
      Hayes veto of 147
Chisholm v. Georgia 57, 190
Christianity, equal protection idea
      in 281. See also
      Protestants
Church and state 41, 235, 239,
      251, 253, 256–57, 264
  bibliography on 241
  Brennan on 204
  in education 235, 241–42, 244,
      258
  Supreme Court and 182, 199,
      242, 258
  See also Prayer in schools
Cinque v. U.S. 269
Circuit courts, Chase's opinions
      from 193
Civil disobedience 276
  argument in favor of 78
  See also Dissent; Rebellion
Civil disorder, presidential power
      and 133. See also
      Riots
Civil Rights Act (1957) 282, 293,
      294
Civil Rights Act (1960) 293
Civil Rights Act (1964) 124,
      277, 282, 289, 296,
      308
  Senator Ervin on 68
Civil Rights Act (1968) 124
Civil rights and liberties 38, 46,
      236, 237, 249, 258–59,
      259–60, 261, 264, 267,
      275, 276, 282–83, 291,
      294, 296
  ability of the political system
      to maintain 47
  bibliographies on 1, 3, 6, 7,
      154, 294–95
  blacks and 203, 206, 207, 235,
      271–72, 282
  Cardozo on 216
  chronology of 292
  cloture and filibuster relating
      to 87
  in the cold war 234
  in colonial America 17, 262
  communism and 250
  concern for at the Constitutional
      convention 24
  Congress and 88, 92, 110
  of defendants 243, 245

Subject Index

Subject Index

Subject Index

Subject Index

Subject Index

Subject Index

Investigatory powers. See Governmental investigations
Iowa, State University of. Benjamin F. Shambough Lectures 185
Iredell, James
    on the Constitution 28
    papers of 212
Ireland, law of obscenity in 261
Italy, judicial review in 80

J

Jackson, Andrew
    destruction of Clay's American system 118
    nullification speech of 125
    papers and biographies of 147, 148, 150, 151, 156, 163, 164, 166, 167, 168
    on representation 276
    Taney's friendship with 217
    use of martial law by 259
    use of the veto by 125
        concerning the Second U.S. Bank bill 129
Jackson, Robert Houghwout 205, 209
Jacksonian period
    bibliographies on 147, 159
    judicial review during 84
    revival of the party system in 128
Japanese Americans, civil liberties of in World War II 246
Jay, John
    on the Constitution 26
    THE FEDERALIST PAPERS and 41
    papers and biographies of 207, 212, 215
    Supreme Court under 190
Jay, William 293
Jay's Treaty 137
Jefferson, Thomas
    attack on the judiciary by 205
    civil liberties and 252
    conflict with Marshall 74, 82, 189
    contribution to constitutional development 35
        war powers 77
    disputes with Hamilton 30, 51
    Johnson's (William) relationship with 215
    papers and biographies of 145, 146, 147–48, 156–58, 161, 167

relationship with Jackson 150
role of in the Declaration of Independence 16
on the U.S. Bank 66, 149
Virginia and Kentucky Resolutions and 62
See also Louisiana Purchase
Jeffersonian period
    analysis of from the view of public administration 32
    coalition between slaveholders and mechanics in 42
    election of 1800 and 141
    Federalist criticism during 45
    judicial review during 84
    judiciary during 82, 122
    nullification in 39
Jehovah's witnesses, right to preach on the streets 241
Jencks v. U.S. 192
Johnson, Andrew 137–38, 285
    impeachment of 44, 108, 115, 121, 127, 132–33, 139–40
    papers and biographies of 158, 168
    use of the veto by 125
Johnson, Lyndon Baines
    appointment of federal judges by 176
    civil rights and 124, 143, 282, 296–97
    the Fortas case and 195
    papers and biographies of 154, 155, 158, 167
    Supreme Court and 187
    on voting rights 50, 274
Johnson, William 215
Jones v. Mayer 275, 295
Judges 37, 178
    appointment of federal 176
    appointment to the Supreme Court 171
    attitudes and ideologies of 195, 196
    bibliographies on 177–78, 186
    directory of 187–88
    in enforcing desegregation 290
    impeachment of and disciplinary measures for 76, 140, 182, 198, 204
    interpretation and application of the law by 175
    as law makers 181, 184
    papers and biographies of 46, 175, 177, 178, 188, 189, 200, 202–19

366

Subject Index

recall of 83
roles of 173
  federal (1789–1801) 142
  in southern black voting 281
support for slavery by 276
tenure of 175
  criticism of 180
See also names of judges (e.g.,
    Warren, Earl)
Judicial Conference 179
Judicial discretion 182
Judicial opinions and decisions 10,
    50, 178, 208–9
  on academic freedom 255
  bibliography on 8
  of Black 207, 209
  on blacks and slavery 274
  of Brandeis 203–4
  of Brennan 204
  of Cardozo 216
  on censorship 238
  on civil rights and liberties 291
  on the Civil War amendments 285
  on discrimination in education
    295
  dissenting 171–72, 200
  of Douglas 205
  on the First Amendment 245
  of Frankfurter 207, 213
  of Goldberg 209
  of Harlan 204–5, 209
  on higher education 238
  of Holmes 202–3, 210
  impacts of 199
  of Jackson (Robert) 216
  of McKenna 214
  of Marshall (John) 202, 214
  on obscenity 235, 253
  on race relations 292
  recall of 83, 182, 193
  on representative government 53
  selections from 4, 201
  on rights of the accused 244
  of Taney 217
  on treaties 120
  of Warren 218
Judicial power 37, 42, 53, 63,
    182, 183, 185, 191, 199
  concern with at the Constitutional
    Convention 24
  during Reconstruction 187
  judicial review as 84
  limits on 249
  organization of 189
  as a protector of individual
    rights 24
  reapportionment and 291

Judicial recall 83, 182, 193
  courts in development of theories
    about 37
Judicial review 35, 38, 39, 46,
    50, 79–86, 94, 173,
    174, 175, 188, 189,
    194, 199, 212, 253
  attacks on 173
  antimajoritan viewpoint in 69
  bibliography on 197
  comparative studies of 80
  of congressional investigating
    power 96
  the executive branch and 69
  forbidden by the Constitutional
    Convention 40
  laws held unconstitutional as a
    result of 198, 199
  origins of 81, 85, 86
  political party strength and 84
  procedures for seeking 199
  under the full faith and credit
    clause 225
  of the validity of amendments
    227
Judicial supremecy. See Judicial
    review
Judiciary 37, 42, 65, 171–219
  antislavery movement and 44
  bibliographies on 7, 8, 186
  Constitutional Convention de-
    bates on 30
  constitutional powers of 36, 52
  departures from the Constitu-
    tion by 55
  in developing American political
    theory 37
  in the economic realm 253
  education and 184, 247
  federalism and 59–60, 173
  foreign affairs and 73
  Fourteenth Amendment and 48
  Frankfurter on 208
  Holmes on 210
  impeachment and 89, 136
  independence of 71, 175
  in the Jeffersonian period 82,
    122, 205
  legislative power of 174, 180,
    183
  organization and administration
    of 179, 192, 228
  pardoning power of 125
  political philosophy in 173, 195
  primary sources on 200–202
  property rights and 93–94
  public evaluations of 191
  reaction to dissent (1960s) by
    122

367

Subject Index

Subject Index

Subject Index

Marshall, John   47, 54, 173
   agreement with Johnson (William)
      by   215
   Brandeis on   207
   in the Burr trial   193
   civil liberties in the court of   250
   conflicts with Jefferson   74, 82,
      189
   contract law and   105
   contribution to constitutional de-
      velopment   45
   correspondence with Story   218
   criticism of the court under   188
   defense of McCulloch v. Maryland
      by   98-99
   Holmes on   210
   implied powers and nationalism ac-
      cording to   106
   on judicial review   85
   papers and biographies of   188,
      200, 202, 203, 205, 206,
      207, 212, 214
   regulation of commerce in the
      court of   61
   reversal of his own opinions   179
   on treason   176
   in Ware v. Jones   190-91
Marshall, Thurgood   203
Martial law   259
   during the Civil War   50, 133
Martin, Luther   33
Mason, George
   anticonstitutional stand of   23
   on the slave trade compromise   27
Massachusetts
   birth control in   240
   challenge to the Vietnamese War
      by   178
   ratification of the Constitution in
      23
   slavery in   281
   See also Boston
Mass media. See Freedom of the
      press
Medical ethics   248
Medicare, Johnson on   154
Medicine. See Health
Mendelson, Wallace, on the Dred
      Scott decision   283
Miami Herald v. Tornillo   244, 262
Michigan, University of
   Thomas M. Cooley Lectures   51,
      187
   William W. Cook Lectures   189
Middle East, Eisenhower on   152
Military
   censorship in   241
   concept of civil control of   137

   desegregation of   282
   effect of the Twenty-seventh
      Amendment on   300
   law of race relations in   280
   role of in a republic   53
   Supreme Court on church and
      state matters concerning
      258
   See also Admiralty law; Conscrip-
      tion; Martial law
Military tribunals, administration of
      justice by   190
Mill, John Stuart, on free speech
      254
Miller (Supreme Court case)   261
Miller, Samuel Freeman   206
Milligan, Ex Parte   137
Milliken v. Bradley   275
Milton, John, on free speech   254
Minnesota Chippewa Tribe v.
      Carlucci   68
Minnesota mortgage moratorium case
      190
Minorities
   attitudes of the suffrage movement
      toward   303
   electoral college and   117, 118
   majority rule and the rights of
      39
   rights of in the Truman administra-
      tion   128
   See also Affirmative action pro-
      grams; Blacks; Ethnic
      groups
Minor v. Happersett   218
Miranda v. Arizona   69, 245, 254,
      265
Misdemeanors, right to counsel for
      247
Mississippi Valley Historical Society,
      presidential address (1959)
      61
Missouri Compromise   55, 118, 147
Missouri v. Holland   117, 125
Monetary policy   101
   congressional power in   95-96
   See also Legal tender
Monroe, James
   papers and biographies of   167,
      168
   support of internal improvements
      by   118
Montesquieu, Charles Louis
   Holmes on   210
   separation of powers doctrine of
      71
Mootness doctrine   190

372

Subject Index

New York County (Manhattan). Supreme Court, delays in 200
New York University
  Anson G. Phelps Lectures 17, 48
  James Madison Lectures 234, 236
New York University. School of Law, papers of a meeting at 174
Nixon, Lawrence A. 273
Nixon, Richard M.
  appointment power under 133
  busing and 272
  civil rights and 290
  congressional-executive relationship of 73, 77, 105, 131, 132
  electronic surveillance in the administration of 241
  free speech under 233
  impeachment of 93, 122, 128, 131, 134, 136, 140
  interpretation of war powers by 143
  relationship with the Supreme Court 177, 187, 188, 195-96, 199
  use of grand juries by 238
  See also Senate Select Committee v. Nixon; Watergate Affair
Nixon v. Condon 273
Nixon v. Herndon 273
Nixon v. Sirica 71
Nixon v. U.S. 116, 118, 182
Nominations for and appointment to office
  presidential power of 133, 139
  Senate role in 78, 89, 93, 100, 105
Norris (Supreme Court case) 236
North Carolina, ratification of the Constitution in 28. See also Greensboro, N.C.
North Carolina, University of. Weil Lectures 61
Northwestern University
  conference papers from 248
  Rosenthal Foundation Lectures 63, 181, 189
Northwest Ordinance 19, 48
  forces important to the development of 20
Nuclear Test Ban, Kennedy (J.F.) on 168
Nullification 39, 57, 62, 81
  of the Alien and Sedition Acts 66

  argument in favor of modern day 78
  Calhoun and 118
  Jackson and 125, 147, 148, 150
  in New England 60
  in South Carolina 58, 82
    documents on 65-66, 148
  of state elections 57-58
  Supreme Court and 197
Nuremberg Trials 200, 205, 209

O

Obscenity 249, 253, 256, 257, 258, 261, 262
  Brennan on 204
  laws of (1940) 242
  the student press and 265
  Supreme Court and 182, 184, 187, 189, 199, 235, 238, 240, 241
  See also Censorship; Pornography
Obscene Publications bill (1955) 261
Office of Education. See U.S. Department of Health, Education, and Welfare. Office of Education
Ohio State University. Law Forum 249
Ohio State University. Law School, lectures at 247, 265
Oleomargarine, regulation through taxation 103
Olmstead (Supreme Court case) 172, 241, 256
Omnibus Crime Control and Safe Streets Act (1968)
  conflict with the Miranda decision 69
  electronic surveillance and 251
Oral argumentation
  role of 200
  transcripts of 201, 202
Oregon, obscenity cases in 189
Organized crime 108
  1920s 237
Orlando, Salvatore 123

P

Pacifism. See Antiwar movement
Palko v. Connecticut 236
Panama Refining (Supreme Court case) 71
Panola County, Miss., civil rights legislation in 296

Subject Index

Subject Index

Subject Index

Roosevelt, Theodore
  papers and biographies of 148,
      165, 169
  view of presidential powers 138
Rostow, Eugene V., on judicial re-
      view 83
Roth (Supreme Court case) 238, 261
Rule of law 236
  federalism as a means of attaining
      41
Rural areas
  apportionment and 270, 281
  electoral college and 118
  role in prohibition 306
Russia, judicial review in 80
Rutledge, John 206, 207

S

St. Clair, Arthur 137
St. Clair, James 93
San Mateo v. Southern Pacific 279
Scandinavian countries, women's suf-
      frage and prohibition in
      305
Schechter Poultry Corp. v. U.S.
      68, 71
Schlesinger v. Reservists Committee
      to Stop the War 72
School desegregation. See Educa-
      tion, desegregation and
School District of Abington Township
      v. Schempp 183, 251,
      255, 260
Schools. See Parochial schools;
      Prayer in schools; Private
      schools
Schwimmer (court case) 246
Scientists, loyalty oaths and 244-45
Scottsboro case 236
Screenwriters. See Motion picture
      industry
Seale, Bobby, trial of 235
Searches and seizures 251
  Brennan on 204
  Supreme Court and 177, 189, 244,
      265
  See also Exclusionary rule
Secession 81, 150, 277, 290
  Buchanan on 167
  Daniel as a proponent of 207
  Jackson on 151
  right of 62
Secessionists, confiscation of the
      property of 154

Sectionalism
  18th-century 24
  Supreme Court and 197
Sedition
  1920s 237
  legitimacy of laws of 40
  state and federal laws on 237
  trials for (1789-1801) 142
  See also Alien and Sedition Acts;
        Espionage and Sedition
        Acts (1917, 1918)
Segregation and desegregation 275
  defacto 241
  in education 180, 187, 194, 196,
        199, 270-71, 273, 275,
        277, 279, 284, 287, 289,
        291, 295, 297
    in Boston 294
    congressional reactions to 75
    federal funds and 289
    in private schools 41, 241, 286
    southern judges charged with
        290
    southern reactions to 64, 66,
        296
    under Nixon 290
  of the military 282
  role of in southern gubernatorial
        campaigns 271
  Supreme Court and 75, 192, 194,
        196, 199, 241, 270-71,
        273, 279, 295, 297
  See also Brown v. Board of Edu-
        cation; Busing; Separate
        but equal doctrine
Self-incrimination 46, 246, 248,
        252, 254
  Brennan on 204
  Supreme Court and 244, 247
  See also Confessions
Self-restraint doctrine, limitations
        of 82
Seminole War (1818), investigation
        of 108
Senate. See U.S. Congress.
        Senate
Senate Select Committee v. Nixon
        116
Senators
  Constitutional Convention on the
        expulsion of 58
  impeachment of 140
Sentencing
  bibliography on 186
  disparities in 244
  See also Capital punishment

Subject Index

Subject Index

Southern states
  black voting in 281, 283–84, 294
  civil rights in 274
  conditions in post–Civil War 291
  education in after 1964 289
  equal justice in 286
  free speech for radicals in 285
  judges charged with implementing
      desegregation in 290
  race relations in after Brown 273
  reactions to desegregation in 64,
      66, 296
  See also Reconstruction
Sovereign immunity, doctrine of 249
Sovereignty
  conflict over location of 36
  Marshall (John) and 206
  Story on 216
  Supreme Court on state 66–67,
      190
  See also Secession, right of;
      States' rights
Speech, freedom of. See Freedom
      of speech
Speedy trial
  delays in 200
  Supreme Court and 244
Spencer, Herbert, influence on
      Sutherland 215
Standing, law of 72, 108, 185–86,
      196
Stanton, Edwin 121
Stare decisis
  Frankfurter on 213
  violation of by the Supreme Court
      195
State action doctrine 288, 296
State Department. See U.S. De-
      partment of State
State government
  assumption of the debts of (1790)
      57
  commerce clause as a limit on the
      power of 87
  conflict and changes in (1775–83)
      48
  constitutional amendments and
      223–24, 226, 227
  contracts and the authority of 214
  expansion of powers after 1933
      51
  Hughes on the power of 209
  police power of 59
  ratification of the Constitution and
      25, 27, 233
  in the regulation of commerce 97

relationship to local government
      60
relationship with the Supreme
      Court 66–67
restricting of alcoholic beverages
      by 300
Stone on 213
taxation and 45, 59, 210
use of martial law by 259
See also Constitutions, state;
      Debt, state; Federal-
      state relations; Interstate
      agreements and compacts;
      Judiciary, state; Law,
      state; Legislatures, state
State of the Union Messages. See
      Presidents and presi-
      dency, writings and
      speeches of
States
  applicability of the Bill of Rights
      to 231
  development of the concept of
      power in 44–45
  federal judicial authority over 256
  Harlan on the suing of 204
  Jay on the Supremacy of 215
  sizes of related to electoral col-
      lege influence 118, 132
States, new, admission of 40, 61–
      62
States' rights 37, 61, 65, 66, 183
  Daniel as a proponent of 207
  desegregation and 64
  disputes over in the Constitutional
      Convention 23, 24, 63
    in the Continental Congress 17,
      20
  federal judiciary and 40
  foreign policy limitations and 79
  of Jefferson 82
  McCulloch v. Maryland and 99
  nationalism and 62–63
  19th-century conflicts over 54
  selection of Senators and 57–58
  War of 1812 and 57
  See also Sovereignty
Steel Seizure Case 119–20, 128,
      136, 137, 142
Stevenson, Adlai 187
Stimson doctrine, Hoover on 164
Stone, Harlan Fiske 54, 172, 200
  biographies of 206, 213, 215
  examination of the Supreme Court
      under 188, 189

Subject Index

Subject Index

Subject Index

Subject Index

    cussions of   121
in the political process   177
searches and seizures and   177,
    189, 251, 265
separation of powers and   71, 72
settlement of interstate disputes
    by   228
slavery and   197, 269
social policies and   56, 109, 187,
    189, 195, 297
the state role in constitutional
    amending and   226
state sovereignty and   66–67, 190
taxation and   106, 193
treaty decisions of   119, 192
use of history by   178, 190
war powers and   135
    Vietnamese War   143
See also Judges; Judiciary; head-
    ings beginning with the
    term Judicial; names of
    Supreme Court cases
    (e.g., McCulloch v.
    Maryland); names of Su-
    preme Court judges (e.g.,
    Warren, Earl)
U.S. Surgeon General, report on
    smoking by   4
Universities and colleges
blacks in   288
discrimination in   271
free speech at   257
judicial opinions concerning   238
reverse discrimination at   278–
    79, 289
See also Academicians; Academic
    freedom
Urban areas
apportionment and   270
bibliography on   154
effect of prohibition on   300
electoral system and   118
judicial response to the affairs of
    184
role of in repeal of prohibition
    306

V

Van Buren, Martin, papers and biog-
    raphies of   167, 169
Venue, change of   254
Verdicts
relationship to pretrial publicity
    262–63
Supreme Court on nonunanimous
    244

Vested rights, doctrine of   93
Veto   129
congressional   77, 100, 113
presidential   77, 125, 144
    pocket   132
Reconstruction era   285
Vice–presidency   136
bibliographies on   131, 139,
    163
history of   122, 142, 143
selection of   124, 139
Twenty–fifth Amendment and
    306, 307
Vietnamese War   249
argument against constitutionality
    of   78, 123, 141–42,
    143, 178
bibliography on   154
executive privilege and   77
foreign policy formation during
    78
Johnson on   154
Kennedy on   168
role of the president in   70,
    116, 127, 131
See also Antiwar movement
Vinson, Frederick Moore   54
examination of the Supreme Court
    under   188
    civil rights in   192
Virginia
educational desegregation in   187,
    287
liberty in early   156
nullification in (1798)   66
opposition to the Second U.S.
    Bank in   57
partition of   50, 133
ratification of the Constitution in
    23
search and seizure in the Bill of
    Rights of (1776)   251
slavery in   281, 183
See also Declaration of Rights
    (Va.)
Virginia, University of.   James W.
    Richards Lectures in
    History   39
Virginia Plan   26
Virginia Resolutions   62, 66
Daniel as a proponent of   207
Volstead Act   299, 304
Voting   283
advances against discrimination
    in (1840s–50s)   84
by blacks   278, 285, 290, 292–
    93
    in Alabama   294

388

in the southern states 283–84, 294

southern judges and 281

concern for in the Johnson (L.B.) administration 50, 124, 143

in the Kennedy administration 143

discrimination in 286

effect of civil rights legislation on 296

guarantee of freedom of 237, 238, 254

legislation on 291

Supreme Court and 176, 178, 270, 277

See also Elections; Poll tax; Presidential elections; Primaries; Suffrage

Voting Rights Act (1965) 124, 176, 274, 281, 293, 294, 296

W

Wade (Supreme Court case) 69

Wagner Act 109

Waite, Morrison

biographies of 214, 218

Fourteenth Amendment and the court of 280

regulation of commerce in the court of 61

Ware v. Jones 190

War of 1812 164

burning of Washington during 108

interpretation of 42

Jackson and 150

policies leading to 60

states' rights and 57

War on poverty. See Poverty program

War powers 38, 50, 56, 72, 79

congressional 76–77, 93, 105, 116, 130–31

presidential 70, 73, 76–77, 78, 105, 115, 116, 119, 121, 123, 126, 127, 128, 139, 141–42

judicial interpretation of 135

under Lincoln 50, 133

Nixon 130–31, 143

related to U.S. United Nations obligations 75

War Powers Act 73

War Powers Resolution (1973) 115, 126

Warren, Earl

civil rights cases argued before 176, 250

compared to the Burger court 182, 188, 199

criticism and analysis of the court under 47, 109, 176–77, 183, 187, 188, 189, 194

education and the court of 270

Fortas case and 195

on interstate compacts 67

Kennedy assassination investigation and 76

mass media in the court of 240

papers and biographies of 194, 212, 216, 218

political offenders in the court of 192

retirement of 176

voting cases in the court of 178, 270

Warren, Samuel, on the right to privacy 235–36, 264

Warren Commission, creation of 154

Washington, Booker T. 274

Washington, D.C.

congressional representation for 307–8

movement for abolition of slavery in 293

Washington, George

administration of 30

court operation in 184

executive privilege in 137

state trials during 142

veto of measure to apportion members of the House 129

election of 29–30

Farewell Address 23

interpretation of war powers by 77

papers and biographies of 149, 153, 155, 161, 167–68, 169–70

Marshall's LIFE OF WASHINGTON 82

Proclamation of Neutrality 119, 125, 127

support of Hamilton's bank proposal by 118

view of the Supreme Court by 191

Subject Index

Watergate affair 71, 93, 115, 116, 118, 122, 126, 131, 182
  bibliographies on 134, 135
  reactions to 124
  See also Nixon, Richard M.
Watergate Reorganization and Reform Act (1975) 115
Watkins v. U.S. 75, 88, 192
Webster, Daniel
  argument of in the Dartmouth College case 278
  influence on the course of constitutional development 36
  interpretation of federalism by 63
Webster, Noah, on the Constitution 26
Welfare state
  civil rights in 257
  Congress' inability to perform in 91
  Supreme Court's relationship to 188
  transition from laissez-faire to 44
  See also Social welfare
West, The, disputes over in the Continental Congress 20. See also Northwest Ordinance
West, Va., creation of 50, 133
Whiskey Rebellion (1794) 30
  Washington on 149
White, Edward Douglas, examination of the decisions of the court of 178
White v. Texas 192
Whittier, John Greenleaf 291
Wickard v. Filburn 104
Wilkinson, James, investigation of 108
Williams, Roger 21
Wilson, James 36
  on the Constitution 26
  ideas on presidential powers 138–39
  separation of powers doctrine and 76
Wilson, Woodrow
  civil liberties under 135
  exercise of war by 130
  papers and biographies of 160, 170
  "New Freedom" creed of and constitutional development 54
  presidential powers under 68, 127-28

Wiretapping. Supreme Court and 244
Women
  discrimination against 271
  equal protection for 275, 299–300, 301, 302, 306, 307, 308
    bibliography on 301
  suffrage for 285, 301, 302, 304, 306
    bibliographies on 304, 305
    interaction with prohibition 304-5
    opposition to 300
  See also Feminist movement
Workmen's compensation, Cardozo on 216
World War I
  civil liberties during 135, 260
  criticism of government expansion during 39
  free speech during 237, 256
  martial law and 259
  presidential power during 128
World War II
  civil rights during 233, 260
    for Japanese Americans 246
  constitutional development and 54
  impact on constitutional interpretation 49
  presidential power during 128
    delegation of 123
Writ of mandamus 186
Writs of assistance, colonial 251

Y

Yale University
  Godkin Lectures 185
  lectures on law delivered at 174
  Storrshect Lectures 177
Yates, Robert
  on the Constitution 26, 28
  notes of on the Constitutional Convention 31, 32-33
Yates v. U.S. 192
Yazoo land fraud 104-5
Youngstown Sheet & Tube Co. v. Sawyer 142. See also Steel seizure case
Youngstown v. Sawyer 120

Z

Zenger, Peter 236, 252